KU-416-603

Industrial Structure and Market Conduct

BY THE SAME AUTHOR

Resale Price Maintenance in Practice Allen and Unwin (1966)

The Small Firm in the Hotel and Catering Industry (with J. A. Greenwood and D. Hunt) H.M.S.O. (1971)

Industrial Structure and Market Conduct

J. F. PICKERING

Martin Robertson

© J. F. Pickering 1974

All rights reserved. No part of this publication may be
reproduced, stored in a retrieval system, or transmitted
in any form or by any means, mechanical, photo-
copying, recording, or otherwise, without the prior
written permission of the copyright holder

First published 1974 and reprinted 1976
by Martin Robertson & Co. Ltd.
17 Quick Street   London   N1 8HL

Reprinted 1978

ISBN 0 85520 040 5 (case edition)
ISBN 0 85520 039 1 (paperback edition)

Reproduced and printed by photolithography and bound in
Great Britain at The Pitman Press, Bath

CONTENTS

dedicated to my Parents

INTRODUCTION

This book deals with a number of issues that are of current relevance to the
industrial economist. A background knowledge of price theory and welfare
economics is assumed. I hope it may be found useful as a source for students
requiring a more empirical approach to supplement their work on the theory
of the firm and as a text for students taking courses in industrial or managerial
economics. The gulf which it is often held exists between business reality and
economic analysis is unfortunate and is not entirely justified by considerations
of the methodology of positive economics. I hope that the material discussed
here will be considered relevant to the experience of the manager in a business
organisation and to those in government responsible for industrial policy
making while still retaining economic validity.

The structure of the chapters offers some recognition of the traditional
distinction between structure and conduct. Broadly speaking, chapters 1 to 5
deal with features of, and influences upon, the structure of industry. Chapters
6 to 9 consider the way the organisation and behaviour of firms influences
structure and conduct, and Chapters 10 to 15 are concerned specifically with
aspects of market conduct. There is no special section that deals with economic
performance. The whole book is about performance and the interest of the
economist in questions of structure and conduct is really because it is thought
they will help in predicting likely performance outcomes. Equally, there is no
separate section concerned with government policy since all the topics covered
create normative issues and they are more appropriately discussed at the
relevant points throughout the book. Because of the magnitude of the topics,
however, chapters 9 and 15 are entirely devoted to considerations of government policy towards mergers and restrictive practices. Many of the subjects
covered impinge upon each other and there is inevitably some overlap in the
material covered in different chapters. Attempt has been made to avoid
substantial duplication between chapters and consequently some cross-
referencing is unavoidable.

The choice of material has been somewhat influenced by a preference for
relevance and consequently use has been made of empirical material –
quantitative and qualitative – to illustrate and support the analysis. The
qualitative or case study material is largely British since in recent years reports

by the Monopolies Commission and the National Board for Prices and Incomes have provided particularly valuable sources of information about different industries which are readily accessible to the student. It is to be hoped that the reader will be able to add his own examples from personal experience or further reading to supplement the material and either to confirm or reject the analysis provided here.

There has in recent years been an increase in the use, especially but not solely by American investigators, of statistical investigations of relationships between different aspects of industry structure, conduct and performance. They provide an important source of quantitative information. Often, however, different studies of the same question do not yield the same result and this diversity of evidence is not hidden in the text. In some cases statistical investigations of British data have produced results that differ in important respects from similar studies of American information. The possible causes and implications of such divergences of experience would seem to be worthy of deeper investigation.

It is right to emphasise that extensive reliance upon empirical material poses difficulties for the analyst. The chances of finding one general model to explain or predict particular aspects of behaviour or performance are greatly limited. Many different arguments and pieces of evidence will have to be reviewed which have some, but not general, applicability. These may not be consistent with each other and so apparent contradictions between explanations cannot always be avoided. There is a real danger that inferences drawn on the basis of one or two case-study examples only may not have general applicability. Econometric investigations create their own problems of measurement, of multicollinearity among the variables and the possibility that the data collected may not relate to dynamic, equilibrium situations.

Often we will find that there is no single position that can be taken about the topics under investigation in each chapter. A particular practice or structural feature may have both advantages and disadvantages, to the firm as well as to the wider public interest. The actual balance of costs and benefits may depend upon the circumstances in each case. It is also likely that different firms will respond in different ways to the same situations. The assumption that firms always follow the most appropriate policy or obtain the greatest private benefit from any situation is not always justified. Where appropriate, I have therefore tried to show how decision-making in firms might be improved by indicating the different factors that must be taken into account. From this it is possible to see how the nature of the decisions taken in firms must inevitably influence the interpretation that the economist will place upon his observations of a particular situation and the implications for the policy maker concerned with government policy towards industry.

The citation of references is a problem in a text that covers an area where the literature is indeed vast. I have endeavoured to indicate sources of information and analysis that I have found of value and that are not generally part of the state of the art. If I have failed to acknowledge any original source of information or ideas that I have utilised, I apologise most sincerely.

I wish to express my sincere appreciation to the many people who have assisted my work on this book, especially the ladies who typed the manuscript and Mr Douglas Parker and my wife who helped with the proofreading. Above all, however, I am grateful to my wife Jane and daughter Rachel for their encouragement and good-humoured tolerance through the many hours that the preparation of this book entailed.

ACKNOWLEDGEMENT

I am grateful to the editors of *Economic Journal* and of the *Journal of Industrial Economics* for permission to reproduce passages that first appeared in articles in those journals.

CHAPTER 1

INDUSTRIAL CONCENTRATION

A frequent starting point for investigations of industrial organisation is a description of market structure. As we shall see in subsequent chapters this is a multi-dimensional concept, but many analyses tend to focus, at least in the first instance, on concentration as a useful and measurable proxy. Market structure, however, may be of little significance in its own right but is often held to be a useful predictor of market conduct and performance. It is therefore because of the assumptions that concentration is an indicator of market structure and that there is a link between structure, conduct and performance that concentration measures are considered to be important. Later in this chapter we shall consider the possibility that a different form of relationship between structure, conduct and performance exists, but initially we shall work on the assumption that market structure does influence performance.

Two separate types of concentration measure may be identified that operate at different levels of aggregation. We may attempt to measure *aggregate concentration* within an economy or we may be more interested in *market concentration,* that is concentration levels in particular industries. Aggregate concentration measures normally indicate the share of (for example) the 100 largest organisations in the total output or employment or assets employed in an economy. A high level of aggregate concentration may be a cause for concern since it indicates the extent to which a few large organisations may influence the success of governmental economic policies, and in so doing may be able to accrue to themselves considerable political influence. How far a society ought to have all its industrial eggs in relatively few baskets may be an important question. High aggregate concentration is likely to indicate the growth of organisations that are large in absolute size and, probably, highly diversified. This may also mean that through their overall strength they are less responsive to market indicators in any individual product market and may be able to use their aggregate power to increase their dominance in individual markets. Interest in measures of aggregate concentration was heightened during the 1930s with the (ultimately inaccurate) prediction by Berle and Means that by 1950 the 200 largest corporations in the United States would be responsible for 70 per cent of all corporate activity.[1] A recent British prediction suggests that, if present trends are continued, by the year 1983 the largest 100 firms in Great Britain would have 70 per cent of net manufacturing output, and by the

1

turn of the century their share would be 90 per cent.[2]

Little research appears to have been conducted on the actual political and economic impact of very large firms in a society and there is not much information at present on the effects of high levels of conglomeration that such high aggregate concentration would imply. However, it is unlikely that such levels of concentration would be economically necessary or socially desirable. The chances are that just as the predictions of Berle and Means were not confirmed in practice, the more recent ones will also not be fulfilled. If they are not to be achieved, however, there will need to be some change in the underlying conditions promoting present trends. This may imply an alteration in government policies towards industrial structure or a change in the underlying conditions influencing the relative growth rates of large and small firms and of conditions influencing the birth and death of firms.

Most studies, however, are more concerned with questions of market or industry concentration and the effect that particular levels of concentration have on competitive behaviour in the industry and the performance outcomes in terms of outputs, prices, profits, productive efficiency and technological progressiveness. High levels of concentration are assumed to indicate tight oligopolies or monopolies and consequently to be associated with particular patterns of market conduct and performance outcomes that are often considered undesirable. In particular it is sometimes feared that high concentration is likely to influence the character and weaken the extent of competition and lead to a reduction in economic welfare by increasing prices and profits, increasing inequalities of income distribution, reducing technical efficiency in production and misallocating productive resources.

A considerable burden is therefore laid upon a single measure of concentration. Not only is it assumed to constitute a measure of monopoly power but from this certain predictions are assumed to be possible as to the likely effects of different concentration (monopoly) levels on economic efficiency. Whether such a link can be assumed is not only an issue for this chapter, it really underlies the whole book, but before we can investigate the nature of this relationship we have first to tackle the difficult problem of deciding how market concentration can be measured at all.

The measurement of market concentration

Market concentration measures pose a fundamental classification problem. How are we to define our industry or market and, having decided that, how are the outputs of multi-product firms or plants to be allocated to appropriate industry classifications?[3] Various alternative breadths of classification have been used.

The broadest classification is the 'order' or in American terminology the two-digit industry. The British Standard Industrial Classification contains 17 industrial orders, 14 of which are for manufacturing industry. These are: food, drink and tobacco; chemicals and allied industries; metal manufacture; engineering and electrical goods; shipbuilding and marine engineering; vehicles; metal goods not elsewhere specified; textiles; leather, leather goods and fur; clothing and footwear; bricks, pottery, glass, cement; timber, furniture, etc.; paper printing and publishing; other manufacturing industries. As will be obvious from the mere listing of these orders, some contain a very wide range of products and activities which may be quite unrelated to each other. Within each order are a number of industries or minimum list headings (three-digit industries in America) and within each industry are a number of separate product groups (four-digit industries). The relation between orders, industries and product groups is set out for a limited number of selected examples in Figure 1.1.

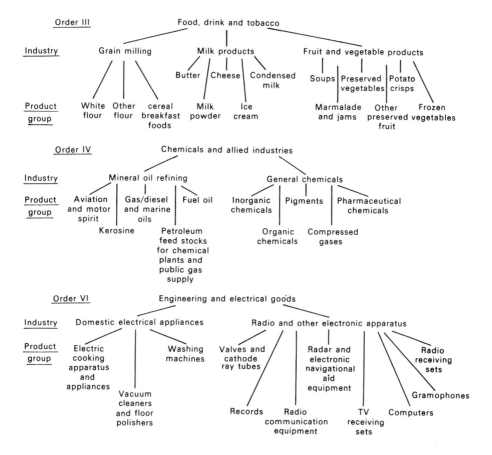

Fig 1.1 Selected examples of the relationship between orders, industries and product groups in industrial classification

4 Industrial Structure & Market Conduct

To be useful as an indicator, the industry for which a concentration measure is calculated needs to be specified in a way that is relevant to the conditions actually prevailing in the market place. The economist defines his market in terms of the level of substitutability (or cross-elasticity of demand) between alternative items. Where the substitutabilities are high the items constitute part of the same market. Where they are low different markets exist. As will be observed from Figure 1.1 the industry (three-digit) grouping may often prove too broad to constitute a single relevant market for analysis. The product group is likely to be more appropriate but may still include products that are not close substitutes. It is also likely to be the case that in some areas quite different products may prove to be close substitutes for each other even though they are not part of the same product group, or industry. The question of the most appropriate definition of a market is something that will frequently recur throughout this book. Having, hopefully, decided on a meaningful basis of industry classification, the next decision is on the actual variable to be measured.

In most cases attention is focused upon the share of a particular market in the hands of a small number of firms – separate decision-making units. On occasion the measure of concentration is based upon the share taken by a small number of plants – production units. Where firms tend to have several plants, the level of concentration of firms will be greater than the level of concentration of plants. Relative outputs of a specified number of firms, the absolute numbers of firms and the degree of instability in market shares through time have all been suggested as the basis of measurement, but most actual statistical series are concerned with relative outputs or sales. Even here, however, difficulties can arise because an unambiguous measure of output is not only hard to specify but equally difficult to collect. Measures of gross output raise problems of double counting where some firms are more vertically integrated than others and create a problem of converting to common value units. Measures of sales overcome the latter problem but are also unsatisfactory in dealing with the problems posed by differing degrees of vertical integration. A measure of net output or value added would be preferable but, even if it could be collected, it would be affected by variations in the profit rates taken by various firms and would not reflect the actual outcome where some goods and services are both produced and consumed in the same industry.

In practice many measures of industrial production and of the relative size of firms tend to use asset or employment levels as the basis of comparison. Neither are reliable, particularly because measures of concentration based upon them will be influenced by varying degrees of capital intensity in the production of a given output. It is likely that capital intensity in an industry will be related systematically to size of firm, with large firms proving to be more capital intensive. Consequently concentration measures based on assets may overstate the level of concentration while a measure based on employment will understate the true level.

Numerous measures of concentration and of monopoly have been proposed in the literature.[4] The measures of concentration normally used are either based upon some measure of the relative importance of a limited number of firms or attempt to offer some information regarding inequality in the size distribution of all firms in an industry.

Measures of relative importance are provided by the concentration curve and the concentration ratio. Hypothetical examples of concentration curves are shown in Figure 1.2. These indicate the proportion of the total output (or size, etc.) of the industry produced by a given number of firms. The curves are plotted in a cumulative manner so that it is possible to read off from the curve either the share of output taken by the n largest firms or to identify the number of firms required to produce a given proportion of total industry output. Normally, it is not possible in practice to construct such a concentration curve since restrictions on the disclosure of information relating to individual firms or plants mean that the data are only available regarding the number of units in each size group and the size groups are so constructed that no fewer

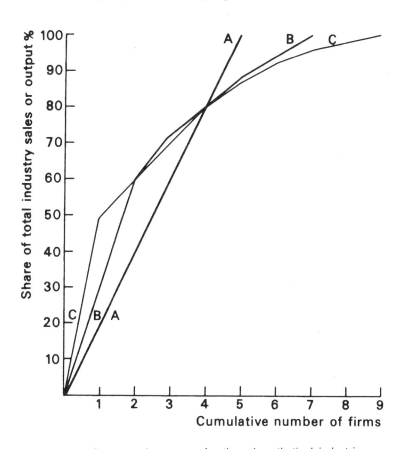

Fig 1.2 Concentration curves for three hypothetical industries

than three firms are grouped together. The concentration ratio is therefore a compromise, indicating one point on the concentration curve. The number of firms on which concentration ratios are based varies from country to country and from time to time, thereby making international or inter-temporal comparisons difficult. Ratios based on the shares of the three, four, five, eight or twenty largest firms have all been used as the basis for analysis.

Leaving on one side for the moment the question whether any measure of concentration is an adequate indicator of market structure, the concentration ratio has important deficiencies as such a statistical measure. Of particular importance is the consequence of producing just one figure reflecting the share of a predetermined, and probably arbitrarily selected, number of firms. We have little conclusive evidence whether three- or four- or twenty-firm ratios are more reliable predictors of market conduct and performance. By presenting a single value reflecting the share of the largest firms the measure fails to provide any indication of the total number of firms in the industry, or of the relative size distribution of the firms concerned in the calculation of the ratio. Are they, for example, all of more or less equal size, or is there one which dominates the industry? The practical conduct and performance implications of the same concentration level may vary considerably according to the answer to that question.

Inter-industry comparisons of concentration may also be unreliable since observations of the relative degree of concentration in different industries may be sensitive to decisions as to the actual number of firms on which the comparative concentration ratios are based. In Figure 1.2 concentration curves were shown for three different hypothetical industries. It will be observed they all have an identical four-firm concentration ratio of 80 per cent and if this is the only information presented about the industries it will be presumed that they have identical market structures, and identical conduct and performance outcomes would be predicted. In fact this would be misleading since the total number of firms varies between the industries and this may be an important influence on the closeness of relations in the industry and the ability to sustain a cartel or otherwise to avoid competition. The size distribution of the firms is also variable with industry C having a single firm with a much greater degree of market dominance than A or B; this would suggest that a form of pricing behaviour might be expected in A which would be different from that in B or C. Finally, it will be observed that a concentration ratio based on different numbers of firms would produce different rank orderings. A one-firm ratio would indicate that C was the most concentrated industry followed by B then A. A five-firm ratio would, however, completely reverse that order. A four-firm ratio would, as we have seen, indicate no difference in concentration between the industries.

An alternative measure that also uses information on the relative sizes of the firms in a particular industry is the Herfindahl index (H) which is derived by summing the squares of the market shares of all firms in the industry. This takes into account both the number of firms and their size differences. The value of H will equal 1 where there is only a single firm in the industry and will tend towards 1 where there are few firms and/or greater degrees of inequality of market shares. Calculating the H values for the three industries in Figure 1.2 we obtain an index of .200 for A, .208 for B and .288 for C. Thus industry C is the most concentrated of the three according to this index and a five-firm concentration ratio would in this case give entirely the reverse ordering of the three industries![5] It has also been argued that the reciprocal of the H index is also useful since this indicates the number of equal-sized firms that would generate the H measure.[6]

In other areas of economics, particularly in questions of income distribution, attention is frequently paid to inequalities in the distribution. These inequalities are often depicted in the shape of a Lorenz curve. This concept has also been applied to questions of industrial structure since it is argued that concentration is fundamentally a measure of inequality and that the size distribution of firms is more important than the actual number of firms as an indication of market structure. A Lorenz curve is fitted by relating the proportion of total industry output (or some other measure of size) to the proportion of firms in the

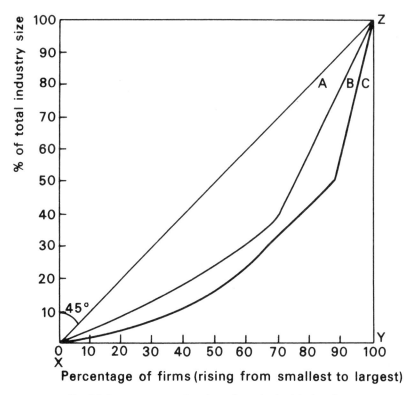

Fig 1.3 Lorenz curves for three hypothetical industries

industry. Figure 1.3 shows Lorenz curves for each of the three hypothetical industries for which a concentration curve was plotted in Figure 1.2.

As industry A has firms of equal size there is no inequality and the Lorenz curve for A is the 45° line. There is some inequality in B and C with the inequality being greatest in C. In practice Lorenz curves that have been plotted for particular industries do indicate that there is often a large amount of inequality between firm sizes.[7] A summary measure of the amount of inequality indicated by the Lorenz curve is provided by the Gini coefficient. This relates the area between the 45° line and the actual Lorenz curve to the area of the triangle under the 45° line, that is triangle XYZ in Figure 1.3. The greater the degree of inequality the nearer the Gini coefficient approaches unity. A high Gini coefficient would therefore lead one to conclude that the market structure was not competitive. Unfortunately this also has its disadvantages as an indicator of market structure and it is less reliable where the number of observations is small. It is less useful than concentration curves and ratios because it takes no account of the number of firms in the industry and it may be over-sensitive for predictive purposes to changes in the population of the industry and to changes in the degree of concentration among the smaller firms in the industry. An alternative indication of inequality may be obtained by comparing the dispersion about the mean of the logarithms of the sizes of the firms concerned. The greater the dispersion the greater is the degree of inequality and the higher is assumed to be the level of concentration. This approach rests upon the assumption that the size of firms follows the log normal distribution.[8]

While concentration and inequality measures attempt to describe market structure and from this to deduce likely competitive consequences, other measures have been proposed that would indicate the degree of monopoly power existing in a market. The best known of these is probably the Lerner index.[9] This measures the degree of monopoly power (m) by the formula:

$$m = \frac{P - MC}{P}$$

where P and MC are price and marginal cost respectively. If $P = MC$ then $m = 0$ and there is no monopoly power. Quite apart from the problems involved in obtaining a measure of marginal costs, this index would overstate the degree of monopoly power held by a firm of superior efficiency and lower marginal costs. It may not be meaningful as a description of actual market structures where monopsony by the firm concerned in factor markets or by purchasers from the firm concerned in product markets is involved. Monopoly power may also be indicated by the cross-elasticities of demand following Triffin[10] or by the elasticity of the firm's demand curve relative to that of the industry.[11] Each of these alternative measures has something to commend it, particularly by offering an indication of the degree of discretion available to individual firms in their decision-making. There are, however, considerable problems in using this information on a regular basis as an indication of the structure of an industry or a market.

Concentration and market structure

It is unlikely that anyone would seriously suggest that a concentration measure alone offers an adequate description of market structure, yet as a quantifiable variable a concentration measure is sometimes used as a basis for anti-trust policy and it does have some empirical success in explaining the variability of particular performance measures between different industries. Yet it is unlikely that a uni-dimensional measure such as a concentration ratio would be an altogether reliable indicator of market structure and an effective predictor of conduct and performance. Some commentators have suggested that the information conveyed by a concentration measure could be enhanced in various ways. Thus Fellner suggested considering together the share of the largest firm, the number of firms with market shares of more than 10 per cent, the joint market share of the firms with shares exceeding say 10 per cent, together with an indication of whether small firms do or do not jointly account for more than 10 per cent of the total market.[12] Stigler has suggested that, as mobility through time is important, a measure of random fluctuations of market shares would be a useful index of concentration[13] and also that a long-run measure of concentration, say averaged over five years, might be more appropriate as it would then allow for adjustments in supply and demand conditions to have taken place.[14]

While such additions might make the measure more informative, they would not overcome the major deficiencies of concentration measures as indicators of market structure. There appear to be four major groups of deficiencies exhibited by concentration measures in this respect. First, the classification of industries may be inappropriate. The problem of identifying close substitutes has already been noted. The assumption in industry concentration ratio calculations that all markets are national markets is also often not justified. The existence of regional markets where concentration will probably be higher than national concentration ratios indicate may be of particular relevance in the United States but it is still undoubtedly applicable in the supply of some goods and services in the United Kingdom and other countries. This is likely to become an important issue in the EEC where it is unlikely that the individual national markets of the member states will become fully integrated into a single international market for many years ahead. This would imply that individual states should continue to maintain an interest in the structure of their own domestic industries.

Secondly, concentration ratios ignore other important elements of market structure. Vertical integration, the conditions of entry, patents and the existence or otherwise of countervailing buying power will all exercise a material influence on the actual market structure of an industry and its likely consequences in terms of conduct and performance outcomes. Some of these influences are discussed in later chapters.

Thirdly, the link between concentration and conduct is likely to be affected by other influences operating in the industry. Concentration measures assume that separate firms are in fact independent of each other and behave independently. In several respects this may be an unjustifiable assumption. It is possible that through interlocking directorates or minority shareholdings one firm may be able to influence the activities of an apparent rival. It may be that a cartel operates in the industry through which prices are fixed, markets shared and competition generally avoided. Concentration ratios cannot provide information on these issues neither can they indicate the degree of interdependence in the structure of the group of firms, which may mean that firm decision-making is based upon a recognition of this interdependence and may be strongly influenced by the past history of the industry. The consequence may well be that concentration measures overstate the likely degree of competition in an industry.

Finally, we should remember that concentration measures may relate solely to shares of domestic production. If imports represent a substantial proportion of total sales in the domestic market the effective degree of concentration may be overstated. If quantities of domestic production are exported and if the contribution of the different firms to exports is not in proportion to their contribution to domestic production the concentration measure may also misrepresent the degree of concentration in the domestic market. If, for example, the largest firms in the industry contribute more than proportionately to exports, their market shares in the domestic market will be lower than a production-based concentration ratio would suggest.

These deficiencies certainly do not mean that a concentration measure is without value. They do, however, suggest that actual conditions must be studied carefully, often qualitatively, in any industry before a final judgement about market structure can be arrived at. They also indicate the substantial caveats that must be borne in mind in interpreting cross-sectional studies of the relation between concentration (as a proxy for market structure) and performance and the possible need to introduce more structural indicators into the analyses.

In suggesting that a concentration ratio is not an unambiguous indicator of market structure and that the link between concentration and performance is not well established, we have also implicitly cast some doubts on the value of the development of an anti-trust policy based upon concentration measures. In both Britain and the USA some facets of anti-trust policy, such as criteria for references of dominant firms and mergers to the Monopolies Commission and the Merger Guidelines issued by the United States Department of Justice,[15] rely upon concentration data. As a basis for indicating the sorts of market situation that should receive most attention this seems unobjectionable. Indeed concentration ratios are often the only reliable form of quantitative information on industry structure available to anti-trust authorities in deciding whether to take action in particular instances. The advantages of pragmatic investigation are that the additional variables can then be added by the investigating authority and over time qualitative evidence may be accumulated which should allow the development of a clearer view as to how far concentration or any other measure is an effective predictor of particular types of performance outcomes that will be of concern to the policy maker.

Whether measured quantitatively by a concentration or inequality indicator or more qualitatively by allowing the introduction of other variables, the structure of industry varies from case to case. Many of the influences appear to be associated with the nature of the product and its production processes. The availability of economies of scale will influence the size of plants and of firms and the number of optimally sized units will therefore depend upon the size of the market relative to the technical optimum. In fact, in their study of concentration in British industry, Eveley and Little found that there was a strong correlation between concentration and the number and size of units.[16] They found that industry concentration and the average size of plant were positively correlated and that concentration was negatively correlated with the number of units in the industry and the ratio of the average size of the three largest units to the average size of all units. It may be that market structure is partly influenced by the stage that the industry has reached in its life cycle with perhaps a progressive tendency for concentration to increase as the industry becomes older. Demand conditions may also be important. The less stable is the pattern of demand the greater the likelihood that the market structure will be more concentrated as a means of reducing uncertainty, while the larger is the total size of the market and the faster the rate of growth of demand the less likely is the industry to be concentrated. In the USA Pashigian found an inverse relation between relative market size and the four-firm concentration ratio while George found that in Britain over the period 1951–8 declining and stagnant industries were more likely to have increased concentration while growing industries tended to have decreasing levels of concentration.[17]

A second group of influences on market structure concern the activities of firms themselves. The numbers and relative sizes of births and deaths of firms will influence the degree of concentration in an industry, so too will the relative rates of growth of surviving firms. Gibrat's law of proportionate growth suggests that all firms irrespective of their starting size will tend to show similar average growth rates. Various studies have largely confirmed that this result does obtain for firms that survive throughout the period under investigation. This alone is sufficient to indicate that concentration will increase as a result of equal average proportionate growth rates for different size classes. If, however, large firms have a greater ability to survive, or if indeed large firms do in fact grow faster, then the rate of increase of concentration will be even greater.[18] The objectives of firms and especially whether they are growth oriented or not are likely to have an important influence on this question and particularly in terms of the extent to which mergers are used as the form of growth and often also of diversification.

The pattern of concentration will also be influenced by the way in which the major existing firms respond to increases in market demand. If they allow a more than proportionate part of any increase to be taken up by the smaller firms and new entrants, concentration will fall. If they meet additional demand by extending the size of existing plants there will be an increase in plant concentration but possibly not in firm concentration, while if they meet the increase in demand by adding additional plants then firm concentration may increase but not plant concentration. British evidence suggests that firms tend to meet rising demand by using larger rather than more plants[19] but American evidence suggests that multi-plant ownership is a more important influence on the level of company concentration than the ownership of larger than average plants.[20] Of course, if multi-plant ownership is an important element in concentration the sale of plants to other operators can be an effective means of reducing firm concentration. American economists often appear to be particularly sceptical of the claims that multi-plant operations bring additional scale economies over and above those available at the single-plant level and tend to consider that firm concentration in excess of plant concentration is indicative of an excessive degree of monopoly in industry.

The conditions of entry exercise an important influence upon the dynamic elements of the structure of industry. Vertical integration; restrictive policies regarding patent licensing; agreements, explicit or tacit, not to enter each others' markets; heavy advertising and restrictive distribution policies; all constitute disincentives to new entrants and so help to preserve any monopoly elements in the existing market structure. Some of these influences, such as vertical integration and patents, are important structural elements in their own right and will be considered separately in later chapters. Advertising is not only an influence on market structure but is also an indicator of a particular form of market conduct.

The final form of influence on market structure that we should note is that of government. This may be exercised in several ways – through tariff policy, through the effects of its fiscal policies on the chances of the birth, survival and growth of small firms, through incentives to rationalise or even cartelise an industry and through the general environment influencing both public and private attitudes regarding the desirability of mergers.

The evidence on concentration levels

In most countries some form of concentration measure is usually now available, normally in the form of a concentration ratio based on the share of output, sales, assets, etc., of the n largest firms. Even if statistical series were directly comparable we would not necessarily expect to be able to make meaningful comparisons of concentration levels across countries if, as is often the case, the industrial composition of the economy differed between countries, or the size of the market differed, or the strategies followed regarding industrialisation policies and industrial structure varied from country to country. In fact we do find that the same industries tend to be highly concentrated and the same industries tend to have low concentration in different countries.[21] Thus, for example, light bulb manufacture, explosives, plastics, shipbuilding and petrol refining are all consistently amongst the most concentrated industries in an economy. This would suggest that there are systematic influences in the nature of the products or the technological processes or the inter-relations between firms in an industry that largely determine relative degrees of concentration.

The most extensive analysis of international differences in market structure has been carried out by Bain[22] in which he compared concentration based on the 20 largest plants for a sample of industries skewed towards those that were more likely to be concentrated. The countries for which he collected data were Canada, France, Great Britain, India, Italy, Sweden and the USA. Comparing returns for other countries with data on the USA, Bain found that the other countries tended to have a higher level of plant concentration but smaller average plant size. Inevitably countries where markets are small in size will be able to support fewer optimally sized plants than in a country such as the USA where for a given average size of plant, the level of plant concentration would be much lower. In several of the industries studied Bain found that even in countries like France, India, Italy and Sweden not more than three firms supplied the whole of the output of the industry. Overall, he found that industry size and plant concentration were negatively correlated. But he found no functional relationship between comparative plant size and comparative plant concentration.

One important question that arises from this study is concerned with whether the smaller size of plant in all the countries other than the USA and, to a lesser extent, Britain indicates that these countries are suffering a loss of technical efficiency through having plants that are sub-optimal in size. A number of possible answers to this question was suggested by Bain. It may be that the smaller plants are not significantly less efficient or indeed that the larger American plants are above the optimum size. It may be that the cost function is such that unit costs rise by little at sub-optimal levels of output. It may be that the outputs and techniques of an industry in different countries are dissimilar, in which case it is less meaningful to attempt to consider international comparisons. Bain was inclined to take the view that plant scale economies were similar in each country. If this is the case, those countries with sub-optimally sized plants are suffering some loss of technical efficiency. This would not, however, necessarily justify further rationalisation measures since to increase plant concentration further might involve a loss of allocative and distributive efficiencies as a result of the inevitable increase in market power. This might more than outweigh any gains in technical efficiency terms. It also does not follow that simply because plants are sub-optimally sized in a country with a small market that industry will be unable to compete in world markets. Competitiveness depends upon the *position* as much as the *shape* of the cost function. Unit costs in a sub-optimum plant in a small country may still be lower than unit costs in an optimally sized American plant.

While British plants tended to be smaller than American plants, they were normally found to be larger than in most of the other countries investigated by Bain. However, by virtue of its smaller market, an equivalent British industry tends to be more highly concentrated than its American counterpart. Studies of British industrial concentration really began with the pioneering work of Leak and Maizels[23] and have been continued in different ways by a number of other researchers. Considerable interest has been shown in the extent to which concentration on average, or in individual industries, has been changing through time. Unfortunately it is not easy to answer these questions since comparisons of changes in concentration in different industries face the problem that official classifications of industries have changed through time while measures of average industrial concentration may be rendered largely meaningless as a result of shifts in the pattern of demand and hence in the volume of activity between different industries.

It does appear that between 1935 and 1951 there was a decline in the overall level of concentration in Britain. This may have been a phenomenon associated with wartime conditions as concentration in the USA appears also to have fallen over the same period. Since 1951 concentration has tended on balance to increase with more industries showing rising concentration than static or declining concentration. It appears that increases in concentration since then have tended to be located in a small number of sectors such as textiles and food[24] and of industries (e.g., aircraft, cars).[25] There has also been some tendency for the existing number of production plants to be operated by fewer enterprises,[26] though in Britain firm concentration still appears to be more closely associated with size of plant than in the USA.[27]

The most detailed indication of concentration levels provided by normal British statistical sources is that on concentration by product group provided in the Report on the Census of Production. Table 1.1 provides a summary of the distribution of concentration levels based on five-firm concentration ratios in 1968 for product groups classified by industrial order. Thus, for example, we find from this table that there are 44 separate product groups identified in the food, drink and tobacco order to which this information relates. Of these, 18 have five-firm concentration ratios of 90 per cent or above and none has a five-firm concentration ratio less than 30 per cent. This table provides the rather surprising information that, over British manufacturing industry as a whole, nearly one-quarter of separately identifiable product groups have five-

Table 1.1 Distribution of concentration ratios by Standard Industrial Classification in 1968

(number of product groups in each Standard Industrial Classification with given concentration ratios)

Order No.	Five-firm concentration ratio (C.R.)									Instances where	
	90-100	80-89	70-79	60-69	50-59	40-49	30-39	Less than 30	Totals	C.R. rose markedly 1963-8	C.R. fell noticeably 1963-8
II Mining and quarrying	2	—	—	—	1	1	1	—	5	2	—
III Food, drink and tobacco	18	7	7	6	3	2	1	—	44	4	3
IV Chemicals and allied	18	12	9	5	3	4	1	—	52	3	2
V Metal manufacture	11	2	4	1	2	2	—	—	22	7	—
VI Engineering and electrical goods	14	14	12	9	14	8	7	5	83	17	10
VII Shipbuilding	—	—	—	—	1	—	—	—	1	1	—
VIII Vehicles	7	—	—	1	—	1	—	—	9	—	—
IX Metal goods n.e.s.	2	2	3	3	4	1	2	4	21	4	1
X Textiles	1	2	2	1	8	5	6	3	28	13	2
XI Leather	—	—	—	—	1	2	—	2	5	2	—
XII Clothing and footwear	—	5	—	—	3	2	4	4	13	10	1
XIII Bricks, pottery, etc.	8	—	—	2	2	1	—	1	19	6	—
XIV Timber, furniture, etc.	—	—	—	—	1	2	3	6	9	2	2
XV Paper and board	—	1	2	4	2	—	1	—	10	1	1
XVI Other Manufactured goods	1	1	—	3	2	2	—	2	14	3	—
TOTALS	82	46	39	35	47	33	26	27	334	77	22

Definition

A marked increase in the concentration ratio was taken as one where the concentration ratio increased by 20 per cent or more and/or where more than ten firms in 1963 were needed to produce the same degree of concentration as that provided by the five largest firms in 1968.

A noticeable fall in the concentration ratio was taken to be a reduction of 10 per cent or more in the five-firm concentration ratio 1963-8.

A few miscellaneous product groups have been omitted from this table.

Where a seven-firm concentration ratio was given it is assumed that the five-firm concentration ratio would leave the product group within the same five-firm concentration ratio range as that indicated by the seven-firm concentration ratio.

Source: Report on the Census of Production 1968 (HMSO 1974), Part 158, Table 44.

firm concentration ratios of 90 per cent and over and that high industrial concentration is particularly associated with the vehicle; metal manufacture; brick, pottery, etc.; food, drink and tobacco; chemical and allied sectors. Many important products also have a five-firm concentration ratio of 90 per cent or over. There are too many to list in full. If, however, we consider only those product groups where sales in 1968 were over £100m we find that high sales and high concentration exists in the following product groups: sugar; ethyl alcohol; blended whisky; cigarettes; coke; various oil products; various products of the iron and steel industry; telegraph and telephone installation, etc.; tractors; cars; commercial vehicles; aircraft; cans and metal boxes; refined precious metals; man-made fibres; tyres and tubes.

We do not know from the census report whether the incidence of high five-firm concentration ratios in each case means that there are five firms each with market shares of about 20 per cent or whether the tendency is for one firm to have almost a complete monopoly of its product group. Undoubtedly the answer would vary from product to product and we should need to know something about the size distribution of the five largest firms and also a lot of other information relating to structural conditions before making confident predictions about the likely conduct and performance of those industries. Nevertheless there are some grounds for thinking that highly concentrated industries may merit particularly close attention for those concerned about the performance of industry and it is clear that quite a high proportion of the product groups in British industry are subject to high concentration.

Of course there are also product groups with low concentration ratios. These are most likely to be found in the timber, furniture, etc., order; in clothing and footwear; in leather; and in textiles. Once again we have no immediate criterion for deciding whether these concentration levels are 'right' or not. It may be that there are no economic reasons necessitating higher levels of concentration. It may be that the determination of product groups was too broadly based and that more narrowly defined product groups might reveal higher levels of concentration. Generally speaking, however, this would not seem to be a major difficulty and low concentration levels do seem to indicate industries with a more atomistic structure.

Concentration levels in different industries will be expected to vary through time and the last two columns of Table 1.1 indicate the number of product groups in each industrial order in which concentration had risen 'markedly' or fallen 'noticeably' (as defined in the table) between 1963 and 1968. Concentration increases considerably outweighed concentration reductions even though the criteria for identifying a marked concentration increase were more severe than for a noticeable concentration reduction. Concentration increases have been particularly marked in the clothing and footwear and in the textile sectors, both of which still remain sectors of low concentration. This may therefore suggest that there is some particular industrial logic providing a stimulus for rationalisation of industries in those sectors. Other instances of marked concentration increases have been spread across most sectors but occur especially in bricks, pottery, etc., and engineering and electrical goods. By definition, sizable concentration increases are most unlikely to occur where concentration is already high and it is not therefore surprising that overall the cases where concentration is most likely to have increased noticeably are less likely to be amongst the most highly concentrated industries or at least among those that were already highly concentrated in 1963.

In a general picture of rising concentration some product groups stand out as having shown very substantial increases in concentration between 1963 and 1968. Taking here cases where the concentration ratio doubled or alternatively rose by 20 or more percentage points 1963–8 we find that 23 product groups recorded concentration increases that met one or other of these criteria. These are set out in Table 1.2. Clearly these represent major changes in the structure of the industry concerned and might be particularly suitable subjects for detailed investigation of the causes and consequences of these changes. In the case of the steel products listed here steel re-nationalisation was presumably the main explanation.

The size of most reductions in concentration between 1963 and 1968 is generally not very big though there are exceptions. The concentration ratio for

Table 1.2   *Substantial concentration increases, 1963–8*

Product group	Five-firm concentration ratio		Product group	Five-firm concentration ratio	
	1963	1968		1963	1968
Coke	65	99	Cutlery	50	71
Cyclic hydrocarbons ...	51	85	Tops or slubbings ...	34	55
Aliphatic hydrocarbons ...	77	99	Socks, stockings,		
Steel blooms, billets and			tights	20	43
slabs	70	97	Infants' wear ...	15	30
Angles, shapes and sections	46	70	Corsets and brassieres	38	59
Steel plates	72	99	Sanitary ware ...	35	67
Pig iron	67	98	Tiles	74	94
Internal combustion			Pottery sanitary ware	66	95
reciprocating engines ...	68	91			
Steel and non-ferrous metal					
rolling mills	67	91			
Transformers for lighting					
and power	45	77			
Gramophones, record					
players, etc.	50	76			
Electric cookers, etc. ...	60	86			

A 'substantial' concentration increase was defined as one where the five-firm concentration ratio either doubled or increased by 20 percentage points.

Source derived from: *Report on the Census of Production 1968* (HMSO 1974), Part 158, Table 44.

blended tea fell from 98 per cent in 1963 to 83 per cent in 1968; for welding and flame cutting machines from 64 to 50 per cent; for powered industrial trucks and industrial tractors from 76 to 56 per cent; for industrial fans from 74 to 60 per cent; for automatic slot machines from 90 to 72 per cent and for rubber footwear from 78 to 57 per cent. Again the causes and consequences of these changes would constitute an interesting subject for investigation. It is likely that concentration declines are due either to the entry of a major new producer to the industry or perhaps to a shift in the pattern of demand between individual items within the product group.

One hypothesis about the level of concentration and changes in the level of concentration that seemed worth investigating was the possibility that there was a systematic difference between the degree and rate of change of concentration in consumer goods industries than in producer goods industries. It is not always easy to be certain that a particular product group falls solely or even mainly into one or other of these two categories; however, it seems reasonably clear that consumer and producer goods industries are equally distributed across concentration levels and in their experience of major concentration changes between 1963 and 1968.

Increased interest has also recently been shown in the question of changes in aggregate concentration in the British economy. Prais has shown that the 100 largest firms in the manufacturing sector of the economy were responsible for 21 per cent of net manufacturing output in 1949 and by 1970 this proportion had risen to 52 per cent.[28] If the same trend continued in the future he estimated that by 1983 the 100 largest firms would have 70 per cent of net manufacturing output and by the year 2000 the share would be 90 per cent. While it does not necessarily mean that just because aggregate concentration increases market concentration also increases, this can only be avoided if all firms achieve the majority of their growth outside the industries in which they have been operating. It is therefore likely that increasing aggregate concentration raises not only its own economic, social and political issues but also the problems of rising market concentration.

Why should this increase in aggregate concentration have come about? Statistically if Gibrat's law, that all firms grow at equal proportionate rates, holds then we should expect there to be some increase in concentration. Against this has to be set the possibility that, as with other statistical phenomena such as heights of children in families, etc., there is a tendency for sizes to regress towards the mean, thereby avoiding substantial increases in concentration.[29] Clearly such regressive influences have, over the last 20 years, been outweighed by anti-regressive influences. Possible factors contributing to the increase in concentration are not hard to find and relate both to circumstances favouring large firms and to others placing small firms at an increasing disadvantage. Changing production conditions may in some cases lead to such an increase in in the minimum optimum size of the firm that, even after allowing for the natural growth of the market, technical efficiency in production has required a significant increase in concentration. It is more likely, however, that changes in aggregate concentration are motivated rather by the pecuniary advantages of increasing size through superior buying power, greater ability to spread risks and to stabilise earnings. Increasing pressures for growth from within the firm and outside it through the influence of the stock market are also relevant. Growth often seems to be an important means of maintaining the independence of the organisation and is therefore a strong influence on company decision-taking. Frequently, rapid growth can only be achieved through the acquisition of other companies and the high price that may be paid for these can only be mortgaged in terms of further earnings increases provided by the next acquisition. The growth through merger movement can, if uncontrolled, be self-generating and must be held to have exercised an important influence on increases in both aggregate and market concentration.

The reverse side of the coin is reflected in the failure of smaller firms to grow sufficiently to ensure that concentration levels do tend over time to regress towards the mean. We shall discuss the position of small firms more extensively in Chapter 2. For present purposes we may observe that small and medium sized firms, especially those with good growth prospects, are often the takeover victims of the growth-oriented larger firms. Shortages of capital and adequate management are also often cited as important hindrances to the growth of smaller firms while estate duty regulations may have an adverse effect on the chances that family concerns will retain their separate independence.

There seems therefore to be a dual problem of too much growth through acquisition by large organisations and too little offsetting expansion by smaller organisations. This is a reflection of many facets of the industrial climate and of governmental policy over industrial structure in Britain in recent decades. One of the areas where the tendency for increasing aggregate concentration might have been tackled is in the formulation of anti-trust policy. The evidence on concentration change seems to be a reflection of the deficiencies of policy towards mergers not only in relation to horizontal mergers but also even more markedly in relation to conglomerate, diversifying acquisitions. It may also be a reflection of the relative imbalance between a stringent policy against cartels and a weak policy towards mergers which may have been adopted by firms as the way of maintaining the stability in the firm and industry that was formerly available through cartels. It is worthy of note that the USA which has a more stringent anti-merger policy, especially where horizontal and vertical mergers are concerned, has a much slower rate of growth of aggregate concentration.

There is little evidence on the economic effects of high levels of aggregate concentration but a substantial concentration of manufacturing resources and employment in a few hands is likely to be a cause for concern. The problem is in knowing what the critical level of concentration might be. It is also necessary to know whether the pattern of aggregate concentration increase is a reliable reflection of changes in actual industrial structure or whether here too other influences on structure have to be taken into account. One consequence of the growth of large firms allied to their product development activities is that they may increasingly come into competitive contact with each other in unexpected industries. Thus firms from such apparently disparate backgrounds as Courtaulds, ICI and Rolls Royce were at one time all working on carbon fibre developments. ICI sells petrol in competition with the major oil companies and Shell and ICI were both marketing detergents, though not in the household market. Increasing aggregate concentration from conglomeration and diversification may therefore imply increasing competition in some product markets but, as the Monopolies Commission report on household detergents showed,[30] it cannot be guaranteed that giant firms will in fact choose in every case to compete with each other, even where they have the technical capability to produce the product.

If it is the more efficient firms that grow and acquire the resources of other less successful companies there should be some gain in technical efficiency. But there may be costs of a loss of competition in some markets and a reduction in the variety of employment and investment opportunities. Beyond some critical level of aggregate concentration there may also be the costs of an undesirable redistribution of political and economic influence. It seems likely that aggregate concentration is approaching a critical level in Britain. The recent large rise in aggregate concentration seems to have been the result both of a very fast rate of growth especially through merger by some firms, and a failure of others, especially smaller units, to grow sufficiently. The prescription is probably a greater attention to the financial and managerial needs of small and medium sized firms and a more healthy scepticism in anti-trust policy of the benefits of allowing mergers between large organisations.

Concentration and economic performance

It is frequently suggested that market structure influences market conduct which influences economic performance. Various attempts, especially using American data, have been made to test at least part of this supposedly causal relationship. In particular, taking market concentration levels as a proxy for market structure, cross-sectional tests have been made of the link between structure and performance for samples of industries. In this section we shall consider the findings in respect of four performance indicators: profits, prices, progressiveness and efficiency. While the structural measure adopted in such investigations is normally a concentration ratio it will also be helpful to consider the results of analyses using size of firm as well. As we shall observe, there are numerous problems that arise both with regard to the quality of the data and the interpretation of relationships that are found to exist. It does not follow, as we have already argued, that a particular concentration measure is an unambiguous indicator of market structure in all industries.

The crucial significance of the degree of concentration as a tool of economic analysis or as a guide to public policy has yet to be established . . . it has not been established that there is a unique correlation between the degree of concentration and either the degree of discretion available to the firm, the types of business practices pursued or the character of the economic effects.[31]

If market structure is multi-dimensional, so too is economic performance where many indicators all contribute to the pattern of information provided about the performance of an industry. Statistical investigations have been based mainly upon single measures of structure and performance. This does not mean that the results are not of interest but their limitations should be recognised. Careful case study analysis of the structure, conduct and performance of individual industries might prove a useful adjunct to the information normally provided by the statistical investigations.

(1)   Concentration and Profits

The technique normally adopted here is to take a range of observations of industry concentration and price levels for a particular point in time, and by using regression analysis to establish whether there is a statistically significant relation between the two and, if so, the proportion of the variation in profit rates for which concentration data alone will account. The value of the partial coefficients obtained will indicate the actual numerical relationship between the two variables, that is the effect on profits of a specified change in the level of concentration. In some cases a dummy variable representing the estimated height of the barriers to entry into an industry is also included as an independent variable along with the concentration ratio. Various measures of profits have been used including $\dfrac{\text{net profits before tax}}{\text{total assets}}$ and $\dfrac{\text{retained earnings}}{\text{net worth}}$ or, as a proxy for a price-cost margin,[32] $\dfrac{\text{gross profits plus pre-tax depreciation}}{\text{value of shipments for the industry}}$

The balance of the evidence suggests that a positive relationship does exist between the level of concentration and the level of profits. But the results indicate that this relationship leaves a large proportion of the variation in profit rates unexplained and that the effect of increasing concentration would not be greatly to increase profits. Whether the relationship is linear or not is not agreed; some research has suggested that profitability levels tend to increase much faster when the eight-firm concentration ratio is at 70 per cent or above,[33] that is where the oligopoly is likely to be particularly tight. One study has however suggested that profit levels tend to be negatively correlated with the share of industry output in the hands of the fifth to the eighth largest firms.[34] The most likely interpretation to place upon this result would be that while a few (up to four) firms dominating a market can behave in a co-operative and joint maximising manner, if there are as many as five to eight firms with not insignificant market shares then it becomes more difficult to preserve the stability of the group and the likelihood increases of independent competitive behaviour in the market which will reduce the profitability of the firms concerned.

Entry barriers, where incorporated in the analysis, are normally found to be significant and positively associated with profits. The more important are regional markets and the more capital intensive the industry the higher are profits likely to be for any given level of concentration.

Very little British evidence on this question is available. What there is is not entirely in keeping with the American findings. Hart[35] found no evidence that high profits and high concentration were correlated although Samuels and Smyth found in another investigation that the more concentrated industries had lower variability of profits.[36]

When size of firm is used rather than concentration level there also appears to be some divergence between American and British results. Hall and Weiss found for American data that there was more of a positive association between size of firm and profits than between concentration and profits and explained this on the grounds that this was consistent with the notion that capital requirements constituted an important barrier to entry.[37] Marcus found, in a study of 118 American industries, that in 35 of these firm size exercised a significant and positive influence on profitability though the extent to which profits rose as firm size rose was not large.[38] In a study of the relation between size and profits in British firms Samuels and Smyth found that although small firms had more variable profits it was the small firms rather than the large firms that tended to have the largest profits.[39] Singh and Whittington also found for the period 1948–60 that the dispersion of profit rates was greater for small British firms than for larger ones. They concluded that there was no systematic tendency for average profitability to increase or decrease as the size of firm changed although they concluded that, if anything, profitability seemed more likely to decline slightly as the size of firm increased.[40]

Whether there really is a difference between the American and the British relationships is unclear on the basis of the evidence so far available. Certainly the possibility that such a difference does exist should encourage rather more attempts to test this question with British data. The vast majority of the American studies generally show that there is a weak but significant positive correlation between concentration or firm size and profits and that this is improved if other structural variables are added in. The British studies often show no significant correlation and if anything a negative relation. If such a difference does exist between the British and American experience the causes and implications ought to be carefully investigated.

But just how reliable are these findings? Several commentators have expressed considerable reservations, both about the nature of the relationship specified, the quality of the data used and the statistical procedures adopted. It is argued that it is not useful to specify such a simple relationship between concentration and profits since profits are influenced by many factors besides monopoly power. Other influences would include the degree of risk, the rate of growth of the industry, absolute size of firms and of market, the firms' product mixes, the factor prices they pay, the optimality of existing sizes of production plant, varying firm efficiencies, different firm objectives and their non-price behaviour. Profit measures may be systematically inaccurate if the existence of a monopoly position acts as a disincentive to earn high profits or if the profits of small, owner-managed firms are understated as a result of the payment of higher wages to management and lower profits to the owner. Profits may not be an unambiguous measure of the welfare consequences of a particular market structure since it is not easy to establish how far high profits arise from superior efficiency and how far from exploitation. Often it is difficult to match completely the profit figures on firms or industries to available concentration data. Finally, it seems that at least some of the studies reported may have obtained spurious relations between concentration and profits by ignoring some other variables that may be correlated with both profits and concentration and by not in most cases standardising for the effects of different absolute sizes of firms and industries or differing degrees of labour intensity.

(2) Concentration and Prices

There are alternative hypotheses regarding the relation between market power and prices. Static neo-classical theory predicts that prices will be higher under conditions of monopoly than under competition. Dynamic theory suggests that once the possibility that a monopolist would gain scale economies not available to firms in an atomistic industry is allowed for, prices may be lower in a more concentrated industry. Empirical testing of this hypothesis is difficult since it does not lend itself to comparisons between industries within a particular economy at a specific point in time. The economist has to make do with analyses of the relation between market power and profits.

There is, however, a related question that has received some attention. This is concerned with the existence or otherwise of a tendency for prices in concentrated industries to move at a different rate from prices in less concentrated industries. This debate has become known as the administered-price controversy and was initiated by work reported by Means in which he argued that prices in some industries with high degrees of market power tended to be less likely to fall in a depression. To this he later added a second strand of argument that prices in some industries with high degrees of market power were more likely to rise when demand was strong. Various people have attempted to test Means's arguments by generalising them into a hypothesis that in more concentrated industries prices tend to move with a ratchet-like effect – being sticky in a depression and flexible in an upward direction in a boom.

This is an interesting hypothesis and seems to have some empirical support in the literature.[41] However, at best it is unlikely that this represents a substantial part of the explanation of the causes of relative price movements and at worst it is arguable that modern technological conditions reduce whatever relevance this explanation may have had at an earlier stage. It is also not at all clear that it is really the degree of market concentration that is the relevant influence. Weiss reported a high degree of collinearity between concentration and wage changes and found that changes in wages were more closely associated with price changes than were concentration levels when both wage changes and concentration were included in the same regression equation.[42] There may be good reasons deriving from their own mutual recognition of interdependence why oligopolists would choose not to lower prices in a depression or alternatively it may be that firms in a capital intensive industry, which by its nature is likely to be oligopolistic in structure, may find it desirable to *raise* prices in a depression as a result of the rising unit costs incurred in production when capacity utilisation falls.[43] Whether oligopolists or monopolists would choose to raise their prices when demand is strong is debatable since their decisions are likely to be strongly influenced by considerations of public goodwill and the likelihood of anti-trust action. The point about market dominance is that it tends to provide firms with a greater degree of independence of the market and makes them less likely to respond to short-term changes in demand conditions. Where cost conditions and capacity utilisation questions are important it is likely that firm behaviour will be different from that predicted in the administered price debate since they are then more likely to wish to *raise* prices when demand is weak and to be better able to keep prices steady or even to lower them (though this latter is unlikely) when demand is strong, capacity utilisation high and unit costs falling.

Although market power allows firms greater discretion in a number of respects, including deciding on the size of profit margin to pursue, there does not seem to be a strong reason for thinking that high concentration is an important cause of ratchet-like price behaviour in industries.

(3)   Concentration and Progressiveness

Debate on the relation between firm size and/or market structure on the one hand and economic progress through effective research and development on the other has a long history. Schumpeter's claim that the large firm (which by implication also has some market power) is the most powerful engine of progress is normally considered the epitome of the argument that large firms and market concentration are important for progress.[44] The converse argument is that monopoly power may, by giving firms increasing discretion and high profits, reduce the incentive to invent and innovate. Clearly, it would be helpful to have a reconciliation of these conflicting arguments, though once again it is unlikely that any clear-cut conclusion will be found.

Before investigating the actual empirical evidence that is available let us first consider the various arguments put forward regarding the relative advantages of large and small firms in research and development (R and D) as this may not only indicate possible economic explanations for the empirical results but will also suggest that it is extremely unlikely that any particular size of firm or degree of market power will consistently give a particular R and D outcome. Large firms may well have important advantages in R and D. There may be a high minimum optimum size of research laboratory up to which scale economies in R and D inputs are available, or the rapid availability of a large market may be an important influence on the profitability of making the necessary investments to exploit a new product or process. The market power enjoyed by large firms may make R and D more likely to take place since there is greater opportunity to enjoy the rewards of successful innovation. By virtue of their size large firms are better able to stand failures in some areas of R and D and to be prepared to accept long lead times before a project is expected to become profitable. Their financial strength may be important for the successful innovation and marketing of a new product and to help them to overcome the negative cash flow problems often associated with new product developments. It has also been suggested that the large firm which is diversified may find advantages because inventions tend to occur in unexpected areas and the diversified organisation has therefore a greater likelihood of capitalising upon these opportunities.[45]

Against this it is often argued that large firms have disadvantages in R and D. They may well be more bureaucratic and consequently less likely to perceive new opportunities and may have a high risk aversion preference, concentrating upon projects with a short period pay off. They may well have a vested interest in existing methods and products and may be unwilling to proceed with an innovation that threatens their own existing investments. They may also find it difficult to attract and retain sufficiently good scientists to enable them to maintain a high level of progressiveness.[46]

The advantages and disadvantages of small firms in R and D are in many cases the obverse of those discussed for large firms. But certain possible advantages of small firms are worthy of note. Organisationally, they may have a more creative staff with a stronger commitment to the job and there may be a less bureaucratic structure which facilitates a closer coupling of the R and D activity to other departments. This will allow better co-ordination between the different product development activities and a shorter lead time between invention and innovation. The owners of small firms may be less motivated by monetary considerations, more willing to take risks and may be more willing to co-operate with other organisations possibly through industrial research associations in order to obtain economies that would be external to the individual organisation.[47] Which set of advantages and disadvantages is more likely to produce the more satisfactory outcome is unclear. It does, however, seem that small firms are more likely to have the edge in *invention* while the financial strengths (and probably established brand reputations and marketing forces) of large firms are likely to give them the advantage in *innovation* and in the *diffusion* of an innovation.

In principle, the question of the relation between industry structure and economic progress might be amenable to the same form of regression analysis that has been used extensively in investigating the relation between concentration and profits. The same problems of industry classification, concentration measurement and the need to assume a constant relation between concentration and market power still remain. There are also problems of determining exactly what it is that is to be used as a measure of progressiveness. Do we really want some indicator of the number of discoveries that are made (inventions), or of the number that are actually turned into something that may be useful (innovations), or of the speed with which a new product or process is generally adopted by an industry (the rate of diffusion of innovations)? All have their economic significance but all pose measurement problems of one sort and another.

In practice the indicator most frequently adopted of R and D outputs is the number of patents issued. But numerous caveats must be borne in mind before accepting its reliability as an indicator. First, there is no means of weighting patents to reflect their relative economic significance or the probability that they will in fact be used in production. Secondly, the propensity to patent is not constant. In industries where the risks of imitation are great or where technological opportunities are substantial the incidence of patenting may be high. In other industries where imitation is difficult and know-how is an important advantage or where government is a major financier of R and D activities and retains the rights on any discoveries, the propensity to patent may be much less. The use of patenting may also vary systematically between different sizes of firms. It is often suggested that large firms are less likely to patent than small firms but it may alternatively be the case that small firms will make less use of patenting because they do not have the financial and legal resources to police and enforce their patents. They may prefer instead to keep their discoveries secret and not to disclose them by applying for a patent.

The use of some measures of input into R and D such as total R and D expenditures or the number of qualified scientists and engineers employed may avoid some of the problems that arise in trying to measure R and D outputs. But these are also not entirely reliable. Much R and D expenditure by industry is concerned with development rather than basic research and in some industries the basic inventions occurred years ago and only a process of gradual improvement is now proceeding. An unweighted analysis of R and D expenditures may therefore give an unreliable prediction of the likely outcome in terms of economic progress. The scope for effective statistical analysis is limited by the concentration of R and D expenditures in only a small number of firms and industries. In those cases where government is the major financier of research expenditures, by using input figures we are not necessarily obtaining any indication of the nature of the firm's own decisions about desirable levels of R and D expenditure. Finally, since we are presumably more interested in knowing what input measures may help us to predict outputs rather than in looking at R and D inputs for their own sake, the possibility that there is no constant relation between R and D input (even after allowing for the differences between basic and applied research) and R and D output must make for further extra caution in using results of analyses where the dependent variable is a measure of inputs. This may not, however, be too serious a problem as one American investigation has shown that there is in fact a high correlation between R and D expenditures and patents.[48]

A number of studies has investigated this aspect of the relation between structure and performance. Some have used input measures and some output measures as indicators of performance. Some have been concerned with the relative performance of different sized firms in the same industry and others have made comparisons between different industries, although it is, in this latter case, important to try to make allowance for the differing degree of technological opportunity that exists to provide an incentive to R and D in each industry. Some studies only consider large and very large firms and do not therefore offer evidence relating to all industrial organisations. When the reader follows up the major sources of empirical work on this question he must therefore be on the look-out for information regarding the actual data used and an indication of the possible limitations on the applicability of the results.

Once again there is not complete agreement among investigators over the link between structure and performance; however, a number of pointers are to be found in the literature.[49] At worst, there is no significant correlation between concentration and R and D intensity or output and at best the relationship is only weak. High levels of concentration, e.g. where the four-firm concentration ratio is greater than about 55 per cent, may hinder progress. Taking large firms rather than market power *per se,* we find that R and D intensity increases absolutely as the size of firm increases, but as a proportion of sales the largest firms spend no more or possibly even less than medium sized firms. Whether the largest firms are obtaining scale economies in their R and D inputs is not clear. The concept of a minimum threshold level of firm size for effective R and D expenditures seems important. While the actual level of the threshold varies from industry to industry, it is unlikely that it is as large as the largest firms in the industries concerned. Large firms tend not to be proportionately more important producers of major inventions. While they are more important as innovators they do not in all cases account for a larger share of innovations in relation to inputs and may still be slow to take up developments that are offered to them by smaller firms. If the level of R and D expenditure is held constant it seems that medium sized firms are likely to be more productive than large firms. Small firms remain important sources of inventions though not of innovations.

This evidence does not lend much support to the view that either high concentration or large firms are unduly conducive to economic progress as measured in terms of either R and D inputs or outputs.[50] While high concentration may act as a positive disincentive it seems that in some circumstances large firms may offer some benefits especially at the innovation stage. There is therefore little apparent reason for increasing market concentration simply to increase economic performance in this area. Whether increasing the number of firms would speed up the rate of invention and/or innovation and/or diffusion of innovations is an open question. The contrast between the conditions favourable for invention and those favourable for innovation seem to be quite strong. It has been suggested from this that a systems approach would favour the location of inventive and innovative activities in different organisations.[51] The work of the National Research Development Corporation is in some sense a reflection of this sort of consideration since it aims to improve the rate of exploitation of inventions that arise from small firms without their own resources to bear the heavy costs of innovating.

(4)   Concentration and Efficiency

Is there any evidence that relative levels of concentration influence the incentive upon firms to increase their operating efficiency? It is certainly arguable that the more competitive an industry is the more likely is productivity to increase because of the increased pressure on costs that competition imposes. In a study of changes in unit labour requirements for a sample of American industries over the period 1899–1937, Stigler found that decreases in unit labour requirements were more associated with less concentrated industries.[52] A more recent study for 19 American industries over the period 1939–64, however, showed that productivity growth rates did not differ significantly by industry concentration class.[53] If data were available this might be a worthwhile area for further analysis, though time series analysis runs into the difficulty that concentration levels change over time both absolutely and relatively to those in other industries.

Performance – conduct – structure?

The discussion in this chapter has largely explicitly assumed that it is industry structure that influences market conduct and economic performance. In most instances it seems correct to assume that if there is a causal relationship this is the direction in which causality will go. However, there has been some suggestion that this does not necessarily follow and that the reverse direction of causality from performance to conduct to structure might also exist.[54] In concluding this chapter we shall consider some circumstances in which this reverse ordering may apply.

The essence of the argument for a reverse ordering is to be found in the attack on static explanations of the relation between structure and performance that are to be found in the neo-classical theories of competition and monopoly. Replacing these with a more dynamic conception of the behaviour of firms, it is argued that there is a feedback relation from a particular performance level that influences *subsequent* structure and conduct. Thus a particular market structure or conduct may well be a consequence of previous performance, or market structure may be a consequence of previous market conduct. This does not seem unreasonable and various possible illustrations can be given to indicate its plausibility.

First, consider the conduct → structure link. This is, for example, embodied in the Monopolies Commission's investigation whether the 'things done' by dominant firms are 'as a result of' (structure → conduct) or 'for the purpose of preserving' (conduct → structure) that position. Aggressive marketing via price discrimination, aggregated rebates, insistence on exclusive purchasing may all be conduct phenomena that influence market structure either by driving out competitors or by so raising the height of entry barriers that potential entrants do not attempt to enter the market. The imposition of legislative constraints on different forms of conduct by firms may cause them to change their structural relationships. For example, it has been argued that by rendering illegal the vast majority of price fixing agreements (a conduct phenomenon) the Restrictive Trade Practices Act 1956 in some industries at least caused an increase in mergers (a structural change), see Chapter 15 below.

Secondly, consider the influence of performance on both conduct and structure. The feedback mechanism is particularly important where firm or industry performance is unsatisfactory. Poor performance measured in terms of profits or efficiency or progressiveness may encourage either the firms concerned or major shareholders in the firms concerned or the government to seek to change either structure or conduct or both. Undoubtedly low profits may encourage firms to consider the possibilities of introducing price fixing or market sharing arrangements or of restructuring the industry through mergers. In some cases, as with the cotton industry in 1959, and depressed industries in the 1920s and 1930s, the initiative may come from the government. In other cases it may come from firms either within or outside the industry concerned who see an opportunity for profitable acquisitions. Considerable rationalisation of both the cotton and the woollen textiles industries has been undertaken as a result of acquisitions especially by some of the major fibre producers.

Patents and other aspects of technological progress also have an impact upon the relationship between performance and structure. Technological progress is an important measure of performance but high rates of technological progress are also likely to lead to changes in market structure. Where know-how and technical expertise are unequally distributed they will cause disparate rates of growth and if it is the dominant firms that have superior know-how, etc., this will increase concentration. Patents and other know-how advantages are also influences on market structure through the possibility that in some cases they may constitute important barriers to entry. Even if it can be shown that a particular form of market structure was, in the first instance, most likely to have contributed to the successful invention or innovation on which the patent was based, the award of an important patent is likely to have a marked effect on subsequent market structure.

The link between structure, conduct and performance does seem to be rather more complicated than is normally assumed. The traditional structure → conduct → performance formulation should not be rejected since there is evidence that structure and conduct do have a reasonably predictable influence on certain aspects of performance. But it does seem that we must recognise that not only is structure an influence on present conduct and performance but in a dynamic framework 'today's' market structure is a result of 'yesterday's' conduct and performance.

CHAPTER 2

ECONOMIES OF SCALE

Production of any commodity is achieved through the combination of different factor inputs, including land, labour, capital, enterprise and the various raw materials, semi-finished products, energy, etc., that go to make up most production processes. The more efficiently factors are combined the more profitably and competitively will the firm be able to operate, all other things being equal. While the identification of least cost combinations of factor inputs is an important part of production planning, our primary interest in this chapter is with the question of the effects which the scale of an operation or organisation has on the unit costs of that particular activity. In current discussions of industrial structure this is a most important issue. To the firm, an awareness of these issues should assist considerations of the size and operations of the organisation. To government policy-making, awareness of the underlying cost and production conditions in certain industries might affect the approach to aggregate demand management in so far as it may be considered likely to affect the operations and capacity utilisation of individual industries. Evidence on economies of scale will also have a direct influence on government thinking on industrial structure and anti-trust policy especially in so far as it impinges on mergers and industrial reorganisation.

While the implications for merger policy will be discussed in a later chapter, it is useful to bear in mind at this point some normative questions that information on scale economies should be able to help in answering. In particular we should want to know the effect that different scales of operation or organisation have on efficiency in production and distribution; whether the structure of economies of scale is such that firms may become too large and ultimately begin to operate under conditions of rising unit costs; how disadvantaged a sub-optimally sized operation is – whether the slope of the unit cost curve is steep or flat as it approaches the optimum; how this bears on the conditions of entry into an industry; whether firms in practice tend to be of optimum size; what market structure gives optimum efficiency; how current industrial structure compares with that required for optimality; whether the achievement of an optimum industry structure if it could be identified would have adverse implications for competition in that particular industry.[1] These are clearly very considerable demands to place upon any economic evidence, especially where measurement of the data is difficult and

31

where, in a dynamic world with changing technology, the evidence from one point in time may well be less relevant to policy-making concerned with a future time period. Nevertheless, considerations of the availability or otherwise of economies of scale are very relevant in both firm and government decision-making.

We must first explain what is meant by the term economies of scale. In the short run where, by definition, a factor of production (maybe the size of the plant) is fixed, variations in the unit costs of producing different outputs arise as returns to the fixed factor of production and the more efficient utilisation of that fixed factor. These then are strictly speaking returns to the fixed factor of production. Genuine economies of scale arise in the long run where all factors of production are variable in respect of the proportions in which they may be used.[2] They may be defined as 'potential reductions in average unit costs associated with higher levels of production capacity, with capacity measured in terms of the number of units of the standard product which can be produced per unit of time'.[3] Thus economies of scale are reflected in the shape of the long-run average cost curve which shows the effects of varying scales of operations on the costs of those operations at a given point in time. To emphasise the actual nature of the long-run average cost curve Pratten has argued that it should be described as a 'scale curve'.[4]

Before we move on to consider the measurement and sources of economies of scale we should note some conceptual reservations that must be borne in mind. While they do not necessarily invalidate the conclusions to be derived later, they do indicate the care that is required in interpreting the data. Discussions of the production function from which the cost function is derived tend to assume constant technology, homogeneous factor inputs and constant factor prices. These are not entirely applicable in a world in which new vintages of plant may be introduced which offer lower unit costs than previous vintages; in which new scales of activity may be introduced using new production techniques that may completely alter the trend in long-run costs in a way that is not predictable in advance; in which factor inputs are clearly not homogeneous either in terms of the quality of successive units employed or when compared between firms; and where it is likely that the supply curve of factors of production is not completely elastic so that when additional units are required a higher price may need to be paid to attract them. Measurement implies that costs can be calculated for different output levels but there are difficulties in the use of accounting data. In multi-product, multi-plant organisations the apportionment of costs between products (and between different levels of productive activity in vertically integrated organisations) is subject to so much discretion that cost information provided by firms may not be a reliable input for the measurement of scale economies. Average costs may not be independent of all variables other than current output since they are often a function of the expected level of sales and hence of output and of the amortisation period determined for fixed costs.

While production economies at the plant level may perhaps be measured with a fair degree of reliability, it is less easy to measure economies of a non-production nature accruing to the organisation. The question also arises of whether a firm or plant that is of optimum size from a production point of view is also minimising actual costs to the fullest extent possible and so is operating on the lowest cost curve that is technically feasible. Where this is not the case there is said to be an element of X-inefficiency equal to the extent of the difference between actual costs and the lowest costs that are technically feasible given the actual level of output.[5] A further drawback in most discussions of scale economies is that they tend to deal with the effect on costs of alternative levels of scale at a given point in time. In fact, as we shall see, many industries find that important economies of scale also accrue through the effects of aggregate output *through* time as well as varying levels of output *at a point in time*. This is the phenomenon normally known as 'learning'.

The measurement of economies of scale

Measurement is concerned with helping to answer the questions posed in the second paragraph of this chapter, particularly: how far are unit costs lowered as output rises; what is the path of the cost function to the optimum; are firms at present of optimum size; what is the significance for concentration of industry of having optimally sized plants and firms? Four main types of technique have been used in endeavouring to assess the incidence of economies of scale.

(1)   Comparisons of Profitability of Firms

The basis here is the assumption that optimally sized firms would be those showing the highest levels of profitability in terms of profit on sales or capital employed or return on shareholder equity, etc. A number of studies have investigated this, and as we saw in Chapter 1 yielded varying results, some showing that small firms have highest profits, others that profitability tends to increase as size expands. Considerable problems arise in using published data here since different accounting conventions in the valuation of assets and even different policies in the declaration of profits make comparability difficult to achieve. With highly diversified firms it becomes particularly difficult to use this information (certainly if using only published data) as a basis for analysis of the optimal scale for production of any given product or range of products. The returns achieved by a company will also be influenced by their market power and by the degree of X-inefficiency persisting in that organisation. Thus profitability comparisons do not seem to be a very promising means of approaching this problem.

(2)   Statistical Cost Analysis

In this method, actual unit costs of production are compared for different sized plants or firms or in the production of different levels of output. If sufficient observations are available for reliable analysis in any industry this suggests that the optimum size of activity is small so that this method is not appropriate to all types of industry, particularly those with large optimal scale and high concentration. Difficulties arise in ensuring comparability between observations in terms of the technology used, factor costs, output mixes, policies in the allocation of overheads and imputation of other costs.[6]

An interesting development of the cross-sectional approach implicit in statistical cost analysis is that used by the Centre for Interfirm Comparison. The Centre operates to provide comparative information for management of different firms in the same industry about their company's performance through time and in comparison with other firms in the same industry (whose returns are grouped and shown anonymously). Much more information is collected than would be available in published accounts, and collection is on a standardised basis, so that direct comparability is achieved. Over 60 industries participate in such schemes organised by the Centre and other similar schemes are run in other industries by trade associations and from university departments. Their value in alerting management to deficiencies in their own performance is widely accepted. The basis of the exercise is the calculation of a wide range of business ratios covering general accounting returns, data on labour force performance, plant and material utilisation, stockholding ratios, space utilisation, marketing performance, financial structure, etc. The basic pyramid of management ratios is shown in Figure 2.1. It will be observed that this alone provides an extensive and informative series of ratios. When firms are subject to the discipline of producing such information, plus information for other ratios which are calculated in individual comparison exercises, this is a particularly important aid to management decision-making and in increasing awareness of cost effectiveness. When to this is added the benefit of comparability with the performance of other firms and comparisons through time it is quite clear that this should be an important aid to management in identifying weak areas in a company's performance.

(3)   The Survivor Technique

It seems that this approach was initially suggested by Stigler.[7] The principle is that firms are grouped into different size classes and their long-run average costs are inferred by observing changes in the shares of output held by the different size classes between two points in time. On the assumption that plant size will tend toward the optimum, those plants observed to be increasing their share of the market through time are assumed to have the lower average costs. The technique has been used by other economists in empirical analysis and it

Fig 2.1 'Pyramid' of ratios

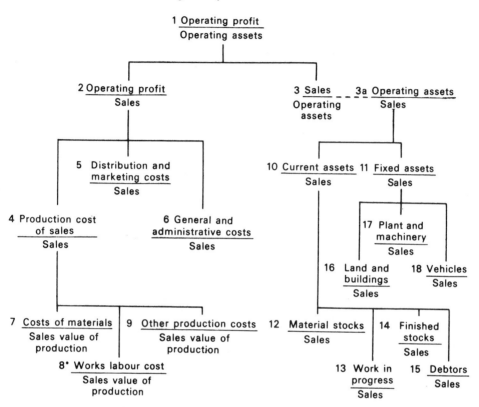

Source: Centre for Interfirm Comparisons

has been found that it is useful in estimating the optimal scale in a number of industries in a welfare as well as a competitive effectiveness sense.[8] The Monopolies Commission inferred a survivor technique in its comments on economies of scale in the production of valves for aerosols, concluding that the existence of a number of small valve makers suggested that this was a field in which there was less scope for economies of scale than there was in the production of aerosols as such.[9]

This technique is likely to be most useful where attention is focused upon questions of the optimum size of plant rather than of firm and where the need is mainly for a rough indication of the shape of the cost curve and the approximate share of industry output required for optimality. It does, however, also have a number of important drawbacks. It is most likely to yield useful information where competition is sufficiently keen for it to generate changing market shares and pressure on costs but where technological change has been limited so that the observed changes in shares of output taken by different plant sizes are not due to the effects of a change in technology. It also has of necessity to assume that the exercise of market power, other forms of market conduct, other circumstances including managerial qualities and performance and the different goals of the firms that may influence the chances of survival and growth of firms with different sized plants do not have a significant bearing on the observed changes in plant market shares. Undoubtedly such assumptions will often be unjustified.

(4)   Engineering Production Functions

The engineering production function approach is based upon estimates by engineers and other technical experts of the hypothetical technical costs of production that would accrue in plants of varying sizes. It is based on ideal rather than actual relations, it applies only to plants using current technologies and cannot readily be used for estimating the cost functions of existing firms, or where expansion takes place through the addition of existing capacity rather than building a brand new plant. Non-technical costs of, for example, management and marketing and differences in their relative effectiveness between firms are ignored in this approach which strictly speaking represents a process function rather than a complete production function.[10] Demand conditions, current or expected, are assumed to be irrelevant and a completely elastic factor supply is once again a basic assumption. While it too therefore has its drawbacks and suffers from a range of unrealistic assumptions, it does have the advantage of overcoming some of the objections, especially relating to measurement, that limit the value of the other techniques. It has been used as the basis of many of the important studies on cost functions carried out in recent years by, for example, Chenery, Bain and Pratten and Dean.[11]

Sources of economies of scale

The benefits of a larger scale of operation may apply at the level of the individual product, the individual plant or at the level of the individual firm. There may also be externalities, that is, benefits accruing from the scale of the industry that are not attainable by any individual firm on its own account. While the sources of economies of scale are not in every case clearly attributable to one or other of the different levels of operation, we shall endeavour to identify distinctions between those economies that are available at the level of the single product or the single plant producing a small range of products on the one hand, and those economies which accrue only to the large multi-plant organisation on the other hand. It should also be noted that while in certain cases a particular feature may be a source of scale economies, in other cases, in different industries or under different sorts of organisational structure and performance, this same source may be a cause of diseconomies rather than economies. The importance of effective management within the firm to harness those possible sources of benefit so that they do in fact prove to the advantage rather than the disadvantage of the organisation is therefore very important.

(1) *Economies at the Single Plant Level*

Economies at the level of the single product or the single plant producing a narrow range of products are mainly those that arise in one way or another from the production process. Many of the costs involved in setting up a particular production process, especially set-up, jigging and tooling costs and indeed a high proportion of labour costs, are not subject to variations in the scale of output. An expanding scale of activity allows these costs to be spread over a larger output and hence the unit costs incurred through these factors fall. The costs of larger sizes of plant will usually not rise as quickly as the volume which they can produce increases. For example, it is often held that while the capacity of a piece of equipment increases in geometric progression, the actual costs of that equipment only rise in an arithmetic progression and so the purchase price of the equipment per unit of the output it helps to produce will fall as the size of the equipment increases. The opportunity to mechanise and perhaps fully automate may allow the use of better equipment, a reduction in material wastage and the achievement of faster machine speeds. Longer runs help to overcome indivisibilities and facilitate the more specialised use of equipment and labour. The move from batch to flow production increases the benefits from an avoidance of retooling and the frequent stopping and starting of equipment. There is therefore often an important argument for rationalisation and standardisation of the product line in order to achieve the benefits of longer runs and also to reduce the high costs of holding stocks of slower moving products.

As the scale of operation increases, so certain benefits from the massing of resources become apparent. With perhaps more machines being used for the same purpose the risks of a breakdown seriously interrupting production are lessened and repair and maintenance work can be more effectively scheduled. Inventory levels in stocks of raw materials and finished products will not rise to the same extent as production increases. Economies in marketing and distribution may become apparent at this level but are more likely to apply to the multi-product firm. One possible exception, however, is the likelihood that there will be a minimum threshold level of sales below which it will be difficult to achieve an effective distribution, whereas once a critical mass of sales is reached it may then be easier to obtain an effective and adequate number of outlets for a product. In this case there is therefore a degree of circularity in the argument. A high level of sales is necessary to be able to achieve effective economies of scale which are themselves necessary to allow prices to be reduced sufficiently so that a mass market for the product can be developed. Thus output and sales levels not only need to be equated in order to avoid excessive stock-piling or lack of production to meet demand, but also the level of sales and the level of output are interdependent.

Not only are there benefits from increases in scale at a point in time, but there are also benefits from the effects of cumulative output through time. This is known as the effect of 'learning' and is depicted in Figure 2.2 where learning causes average costs to fall through successive periods of time. If the same level of output OM is produced in each time period the unit costs of achieving that output fall progressively from OC_t to OC_{t+n}. Whereas normal economies of scale are based on the assumption that the scale of activity may vary while technical knowledge remains constant, learning effects derive from changes in technical knowledge while the size of plant and scale of operations is constant.

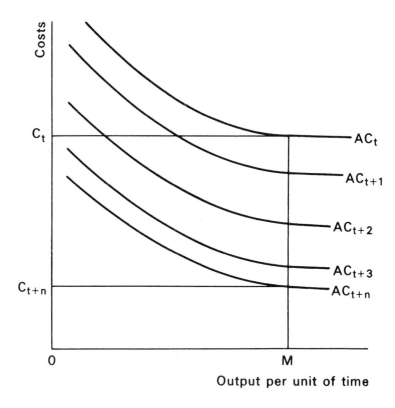

Fig 2.2 Movements in average costs through time

Learning is normally held to occur as a result of the repeated execution of the same task, so direct labour functions, especially in assembly, are normally considered to be an important source of cost savings through learning. But it seems likely that all parts of an organisation learn to a greater or lesser degree.

For example, it has been claimed that learning may also occur in machine-intensive industries as a result of the adaptive, debugging work of engineers, supervisors, machine operators, quality control staff, etc.[12] Much of the discussion of the economics of learning has been in terms of the aircraft industry[13] where it is often assumed that as output doubles so the level of unit costs falls to 80 per cent of its previous level. A typical curve depicting the path of costs under such conditions is shown in Figure 2.3. The concept appears to be relevant in other industries too.[14] In the semi-conductor industry a learning effect has been reported in which costs may fall by 20 or 30 per cent as output doubles[15] and in different machine tool activities a reduction in labour costs of 16 to 25 per cent has been found as output doubles.[16]

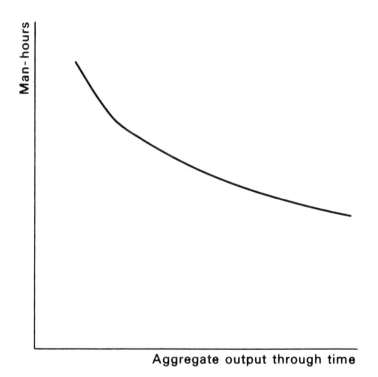

Aggregate output through time

Fig 2.3 The learning cure

Management consultants talk of the 'experience curve' and show how the overall profitability of firms in an industry is often positively related to their aggregate outputs through time. This seems also to be derived from the same basic concept as the learning curve. Learning may be an important source of cost savings and certainly the scope for learning is taken into account in government pricing of aircraft contracts,[17] but in some industries the time taken and costs incurred while learning is taking place can be unwelcome and it may be preferable so to organise production in order to reduce the scope for learning altogether.[18]

(2)   Multi-plant Economies

Most of the production benefits from increasing scale will be expected to be available at the individual product and plant level. But the firm that produces a large number of products, often in several different plants, may also derive benefits from expanding the scale of its overall activities. The ability to pool common overhead services and costs of accounting, market research, research and development and other specialist management and technical functions can be an important source of cost savings. A large firm may find it easier to recruit and retain good quality staff, since the range of opportunities for experience and promotion will probably be greater than in smaller firms. It may be possible by planning and reallocating production between plants to achieve further standardisation and specialisation in production and hence further economies of long runs. It may prove possible to transfer supplies and outputs from one plant to another in order to meet demands as they vary from one geographical area to another. Control and co-ordination may also be achieved in the large organisation through vertical integration which offers not only production cost savings but also the possibility of pecuniary advantages.

The large firm will be expected to gain several marketing and pecuniary benefits. It may find that a well-established corporate and brand image will facilitate the introduction of new products. The benefits of profits accruing across a range of products will enable the firm to devote a disproportionate level of marketing outlay to a new product or one whose sales a company wishes to promote extensively. It is possible for the sales force to handle several products in their personal selling activities and so the unit costs of sales representation for each successive product fall, and the marginal costs of taking on an extra product may be very low indeed up to the point at which no more products can be handled effectively by the same person. Similarly, a distribution and transport network normally handles several products with very little addition to the total cost that would have to be incurred from handling only one.

The financial strengths normally to be expected in a large firm mean that additional research and development can be financed and a large number of new product possibilities investigated while short-term losses can be borne with less difficulty. Large organisations will often have a higher credit rating and hence find the cost of external supplies of capital cheaper while also being more likely to be able to provide considerable amounts of new capital by internal financing. As purchasers of raw materials and semi-finished products, large firms will expect to place orders for bulk supplies which will be reflected in more favourable supply prices and conditions than would be available to their smaller competitors. To some extent the lower prices may reflect the scope a large order allows to a supplier also to achieve economies in production through longer runs, but in part they are a reflection of the fact that the large firm is an important and powerful customer, the loss of whose order could be very serious to the supplier. In this case the effects of the exercise of counter-vailing buying power do not depend simply on the cost advantage offered to the supplier but on an estimate by the supplier of the opportunity costs of losing a large order.

(3)   Diseconomies

It does not follow that economies of scale continue indefinitely. In some cases after a point unit costs may simply remain constant and in other cases diseconomies and hence rising unit costs may occur. In the short run the difficulties of squeezing extra production out of a situation where the fixed factor is almost fully utilised may cause sharply rising costs in a bottleneck situation, either through the need to pay higher overtime rates or the conse-quences of a higher breakdown rate on equipment. In the long run the adjustment path of the firm should enable it to overcome this particular cause of diseconomies but others may still arise. Factor costs will rise when the supply of factors is not completely elastic. This is quite likely in the case of labour where higher wages have to be offered to recruit more staff and the possibility that later units taken on may be less efficient and consequently labour costs per extra unit of output will be higher. (Even if the wage rate offered remains constant but labour inputs are of declining quality the labour cost per unit of output will of course rise.) While large-scale operations may offer benefits in marketing and distribution, under some circumstances these costs may also rise as the need to ensure a high, continuous level of demand necessitates increas-ingly heavy marketing costs per unit sold to clear the extra output or imposes heavier costs of distributing in a wider market area.

Co-ordination and management may pose particular problems in the larger organisation. Although computers and other management aids, together with new approaches to techniques of management and delegation, reduce some of the difficulties, there is a danger of increasing bureaucratisation and loss of flexibility in the decision-making process. Increasing hierarchical levels mean that control loss may occur, while information flow may become increasingly distorted as it passes across different levels.[19] It may be increasingly difficult to encourage staff to identify with the organisation and higher levels of labour turnover will impose additional costs, not only in recruitment and training but in the benefits from learning that will be foregone.

Some managerial implications

To the individual firm the availability and attainment of scale economies may be very important influences both on the size of plant, the nature of the operations of the firm and its policies regarding the desirability of growth internally and through merger. Scale economies may be both a major motive for, and a source of growth for the firm. Improved utilisation of plant and the benefits of learning will both, in effect, increase the real capacity of the plant and therefore assist the growth of sales without necessitating the growth of assets. One of the features of many modern industries is the high incidence of fixed and semi-fixed costs. The implication of this is that the overall level of unit costs is very much dependent upon the ability to achieve large levels of output in order to spread the fixed costs more thinly. Thus changes in capacity utilisation will have substantial effects on the overall profitability of the organisation. A few industries which may be cited as examples where this phenomenon has been discussed recently would include consumer durables, fertilisers, butyl rubber, cement, dyestuffs and hotels.[20] This is of course an important reason why some industries, notably the motor manufacturers, have traditionally been anxious to try to persuade governments to maintain a high level of effective demand since fluctuations in demand hinder the achievement of a high level of capacity utilisation and therefore cause either price increases or reductions in profits through consequent higher unit costs. Where the benefits of high capacity utilisation and long runs are achieved one would expect that not only would profits increase but that prices should be reduced or at least maintained at a more stable level. Certainly it does appear in a number of industries with high fixed cost structures that prices were kept substantially stable during much of the late 1950s and early 1960s, no doubt as a result of expanding markets and consequent additional economies of scale.

Just because scale economies are available this does not mean that in all cases firms will necessarily seek to achieve them to the full even if they are able to do so. Their availability does, however, point to a number of decisions (especially production decisions) that management will have to take and the possibility that other considerations will on balance over-ride the search for optimum scale. First, the firm will need to decide on its market and production policy, whether it is to aim to produce a few standardised lines for a mass market or whether it will produce a wider range of less standardised products. If it decides on fewer, more standardised, lines it will look to attain the benefit of long production runs. If it chooses to offer a wide range of products then it will have the benefits from increased representation in a market and spreading of some administrative and distributive overheads but will probably have to accept the additional costs of increased stockholding of slower-moving products and the costs of re-tooling and adjusting machines to produce the different lines. Metal Box, for example, found that it took up to eight hours to adjust machinery in order to change from production of one size of can to another.[21] Of course it is not always possible to choose between the two alternatives as the nature of the market will often dictate this, but many firms do find themselves faced with such a choice.[22]

Decisions also have to be made on production method. Sometimes there is a choice between labour intensive and capital intensive processes, the balance of advantage of which may depend upon the size of the expected output.[23] Sometimes firms may find themselves faced with a choice between alternative techniques of producing the same product, the ultimate choice of technique again depending upon the expected length of the production run. For example in the printing industry the choice between letterpress, gravure and lithograph printing depends partly on the quality of printing required but also on the expected scale of production. Letterpress printing offers lower unit costs for small runs but gravure printing is cheaper for longer runs. Another important decision is between the search for maximum scale economies through high capacity utilisation and the adjustment of output to meet fluctuations in demand. In some industries[24] although the costs of stockholding are high the costs of temporarily reducing the level of output are even more substantial and so production is maintained at a constant level. In other cases where seasonal fluctuations are important influences on the overall pattern of working of the firm, this may be a signal for increased marketing effort to build demand in the off-peak periods or to add another product to the firm's overall range that will offset the seasonal variation. Walls apparently did this by pairing ice cream for the summer and sausages for the winter.

The search for the benefits of increased scale may impose other costs which may ultimately prove to outweigh the advantages. The outputs of longer production runs have to be sold and this may require additional transport or marketing costs per unit. The use of faster machines may necessitate better quality and therefore more costly materials in the production process. Continuous working may mean that more than proportionate increases are incurred in labour costs together with the increased costs of supervision on a night shift and the loss of flexibility in dealing with breakdowns or temporary increases in demand. There may be fire risks which may make increasing the scale of plant a most unwise step. Decisions to increase the scale of a firm's operations may well mean that a substantial new investment has to be undertaken, since the growth path of operations in a particular industry may well not be smooth and continuous but may involve expansions in large, discrete and costly steps.

The nature of the implications for management and the balancing of advantages and disadvantages will of course vary from industry to industry. But it is clear that it does not follow in every case that the pursuit of the technical production optimum scale is necessarily in the best interests of the firm. We should also note in passing that economies of scale are but one source of cost savings available to the firm. Continuous improvements in the performance of firms may well be looked for through the achievement of other sorts of cost saving. For example, the use of modern techniques such as value analysis, operations research, work scheduling, improved stock control may generally lead to an improved organisation of production and hence lower unit costs. In some cases production of a given product may be achieved through the use of alternative mixes of factor inputs. Thus a range of different combinations of oils can be used to produce margarine,[25] while it is possible to substitute de-inked waste paper for pulp in the production of certain items in the paper and board industry. In these and other cases careful attention to the least cost combinations of different factor inputs would be expected to yield considerable cost savings. Control over material usage and other aspects of worker performance, including perhaps the use of productivity bargaining may also be expected to yield benefits. Some firms have been known to go to quite novel lengths to encourage their workers to identify with the objectives of the firm and to improve the usage of the raw materials that go into the production process. For example, one weaving firm which was bothered by the problem that its operatives frequently broke the cotton before using up the whole spindle, successfully hit on the idea of putting trading stamps round the inside of the reel which could only be collected by the operative when all the cotton had been used up in the production process!

Empirical evidence regarding economies of scale

Our discussion of alternative methods of estimating cost functions will have indicated how difficult it is to obtain completely reliable and meaningful information on this issue, and it is possible that the alternative techniques available may yield different results for the same industry. Yet not only management but also government policy-making concerning the structure of industry requires information on the question whether economies of scale do exist and how important they are. If possible we need to be able to answer four questions: are the economies primarily at the single or the multi-plant level; at what point is the minimum optimum scale of activity; how fast does the average cost curve fall as it approaches the minimum point and what happens after the minimum point, does the curve turn up immediately, remain flat thereafter or remain flat for a time and then turn up? We shall attempt to indicate in the light of such information as is available[26] where the balance of economic opinion exists on these questions. It must be remembered, however, that the views summarised here represent a general synthesis across the results of a variety of commentators working on different industries. It would be extremely surprising to find only one unequivocal answer to the questions posed irrespective of the industry for which the data was collected.

In the short run it seems to be largely agreed that average costs fall as output increases more or less as far as the normal or planned output level of the firm. Some would argue that the curve rises sharply if an attempt is made to obtain an expansion of output beyond the normal or planned level due to the effect of increased breakdowns of equipment, the need to use extra-marginal equipment and an increase in labour costs per unit of output. Short-run average variable costs and therefore marginal costs are normally considered to be constant over the range in which average total costs are falling on the assumption that all factors are infinitely divisible and that all costs of production rise proportionately. If these did not hold then the marginal cost curve would also fall.

Turning to the long run we find that economies of scale are considered to arise more from technical factors and to be largely attainable at the level of the individual plant. This also suggests that pecuniary economies are not particularly important although as we shall see in Chapter 8 they are often thought to be important sources of cost savings as a result of mergers.

The optimum scale of output will vary from industry to industry according to the prevailing technical production conditions. Information on this question is normally provided through a discussion of the share of total domestic output that an optimally sized plant would take since (ignoring the effects of imports and exports and assuming that all major economies can be obtained at the single plant level) this is thought to offer a clear guide to the number of firms that can be economically sustained in an industry. Bain's studies showed that in the USA in only two of the twenty industries he investigated (cars and typewriters) did an optimally sized plant require more than ten per cent of the total market capacity.[27] Since the American market is larger than most other markets, and although somewhat different technologies of production might be used in the USA thereby raising the optimal level in absolute terms over that which would apply in other countries, it is likely that similar industries in other countries might require greater concentration if optimally sized plants are to exist. As we saw in Chapter 1 Bain's own later work on international differences in industrial structure does give strong support to this hypothesis.[28]

An extensive British study has attempted to identify, using engineering production functions, the extent of scale economies in a large number of industries.[29] The general results of this investigation as it relates to the question of the optimal size of plant (described in the study as the minimum efficient scale) as a proportion of UK output in 1969 are shown in Table 2.1. From this it appears that although a few products require very high proportions of UK output for maximum productive efficiency and in some cases production of individual products or titles or designs should not be dispersed at all, generally speaking the level of concentration required for minimum efficient scale is quite low and would support several firms in the British market. In other words optimum outputs to achieve maximum scale economies do not appear to represent large proportions of total output in many British industries.

The next question concerns the slope of the long-run average cost curve.

Table 2.1.   *Minimum efficient scale of plant as a proportion of UK output, 1969*

Industries where minimum efficient scale of plant would require:

80 to 100 per cent of UK output	50 to 79 per cent of UK output	15 to 49 per cent of UK output	0 to 15 per cent of UK output
Dye	Turbo generator production	Ethylene plant	Oil refining
Steel-rolled products	Electric motors	Sulphuric acid plant	Beer
Aircraft		Synthetic fibres	Cement
Machine tool models		Synthetic detergents	Non-fletton bricks
Design of chemical plant		Steel produced by blast and electric arc furnaces	Plant bakery
Design of turbo generator		Motor car models	Steel rods and bars produced from billets
Electronic capital parts		Domestic electrical appliances	Foundry making
Single plastic products		Newspapers	Cylinder blocks
Single title of a book			Foundry making small engineering castings
			Bicycles
			Manufacture of machine tools
			Diesel engines
			Spinning mills
			Weaving mills
			Warp knitting mills
			Footwear
			Book printing
			Range of plastic products

Source: derived from C. F. Pratten *Economies of Scale in Manufacturing Industry* Cambridge University Press (1971).

Clearly if a curve falls sharply towards the optimum the importance of having optimally sized plants is much greater than if the slope down towards the optimum tends towards the horizontal, since the latter would imply that sub-optimally sized operations do not suffer much cost disadvantage. Indeed where the comparison is on the basis of engineering production functions it may well be that a disadvantage from the point of view of the ideal scale of production may in reality be more than compensated by superiority in management or other factors that are not included in the assessment of scale economies. Generally speaking we find that the greater the degree of capital intensity in the production process the more steeply the long-run average cost curve falls.[30] Bain found that in seven of his twenty industries firms operating at half the optimal plant scale would have unit costs five per cent or more above the level prevailing at the optimum scale. Pratten's study showed rather fewer industries where the increase in unit costs at 50 per cent of optimal capacity would be less than five per cent but not many where the disadvantage would be more than ten per cent. Ignoring those cases where individual products or designs or titles are involved, steeply sloping average cost curves could be inferred to be most apparent in bread baking, the production of non-fletton bricks and electric motors. This is not of course a complete listing of industries in which a steeply falling average cost curve can be inferred, but it does perhaps suggest that the slope of the average cost curve for plants as they approach towards optimum scale is not in most cases such that sub-optimally sized plants are placed at a serious cost disadvantage.

The final question to be considered is the shape of the average cost curve beyond the minimum optimum scale. Does the curve remain horizontal there-after or flat for a while and then rise or is it, as traditional economic theory suggests, U shaped? The majority of views, theoretical and empirical, would now suggest that the long-run average cost is L shaped, at least over the range of output that firms would consider in practice. But Walters remained unconvinced of this, especially where industries in the private sector were concerned. At the end of his survey article he concluded that 'at least there is no large body of data which convincingly contradicts the hypothesis of a U-shaped long-run cost curve and the fruitful results which depend on it'.[31]

On balance, while experience will vary in different industries, it does not seem unreasonable to conclude on the basis of all the evidence that economies are mainly at the individual plant level; in both the American and British cases optimum scale is often not large as a proportion of total industry output; while some plants in some industries may suffer significant cost disadvantages from being of sub-optimum size, many probably do not and may compensate with other cost advantages; the long-run average cost curve tends to be flat over quite a wide range of output. Economies of scale are clearly of practical importance in many industries, though perhaps not quite as important as some would have us believe. It is, however, also possible that they are becoming increasingly important through time. Certainly Pratten advances cogent reasons for thinking that this is so. Among his reasons are the increasing experience and assistance available in building and managing large units, changing technologies and larger plant sizes that offer considerable savings, increasing initial set-up and R and D costs that have to be spread over larger outputs and the use of synthetic materials that make for some consistent quality in the production process.

The evidence is clearly relevant to policy making. The availability of scale economies and the costs of operating below full capacity may point to the importance, from the point of view of the pursuit of technical efficiency, of maintaining high and stable levels of demand while the possibility of over-coming indivisibilities and spreading set-up costs may justify policies designed to facilitate fast rates of growth of new operations. The evidence on scale economies should help in formulating policy towards the structure of industry. Where firm activities are known to be subject to constant returns to scale there may be little point in allowing firms to expand beyond the minimum optimal size if, although they are unlikely to incur diseconomies, their future growth will result in a reduction in competition. Bain's investigations led him to the conclusion that there was more concentration than scale economies justified, and Pratten[32] concluded that there would not be much net loss of scale economies if ICI were to be dissolved into several smaller firms. Even if firm sizes are such that they satisfy technical criteria of optimum scale, this need not necessarily be the over-riding objective in all cases. Non-technical optima may occur at different scales and may outweigh the benefits of an optimum scale of production. Government may consider that the pressures of competition through maintaining more, smaller firms may outweigh the losses from a failure to achieve the maximum possible economies of scale in production. We are still a long way from precision in this area and it must always be borne in mind that there is not necessarily a perfect relation between maximum economies of scale and minimisation of actual costs.

The economic position of small firms

If there are so many possible sources of scale economies, we might ask how far small firms can survive at all. Yet not only do they survive but they still remain numerically very important. Although a downward trend is clearly apparent, in 1963 it was estimated that 93 per cent of all firms in a wide range of activities covering manufacturing industry and many primary and tertiary activities were still 'small' in that they employed fewer than 200 workers. Obviously their contribution to total employment, investment or output was much lower than this and it was estimated that 21 per cent of all output of the activities covered was produced by small firms.[33] Not only do they have an important role at the present time but it is through the success and expansion of some firms, small at present, that successive generations of major organisations will arise. So there may well be a strong case for paying particular attention to the problem of the small firm since if there are hindrances to the birth and initial development of small firms this may imply a weakness in the economy at a later stage. It might also be argued that there is a certain social value in the presence of small firms in a local community and this should not be lightly disregarded.

There is little doubt that small firms face important disadvantages in comparison with large organisations. They are often particularly weak where the pattern of demand is changing away from locally produced, unstandardised goods to mass produced, standardised products, and this trend is facilitated by growing urbanisation and easier national and international marketing and distribution. Technical change often requires the use of more capital intensive production methods with rising technical optima. The inability of small firms in many industries to obtain full economies in production, marketing and the pecuniary benefits of large scale can be a serious competitive disadvantage. Their small scale often militates against effective bargaining with large firms to whom they are supplying goods or from whom they are obtaining supplies. Small firms also tend to complain that the increasing role of state procurement tends to favour large firms and that restrictive practices legislation has made it difficult for them to undertake desirable collusion and receive advice from their trade associations. Certainly restrictive practices legislation and particularly that on resale price maintenance has increased competition, but it is not clear that the sort of collusion and advice that small firms would look for would always be in the public interest or even in the interests of the more outward looking of the firms concerned.

Through all the investigations on the problems of small firms two major difficulties are strongly emphasised – finance and management – and these are to some extent inter-related. The quality of management in small firms is often criticised as lacking in basic skills, failing to utilise or even to look for available sources of assistance and advice, failure to use adequate costing and pricing techniques or to appraise new opportunities and a failure to adopt an outward-looking, marketing orientation. Obviously such a description of the managerial weaknesses of small firms is grossly unfair to a large number of them and their owner-managers, and it is also quite clear that the quality of management in large firms is often not creditable either. But it does appear true to say that on balance the quality of management of small firms is not as high as in larger organisations. Owner-managers of small firms are often less well qualified but it is also relevant that in a small organisation they do not have the support of other managers in particular functional fields to enable them to overcome indivisibilities and achieve some degree of specialisation and division of labour. This is also, of course, a scale problem though this time in management. As this does seem to be such an important influence it is a pity that owners of small firms are all too often unwilling to use available specialist services, external to the firm, that could assist them.

The other major deficiency in small firms is normally considered to be a lack of finance. The firms themselves claim that they suffer particularly from the effects of heavy taxation and that as they are small the absolute level of profits available for ploughing back is also small, so internally financed growth is hindered. Many small firms appear to be unaware of external sources of financial assistance other than their bank manager, and those that do seek loans from this or another source often find that their credit rating is low and the costs of capital consequently much higher than to larger organisations. Again the structure of management and its dependence on the health of one man is often a contributory cause of the reluctance to lend money. However, those firms that are prepared to make a positive case for funds, properly supported by relevant data, are more likely to find it possible to raise money,[34] so the moral is clear: effective management can improve access to credit sources.

Yet many small firms not only survive but have a profitable existence. They tend to be found mainly in industries where there is easy entry and where therefore scale economies are not large enough to act as a major barrier to the entry and competition of new firms. Frequently this occurs in industries or particular product markets where capital intensive technology is not appropriate, and where therefore capital/output ratios are low. Often small firms survive effectively by supplying goods and services for which the market is local and/or, due to the perishability of the products, is unlikely to become suitable for a large organisation. Again small firms may be important in a particular market segment where small specific jobs are required or where a premium product requiring much attention to detail rather than mass production is appropriate. Even within a specific industry different sizes of firms may be appropriate for different activities. Thus, in the production of aluminium semi-manufacturers, small firms produce extrusions successfully though they would not be able to compete with larger firms in the market for rolled products.[35] In other industries small firms exist as specialist component suppliers offering a degree of vertical disintegration, and others find it possible to continue effectively as producers of goods to be sold under a retailer's own brand and so avoid having to incur their own marketing costs.

If there are certain types of activity where small firms are most likely to be found there are also a number of reasons why they continue to exist successfully. The owner-manager may choose to set up his own business to achieve independence and to satisfy some personal aspirations. Consequently he is likely to be highly motivated to ensure its success and may not look for a high remuneration from it. Indeed an owner-manager may consider the non-monetary benefits of being his own boss sufficient to justify paying himself a lower salary than he would receive as an employee elsewhere. Consequntly a small firm may also stay in existence longer than might be considered justified in terms of simple monetary returns. Of course, the distinction between a salary to the owner and profits is hard to draw where the same person receives both payments and the decision how to distribute the balance between salary and profits may depend upon tax conditions. In consequence studies of the profitability of small firms and their comparison with larger organisations may be misleading. Another advantage on the financial front is the possibility that a small firm may be more willing and better able to plough back profits into the firm since the owner may be more prepared to waive profits in the short run in the anticipation of better returns in the longer term than shareholders in larger organisations would accept. Staffing may pose less problems in small firms, a more informal working atmosphere may exist in which workers identify more effectively with the organisation, and as a result of which labour relations are much easier, and demarcation problems possibly non-existent. In some cases, where the pattern of labour utilisation is very uneven, as in retailing and hotels and catering, family labour may offer additional flexibility and some of the usual problems of indivisibility of a unit of labour can be overcome.

Particular production advantages have already been touched upon in the discussion of the sectors where small firms are most likely to be found. While in many respects technical change involves the adoption of larger scales of operation, in some, such as the development of numerically controlled machine tools and the development of continuous castings, together with the availability of more flexible machines, the optimum scale of production could actually be falling. Small firms may also succeed in remaining competitive by buying out many of the semi-finished goods used in their own production process so obtaining the benefit of others' scale economies. Or they may use less costly techniques and materials including maybe older, fully depreciated plants so that the capital and depreciation charge elements in the final price are lower. Another source of ability to set lower prices is through the avoidance of the heavy central overhead charges that large organisations tend to impose on their operating units and which can completely swamp a small subsidiary and radically affect its overall profitability. Small firms may also be able to improve their competitiveness through various forms of co-operation in purchasing and marketing. Voluntary groups are well known in various branches of retailing but also have a role in other sectors, as for example in hotels. Finally it may well be the case that large firms in an industry may deliberately seek to preserve the existence of smaller firms in order to avoid accusations of monopolising and to achieve this may formally or tacitly operate a market sharing arrangement or may decide to raise a price 'umbrella' to enable small firms to continue in existence.

It is clear that there is scope for the continued existence of small firms in the economy generally and they are likely to continue to have a major role in some industries. Forecasts of the future path of technical change in terms of the implications for optimal scale of operation may be unclear at the moment and there is a possibility that with some developments facilitating lower optimum scales of production, together with the effects of rising personal incomes perhaps encouraging less willingness to accept the results of mass production, the future for small firms may be more promising. The Committee on Small Firms was at pains to emphasise the importance of creating a situation in which a sufficient number of births of new firms could be undertaken, and this is clearly most important. What is also required is a policy on industrial structure that does not allow firms to grow beyond the minimum optimum scale at the expense of smaller units and of competition and a fiscal and anti-trust policy that increases the chances that vigorous and efficient small firms will be able to sustain their own independent existence. Small firms as a group are highly heterogeneous and what applies to one does not necessarily apply to others. But there appears to be considerable scope for improvement in management techniques and orientation, the adoption of a less protectionist stance and the identification of ways in which either singly or in co-operation with others they can identify and develop particular market segments and improve their competitiveness and marketing efficiency.

CHAPTER 3
VERTICAL INTEGRATION

The production and distribution of any single product normally involves a very large number of separate processes and activities. Where any two or more of these are carried on by the same organisation this constitutes, strictly speaking, vertical integration. Inevitably therefore most manufacturing organisations as well as some primary producers and some distributors are to a greater or lesser degree vertically integrated. Some, however, have taken this process to a much greater length than others by bringing under one control a range of activities that might have remained the responsibility of a separate organisation. Where a firm performs a preceding function it is said to be backward integrated, where it performs a succeeding function, it is forward integrated.

Interest in vertical integration does not normally concentrate so much on inter-linked processes that have to be performed in a continuous operation but on the integration of quite disparate activities such as the production and processing of a raw material or the ownership by a manufacturer of his own retail outlets. This integration may either take the form of the acquisition of other firms or it may involve the creation of new capacity. It does not, of course, mean that all operations are carried out in a single plant but rather that they are carried out under a unified control system where prices and quantities are often determined by administrative decision rather than the free inter-play of the market. Vertical integration is likely to occur in the absence of formal controls where firms believe that other functions are not best carried on by specialists, where specialisation of function and division of labour is not required or where it can be obtained within their own organisation. In addition it may be that in some cases vertical integration occurs not only because of the cost savings that are thereby attainable, but because there are other forms of economic advantage that are available to a vertically integrated firm.

The incidence of vertical integration

Reliable data on the extent of vertical integration are not available, primarily because it is a concept that is very difficult to measure statistically. *In principle* we could say that vertical integration increases as the ratio of the value added to total sales of the firm rises. However, there are particular measurement problems which reduce the validity of this approach.[1] An inventory/sales ratio has also been discussed but rejected as inadequate. Alternative approaches which, though less amenable to aggregate analysis, may be more reliable in individual cases, would involve a comparison of the proportion of total inputs bought outside the company, or of total products sold or distributed in the open market rather than through the firm's own outlets. Little work appears to have been undertaken which deals in any aggregative sense with the incidence of vertical integration although an investigation of vertical integration in the USA since 1929 has argued that, if anything, it has tended to decline there.[2]

We cannot offer any clear view as to the incidence of vertical integration in the British economy or its tendency to increase or decrease. Certain impressions might, however, be noted. It would appear that vertical integration is a highly important influence on the structure of a number of major industries including beer, flour milling and baking, man-made fibres, motor assembly, paper and board. In some cases the vertical relationship is a very important and extensive part of a firm's activity. Thus for example, it was reported that 75 per cent of the fixed assets in the brewing industry were represented by retail outlets[3] and that over 80 per cent of on-licence outlets (mainly public houses) were owned by the brewers.[4] In the flour milling and bread baking industry, each of the five major baking groups obtains nearly all its flour from within its own group.[5]

It is probable that all firms in an industry may tend to have more or less the same degree of vertical integration. Indeed competition between firms may well take the form of the acquisition of outlets, and the desire to ensure continuity of supply, etc., may well cause firms to keep in step with each other in this respect.[6]

It does not always follow that formal vertical integration is necessary to achieve the apparent benefits of this form of industrial structure. In some cases, as in the case of the Solus System of selling petrol in which many garages are owned by the retailers but are tied as to their source of supply, the end result may not be very different from one in which the oil company did own its outlets. In others, customer and supplier may work closely with each other, co-operating over questions of quantities, prices and delivery dates, and on technical matters. Again, other forms of exclusive dealing and tying contract may be an alternative. These tendencies are perhaps particularly noticeable in agriculture and horticulture where large retailers are entering into long-term supply arrangements with growers and so by-passing the normal wholesale markets.

Not all industries are as highly vertically integrated as technological considerations might at first sight appear to justify. The supply of tin cans is an activity which might conceivably encourage some backward integration by canners. Metal Box, the dominant supplier of tin cans in Britain, has however argued that formal vertical integration is not necessary if effective customer relations are established and has on occasion successfully dissuaded canners from producing their own cans. It appears that this company has close and effective relationships with its major customers.[7] In the British motor industry the assemblers have not taken vertical integration as far as their American counterparts[8] and continue to buy many components from independent suppliers, often at prices as low as they could produce for themselves.[9] Here the viability of the supply industry, considerations of the security of supplies and the level of prices charged reduce the incentive for the manufacturers to make their own components. Where this is no longer assured, vertical integration is likely to occur as has happened in the case of car bodies which are now produced by the assemblers.[10]

The degree of vertical integration in an industry may also be explicable in terms of the age of the industry: in other words there may well be a life-cycle element. In the early days of an industry there is often no specialist supply industry so manufacturers must engage in some backward integration producing their own semi-finished goods or components. Equally a manufacturer of a sophisticated new product may integrate forwards to control the distribution of his product in order to ensure its resale under satisfactory conditions. In time, as the specialist supply industry develops, and independent distributors acquire expertise, manufacturers can, if they choose, run down their own vertical involvement. Examples of vertical disintegration of this sort through time can be found in food packaging with the growth of Metal Box, in the motor industry where until the 1930s British vehicle manufacturers made their own propeller shafts and other components, and in photographic goods where Kodak, again in the 1930s, decided that it was no longer necessary to own its own retail outlets as other retailers were now proving satisfactory distributors of its products. At the other end of the life cycle for a product or industry, as the rate of expansion of the market decreases, it becomes likely that there will be an increase in both horizontal and vertical integration. The vertical integration here may be a reflection of the particular horizontal competitive pressures for market shares which will often encourage attempts particularly to increase control over retail outlets.[11]

This particular pattern is indicated in Figure 3.1. At the beginning of the product cycle the level of vertical integration is shown to be high. As the product becomes established and a supply industry develops the necessary level of vertical integration falls. As the product life begins to tail off then competition to maintain outlets and desire to preserve the security of investment in production activities causes the level of vertical integration to increase. This is clearly a hypothesis that needs quantitative testing to supplement casual empirical observation. If this hypothesis is substantiated in practice then it would appear that vertical integration often tends to occur as a response to particular necessities or market difficulties.

In some industrial situations vertical integration is not likely to occur in any substantial degree. In the case of many consumer goods, especially non-durables there are considerable economies of scale to the distributor from

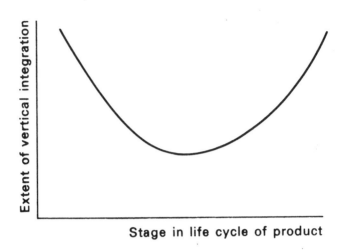

Fig 3.1 Hypothetical life-cycle influence on the degree of vertical integration

handling a large number of lines, only a few of which will be produced by any one manufacturer. Thus forward integration into retailing is unlikely under these circumstances, and manufacturer ownership of, for example, supermarket chains as specialist outlets for their products is highly unlikely. Similarly backward integration may not be feasible or an efficient use of resources in industries where technical progress in the supply industry is faster than a converter can keep up with or where one process offers greater scale advantages than its related activity. Where a vertically integrated firm has quite unequal market shares at different levels of productive activity, it may also be preferable not to look for substantial intra-group trade in order to avoid the accusation of competing at one level or another with one's own customer.

Motivations for vertical integration

Discussion of the motivations for vertical integration normally suggests that firms are motivated either by considerations of efficiency in terms of the availability of technological joint economies and the ability to by-pass imperfect markets, or security, and that while the pursuit of efficiency is acceptable in economic welfare terms the desire for security is not. While there is some value in this particular dichotomy, the issue is less clear cut and the normative implications do not follow quite so easily from the motivations. Let us consider first the question of motivation. Four main categories of reason may be identified.

(1) Production Savings

There are two main types of benefit here. The first occurs where technologically complementary processes can be carried out in quick succession
thereby avoiding intermediary costs and attendant disadvantages. Thus the
ability to roll steel while still hot from refining offers an advantage, so too
does the ability to turn pulp into newsprint without the need for the drying
and reconstitution that would be involved if the pulp had to be delivered to a
different organisation between processes. Equally in a vertically integrated
organisation it becomes possible to treat metals with finishes before they are
exposed to oxygen corrosion. In all these cases, not only is production under
a common ownership implied but production in the same plant is also most
advantageous.

The second form of production saving arises from the easier consultation,
planning and co-ordination of adjacent processes that is made possible in a
vertically integrated organisation. Forward scheduling is facilitated, the economies of longer runs may be achieved and a steadier pattern of production
activity and/or more intensive utilisation of capacity and spreading of overheads may ensue. The benefits of having technologically complementary
processes under one administrative control have, for example, encouraged
ICI to increase its own vertical integration in the man-made fibre industry
on the grounds that as the bulking process has now become more adjacent to
the texturising process some vertical integration will allow it to plan and
co-ordinate the introduction of new processes.[12] Inventory and stock levels
may be kept at a lower level than would apply where unintegrated activities
were carried on. More reliable product quality may be assured.

In some cases forward integration may be sought to help stabilise the level
of production activity and to avoid seasonal fluctuations. Thus, for example,
Thorn Electrical Industries told the Monopolies Commission that it moved
into television renting in order to avoid the seasonal unemployment patterns
which had prevailed in radio manufacture but which were unacceptable for
television set manufacture because of the technical complexity of the production process.[13] In this case, therefore, the efficiency of continuous production
was assisted by the existence of a captive outlet for the product.

(2) Avoidance of the Market

By replacing purchasing and selling in the market with more direct administrative contact certain cost savings may be effected. Professional buying and
selling functions, including the costs of information collection, hedging and
promotion are reduced or eliminated. No profits need be paid to middlemen,
lower inventories and stocks need to be maintained because of the easier and
more accurate production scheduling that is possible. Backward integration

ensures a greater security of supply at more readily guaranteed prices and qualities.

(3) Distribution Cost Savings

Intra-group trading should also allow costs of distribution to be lowered through easier storage and handling and possibly more economical delivery arrangements. In some cases ownership of distributive outlets may be necessary if required standards of service with a complex product are to be provided, especially with a new product or entry of a manufacturer into a new market. We have already observed that this was an important consideration with Kodak in the early years. Volkswagen's rapid and successful entry into the American motor car market clearly owes a substantial amount to its acquisition of distributive outlets and hence its ability to obtain effective and speedy display for its products.

(4) Security of Market and Investment

Manufacturers may argue that forward vertical integration into distribution is necessary to provide security for heavy capital investment in manufacturing plant. The move forward is one means of increasing the element of 'planning' or effective control over demand in the market and may be particularly important where retailers are the main promotors of the product and are able to influence a consumer's choice of brands, etc. In some cases forward integration may be a means of influencing demand for the output of the preceding stages (this was apparently the reason why the flour milling groups became major bread bakers). It is also a reason why airline companies are controlling hotels since in this way they are able effectively to boost their sales of airline tickets on the package holiday trade.[14]

Managerial implications

Discussions of the advantages of vertical integration tend to make three implicit assumptions: that communications within an organisation are of a high quality and certainly better than those between different organisations; that all parts of an organisation have common non-conflicting objectives and that where intra-group trading is possible it does take place. None of these is necessarily correct.

In some cases production planning can be more difficult within an organisation than in dealing with a completely separate concern. There may be internal conflicts to resolve and a balance to maintain between different parts of the organisation that quite negate the benefits of vertical integration. All in all there are certainly administrative costs which have to be accepted if intra-group trading is to take place, even though other costs are avoided or reduced. The pursuit of vertical integration may mean that activities are added by internal expansion for which there is insufficient know-how available to the firm and this can prove very costly. Even vertical integration by merger may not entirely overcome this problem and it poses other difficulties of co-ordination between the two organisations. Care has therefore to be taken in looking for vertical integration since it may be more difficult to cease trading with an inefficient part of the same organisation than to drop an independent, inefficient supplier. A further hidden threat to the vertically integrated organisation arises where two linked activities are treated as a joint activity. Here there may be a source of internal conflict between, for example, marketing efficiency considerations which may require the closure of some outlets and the production interest in the firm which may argue for the retention of all outlets in order to maintain a given level of sales and therefore of production. Failure to identify the true economic performance of the different levels of activity may well conceal inefficiences at one stage or another and may encourage the retention of an activity even if its true rate of return should, strictly speaking, be considered unacceptable.

Strange as it may seem, it does not necessarily follow that intra-group trading does take place in every case where it is possible. Much apparent vertical integration in modern large organisations seems to have grown up as if by chance as a result for example of mergers pursued for quite different reasons. Often it may be found that, although two parts of an organisation are producing at successive stages, they may well produce and require different qualities of product and so may hardly deal with each other at all, but instead may both be buying and selling in the open market. Different companies also have different attitudes and policies towards intra-group trading. Some companies insist on intra-group trading wherever possible, others require purchases to be made within the group all other things being equal and require explanations of the reasons why purchases are made outside,[15] while in other companies again each unit is left free to buy in whatever it judges to be the most favourable market. Unilever, for example, told the Monopolies Commission that the individual businesses within the group would never be compelled to buy Unilever products since this would require a reversal of the policy that the operating unit is responsible for its own profits.[16]

Undoubtedly policy regarding intra-group trading would be expected to be influenced by the company's policy regarding accounting performance and the nature of profit centres within the organisation. It is unlikely that an organisation that makes each of its activities separate profit centres could also exist successfully on intra-group trading irrespective of the difference between internal prices and free market prices. On the other hand a company which does not have a large number of profit centres may be more prone to insist on intra-group trading irrespective of relative prices and costs since it would be able to average the overall effect of a loss of profitability at one level over increased profitability at another level of the company's activities. Where this is so, of course, it does again mean that there is less indication of the relative performance of different activities in the company.

Whatever policy is adopted it offers both advantages and disadvantages. If intra-group trading does occur then costs may be saved, efficiency raised and orders gained if one part of an organisation is able to help another by quoting a special price or delivery date. But insistence on intra-group trading may create dissatisfaction and tensions within the group and a loss of flexibility. If, on the other hand, intra-group trading is not in force where it might be then the efficiencies claimed for vertical integration cannot be achieved.

The question of pricing policy on intra-group sales is difficult. Firms seem to pursue one of three different strategies. They may arrange that prices paid for intermediate goods and services supplied shall be particularly cheap in order to make it possible for the final output to be competitive in price. This creates difficulties since it means that internal checks on the efficiency of separate operating divisions cannot be undertaken using normal profit and loss accounting criteria. It is also a policy that is more or less guaranteed to raise objections from less integrated competitors who may feel that the competition they are facing is unfair, especially if they have to pay higher prices for the intermediate product.

Some firms allow bargaining to take place between the divisions. Each division will act rather as in a bilateral monopoly situation, though information on prices prevailing on the open market should set an upper limit to the price that a buying division would be prepared to pay and a lower limit to the price at which a supplying division would be prepared to sell. This procedure will also affect the ability to appraise objectively the performance of individual divisions. It has been argued that this is especially likely to cause problems where the fixing of a transfer price is based on an exchange of information between divisions since this provides an incentive to divisional managers to cheat by giving false information in an attempt to rig the transfer price determination procedure.[17]

In other cases firms adopt a transfer price equal to the price prevailing on the open market. In an extensive analysis of the correct pricing policy for an optimising firm, Hirshleifer showed that this is only the correct policy where the product being transferred is produced in a competitive market in which no one producer can influence the price. In all other situations setting transfer prices equal to the open market price for the product will lead to a loss of aggregate profits to the firm. So while the use of market prices may well be effective from the point of view of control over the performance of individual divisions it may not be compatible with profit maximising aspirations of the firm as a whole. In most other situations Hirshleifer showed that the rule is that the transfer price should be equal to the marginal costs of the selling division. (This is, of course, also the market price in a perfectly competitive market.) Greater difficulties arise where there is interdependence either in technology between different divisions or in demand such that the sale of one unit to a buying division within the organisation has an effect on the level of sales to independent customers. Where there is demand dependence the correct transfer price is between the marginal cost price and the market price. Where there is technological dependence Hirshleifer concluded there could not be a general solution and thought there was little scope for preserving divisional autonomy.[18]

Such optimising policy would often be difficult to pursue in practice. It also has the disadvantages that in emphasising the overall performance of the organisation it involves a loss of information about the performance of individual divisions and possibly a weakening of financial incentives upon divisional management. Where marginal cost prices are set on intra-group sales but higher, market prices are charged for the same product on sale to other firms, the possibility of customer accusations of price discrimination and predatory pricing to preserve or enhance a position of market dominance also becomes likely.

Economic implications

As we have seen, just because two activities in the same organisation are vertically related to each other it does not necessarily mean that a captive market inevitably exists or that any particular form of pricing policy can be assumed to operate. Equally it should not be assumed that an increase in vertical integration is necessarily for some predatory or exclusionary purpose. Nevertheless the distinction between sensible business conduct and predatory behaviour is not at all clear cut and attention has been paid to the public interest implications by the courts in the USA[19] and the Monopolies Commission in Britain. This attention has also been supported by the doubts expressed by some economists regarding the motivations for and the consequences of the practice.[20] There are three main respects in which concern over the consequences of vertical integration has normally been expressed: these are effect on new entry, the effect on existing competition and the general implications for economic welfare.

(1) Effect on New Entry

Either backward or forward integration may hinder new entry and foreclose an industry. Entry may well be barred if existing firms control all readily available sources of supply of raw materials or semi-finished goods or if they will not supply a potential competitor on terms equivalent to those at which intra-group sales occur, after allowing for any economic differences in the cost of supply, and if the creation of new sources of supply would involve extra costs per unit obtained. The need to integrate forward because existing firms control their own outlets and pursue a restrictive or preferential trading policy is also highly costly and therefore a deterrent to new entry competition. As we have seen, the acquisition of outlets is a particularly important form of competition in some industries and may well bid up the costs of new entry still further. In trades such as brewing and petrol, where the number of retail outlets is controlled by some form of licensing system, this becomes even more expensive.

(2)   Effect on Existing Competition

A vertically integrated firm supplying competitors as well as its own subsidiaries is often thought to be in a particularly strong position to control the competitive strength of its rivals and even in extreme cases to decide whether they may exist at all. Such control over existing competition could come about through a price 'squeeze' whereby a producer supplied its own subsidiaries at a much lower price than its competitors, or alternatively through equivalent influences on the quality of the product supplied or the speed of service or the frequency of supply, especially where supplies are scarce. This allows it either to take much larger profits at the next level of production or to charge a lower price which its competitors cannot match because they are having to pay a higher price for factor inputs.

An example of such squeeze activities was apparently used by United States Steel Corporation, which in 1948 squeezed non-integrated companies that purchased semi-finished steel from it by raising its semi-finished steel prices but not raising finished steel prices, and then three months later actually *reduced* the price of its finished steel products.[21] The Monopolies Commission found that Courtaulds had engaged in price discrimination by selling to its own subsidiaries at lower prices than it supplied to its competitors and that this had been a means of preserving its monopoly position.[22] In some cases it also appears that a more heavily vertically integrated dominant firm may be able to encourage its less integrated competitors to follow its price leadership for fear that they would otherwise be deprived of their basic raw materials.[23] Clearly such activities are open to dominant firms and can affect the extent and pattern of competition that they face. It is, however, possible that there may often be more suspicion and fear of squeeze operations than is actually to be found in practice. If, however, the correct strategy for a vertically integrated firm is to set its transfer prices equal to marginal costs and if these operations are subject to increasing returns to scale, price discrimination is inevitable and the private and social interest in these circumstances may well appear to be in conflict.

A different form of hindrance to competition may be applied where a vertically integrated company controls outlets which its competitors require for distribution of their own products. The Monopolies Commission found that this was a particular problem with the tied house system of selling beer.

Not only did this mean that competition from other beers and brewers was hindered, but also it enabled the brewers to influence the distribution of proprietary brands of wines and spirits, cider and soft drinks and to promote their own house brands instead.[24]

(3) Welfare Implications

We have sought to show that there are a range of motivations for vertical integration and a variety of ways in which the practice may operate. It is impossible therefore to state categorically whether the welfare consequences of this particular aspect of market structure are favourable or not. The net consequences are likely to be detrimental if market power is substantially raised through the creation of barriers to entry or other hindrances to competition, or if it gives so much security that the search for cost savings is reduced. Vertical integration may cause a waste of resources if it hinders standardisation of intermediate products by retaining too many separate producers, if it leads to unnecessary duplication of outlets, or a failure to rationalise the distribution system. It will probably be undesirable if it deflects competition from price savings and product innovation towards the competitive acquisition of outlets, and is particularly likely to be so if firms, in their search for security, fail to consider the full financial implications of heavy expenditures.[25]

To set against these possible detriments are a range of important potential benefits, particularly if the alternative to vertical integration is the apparent inefficiency of bilateral monopoly.[26] The efficiency gains should yield cost savings, may reduce mark-ups at the intermediate stages, and may give lower profits than would persist under bilateral monopoly. Prices may therefore be lower and output greater under vertical integration and price discrimination may be advantageous since it will extract a greater degree of consumer surplus.

There is therefore no clear-cut answer on the economic consequences of vertical integration. While not condemning vertical integration as such, public policy would be expected to look at the reasons why a particular movement towards increased vertical integration was undertaken, the way in which the integrated firm proceeded to behave in relation to its provision of supplies to competitors and its attitude to the handling of competitors' products, the effect of this on other firms, and the extent to which by opting for vertical integration the firm had obtained an excessive degree of security which allowed it to follow a quiet life.

The Solus System in petrol retailing:

a special case of vertical integration

Petrol is an industry with, in general, a very high degree of vertical integration from extracting through refining to the final distribution. Considerable interest has been shown in Britain in recent years in the question of the oil companies' involvement in the retailing of their petrol. This tends to occur either through their ownership of sites or through a form of arrangement known as the Solus System whereby independent garage proprietors undertake to tie themselves solely to a particular oil company's supply for a minimum period of time in return for certain financial advantages – usually loans at low rates of interest and a solus rebate. The economic desirability of the Solus System has been considered by the Monopolies Commission.[27] The courts have investigated whether it is contrary to the public interest as a restraint of trade and therefore unenforceable at law.[28] The legal position is that the courts have found the Solus System not to be a restraint of trade while the majority of the Monopolies Commission found that in principle its operation was not contrary to the public interest but recommended that the duration of the solus tie should be reduced from about twenty years to a maximum of five years.

As the oil companies do not own the outlets with which they have solus agreements this is clearly not a true example of vertical integration. However, it is seen by the oil companies to be very much an alternative to the direct ownership of retail outlets and may therefore be classed as largely equivalent in its outcome to vertical integration. In view of the importance of this question and the extent to which the primary issues have been debated we shall look briefly at the main arguments.

Initially it appears that the motivation for the introduction of the Solus System in 1950 was to improve retailer performance since Esso introduced the scheme in order to encourage retailers to improve the service they offered, so linking retailer goals to the goals of Esso and increasing the interdependence between the oil company and its distributive outlets.[29] The response by the other oil companies also to introduce a form of solus trading was in effect simply a competitive response to Esso's move. Subsequently, however, a number of other arguments have been advanced in support of solus trading. In particular it is claimed that:

(1) Oil company investments in petroleum production, refining and distribution have a long gestation period and the Solus System offers the market stability necessary to justify these expenditures by making the investments more secure;

(2) Administrative integration of the different levels of productive and distributive activities have been made easier and in consequence it is easier and cheaper to match capacity to demand and so achieve security and continuity of the operation;

(3) Costs of administration and distribution have been reduced;

(4) Petrol stations have been improved through the provision of funds at below market rates of interest;

(5) Prices have been kept stable.

Against this the detriments to which it is claimed the Solus System gives rise are largely:[30]

(1) The provision of loans to retailers at low rates of interest is a wasteful expenditure and a misallocation of resources. The combination of low rates of interest and high wholesale prices represents inefficient pricing and may lead to excessive investment in retailing if investment decisions are influenced by the rate of interest. It may also lead to higher retail prices if, as is likely, the wholesale price is a major influence in retail pricing decisions;

(2) The system of distribution to which the Solus System gives rise is inefficient since costs are averaged across customers and there are no quantity discount arrangements to encourage the acceptance of large drops. Consequently the less efficient retailers are preserved in business;

(3) There is no evidence that petroleum refining capacity (as opposed to capacity for other petroleum products) adequately meets the demand, and it is not accepted that investment in refining capacity would be any lower in the absence of a Solus System;

(4) The Solus System has been used by the major oil companies to preserve their own position and hinder competition from the cut-price companies and from other suppliers of non-petroleum products, especially oil, but also tyres, batteries and accessories;

(5) While the system may be advantageous to the supplier it may not be so in the long run to retailers and certainly is not so to consumers who have to pay higher prices.

The majority of the Monopolies Commission concluded that on balance the solus tie would not be contrary to the public interest so long as it was not for more than five years and did not apply to goods other than petrol. Longer-term agreements were held to be not in the public interest since they rigidified the structure and hindered entry into the trade. Although it found in favour in general of solus arrangements it is clear that the Monopolies Commission was sceptical over many of the benefits claimed for the Solus System. For example, it pointed out that the average size of drop had not increased much as a result of the system, competition did not ensure that all the savings in distribution costs were passed on, not all the benefits did in fact go to the consumer since the retailer gained from having much higher margins on a higher turnover, too much security was not good since it rigidified the trade and raised barriers to entry and a quantity discount system might be preferable to a Solus System.[31]

The reader will have to make up his own mind on the issues posed. However, it may be helpful to point to some considerations that are relevant in reaching a view. First, as Dixon pointed out, a distinction ought to be drawn between the three separate features of the Solus Agreement – exclusive dealing, co-operation between producer and retailer, and the continuity of trading relations through time. Viewed separately there is no apparent reason why if these are commercially sensible, as they presumably are, they would not individually continue in the absence of a solus agreement. Secondly, we must ask with the Monopolies Commission whether petrol is distributed as conveniently, efficiently, and cheaply as under any alternative system, or whether there are more effective ways in which the benefits could be obtained. This requires a consideration not only of how the existing system is worked, but if at all possible how an alternative system would operate. Next we need to reach a view on the question of whether petrol is unique by virtue of the heavy investment and long gestation period involved before investments become profitable, and therefore requires a particular form of market planning in order to obtain desirable economic benefits. Is it really the case that the primary motivation underlying the Solus System is the search on the part of the oil companies for additional efficiency gains or is it, alternatively, simply an attempt to find and preserve outlets for the suppliers' products? Are the oil companies making the right decisions by offering cheap loans rather than encouraging garages to meet the competition from the cut-price companies through lowering prices, and does the commercial decision of a businessman necessarily, or in this particular case, equate to the wider public interest? Finally, we have to ask whether an increase in ownership of retail outlets by the oil companies and hence in formal vertical integration is a likely alternative if the Solus System were to be abandoned. If so, would the consequences of this be more or less desirable than the consequences of the Solus System and if both are considered to be undesirable could an effective way be found of achieving more effective control over the structure of this industry?

Although the Solus System is not identical to vertical integration, in practice it seems to lead to very similar consequences and poses similar policy questions. Four years after reporting on petrol the Monopolies Commission also produced a report on the supply of beer[32] which dealt particularly with the effect of the tied house system, which is a form of vertical integration. There are numerous similarities in the two cases as the Commission found them at the time. In both cases investments in retailing constituted an important use of producer funds; the acquisition of outlets was recognised as an important form of competition for market shares and a means of protecting investments in production; supply was on terms which restricted the retailer's ability to sell different brands and other goods; producers of specialist products consequently found difficulty in obtaining access to outlets; the terms of supply constituted a disincentive to competitive enterprise and there was little effective competition from other types of outlet and new entry into both industries was controlled by various forms of legal provision. Whereas the Monopolies Commission gave positive if guarded approval to the Solus

System for petrol, it strongly criticised the tied house system in the report on beer. It found that the tied house system was contrary to the public interest since the restrictions on competition which this system involved meant that it hindered the elimination of inefficient traders; it hindered the development of an efficient system of distribution; it hindered the growth of independent wholesalers; it hindered the entry of new producers and products and made retailing less competitive since the competition between producers was for captive outlets.

We cannot of course be sure whether the Monopolies Commission did consider that there were significant differences between the two cases to justify different conclusions, or whether in view of the similarities pointed to above the view of the Monopolies Commission about the public interest aspects of this form of vertical integration had changed.

CHAPTER 4

THE CONDITIONS OF ENTRY

In any analysis of the structure of a particular market attention needs to be paid not only to existing objective conditions such as buyer and seller concentration, product differentiation, vertical integration, the geographical structure of the market and the secular pattern of market demand, but also to the possibility that competition may be increased as a result of the entry into an industry of additional suppliers. In addition it is necessary to take into account the possibility that the market conduct of existing firms may be constrained simply by the possibility of such new entry. The concept of potential competition does therefore introduce an important dynamic element into discussions of market structure and performance.

In Ricardian discussions of the competitive system it was assumed that the free entry and exit of firms in a perfectly competitive market was an important equilibrating mechanism since in this way super-normal profits were competed away. In modern economies such adjustments do not often occur and attention must inevitably turn away from discussions of free entry and exit to the hindrances or barriers to entry.

Interest in the conditions of entry was renewed in the mid–1950s by the publication of two books[1] offering rather different approaches to this issue. As a result it has played an increasingly important role in recent discussions of industrial organisation. There appear to be three respects in which this concept can make a useful contribution to our understanding. First, it rightly emphasises that conditions of entry may well significantly affect effective competition and the form that new competition may take in an industry. Secondly, it makes an explicit contribution to discussion of pricing behaviour of firms especially in relation to oligopolistic markets.[2] Thirdly, it offers scope to identify certain normative implications in the distinction between natural and predatory barriers to entry.

Bain's classification

On the basis of empirical studies in twenty industries, Bain identified three sources or types of barrier to entry. He described these as product differentiation, absolute cost disadvantages, and economies of scale barriers.

(a) *Product differentiation* barriers were most likely to be important in consumer goods industries. They occurred through various forms of differentiation in terms of price, design, selling costs, franchises and customer services. They arose i) because buyer preferences were established due to goodwill, the effects of brand names, loyalty, or simply inertia; ii) from superior product design as a result of the control of patents or simply the preservation of secret know-how; iii) through the control of distributive outlets where alternative channels of distribution would be costly to establish. Whatever the source of this barrier, the consequences tended to be the same; the potential new entrant would have to incur heavy marketing costs in the form of extra advertising outlays, higher distributor margins, etc, in order to be able to compete successfully with the established firm.

(b) *Absolute cost disadvantages* exist where the established firms have i) superior production techniques in terms of patents and know-how which are not therefore available readily and without cost to others; ii) control over, or favourable access to, supplies of important factor inputs such as raw materials, management and operatives which cannot be obtained from alternative sources at the same price; iii) lower costs of finance. Bain concluded that absolute cost disadvantages were not normally an important barrier though they could be in particular situations where major patents existed or where the capital costs of entry were high, or where sources of raw material supplies were controlled, thereby necessitating new explorations.

(c) *Economies of scale* are said to constitute a barrier where i) the minimum optimal scale of production represents a large proportion of total industry output, in which case new entry at an optimal scale cannot occur without established firms being affected and possibly reacting; ii) unit costs at a sub-optimal level of output are substantially above those at the optimum output. Where these two circumstances co-exist new entry can prove very difficult indeed. Bain found that economies of scale were frequently perceptible but only as mild barriers in the industries he investigated. He did, however, recognise that British economists tend to place greater emphasis on the existence of economies of scale than do their American counterparts. To the extent that this *may* represent the effects of a smaller market for British producers while they operate under similar technological production conditions, one might expect that at any point in time economies of scale would constitute a greater barrier to entry in a British industry than an equivalent American one.

The consequence of these barriers is that potential new entrants are put at a cost and profit disadvantage, vis-à-vis established firms. In an industry with high barriers to entry an established firm or group of firms acting collusively can safely set prices near to a profit maximising price, without fear that this will encourage new entrants, while in industries where barriers to entry are low and therefore a threat of potential competition is stronger, prices will necessarily be set lower and will tend towards the perfectly competitive price. If existing firms wish to exclude new entrants they will set an entry forestalling price at a level just below the price which the least disadvantaged potential entrant would need to charge. The extent to which the entry forestalling price exceeds the perfectly competitive price is a measure of the height of the entry barrier. On the basis of this approach, we would be encouraged to conclude that the mere threat of potential competition can be as effective as actual competition in constraining pricing policy by existing firms.

Although an existing barrier to entry may appear to have a pervasive and enduring effect on the structure of an industry it can and often will be changed. Endogenous influences will be important but exogenous influences may be particularly significant where they take the form of anti-trust action, the expiry of patents, availability of new sources of supply, technological change or the expansion or contraction of the market.

The nature of new entry

Although much of the developmental work on the concept of barriers to entry has been undertaken by Bain, there are a number of extensions which could be explicitly added with advantage. Not only do these apply to questions of the pricing strategy and the categorisation of types of barrier which will be discussed in later sections of this chapter, they apply also to the nature of the new entry and the origins of the entrant firms.

Whereas Bain's work is based primarily on the costs of entry for newly established firms, other writers[3] have emphasised that entry is more likely to occur through the expansion into new markets and product areas of already established firms. This may include entry by firms already producing broadly similar products in the same industry (called cross-entry by Andrews[4]) or it may be through the decision of customers to set up their own production plant and so integrate backwards, or it may involve geographical diversification with companies producing the same range of goods in a new market. The same consequences may of course also occur through a liberalisation of trade, either through lower tariffs or a relaxation of quota restrictions. Our interest is, however, more concerned with new entry that represents a direct investment in manufacturing plant, though much of the analysis can quite easily be extended to the international trade situation if it is simply assumed that tariffs represent a barrier to competition. In practice, however, it is sometimes the case that tariff barriers encourage new entry by increasing the advantages of setting up a production plant in the market that is apparently protected by tariffs.

The reasons for new entry may well be associated either with expectations about the level of profits[5] or the rate of growth in that particular market. New entry is less likely to occur in static or declining or unprofitable industries. But this is normally an incomplete explanation of the actual reasons for a particular new entry. New entry may come about, not for reasons associated primarily with existing market conditions, but as part of a particular diversification strategy of the firm concerned[6] (which if undertaken without due regard to the profits or growth prospects in an industry may depress the market and encourage weak selling) or in response to encouragement from potential customers. Thus, for example, GKN's decision in 1959 to move into the production of propeller shafts in competition with Hardy Spicer was a response to encouragement from the motor manufacturers backed up by a guaranteed market for two years and an offer to pay higher prices in the initial period. Similarly, British Insulated Callender's Cables began production of mineral-insulated cables in 1948 at the instigation of the manufacturers of rubber cables.[7] Alternatively, the reason for entry may be to utilise a joint product or byproduct arising from another production activity as is the case with ICI's entry into petroleum distribution. For ICI petroleum is essentially a byproduct from one of its other chemical processes.

Changing technological processes and the effects of R and D activities will influence the type of firm that can successfully enter an industry and may have the effect of bringing firms from quite different industries into close contact with each other. Thus the firms constituting the major man-made fibre producers tend to come more from the chemical industry than from traditional textile manufacturers since modern man-made fibre production needs a considerable degree of chemistry know-how. Other examples of this phenomenon were discussed in Chapter 1. The petroleum industry in the United Kingdom also offers evidence that some of the new entry occurring in this market in the late 1960s was due primarily to a world surplus of crude oil supplies. Again, some new entry, especially of a geographical kind, may occur out of a desire to discipline a particular competitor or to preserve a balance in relation to some other market altogether.[8]

Questions of the timing of new entry are also important. It does not necessarily follow that any time is as good as any other for new entry to take place. Particularly in highly technologically oriented industries, it is quite often the case that new entry is most likely to occur at times when a major new innovation has just arisen. This is the time at which knowledge barriers are lowest and new entrant firms, at least from that point of view, are at less of a disadvantage than they would be at other periods of time where there is a static technology and where substantial learning effects have already been achieved by existing firms.

The method of new entry is also subject to variation. In some cases entry will involve the immediate creation of new manufacturing capacity. In others it may be achieved by the establishment of a distribution organisation in the first instance to distribute supplies imported from abroad or produced by some other company. This can offer a particularly effective means of overcoming any initial economies of scale disadvantages. New entry does not necessarily mean that an entrant will enter the whole of a market (defined either in product or geographical terms) and certain benefits of specialisation through operation in a limited market may therefore be available. Strictly speaking, a mere change in the ownership of assets from one firm to another as a result of a merger does not constitute new entry. However, it is sometimes the case that the acquiring firms may plan to operate more aggressively and possibly to expand the output and sales above that achieved by the acquired firm. Where this occurs, the economic implications may be tantamount to new entry.

This discussion of the form and motivations for new entry points to some important implications. It is clear that the height of a particular entry barrier cannot be considered to be uniquely determined. Where new entrants are established firms they will normally have some technological or marketing links with the product market into which they are moving. This may allow them to overcome production disadvantages by sharing a common production line with existing outputs, using the same raw materials inputs and benefiting from superior buying power. An established firm is likely to have available technical experts or be more readily able to recruit them to cope with difficulties. An established company may be able to overcome disadvantages caused through the existence of patents by arranging an exchange of patents or entering into some form of cross-licensing arrangement. Established companies would be expected to have made a more thorough investigation of market possibilities before committing capital to an enterprise and may be helped in their market penetration by the existence of an established dealer organisation or distributive network and the acceptance by potential users of the company name or brand names which will assist the initial effort to establish an adequate volume of sales for the new product. Where the entry occurs through acquisition, brand names may again be available to assist the expansion. 'Geographical' new entry by multinational organisations is likely to be made even easier in respect of many of these considerations as such companies are likely to have many of their production difficulties and marketing strategies already sorted out.

Perhaps even more important is the fact that an established multi-product organisation will have easier access to capital and a greater ability to take a long-term view of the new activity while accepting losses or very low returns in the short run. Bain's discussion does not appear to take account of the likelihood of short-term losses though this is realistic, at least for UK firms entering new markets. Bhagwati's recent formulation does, however, recognise this explicitly.

Of course not all new entries by established firms will be successful but it is highly probable that for the reasons given the height and duration of any given barrier will be lower where established firms are the most likely new entrants. Such new entry may not only be more competitive by introducing more aggressive managerial attitudes, greater ability to attack quickly at the heart of the industry and improved R and D performance, but it may also reduce substantially the lead time before the new entry becomes effective competition.

Implications for pricing strategy

We have shown that the higher are the barriers to entry the greater could be the premium over the competitive price taken by existing firms without inducing new entry. There has, however, been considerable interest shown in the wider implications that considerations of the threat of potential competition may have in understanding firm pricing behaviour, especially in oligopoly.

There are a number of problems in undertaking such an analysis.[9] To be able to identify a single, entry deterring price it needs to be assumed that all firms (existing and potential entrants alike) have the same objectives.[10] In addition it is necessary to predict the output levels decided upon by both the existing firms and the new entrants after the entry has taken place and the effect that alternative output decisions will have on prices. If, for example, existing firms maintain their existing outputs after the entry has taken place this would be expected to depress market prices and would reduce the attractions of that market to the potential new entrant. If the products of the new entrant are not direct substitutes for those of existing firms and/or if the market is expanding at a rapid rate, output decisions may be less important influences on the price level to be expected after new entry has occurred. The relevant price to consider in limit price analysis is the price after the anticipated new entry has occurred and not the pre-entry price. Considerations of conjectural interdependence have their role in limit price approaches to oligopoly as in other theories of oligopoly.

What then can we say on the extent to which existing firms can set a premium over the competitive price and still forestall entry? If it is assumed that the results can be quantified in revenue terms, then the aim of the existing firm will be to set a price which 'causes the entrant to suffer a larger present value of losses than the monopolist suffers if entry did occur'.[11]

Certain general pointers can be identified as to the conditions under which the relative size of the premium will vary.[12] It will tend to be higher if the new entrants are expected to be completely new firms who would not be able to bear short-run losses or if the extra output the new entrant would produce would cause market prices to fall. It is also likely to be greater where the minimum optimum scale of production is larger and where the cost of increasing the rate of output is high. The premium would be expected to be lower where the price elasticity of demand facing existing firms is high, where new entrants are more likely to be willing to accept short-term losses and if the rate of expansion of the market is rapid. According to Bhagwati, an expanding market may not even allow a premium at all since the appropriate entry forestalling price would be at a level below (existing) average costs. Under such circumstances the firm would be best advised to concentrate on maximising its own share of the increasing market segment.

The likelihood of new firms coming into an industry even granted a particular level of prices is not of course something which existing firms can normally pronounce on with any degree of certainty. It has therefore been suggested that firms could establish the probabilities of new entry taking place for each possible price that they might set. The size of the premium above the entry forestalling price that they would be justified in taking in practice would be smaller the greater the desire to exclude new entrants and the higher the probability of new entry.[13] It does not even follow that an appropriate pricing strategy in all cases is to set an entry forestalling price. If a firm has a high time preference and if lead times are long before new entry can become effective, it may well pay the firm to set a profit maximising price in the short run. Equally, if the objectives of existing firms are expressed in terms of market expansion or a stable stream of profit then it may be appropriate to set a price that earns only normal profits and is therefore below an equivalent entry forestalling price.

There is no simple limit price rule that a firm may take into account in setting its own prices. The correct decision will vary according to the objective conditions existing in the market and the expectations of both the existing and potential new entrant firms about the consequences of any new entry that did occur. Nevertheless it seems that firms would be well advised to allow the prospect of potential competition to influence their price determination. Certainly examples do exist of firms setting a low price to discourage entry into an industry and in some cases the expiry of an important patent which had constituted a major barrier to entry marked the decision to lower prices in order to discourage new entrants.[14] Andrews found that the conditions of entry had an important influence on the size of firms' costing margins and hence on prices.[15] In other cases it seems that by failing to consider the threat of potential competition existing firms have set high prices that have either encouraged new entry or have appeared likely to have that effect.[16]

Barriers and public policy

There is evidence that very high barriers to entry are associated with high profitability in industry.[17] In Britain the Monopolies Commission in its investigations of particular firms and industries has appeared implicity to accept this view in treating the continued existence of high profits as evidence of the incidence of high barriers to entry. There is therefore a strong public policy interest in the question of the way in which barriers to entry occur and the way in which they affect the performance of industries in which they are an important feature of market structure.

The three general categories of barrier to entry identified by Bain and discussed earlier in this chapter are less helpful to consideration of this aspect of the problem. It is necessary to look again at sources of empirical evidence on the nature of barriers to entry and the way in which they perform. For Britain this becomes possible by using in particular the reports of the Monopolies Commission. It should, however, be noted that this source may well distort the pattern of information obtained since Monopolies Commission references tend to be of dominant firms as indicated by a concentration ratio and the Commission's investigations are primarily concerned with the question of whether the position of such a dominant firm operates against the public interest and whether there are any 'things done' as a result of, or for the purpose of preserving, a monopoly position. Thus, if different types of barrier to entry occur in industries with different concentration levels, then the use of information obtained primarily from studies of dominant firms may well have the effect of excluding from consideration certain types of barrier to entry altogether. Nevertheless, from this source of case material, we are able to identify a number of types of barrier to entry, some of which at least would not fit easily into Bain's three categories and we are also able to say something about the way in which the particular barrier has arisen and the effects of its operation in practice. As the Monopolies Commission observed in its report on Metal Box, 'the proper question to ask is whether Metal Box has created barriers to competition over and above those attributable to its cost advantages'.[18] The main types of barrier identified are as follows:[19]

(a) *Barriers from the scale of investments and operations.* The large size of initial investment required appears to constitute an important barrier in a number of industries especially, of course, those where technology is advanced and continuous production necessary. The ability to spread overhead costs thinly over a large scale of production means that scale economies are important. For a firm contemplating entry it is necessary under such circumstances to grow large quickly. This may also mean of course that heavy marketing outlays will have to be incurred to achieve this rapid growth and so there may well be an interdependence between production barriers and marketing barriers. Difficulties in raising finance are faced particularly by small and medium sized firms and constitute part of this barrier. Heavy advertising expenditures may also constitute a barrier, especially if they are also subject to economies of scale so that there is a high minimum threshold level of expenditure before advertising becomes economical at all. This applies primarily in consumer goods industries (e.g. detergents and breakfast cereals). This aspect is also considered in Chapter 11 below.

(b) *The established position and size of an existing large firm* may often constitute a barrier, especially where it is reliable, efficient and has adequate financial resources. It is not only that such a large firm is likely to have taken reasonable advantage of the scale benefits open to it but it is likely to have strongly established know-how and access to raw material and financial resources that would allow it to withstand competitive pressures. Well-established brand names will make the required marketing outlays of new entrants larger and may hinder their access to channels of distribution. This seemed to be a problem hindering the development of new competition in the supply of electric lamps.

(c) *The size and rate of growth of the market.* A small market or a low or variable rate of growth of market demand are likely to constitute a barrier to entry. If there is uncertainty about the future prospects for a particular product or industry this will also reduce the incentive for new competitors.

(d) *Patents and R and D.* The relationship between patents and entry seems to vary from industry to industry. In some cases, e.g. metal containers, the Monopolies Commission has found that the existence of patents has not hindered competition, while in others, e.g. man-made cellulosic fibres, it has found that patents did constitute an early barrier to entry. High royalties where licences were granted on tranquillizers made it difficult for rival producers to undercut the dominant suppliers. In the case of cellophane the Monopolies Commission reported that it might take five to seven years for a firm to make up a deficiency in its know-how and so this would constitute a very serious barrier to entry.

Other writers have offered their analysis of the effects of patents on the conditions of entry. Sylos Labini has argued that patents may offer only short period protection and then only of the production *method*. In an interesting article, though admittedly lacking in empirical data, Mueller and Tilton argued that patents do not often constitute an important barrier since firms may prefer to licence rather than appear to be a conspicuous monopoly. This they thought was particularly likely to be the case in the early stages of the adoption of an innovation. Later on, at what they called the 'technological competition stage' royalty payments for licences might have to be made and other barriers in terms of the acquisition of know-how would increase. At the end of the cycle, when the product is standardised, no more technological competition would occur, patents would expire and the size of the R and D barrier would decline.[20] The economic implications of patents are discussed at length in Chapter 5.

(e) *The 'Rules of the Game'.* Pursuing the argument that because the large size of existing firms constitutes an important general barrier to entry, Marris stated 'consequently existing giants are the most effective rivals to other existing giants, except where small firms have a special advantage'.[21] Unfortunately it often appears to be the case that the 'existing giants' succeed in finding ways of not competing directly with each other when such competition would appear to be a natural extension of their product policy and the existence of other barriers may ensure that smaller firms do not enter the market. Thus, for example, the Monopolies Commission expressed some surprise that Shell and ICI, while producing a product that was to all intents and purposes a household detergent and while marketing this to industrial users, had chosen not to enter the household detergent market in competition with Unilever and Procter and Gamble. In some cases the rules of the game may take the form of tacit arrangements not to diversify into product or geographical markets that are the preserve of other firms (e.g. metal containers and man-made cellulosic fibres). In others it may take the form of covenants or agreements between firms not to compete with each other and to divide international markets between them (e.g. cellophane and matches). The interdependence that is frequently to be found in individual oligopolistic markets seems therefore often to transcend individual markets and to influence potential competition between giant organisations on a product-wide and even a global market basis.

(f) *Direct controls on competition* may be exercised by buying up any competitors who do succeed in breaking into a market (wallpaper) or by the exercise of import agreements to keep imports into a domestic country low (cellophane and man-made cellulosic fibres). Stigler has claimed that new entry in the USA has sometimes been hindered by, amongst other things, coercion of potential sellers.[22]

(g) *Price policies.* The setting of a low price would normally be considered to be a perfectly reasonable entry forestalling tactic. In some cases, however, lowering prices, especially after entry has taken place either generally or selectively by use of fighting companies, may constitute a hindrance to competition (e.g. metal containers, man-made cellulosic fibres and industrial gases). The knowledge that this sort of tactic is used in some markets may itself be sufficient to discourage other firms from attempting to enter. The charging of uneconomically low prices in initial equipment markets may also make it difficult for new competitors to break into the market. This was a well-established practice in the supply of motor accessories (electrical equipment and clutches). A variant of the same practice appeared to exist in the case of tranquillizers where the supply of the drug at very low prices to hospitals effectively kept competitors out of that part of the market and maintained the position with general practitioners' prescriptions since they tended to prescribe the same drug that a patient had received in hospital.

(h) *Action through distributors*. Tactics of full-line forcing and insistence on exclusive dealing, offering preferential terms, incentive discounts or loyalty rebates to ensure favourable or even sole representation have frequently been found (e.g. dental goods, cigarettes, clutches and lubricants). This makes it difficult or even impossible for new entrants to obtain distributive outlets. A graduated discount structure may make it very difficult for another supplier to break into a market. The opportunity costs to a customer of giving part of an order to a second supplier may well be very high in terms of discounts foregone from the first supplier and the second producer would need to offer a high discount to compensate. Thus the marginal costs of gaining distribution are high. The Monopolies Commission brought out this issue in their report on metal containers. In some instances the ownership of tied outlets with a refusal to stock competitors' products raises the costs of new entry very substantially since the new entry by the manufacturer may also require the heavy additional investment in a complete distributive network.[23]

(i) *Action through suppliers*. Some manufacturers are in the favourable position of controlling supplies of an important raw material or machine which their competitors will need to obtain from them. Refusal to supply or agreement to supply only on unfavourable terms may ensue. In some instances it appears that even independent suppliers can be persuaded by a dominant firm to refuse to supply at all or to practise price discrimination by charging prices that are excessively high in relation to the actual costs of supply.

Although a number of other barriers are identified in the reports of the Monopolies Commission, the categories listed above appear to be the most important and prone to occur in several different situations. It must be emphasised again that they cannot claim to be a representative selection of the types of barrier that are found in British industry because the Monopolies Commission does not investigate firms and industries selected on a random or representative basis. What is apparent, however, is that in a number of monopolistic and oligopolistic industries of the sort with which discussions of the conditions of entry are most concerned, a series of barriers to entry and hindrances to competition are to be found which do not fit easily into Bain's categories and in some cases extend quite considerably awareness of the existence and operation of different types of barrier not identified in Bain's initial studies. We can perhaps also begin to observe a distinction between barriers that appear to exist naturally in a particular industry as a result of specific technological conditions in that industry and others that are created as a result of deliberate action by one or more firms with a view to preserving their dominant position. Hindrances to competition through various forms of direct and indirect action as indicated under the headings (e) to (i) above seem to occur quite frequently. Most of these fall outside Bain's categories. It is interesting to note that the majority of them occur in relation to marketing activities by existing firms and/or frequently arise out of particular vertical relationships that these firms have with or as suppliers or distributors.

It would be unwise to attempt to make a clear-cut distinction between natural and predatory barriers. But if barriers arising from technological aspects of production or the rate of growth of the market may be deemed 'natural', such tactics as full-line forcing and fighting companies are clearly 'predatory'. But all is not black and white, and it is in respect of the shades of grey, which probably include advertising and patent policies of firms and their vertical trading relationships, that greatest difficulties may occur in establishing the causes and consequences of a particular barrier. In these cases a firm with a monopoly position should be prepared to justify its practices and Bain's general policy prescription that action should be taken to shorten the time lag before a new entrant can compete on equal terms is appropriate. The greatest difficulty is, however, going to lie in policing those agreements, tacit or otherwise, between large organisations who refrain from competing in each others' territory, whether product or geographical. Since we have argued that it is potential competition that comes from entry of existing firms into new markets that is most important, it follows that in terms of their potential practical consequences, the barriers arising from the observance of the rules of the game and the predatory behaviour of dominant firms are the most serious in their implications.

CHAPTER 5

PATENTS

A patent is a property right which may be conferred upon an inventor as a result of some original invention. As with other forms of property it may be assigned, sold, licensed or shared, normally at the sole discretion of the owner. In return for disclosing the details of the invention the inventor is usually allowed, under the terms of the patent, to control and even to prevent rival production or use of the patented item or process. The duration of a patent varies somewhat from country to country; in Britain at present it is 16 years. Although the use of a patent may occasionally be circumscribed by other controls, it is clear that to hold a patent can constitute an important potential form of monopoly power over both existing and potential competition. Patents may therefore represent a major structural influence in at least some industries. In this chapter we shall consider the likely economic consequences of this element of industry structure. One word of warning is, however, in order. The general economic principles are likely to remain reasonably applicable to most societies in which the domestic private sector is important in industrial invention and innovation but they may be less relevant to economies with a high level of technological dependence on others. In addition the actual practical implications will depend upon the particular patent system adopted. This varies from country to country, especially in terms of the legal provisions, the nature of the administration of the system and its relation to the anti-trust laws of the state concerned. We shall be primarily concerned with the situation in Britain, although some comment will also be made about experience in other countries.

Administrative aspects of the patent system

The practice of rewarding inventors dates back some 500 years or more. From an early stage (as for example in the Statute of Monopolies 1621) a distinction was made between the monopoly power conferred by a patent which was permitted and other forms of monopoly which were more likely to be prohibited. The basic principles of the patent system have not greatly changed since then and it has been suggested that the system as we know it is still in fact a pre-industrial one. However, in the last hundred years or so there has been a substantial increase in the use made of the system.

The general principle of the patent system is that all patents carry equal rights irrespective of the intrinsic merit of the invention. There is no attempt to reward the inventor according to the merit or value of his invention. Provision may, however, be made for the patent and hence the monopoly power so created to be extended beyond the normal maximum period of the patent in order that the inventor may be enabled to obtain a fair reward if for one reason or another, not the fault of the inventor, this has not been possible within a normal patent period. Most countries grant patents for a period of 16 to 20 years, although the trend is for the length of the period to increase rather than to be reduced. The criteria for the grant of a patent tend to vary slightly from country to country but in general patents may be granted for any invention which is susceptible of industrial application in industry or agriculture, which is new and which involves an inventive step and does not form part of the existing state of the art. The concept of an 'inventive step' means that there must be some element in the invention which was not obvious or predictable granted the existing state of the art. The concept of the 'state of the art' is essentially to be understood to mean any knowledge that is available to the public. Patents will not be granted where an invention would be contrary to public order or morality or in respect of any plant or animal varieties which may be developed or in relation to essentially biological processes for the production of plants or animals.[1] The range of products and ideas that are considered to be patentable tends to vary slightly from country to country. For example, some countries restrict the patentability of food and/or drug products and processes. The USA on the other hand has actually extended the area of patentability to include known and naturally occurring substances and processes including fermentation and has also allowed the patenting of combinations of old drugs.

Administration of patent policy also tends to vary from country to country. At one extreme a system may be adopted based simply upon the registration of patent applications with very little provision for testing the validity of an application unless the patent is challenged by a third party. At the other extreme is a system based upon a detailed examination of the validity of individual patent applications. With a substantial number of patents being sought each year and the backlog of patent applications to be dealt with progressively increasing, many countries choose not to conduct a rigorous examination of applications, leaving it instead to interested parties to challenge and initiate more extensive examination of a patent that may not be entirely justified.

The British system is a compromise between the two extremes, though it tends towards a registration procedure. A limited examination of the novelty of an invention is conducted to check whether it has been anticipated by prior publication or patent claim. Questions of priority and obviousness are really

only investigated if there is an opposition to a patent application. The useful-
ness and inventiveness of the invention and the public interest aspects of the
patent grant are only considered if proceedings are instituted for a revocation
of the patent. Only about 15 per cent of patent applications in Britain are
rejected[2] and it is reported that 'in practice the Patent Office makes every
effort to give the benefit of the doubt to the applicant and does everything
it can to grant some sort of a patent even if it is very weak'.[3] The effect of
this is that many patents are granted that are of little economic significance
and, more important, are of doubtful validity. Hence some patent monopolies
may be created which do not have much justification in terms of the reasons
for which patents are normally granted.

The protection of the public interest under a registration oriented patent
system relies heavily upon the assumption that the self-interest of other manufacturers will be sufficient to ensure that dubious patents are challenged.
This assumption may not be justified. The evidence is that less than two per
cent of patents in Britain are challenged.[4] It seems that a much higher
proportion could be challenged if firms were willing to bear the costs of litigation and assuming that they had not been persuaded by cross-licensing not
to challenge doubtful patents. The alternative, of a fuller examination of
patent applications such as that used in the USA or Germany, would
necessitate a much more extensive search procedure, probably based upon an
improved and more extensive information retrieval system within the Patent
Office. Without other compensating adjustments in the procedure this would
impose the disadvantage of a longer delay before a patent could be granted
and the invention for which the patent is granted made public.

If a patent application is to be successful, it is most important to establish
priority in invention. But priority is not an unambiguous concept. The
American patent system interprets priority as being the first to produce the
invention, whereas the British system accords priority to the first person to
file a specification for the invention, without necessarily having actually produced it. In Britain the situation is taken even further by allowing an inventor
to file a provisional specification in order to establish his priority and then at
a later date to file a full specification for his invention. The actual date from
which the patent runs is the date at which the patent is in fact sealed and
this is therefore based upon the filing of the full specification rather than the
provisional specification.

Although the legal life of a patent in Britain is 16 years, the effective life
can be very variable. Many patents are not renewed for the full period of
time. But some patents may be extended beyond 16 years if it is considered
that the invention is of considerable value to the public, but that the inventor
has not over that period been adequately rewarded for his invention. Equally,
the terms of the Patent Act 1949 allow for a termination or reduction of the
monopoly power given by a patent. Other firms may apply for the revocation
of a patent on the grounds that the patentee did not have priority in publica-

tion, that the specification filed contained insufficient information, or that the invention was obvious, that is, it was lacking a genuine inventive step. Although, as we have noted, the proportion of oppositions to patent applications is very small, occasional patent cases can be long drawn out and bitterly fought where a key or master patent is involved.

After a patent has been in existence for three years, other firms may apply to the Comptroller-General of Patents for the grant of a compulsory licence of right enabling them also to engage in production of the patented product or use of the patented process if it appears that the monopoly power granted by the patent is being abused. Abuses may be held to have occurred if the patented invention is not being worked commercially in the United Kingdom to the furthest practicable extent, if existing demand is not being reasonably met, if an export market is not being supplied because of the patentee's refusal to grant a licence on reasonable terms, if the production of any other patented invention that makes a substantial contribution to the art is hindered, or if the establishment or development of commercial or industrial activities in the United Kingdom is unfairly prejudiced. Clearly the aim of this section is to attempt to overcome at least some of the artificial restrictions of output that are normally held to be a consequence of monopoly power. It is, however, often difficult for firms to show that demand is not being reasonably met as the unsatisfied demand has to be demonstrated to be actual rather than potential. In addition, a patentee can, if he wishes, cause extensive delays in the hearing of applications for a compulsory licence of right and may involve an applicant in heavy financial costs which could well reduce the incentive to apply for a compulsory licence. It may be, however, that threats to seek compulsory licences are sometimes sufficient to induce patentees to be more willing to agree to grant a voluntary licence of right to a competitor.

Drugs often have a special position under patent laws, and it has been reported that only three countries – USA, Panama and Belgium – allow unrestricted patents on drugs.[5] Some countries disallow patents on drugs altogether. Britain and a number of other countries allow drugs to be patented but impose additional provisions regarding the grant of compulsory licences. Section 41 of the Patents Act 1949 provides that compulsory licences for the production of both food and drugs shall be granted at any time by the Comptroller if an applicant for a licence is suitable. The terms of the licence are to be as the Comptroller thinks appropriate. In this case it is not necessary for an applicant to prove that abuses have followed from the existence of a patent monopoly and the aim of this section seems to be to ensure that the lowest possible prices are charged for food and drugs consistent with the provision of a reasonable advantage to the patentee from his invention. Although this may seem a very powerful provision, experience has shown that the legal and administrative procedures are cumbersome and protracted and give considerable scope to a patentee to delay the actual grant of a licence.

In its report on the supply of tranquillizers the Monopolies Commission showed that it took three to four years for other firms to obtain a compulsory licence to supply tranquillizers under the terms of Section 41. From the report it seems that Roche, the holder of the patents, made strenuous efforts to delay the execution of the licence of right and also sought to prevent the licensees from marketing the tranquillizers in a form similar to that used by Roche. All in all, the expenses of obtaining the licence together with the high royalty rate that the Comptroller decided should be payable meant that a licence to produce the drugs was not particularly profitable to the licensees.[6]

The final provision under the 1949 Patents Act for curtailment of a patentee's monopoly power appears under Section 46 in what is known as the Crown User Provision. Under this a government department may ignore existing patent rights and acquire any patented invention from a cheaper supplier where the supplies are intended for the service of the Crown. Again, this provision may be exercised at any time during the life of the patent. This provision has also been invoked in relation to the supply of drugs. In 1961 it was used for the first time in order that supplies of tetracycline drugs could be obtained for hospitals at lower prices than those being charged by the holders of the British patents. Invitations to supply the hospital service were put out to tender and much lower prices obtained from foreign suppliers, thereby producing savings estimated at about £1 million a year.[7] At that time it was considered that only supplies for the hospitals and the armed forces could be counted as supplies of drugs for the service of the Crown. However, since the National Health Service Act 1968 it has been possible for the Crown User Provision to be applied in relation to the purchase of drugs to meet prescriptions from general practitioners as well.

The economics of the patent system

(1)   *The Incidence of Patenting*

It is only recently that much statistical information has been available on the economic importance of the patent system. The Banks Committee reported that over 60,000 patent applications were received in the United Kingdom in 1968 and that over half of these were from foreign applicants, especially from Europe and the USA. It appears that the preponderance of foreign patent applications is a phenomenon in a number of countries including Australia, Canada, France, Sweden and Switzerland, though not of applications in the USA, Japan and Germany. The increase in the proportion of foreign applications has had an important effect on the total number of patent applications but the Banks Committee also attributed the increase and its attendant administrative problems to recent technological advances.

Unfortunately the trend in the level of patent applications may be only a limited indicator of trends in technological progress. Through time it appears that attitudes to patenting have varied and the limited examination system currently in force in Britain means that patent protection may be sought for trivial inventions that do not constitute a major technical development. Conversely, a high proportion of new ideas and developments may well not be patented and it appears that the propensity to patent is variable from industry to industry. It is generally agreed that the vast majority of patents are in fact not worked. A very small survey conducted by the Banks Committee indicated that only about 30 per cent of patented inventions were in commercial use and it was admitted that this proportion was higher than was usually thought to exist. In the chemical industry where the incidence of patenting was found to be greatest it was also found that less than one patent in five was actually in commercial use.

Not only may the propensity to patent vary from industry to industry, it is also highly likely that the degree of monopolistic protection provided by the patent will also vary from product to product. Some patents are 'master' patents which means they cannot easily be avoided in production. For example, the tranquillizer patents and those on some of the less frequently found forms of electric lamp, especially mercury and sodium discharge lamps, fall into this category. Other patents are less strong and firms may be able to produce similar competing products by using an alternative process or input at little additional cost. The patents on acrylic fibres, for example, were not particularly strong and competition was more easily introduced there than in the case of the polyester patents which preserved a much stronger monopoly position to the holders.

In some though not all instances it seems that while master patents may have been important at some stage in the development of an industry their impact is no longer as great.[8] In the production of viscose fibres there had been seven master patents all of which had expired by the mid-1920s and the key patents on clutches, colour film, detergents and metal containers had all expired at least 25 years ago. Metal Box, for example, told the Monopolies Commission that since 1945 less than one per cent of the cans sold had been covered by patents that prevented a competitor selling an identical item. Even if patents are of less significance in some industries, know-how is often very important, and may exercise a major influence on the structure of an industry. Licensing applications may be less concerned with access to the subject matter of the patent than with obtaining the know-how underlying a development. In some cases a firm may choose not to seek a patent in order to avoid disclosing its own know-how.

Firm motivations in seeking patents appear to be varied. Some patents are sought for defensive reasons. Small firms may feel that a patent offers greater security, especially in their search for financial assistance to develop their inventions. However, all a patent may do in such cases is confirm the right of the organisation or inventor concerned to sell the rights to the invention; it does not seem to help preserve the independence of the inventing organisation. Firms of all sizes may find that where a development is easily imitated a patent is helpful in preventing copying by firms that have made no research and development contribution on their own account. The existence of a patent allows a firm to control the expansion of production facilities through its licensing decisions. This reduces the fear that too many firms attempting to produce a new product might lead to the creation of excess capacity in the early stages of the life of the product and the possibility that this would cause weak selling and make commercial production generally unprofitable. Finally, since patents are granted on the basis of claims of priority, a firm may seek a patent not because it desires the monopoly protection that this offers, but simply because it removes the possibility that it could otherwise be excluded from the market and blocked from using a development it has pioneered if a later firm actually applied for a patent and was successful because there was no evidence that the prior claims of another organisation had been established. However, publication of results can be an alternative to patenting for this purpose.

But there are more positive reasons as to why a firm should seek the benefits that a patent confers. It will give a commercial advantage to the patentee by giving it a head start in the competitive process: 'The importance of the patent is time – time to recoup expenditure on research and development and time to discover and develop the next step'.[9] Where the establishment of a viable market requires heavy marketing outlays the protection of a patent offers the incentive to make the required major marketing and promotional effort in order to develop the market. This appears to have been an important advantage that patents offered in assisting the early development of nylon and terylene.[10] Some patents are taken out in order that a firm may have something worthwhile to offer in exchange for a licence of right on a major patent owned by a competitor. Such bartering of patents appears to be a regular practice in some industries.

Whether a firm actually chooses to patent a particular development will depend upon a range of considerations of the likely benefits that may be available from patenting or of the costs that might be incurred if a patent is not obtained. The actual calculus would require consideration whether the revenue derived as a result of the patent, net of the costs of obtaining and enforcing it, was greater than the expected revenue from the development of the invention without the patent. It is not such a straightforward task to estimate this as there are risks and hence probabilities to be estimated on both sides. If a patent is obtained there may be losses from the disclosure of the development and costs of litigation, while if a patent is not sought there is a risk of being copied or of being shut out by an alternative patent claim.

Of course, it does not follow that just because a firm receives a patent it will choose to work that patent as a single firm monopoly. Many patentees do grant licences to other producers and receive in return royalties related to the volume of sales. ICI's licence on its terylene patents was estimated to have brought in £25 million in royalties and Pilkington's generous licensing provisions (for which it received a lump sum for know-how and a royalty based on the level of production) was approved by the Monopolies Commission as it was thereby exposing itself to competition. A licence may offer widely varying benefits to the licensee, often depending on the strength of the initial patent. In some cases it may simply be a means of saving the time and effort of inventing round the patent, or it may be an opportunity to acquire the know-how involved rather than the right to produce as such. In other cases where a strong patent exists a licence may be the only means of legitimately entering that particular product market. Probably the best-known patent licensing activities in Britain in recent years have centred round the formation and operation of the 'crimplene club' in which a small group of firms has been licensed by ICI to produce and sell crimplene. This licence has been keenly sought and is now considered to be highly profitable for those who hold it.

(2) The Case for Patents

It is claimed that the general advantage of a patent system is that it maintains a balance between the legitimate property rights that an inventor should have in his invention and the social desire for increased dissemination of knowledge. By disclosing his knowledge the inventor is able to obtain the benefits of a monopoly from his invention and is thereby saved from the possibly expensive consequences of a rival appropriating his own knowledge without necessarily having incurred any research expenditures on his own account.

Of perhaps rather more immediate economic relevance, however, are claims that relate to the effect on the level and direction of inventive effort. It is argued that the market will obtain a better allocation of inventive effort by offering the possibility of monetary benefits through the patent system and this therefore encourages a socially desirable increase in the level of inventive and innovative effort which will secure a more rapid rate of technical progress than would exist if there were no property rights.[11] By allowing time for research and development outlays to be recouped it particularly encourages firms to undertake outlays on risky innovations and developments and where long gestation periods are to be expected.[12]

(3) Economic Criticisms of Patents

Criticisms of the economic effects of the patent system are based mainly on three broad grounds: concerning the degree and form of monopoly power that is exercised by patentees; the effect that the system has on the type and volume of inventive effort; and the effects of the particular administrative features of most patent systems.

(a) Patents lead to an increase in the exercise of monopoly power   Although many patents do not appear to create a major monopoly position for the holder, there is no doubt that the more limited number of major or key patents does offer a high degree of monopoly power. This inevitably gives rise to concern that holders of major patents may take undue advantage of the monopoly position their patents offer and set prices and profits substantially above the level that would be necessary to produce a proper reward for the research and development effort that had been undertaken. Although *ad hoc* investigations may conclude that the level of prices and profits on a product is too high and may attribute this to the influence of patents, it is rarely possible to investigate whether prices are higher under a patent system than they would be without patents since there is little variation in national policies to allow investigation of this question. However, the rather greater diversity of national patent policies on drugs does offer some scope for such a test. Using information from the US Senate Administered Prices Report on Drugs, J. M. Blair [13] found that drug prices tended to be higher in countries with patent protection on drugs than in those without. This does not, of course, demonstrate causality but another investigator did argue that there was a direct link between patents and high prices and profits. The high profits in turn allow additional advertising and promotional expenditure to be undertaken on both the patented items and on unpatented items which creates a barrier to entry and again leads to higher prices. In this way, he argued, patents may not only affect the conditions of entry and hence prices and profits on the patented goods but also on other items produced by the same manufacturer.[14]

It seems that possession of a patent may well allow a manufacturer to extend his monopoly power well beyond that initially allowed by the patent. 'Improving patents' which embody minor adjustments to the basic design may be used to extend the life of a basic patent and competitors may be acquired in order to obtain control of important rival developments. A patent holder may refuse to grant licences of right to competitors or may do so only upon terms that are so onerous that it becomes impossible for the licensee to offer the product at more competitive prices. Again licences may only be granted subject to restrictions on the level of output that may be produced, the geographical area in which supplies may be sold or on the use to which the patent licence may be put. In their investigations Silberston and Taylor found that the most onerous restrictions in licensing agreements were more likely to be those imposing restrictions on the markets to be supplied and on the exchange and use of know-how covered by a licensing agreement. They reported that licensing tends mainly to be international in character with the licensee undertaking not to sell in the licensor's home or main export markets.[15] Consequently, licensing under those conditions will not increase competition in the domestic market of the patent holder.

The grant of compulsory licences of right imposed by governmental authority would, of course, be likely to increase competition. But this may also be ineffective if the holder of the patent is able to delay the operation of such an order or if the royalty rate laid down reduces the possibility of lower prices. The Banks Committee [16] was of the opinion that the compulsory licensing provisions had not worked well and it would seem from the Monopolies Commission's report on tranquillizers that this was also consistent with its evidence since it reported that it took three to four years for compulsory licences to be finally granted.[17]

Much patenting activity is based on a co-operative arrangement between groups of firms who form a common patent pool. In some cases this may operate on an international basis and it is often exempt from normal regulations controlling the behaviour of cartels. Patent pooling may make competition more difficult for independent firms outside the cartel and threats of litigation may be used as a means of preventing or restraining competition, possibly by forcing the competitor to join the cartel and to accept the common restrictions. The earlier history of the electric lamp industry was a good example of the operation of a patent sharing cartel. The members agreed that they would not oppose each other's patent applications and would not even challenge doubtful patents. All parties were entitled to be cross–licensed on normal commercial terms, production quotas were fixed and an approved list of manufacturers maintained. This was used for both aggressive and defensive purposes against competitors and clearly represents an example of the extent to which such a cartel may exercise undue monopoly power.[18]

(b) Patents lead to a misallocation of resources It is argued that the marginal cost of producing information is zero and, as there is unlikely to be congestion in the use of knowledge, effective resource allocation would require that the supply price of information should also be zero. The effect of the patent and the price charged for the information embodied in the patent is to create scarcity. This means that demand will be at a sub-optimal level and there will be an under-utilisation of the results of the inventive activity.[19] The implications of such arguments are that a distinction should be made between the provision of rewards to inventors and charges to the users of the information provided.

If the main resource allocation objection relates to the impact on the demand for information, criticisms are also levelled at the effect on the effort to supply information. It is argued that speculative pursuit of a patent monopoly may encourage too much effort to produce patentable but not particularly useful inventions. Perhaps this is not an important objection since if it was known that there would not be much demand for a particular invention the prospective return to the producer, whether protected by a patent or not, would not be high enough to warrant the initial research and development expenditure. Of much greater importance is the claim that the presence of patents in certain fields leads to a misallocation of other inventive efforts since too much attention is paid to attempts to circumvent existing patents rather than to make major new developments. The Sainsbury Committee, for example, commented, 'the imitation of existing products by the minimum of molecular manipulation required to circumvent patents has clearly proved profitable and the number of 'me-too' products that follow a new therapeutic fashion shows that it is widely used'.[20] It is, however, fair to add that in their investigation covering a wider area of industry Silberston and Taylor did not find much evidence that firms were forced to design around a patent although it is equally true that their information was collected from the larger firms in the relevant industries. Had they approached smaller units too their conclusions on this aspect might have been different.

(c)   The patent system operates unsatisfactorily   The crucial administrative criticism concerns the provision that only one patent may be granted for a particular invention and that it is only where a successful invention is achieved that the inventor is entitled to any reward. In other words, the patent system only backs success and there can only be one winner in each competition. This means that if it is socially desirable that some efforts to discover a new product or process should be made which ultimately turn out to be unsuccessful the researching firm is not compensated for its efforts. It simply has to bear the losses out of its profits from more successful research activities elsewhere. Some financing of such efforts may be provided by the government where a particular social need has been identified, but this is not necessarily to be relied upon. Disadvantages may also arise if there is 'too much' success. It may be the case that several firms are making research efforts in the same field and come up with the same patentable invention more or less simultaneously. But only the first firm to have its patent application registered and accepted can hold the patent. At best, the other firms will have to pay the royalties to be able to work an invention they also discovered. At worst, they may be unable to produce at all if licences of right are not granted. This is not an unlikely situation. Boehm [22] reported that not infrequently identical patent applications, especially in the fields of chemicals and pharmaceuticals are made within a day or two of each other. Steele [23] found a similar situation in the USA where six firms claimed priority on the drug prednisone at about the same time. The race to the Patent Office may lead to injustices and wasted research and productive effort.

The absence of an effective examination procedure in Britain means that patentees cannot be sure that they are entitled to manufacture as they cannot be certain that a prior patent does not exist. The delays in dealing with patent applications, partly accounted for by the large number of trivial or worthless inventions, means that there is considerable uncertainty as to whether other firms are entitled to produce or whether, possibly having invested in new plant and equipment, they may subsequently find themselves unable to use these productive facilities. Such delays also mean that the dissemination of knowledge is retarded.

A basic failing of patent law and administration seems to be a lack of a clear concept of just what does constitute the public interest. Boehm reported that the Patent Office gives every help to a manufacturer to obtain a patent [24] and the Banks Committee stated that 'we have considered it our duty to make broad recommendations which we believe to be of general benefit to industry'.[25] The impression is conveyed that in this area the public interest is presumed to equate to that of the inventor since on the following page the committee stated that its recommendations were based on what would be best for the national economy. Boehm did recognise that a trade-off was involved in getting the 'right balance between the public interest in restricting the grant of monopolies and the private interests of the patentee'.[26] But it is arguable that even this does not present the correct trade-off, which should be between the public costs of monopolies and the public benefits of progress. The private interest of the inventor is only relevant if it can be shown to be compatible with the public benefits of progress. Much of the evidence and reasoning in this chapter suggests that while there is undoubtedly a similarity between the private and public interest it is not identical. Much recent writing and practice seems to have paid little heed to Machlup's warning that the purpose of the patent laws is to serve the public interest through the early and intensive use of new technologies and not to serve the private interest of inventors.[27]

An equally unsatisfactory situation seems to have existed over the position of patents under the anti-trust laws. Under the terms of the 1948 Monopolies and Restrictive Practices Act the powers of the Monopolies Commission were more limited in dealing with abuses arising from patent protection than from other forms of monopolistic behaviour. The Commission had no power to investigate patents *per se* though it could make recommendations if patent abuses came to light in the normal course of an investigation. When this did occur procedures to remedy abuses were at the discretion of the Comptroller of Patents and were therefore likely to be slower to take effect than action upon other Monopolies Commission recommendations. 'It is difficult to avoid the impression that the provisions in the new [1949] Patents Act were so carefully framed to safeguard the interests of the patentee that it would have been extremely difficult to employ them against the abuses which they were intended to check.'[28] The Restrictive Trade Practices Act 1956 gave a similarly favourable position to patent licensing agreements which under Section 8 (4) did not have to be registered as long as they related only to articles to which the patents related and did not raise an expectation regarding other aspects of behaviour. The implication was, however, that many normal cartel activities became unregisterable where they were based on a patent.[29] However, under Section 101 of the Fair Trading Act 1973 patent pooling and licensing agreements have been made registerable and referable to the Restrictive Practices Court.

Appraisal and proposals for amendment

There is no doubt that, in terms of the sheer volume of applications, the patent system is a major industrial phenomenon. It seems, however, that the increase in volume does not relate closely to an increasing rate of technical progress. In general it also does not seem to be a major cause of increasing monopoly. In some cases, however, it is clear that the existence of important patents does have a major influence on the degree of monopoly power that can be exercised in particular markets. While this serves to emphasise that the consequences of the patent system should be investigated primarily on an industry by industry basis, it does not remove the possibility that the overall strengths or weaknesses of the system as a whole may not affect its effectiveness in any one sector.

In appraising the patent system, two questions should be considered. First, how does the balance of costs and benefits stand from the system as it operates at present? Secondly, what would be the effect of changing the system? Generally it seems that while there may be abuses which should be controlled, most commentators would conclude that a patent system offered net benefits.

This is the conclusion, for example, of Silberston and Taylor, who also investigated the likely consequences of a change in the system. Strictly, such an investigation should consider the effects of a marginal adjustment in the degree of patent protection.[30] But a marginal change would be difficult to envisage, as indeed would a complete abandonment of the patent system. So they asked firms to tell them what they thought would be the effect of a thorough–going worldwide compulsory licensing system. They found that such a change was unlikely to have much impact on either inventive or innovative effort or on prices and profits other than in the pharmaceutical industry where they were led to believe that compulsory licensing would have a serious adverse effect on efforts to discover and develop new drugs. They did also conclude that a compulsory licensing system would create an atmosphere of secrecy and insecurity that would hinder the exchange of know-how in industries where process technology is important. This they thought would be an appreciable loss to the economy.[31]

However, there are still one or two questions that need to be asked about the patent system. We might consider whether it is really relevant to the needs of the person it is supposed to help – the inventor – through whose efforts the public interest is presumed to be advanced. Nowadays invention and innovation are often treated as separate activities. The individual or small firm remains relatively more important in invention [32] while the more expensive innovative activities are increasingly the responsibility of larger organisations. It is not necessarily the case that a patent system is required to encourage invention. Earlier periods have shown technical progress without heavy reliance on patents. Much of the nineteenth century, for example, has been described as an 'age of patentless invention' [33] and even at the present time some industries, notably vehicles, are heavy spenders on R and D but have a low propensity to patent. It is certainly arguable that the motives of inventors may not be responsive to the prospect of a monopolistic advantage through patents and that there may be more effective ways of recognising and preserving their property rights. The main impact of patents may be to give a monopoly to an innovator. Is this really required? Is it not at least arguable that competition rather than monopoly is likely to stimulate innovation?

Concern about the resource allocation effects of the patent system has led to the suggestion that a distinction should be made between the method of rewarding an inventor and the imposition of charges to users of the knowledge produced. As we have noted, some economists argue that the supply price for knowledge should be zero in order to avoid under-utilisation of that resource. One possibility would be to pay an inventor a lump sum from the public purse that reflected the contribution of that piece of knowledge to the national income or welfare.[34]

Numerous other proposals for amendment to the patent system have come from various commentators through the years. One major set of proposals relates to the tightening of conditions for the grant of patents. It is often argued that the number of patents should be reduced and that patents should only be awarded for meritorious inventions. This would require a more extensive examination when an application for a patent was received. For example, worldwide literature and patent searches might have to be undertaken, obviousness could be included as a basic criterion in the examination and the general standards of invention required should be raised in order to avoid the possible abuses that arise from inventing around a patent and the patenting of trivial inventions. A more stringent investigation procedure would be expected to reduce the number of patent applications filed and should allow for more careful consideration of the claims that were made. It might be appropriate at the same time to liberalise the provisions to deal with the situation where more than one firm discovers the same patentable invention simultaneously.

A second set of proposals broadly relates to possible controls on the exercise of the monopoly power that is created by a patent. It has been suggested that the monopoly benefits conveyed by a patent should be limited so that they are no greater than the assessed social value of the invention, and that the size of the benefits obtained from patents should be subject to rather greater scrutiny. At present in Britain a firm may apply to have its patent extended beyond the normal time limit if it can demonstrate that it has not earned a reasonable return through no fault of its own during the normal life of a patent. If this is to remain an element of patent policy then the question should be considered whether a patent ought not also to be terminable when a reasonable return has been achieved if this should occur before the normal expiry of the patent. Licensing policies are of course a very important influence on the actual competitive situation. More attention should be paid to ensure that refusal to licence at all or only on penal terms is not unjustifiably used to restrain competition. Various possible developments in terms of a two-tier patent system have been suggested. A short first stage with full patent rights might be followed by a second stage in which licences of right were automatically granted. Alternatively any applicant might be given a short–term patent without examination but a long-term patent would only be given after extensive examination of the validity of the patent claims.

In closing this chapter it is helpful to look critically at two sets of proposals that have been made for reform of the patent system – the Banks Committee Report in Britain and the Second Preliminary Draft European Patent Convention.

(1) The Banks Committee Report

In setting up the Banks Committee to report on the British patent system it is clear that the government expected a thorough reappraisal of the whole system.[35] It can hardly be said that the Committee provided this. It did not greatly help to remedy the lack of analysis and information of the effects of the patent system that it noted existed. Its concern seems to have been simply to make recommendations for the best interests of industry rather than on a more broadly conceived public interest basis. To deal with the problem of the overloading of the patent administration arrangements the Committee thought that tighter criteria should be introduced to reduce the propensity to grant patents unjustifiably. More extensive search procedures were recommended and in particular it was suggested that the Patent Office should undertake a wider search to cover other countries and older and more technical publications. In addition it was recommended that the office should consider criteria of obviousness and inventive merit before granting a patent.

The Committee favoured an extension of the life of a patent to 20 years which it said was in keeping with general international trends. It suggested that the patent should in future run from its priority date rather than the date of granting of the patent; this would have the effect of reducing its average life by one year. The Committee also considered the question of extensions to the patent life on the grounds that the patentee had been inadequately remunerated but decided that this was not an appropriate ground for extension of a patent:

> In our view the patent system is not meant to guarantee a reward to the inventor which purports to be commensurate with the merits of his invention. What it does is to give the inventor an opportunity of obtaining some reward for his invention by granting him a monopoly for a specified period of time. The reward obtained may be great in some cases and small in others and we can see no more justification for extending the period where the patentee does not consider the reward obtained to be sufficient than for shortening the term in those cases where the reward is large.[36]

This is certainly an interesting philosophy. We have already suggested that symmetry in dealing with the life of a patent in terms of the remuneration obtained would be equitable. But the Banks Committee really appeared to be saying that the grant of a monopoly right under a patent should not be related to any criteria of the reasonableness or appropriateness of the reward obtained. If this is valid, one wonders whether the patent system is not altogether too haphazard a means of promoting invention. It is also difficult to reconcile the Committee's view on this question with its argument that invention would be likely to continue in the absence of a patent system and that the main aim of such a system is to encourage the industrial application of inventions.

The Sainsbury Committee had clearly placed in the Banks Committee's court the suggestion that the patent law relating to pharmaceuticals might be amended in such a way that a shorter period of monopoly should be granted followed by a right to receive royalties from production under a licence of right. The Sainsbury Committee thought that this system would be quite adequate while reducing the degree of monopoly in the marketing of pharmaceuticals. The Banks Committee reviewed the issues and in particular pointed to what it considered was a trade-off between the desire for low prices on existing drugs and the need for new remedies which were the products of expensive and lengthy research programmes. It concluded that it was not possible to say whether patents had caused high prices but decided that the patent system was an effective incentive to research and development not least in the field of drugs. The Committee believed that the community stood to benefit greatly from the discovery of new drugs, that their discovery and development was becoming increasingly difficult and concluded that the full protection of the patent system would be necessary to provide a sufficient stimulus to innovation. Thus the Committee felt that drugs should have the same basic patent rights as other products and that any diminution of patent protection for drugs would work against the long-term interests of the public. The provision for the grant of compulsory licences on drugs was not favoured since this would deprive effective researchers of some of the benefits and would benefit those manufacturers who had not undertaken any research. The Committee did, however, think that it was appropriate that the Department of Health and Social Security should continue to have the sanction of obtaining supplies of drugs at competitive prices.

At the time of writing, legislation on the Banks Report is awaited. If the recommendations are implemented they will be in the direction of a further strengthening of the market power conveyed by the patent system, at least for those with a strong case for a patent. The analysis underlying the recommendations is not convincing. It is unfortunate that the Committee apparently failed to recognise the likelihood of a divergence between the public and the private interest before making its proposals. In any legislation that did attempt to enhance the public benefits of the patent system, a strengthening of the powers to prevent abuses of a monopoly position provided by a patent would seem to be a high priority.

(2) The Second Draft European Patent Convention [37]

The objective of the convention is to abolish territorial limits within Europe for the marketing of patented goods. A two-tier procedure of investigation is proposed. The first stage involves a formal examination to check whether the criteria for the grant of a patent are satisfied. These are that an inventive step is involved; that it is susceptible of industrial application and that the details are sufficiently clear for a person skilled in the art to be able to carry it out. Developments that are contrary to public morality or relate to biological processes for the production of plants or animals or to materials existing in nature would not be patentable. Pharmaceutical developments would be patentable. If these conditions are satisfied a novelty investigation would be undertaken. If this too is satisfied a European patent would be granted and it is expected that this would be available within about 18 months of the application or the date of priority whichever is first. This is therefore considered to offer the benefit of speedy publication and action.

The second tier consists of a detailed examination by the European Patent Office to establish whether the requirements of the Convention are satisfied. This must be requested within six months of the publication of the grant of the patent. If this is not requested the patent lapses. This reflects the fact that many patents are allowed to lapse after a short while and so the opportunity is retained to investigate thoroughly the claim for an important patent while saving time by not making such a complete investigation of unimportant patents that would be likely to lapse quickly. Oppositions may be lodged by anyone upon certain specified grounds: that the subject matter is not patentable; that the invention is not sufficiently disclosed; that the subject matter of the patent extends beyond the content of the patent as filed. If an opposition is lodged an adversary procedure between applicant and opponent is envisaged to resolve this issue.

A patent if approved will be granted on the basis of priority which will be determined on the date of filing of an application. It will last for 20 years from that date. Patents of addition may be granted and will date from the date of filing of the parent patent. This means that improvement patents would not be a means of extending the effective duration of a basic patent. Renewal fees would be payable from the third year from the date of filing.

Some scope exists for revocation proceedings, but only on a limited range of legal and administrative objections: that the subject matter was not patentable; that the patent does not disclose the invention sufficiently clearly; that the subject matter extends beyond the content of the application; or if the extent of the patent has been extended illegally during opposition proceedings.

It is not at all clear that this scheme will in fact be implemented. Certainly it diverges at important points from the one outlined in the first draft European patent convention. As it stands it meets some of the main objections to a registration-oriented system. It seems likely that a high proportion of patents would lapse without detailed examination and this would be beneficial. Two main criticisms are relevant. First, the possible wastes of just failing to establish priority become much greater as the geographical coverage of the patent system increases. Secondly, it is regrettable that there seem to be no public interest criteria to be applied either in the detailed examination or in the revocation procedure. This would represent a weakening of the already unsatisfactory British legislation on this aspect. The great danger seems to be that what ought to be a major piece of economic policy is treated as simply a means of tidying up administrative arrangements.

CHAPTER 6
THE ORGANISATION AND GOALS OF THE FIRM

One of the areas that has generated much controversy in recent decades is the question of the objectives and decision-making processes of the firm. The traditional assumption that the objective of the firm is to maximise profits has been challenged, as has the assumption that once that objective function has been specified then an adequate description is thereby available of the way in which price and output decisions are arrived at. Criticisms of the profit maximisation approach have come from investigators who have carried out studies of the way in which decisions, particularly price decisions, are reached in firms. Attention in recent discussions of the theory of the firm has tended to focus on managerial, behavioural and organisational theories, though often with only an imperfect awareness of the extent to which a firm distinction has to be drawn between attempts to explain the objectives of the firm on the one hand and the processes of organisational decision-making on the other.[1]

The classical theory of the firm relied heavily on the notion that firms are small, owner-managed organisations operating in highly competitive markets whose demand functions are given and where only normal profits can be earned. If the firm did not therefore maximise profits it would fail to survive under those conditions. Setting aside the question as to whether this ever was a valid description (and of course the incidence of monopoly was clearly recognised in the Marshallian analysis) it is certainly far removed from the actual characteristics of firms in many branches of economic activity today. It is only when the main features of the organisation of modern corporations are taken into account that the questions of the goals of the firm and its decision processes can be effectively discussed.

Features of modern organisations

In industrial markets the leading organisations at the present time tend to be very large in absolute terms when measured by capital employed, level of sales and number of employees. Their shares of individual markets are often substantial. Their growth has been facilitated by the development of limited liability during the present century and has been financed to some extent at least by funds provided outside the organisation – from banks or other financial institutions or by raising money from members of the public through share issues. This has had the effect of introducing a large number of 'owners' into the organisation but in practice has meant that owners play very little part in the running of the business. Thus there is a divorce between ownership and control. The growth of firms has come about not only through the expansion of any single market, but also through the diversification of the firm's productive process. Thus firms now tend to be multi-product organisations often operating in multiple divisions and producing in multiple plants. Many firms have positions of considerable market dominance which, allied to the consequences of the divorce between ownership and control, means that there is a much greater degree of discretion in relation to the choice of policies to be pursued. Yet although the modern firm has a substantial degree of decision-making discretion it is operating in a world that is complex and uncertain and the firm is often simply ignorant of much information that would improve its decision-taking performance. Consequently the risks of loss may be high and the outcome of business decisions cannot be forecast with certainty.

The actual organisational structure of these large firms has an important impact on the nature of the decision-making process. In particular, instead of a single clearly identifiable decision-maker, many different people and interest groups participate. Decision-making is shared by people with a complex pattern of personal relationships, different temperaments and personalities, all of which affect the ultimate outcome. They will all have varying personal goals which will make up part of the value system of the organisation. The firm will tend to adopt a bureaucratic form with an information system that plays an important part in influencing the decision process. But this system is by no means perfect and often may be distorted by 'noise'. It will have problems of control, will be constrained by a budget, standard operating procedures and will have an aspiring middle management.[2]

If this is an accurate indication of some of the features of the organisation, what are the implications for our understanding of the decision–making process within the firm? It is clear that the firm cannot be considered to be a perfectly adapting organism which is always in equilibrium.[3] Instead its decisions will be strongly influenced by its current financial position as well as by the history of the firm. Its internal structure will also exercise considerable influence on both the speed and direction of reactions. Thus the mechanism of adaptation is important. Recognising this it then becomes necessary to acknowledge that it is *people* who act rather than an anonymous, inanimate organism of the sort implied in the concept of the holistic firm.[4] The responses will therefore depend on the competence and knowledge of the people involved and on the outcome of bargaining and conflict resolution between members of the coalition or technostructure.[5] Further, it has been found that senior people in organisations consistently bend the rules in order to achieve goals of their own so this also has some influence on the actual implementation of the decisions.[6] Although this suggests that consistency of choice of goals is unlikely to be achieved, it is likely that there will be some underlying motivation to ensure the survival of the organisation and hence to maintain the job prospects of the individual participants in the decision-making process.

The market and response problems are therefore seen by the participants through an organisational filter and prediction of responses depends on a view of the perceptual and cognitive processes of the parties to the decision and the cybernetic system through which they receive information.[7] Thus the decision-making process is seen as a loosely coupled, partially decentralised structure in which goals are adaptive, complex, often made simultaneously and tend to enter in as constraints at other parts of the organisation.[8]

If, as seems likely, this is a reasonably accurate indication of some of the relevant aspects of organisation structure and its likely influence on the decision-making process, we must ask what relevance it has to economic analysis. Even if it is a more accurate picture of the complex human influences affecting the way in which decisions are made, does it also point to a more realistic indication of the type of decisions that will result; in other words, does it improve our ability to predict the sort of decision that firms will reach?

The attack on profit maximisation

An early attack on profit maximisation is to be found in the pricing studies of Hall and Hitch [9] and the controversy has continued on both sides of the Atlantic.[10] Although there is some vigorous dissent, the general consensus of opinion would seem to be that profit maximisation is unsatisfactory as a description of the goals of the firm and of the processes by which business decisions are arrived at. The criticisms may be grouped into two broad, though overlapping categories – organisational objections and operational objections. They relate both to the question as to whether it is reasonable to assume that any variable is likely to be maximised and, even if something is to be maximised, whether that 'something' is profit.

As far as organisational objections are concerned, it follows from the foregoing discussion of organisation structure that a single maximand is unlikely to be agreed upon, let alone attained. Even though some of the 'managerial' theories to be considered later in this chapter assume that a utility function is to be maximised it seems reasonable to point out that in a complex organisation with bargaining over competing departmental goals and adaptive behaviour by individuals this outcome is unlikely. A reluctance to disturb established routines will hinder the attainment of an optimum. Managers may have a high risk aversion preference and in an organisation that has a certain degree of discretion in its market operations the incentive to minimize costs may well be weakened.

The implications of the distribution of benefits from the operations of the firm are also important. Why should managers seek to maximise returns for shareholders rather than pursue other objectives more likely to satisfy their own interests and aspirations? Certainly the pressure to maximise profits can be quite weak for a firm with some market power. It is likely that a board of directors will normally tend to follow the guidance of its management team rather than act specifically in the interests of the shareholders. Private shareholders are frequently ineffective and unimportant influences on the performance of a company. Institutional shareholders, at least in Britain, have traditionally tended to be passive and are also hindered by imperfect information, a failure to appraise a situation sufficiently and an apparent tendency to rely on a subjective assessment of relevant managerial issues in appraising a company. The consequence is that the discipline exercised by the stock market through the threat of takeover works very imperfectly and managerial discretion is normally not much circumscribed by fears of losing the confidence of shareholders.

One interesting empirical study has indicated that profit maximisation may be a less relevant assumption in a manager controlled firm than an owner controlled organisation. Taking 36 owner controlled firms and 36 manager controlled firms in 12 American industries, Monsen and his colleagues compared the performance of the two groups. They found that owner controlled firms had 75 per cent higher performance than manager controlled organisations and concluded from this that the motivations were different in the two cases.[11] It may also be that an observation at a point in time may hide the effects of different time horizons on the objectives of different types of organisation, which may mean that different dynamic long-run consequences will appear in contrast to a particular set of short-run outcomes. It seems, for example, that because Pilkington the glass manufacturer was, at the time, a private company it was able to take a much longer-term view of development of the float glass process because it was not concerned with the need to satisfy shareholders on a year-by-year basis and so while its short-run performance might be inferior, its long-run performance would be improved by being able to take a long-term view and to continue to invest money in new developments.

Turning to operational objections, it is clear that the concept of profit maximisation is too vague (and indeed the concept of profit itself as traditionally used is also vague[12]) to be specified in operational terms. There is a divergence between accountancy practice and economists' preferences as to the costs that ought to be included in the calculation of profit. The emphasis on the short run is unsatisfactory but if a long-run, dynamic view is to be utilised, it runs into a range of additional conceptual and measurement problems. In an uncertain world long-run profits can only be forecast on some probability basis and it is very difficult to be clear just what is rational under uncertainty. Such a view also makes it difficult to take into account differing rates of time preference and varying levels of risk aversion. It also makes it difficult to take into account the relation between today's action and both yesterday's actions and tomorrow's opportunities. Firms do not live in discrete periods in which their actions through time are unrelated, rather they should be seen as having a continuum of actions in which a previous action may operate as a constraint in a future pattern of choices. Thus the commitment of resources today influences the use to which they can be put tomorrow, and the present range of operations influences the level of profits available to finance new activities and the type of information feed-back that is available.[13]

An optimising policy may also be held to require a firm to operate in a more predictable environment than is usual in the real world and also to assume that firms have perfect knowledge of all alternatives. This again is not possible in practice. Firms tend not to have the information, including knowledge of their marginal conditions, to allow them to maximise and will be unable to make the continual adjustments that would be required in an optimising policy. Their knowledge of alternatives is limited and information is often costly to acquire in both time and money terms. Search procedures tend therefore to be problem oriented, sequential, and satisficing rather than optimising. In markets where interdependence is recognised by firms an optimal policy can only be determined when the likely outcome of the other firms is also known and so to seek for a maximising policy under these circumstances is equally difficult. Thus it seems that granted the major influences of dynamic market conditions, uncertainty and ignorance, and oligopoly, a maximising policy is not feasible even if the technical difficulties of identifying in practice just what the maximising decisions should be could be overcome. Thus there are doubts not only about the role of profit maximisation as an objective, but also about the firm's ability to maximise anything. Certainly the observed behaviour of firms using sticky prices, standard costing margins etc, throws considerable doubt on the empirical validity of the concept in its strict form.

The defence of profit maximisation

It has been argued that much of the attack on the profit maximisation approach is inappropriate because its critics have failed to recognise that profit maximisation is not a hypothesis that can be tested, but a paradigm that is not itself testable but in which a set of possible hypotheses can be defined for subsequent validation.[14] The justification for the profit maximisation assumption has been defended in varying degrees by a number of writers including Machlup, Maguire, and Baldwin.[15] Machlup has argued that to maximise profits firms do not need an accurate knowledge of their marginal revenue and cost conditions. These are merely subjective and firms 'size up' the situation.

He suggested that many firms earn only normal profits and are therefore forced to be profit maximisers. Baldwin also argued that there are many internal and external constraints influencing the operations of firms and limiting the freedom of managers to pursue their own personal objectives. These are so strong that he considered profit maximisation to be a fairly close approximation to the actual goals of large companies.

The growing sophistication in budgeting and cost accounting on the one hand and in market research on the other, means that it is now more likely that firms could take a fairly accurate view of their marginal conditions which are necessary for profit maximisation. Profits are certainly important to any organisation, even if not maximum profits. They are crucial as a means of financing growth,[16] as an indicator of management performance and a means of satisfying shareholders. The need to keep shareholders happy may be a very important means of focusing the attention of management on the profit performance of the company and this, allied to the development of stock option schemes, may well mean that, in so far as share prices and profits are directly correlated, management is increasingly forced to have regard to its overall profit achievements.

Institutional shareholders are becoming increasingly important.[17] Not only are their holdings important in determining the success or failure of takeover raids but they are now (in Britain) becoming more involved in the actual operations of an organisation. Often an institutional shareholder has such large holdings in a company that even if it wished to sell on the open market, it could hardly do so without severely depressing the price for the shares and would not thereby greatly serve its own advantage. Consequently, the institutions are having to take rather more direct action with the companies whose shares they hold. Various examples are already known where a takeover bidder has been sought for a company with a poor management performance and where internal management shake-ups have come about as a result of the initiatives of institutional shareholders. Unit trust funds have been established to invest in recovery situations and the intention has been announced that where appropriate the managers of the trust will participate in the active management of the companies in which they are investing.

In terms of the development of improved managerial techniques, the role of profit in the overall activities of the company and the growing importance and involvement of the institutional investor, it does appear that the technical ability to approach towards profit maximisation under conditions of certainty is increasing and the pressures on management to attempt this are to some degree growing. It is also clear that in certain types of organisation and under some market conditions it may well be that the pressures to approach towards profit maximisation are actually receding. The same sets of consideration are often relevant to both types of argument, the balance of view depends largely upon the sort of firm that is under consideration and the nature of the information available to the commentator.

Alternative explanations of the behaviour of firms

The search for alternative explanations of the goals and decision-making processes of the firm offers a wide range of choices. In general, however, we can identify two main groups. First, there are the managerial theories that are still concerned with explaining the objectives of the firm in terms of the maximisation of something other than profits. Secondly, there are the behavioural theories which offer perhaps greater insight into the decision-making processes of organisations and in discussions of goal formation tend to emphasise the importance of multiple, satisfactory outcomes rather than optimisation as such. Appraisal of the value of alternative theories tends to be based upon considerations of the realism of their predictions especially with reference to the effect of changes in demand, increases in fixed costs and in a profits tax on prices and outputs.[18]

MANAGERIAL THEORIES

The alternative formulation that has received most attention so far has been Baumol's sales revenue maximisation hypothesis.[19] The essence of this is that firms seek to maximise sales revenue subject to a minimum profit constraint necessary to keep shareholders content. The consequence of this is that so long as the required profit is less than a profit maximising level the sales revenue maximiser will set prices lower and output higher than the profit maximiser. Baumol claimed empirical validity for his theory. He argued that firms do treat a small fall in sales or market shares seriously because this means a loss of income, a loss of distributors and an unhappy atmosphere within the firm. He argued that salaries tend to be related more to the scale of operation than to profitability, and found that firms are reluctant to abandon unprofitable markets because this would have an adverse effect on their sales. Two implications of the price aspects of his model are also claimed to fit the real world situation. When fixed costs rise the sales revenue maximiser will pass them on to customers or will reduce expenses, whereas the profit maximisation model would postulate a 'no change' position. The sales revenue maximisation hypothesis also recognises there is a strong incentive to firms to go for non-price rather than price competition. Certainly much of this does seem valid. It is clear that changes in fixed costs [20] do enter into the pricing decision of firms. There is evidence as Baumol claims that firms are more concerned with the level of revenue rather than profits [21] and other studies have confirmed the view that salaries of senior management are closely correlated with the size of the organisation [22] and this is likely to constitute strong reason for pursuing some form of a growth oriented policy.

Various comments on this hypothesis have appeared in the literature.

Shepherd sought to show that it would not apply in markets in which there was considerable interdependence between firms[23] and although Hawkins has shown that this is not necessarily the case when non-price competition occurs, he was doubtful of its value in explaining the behaviour of multi-product organisations.[24] Alchian has also criticised the theory on the grounds that it is not supported by observed behaviour of firms and that it is unlikely that management would attempt to maximise sales regardless of how much they could increase profit.[25] One attempt to provide an empirical test of the main implications of this hypothesis was not successful[26] but other studies show that in merger situations in the USA firms tend to maximise sales per share,[27] and a study by the National Industrial Conference Board of 100 leading American companies showed that they evaluated new investment opportunities in terms of market opportunities rather than the rate of return.[28] These are both consistent with the sales revenue maximisation hypothesis as an explanation of the objective of the firm. So too is the suggestion[29] that the role of the firm is to maximise the physical size of the organisation and this may be an important explanation not only for the internal growth policies of the organisation but also for the propensity to use the takeover bid as a means of achieving a rapid increase in the physical size of a company.

Related to these explanations are a further set of 'managerial' theories propounded by Marris,[30] Oliver Williamson[31] and Mrs Penrose.[32] Here the emphasis is explicitly on the utility function of the manager or the management team. Williamson's model is static and like the others applies in conditions when management has discretion. He argues that, subject to a modest profit constraint, managers seek to satisfy a utility function that consists of hierarchical expense on staff, salaries and perquisites over and above those strictly necessary for the firm's operation. These non-pecuniary objectives are most likely to help the manager in his own pursuit of status, power and prestige. The expenditures are likely to be at their peak when business conditions are most favourable. They will fall when demand is weak. Expenditure on staff and emoluments will increase in response to a rise in profits tax in order to reduce reported profits. This model offers little in the way of prediction regarding prices and outputs but its predictions about the way in which firms react to changes in environmental conditions by adjusting their discretionary activities does seem to have empirical relevance.

In his more recent writings Oliver Williamson appears to have made a major shift of position.[33] He built his new analysis on the distinction between what he called the U and the M form of organisations. The U form is organised by functional division and is, in his view, inadequate because of the consequent control loss between hierarchical levels, the conflict between operating and strategic decisions and because it allows too much scope for the exercise of discretionary behaviour by management.

The M form is organised on a basis of product divisions with an elite general office staff exercising overall auditing, advisory and control functions over the divisions and making strategic decisions. Williamson claims that three benefits will follow from the M form organisation. First, by reducing the degree of control loss implicit in U form organisations it improves the internal organisation of firms. Secondly, the head office acts very much as the capital market for the firm and achieves a better allocation of resources, especially for investment, than the capital market would obtain since the head office has more information and can make a finer tuning of the system. Thirdly, and most significant, Williamson argues the M form will cause a shift in the nature of the goals that the firm pursues, away from policies favouring staff or managerial slack and in favour of profits. He claims that this form of organisation reduces the implications of the separation of ownership and control for discussions of goal formation and suggests that in discussions of the goals of firms a multi-goal utility function is no longer needed and that a profit maximising goal will suffice.

Williamson recognises that there is no guarantee that profits will be maximised since there may be laxity in surveillance, discretionary behaviour at the top and carelessness in the selection and training of staff. While each of these may permit the pursuit of sub-goals at lower levels, he claims that this will not persist in the long run when the emphasis will return to profitability.

Accepting that some firms do adopt a structure and form of operation in keeping with Williamson's description, some queries arise before accepting his analysis of the likely consequences. What is the relative distribution of M and U form firms in a society? Is there any more reason why head office staff in an M form firm should seek to maximise the return to shareholders and if not, why is profitability to be assumed to be the sole goal of the organisation? (Williamson does indicate that if a multi-goal function were still considered necessary he would add growth to the profit goal.) In this form of organisation there are often resentments at the influence exercised by the head office and the apparent propensity to reduce such staff severely when economic conditions become difficult for the firm suggests that many firms may (rightly or wrongly) view their control staff as dispensable and therefore an element of organisational slack. Certainly such behaviour is not consistent with the status Williamson's analysis accords to such staff. There is, as Williamson recognises, still a problem of ensuring effective performance in the divisions. Is it not more likely that a non-operating head office may find greater difficulty in motivating staff? If the setting of targets upon which the following period's performance is to be appraised is based upon the provision of information from the divisions, is there not an incentive to staff in the divisions to distort the information provided so that targets set are lower and less challenging and less likely to disturb the pursuit of a divisional quiet life? Finally, it is implicit in all Williamson's writings that firms seek to optimise rather than satisfice. Is there really any reason for thinking that this structure will increase either the incentive to optimise or the chance of success in doing so?

Despite these uncertainties there is much in Williamson's analysis that has interest and possible validity. It does also constitute a further major defence of the profit maximising position.

Marris's dynamic theory is also based on the hypothesis that decision-takers subject the policy decisions of the firm to their own utility function. Since their goals are associated with considerations of power, prestige, etc., these are more dependent upon consideration of the size and hence the rate of growth of the firm rather than its profits. The pursuit of growth is there-fore a key feature of this model and indeed Marris emphasised that the planning of growth and diversification in the firm is an important function of top management. But the pursuit of growth has to be tempered if it may so weaken the firm that by depressing the current dividend it increases the risk of a takeover. The desire to avoid being taken over is therefore an important constraint on the growth rate that is to be maximised. The constraint is indi-cated by a minimum level of the firm's valuation ratio (the ratio of the market value of the firm to the value of its assets) that should be maintained. This model has stimulated various attempts at empirical testing, particularly of the relationship between the valuation ratio and the probability of takeover. These results are considered in the next chapter but we may note in passing that they do not entirely support Marris's hypothesis. Indeed it seems quite likely that growth oriented companies may obtain high stock market ratings almost irrespective of their current profit levels and in this case the rate of growth and the valuation ratio may be positively related rather than competitive.

Clearly the emphasis on growth is a very valuable element of managerial theories and seems to be consistent with the objectives of decision takers. It also has the great merit that it introduces a more explicit dynamic element into the theory of the firm than existed in neo-classical models. An earlier formulation emphasising growth was provided by Mrs Penrose. In her model growth and profits were treated as interdependent with the one strongly influencing the other. Consequently her approach represents a less substantial decline in the status of the profit motive than is apparent in the later managerial theories.

BEHAVIOURAL THEORIES

Behavioural theories emphasise description of the decision-making process of the firm on the basis of observation rather than *a priori* reasoning. There are two important strands in their approach. First, they emphasise that people count in the decision-making process, both individually and collectively,[34] and that therefore the internal organisational characteristics of the company must be investigated. The actual decisions that are taken are influenced by the cognition, perception, beliefs and knowledge of the actors and their inter-personal relationships. Bargaining takes place between individuals and groups and the outcome of this bargaining is a complex set of objectives which are at the same time also constraints upon another element in the firm's activities. Secondly, the behavioural approach recognises that in a world of uncertainty and lack of knowledge, maximising behaviour is not feasible. It is also psychologically unlikely according to Simon since the motives to act stem from drives and the actions terminate when the drives are satisfied.[35] Satisficing is therefore an integral part of the decision processes of the firm and rules of thumb are followed. Past experience has a considerable influence on the outcome as also has the firm's present situation. Learning and the way the firm receives and processes information and adapts to it is the key to the success of the firm.

(1)   *Essential Elements in the Behavioural Approach*[36]

(a)   *Bargaining* Conflict or bargaining is an essential element in goal formation. Conflict is never fully resolved and in consequence some decisions may be taken which are inconsistent with other decisions. Side payments may occur as part of the bargaining process and may be in cash or non-cash forms including a commitment to adopt some particular policy.

(b)   *Goals* The basic assumption is that survival is the underlying motivation and various practices, including uncertainty reduction, are compatible with this. Once this is ensured other multiple goals will be pursued which arise from the bargaining process. These will be partial, maybe departmental, objectives, set in the light of past experience and the present situation and they may even be in conflict with one another. Decision-making is concerned with finding a course of action which will satisfy these and they are therefore constraints as well as goals. Although attention shifts between goals from time to time, and although membership of the coalition and relative bargaining power may change, organisational objectives tend to be stable through time. This is due to the influence of the corporate budget and of precedents, and because it is difficult and costly to change long-term decisions (e.g. major capital expenditures). Although the set of objectives will be stable, the emphasis given to each and the inter-departmental allocation of resources will be subject to adjustment. Above all, however, in this formulation goals will be satisficing rather than maximising, sub-optimal rather than optimal. The drive is therefore to attain a target that is set as a constraint. It will be based on an aspiration level that will be partly influenced by past attainment and partly by what is currently considered to be attainable. Although such behaviour is not optimising it may be rational when the costs of obtaining additional information are considered. In any efficient, profit conscious organisation it is likely that the trend in the pattern of aspirations will be to move it nearer to the optimum.

(c) *Problemistic search* Organisations are assumed to be essentially static, acting only when necessary because some goal has not been achieved. Their search procedures where required are sequential, limited, and specifically problem oriented. Only a few of the alternatives are considered, starting with the least cost ones. Directly a solution has been found which satisfies the constraints imposed by the organisation's goals the search ceases.[37] Thus search procedures are also essentially satisficing rather than optimising.

(d) *The nature of choice* Choice hinges on information which comes partly from search procedures. The organisation must seek, collect and process information but the communication system may bias the information received and therefore the consequential decisions taken upon it. Firms prefer to react to feed-back rather than to predict the environment but decision-making must take into account the effects of uncertainty. This means therefore that some prediction and the formation of expectations are required. Learning and feed-back will reduce the amount of formal decision-making required and standard operating procedures and rules of thumb will assist the implementation of the decisions. Where formal decisions are required, these are taken within an environment the dimensions of which depend on the personality of the decision makers, previous experience and information conditions. The complexity and instability of the organisation are therefore important influences on the decision reached.

(e) *Adaptation* The structure of the organisation allows employees at all levels to modify in practice the goals of top management or of the owners. For this reason, it is argued, one cannot explain organisational goals in terms of the goals of any individual members of that organisation. There may be dysfunctional elements that retard the tendency of firms to adapt themselves to their environment, create greater conformity, reduce innovation and raise barriers to the achievement of goals.[38]

(2) *The Resultant Predictive Theory*

The major theoretical model is that of Cyert and March in which they attempted to predict particular decisions on price, output and resource allocation. In the process they used four sub-theories:

(a) *Organisational goals,* to explain how goals are formed, altered and their influence on organisational behaviour.

(b) *Organisational expectations,* to explain the search procedure and information gathering behaviour of organisations – the drawing of inferences, the nature of search activity and the methods of processing information.

(c) *Organisation choice,* the ordering of alternatives, the way in which selection is made.

(d) *Organisational control,* to explain the difference between executive choice and the decisions that are actually implemented.

They identified five goals which could then be predicted; these are all satisficing or attainable goals deriving from the firm's aspirations. They relate to production, inventory levels, sales, market shares and profits. Decisions on price, output, and sales strategy are made on the basis of these goals. Firms make an approximate sequential consideration of alternatives selecting the first satisfactory alternative found; regular procedures and a policy of reacting to feed-back are used and the organisation uses standard operating procedures and rules of thumb to make and implement choices. In the short run these dominate the decisions made.[39]

(3)   Comment on the Behavioural Approach

As an explanation of the factors influencing the decision-making process within the firm the work by Cyert and March, Simon and others give grounds for thinking that they are dealing with the right sort of variables. Other information also gives at least weak support for some of the ideas implicit in the behavioural approach. In a study of project evaluations in 20 New Zealand companies it was found that under the primary objective of an emphasis on long-run profits, conflicting aims of managers did produce restraints on the nature and direction of the firm's operations and showed that personal aspirations and motives limited the manner and scope of the pursuit of profit.[40] Hague's studies led him to conclude that satisficing behaviour was prevalent amongst the firms he investigated and was often selected when there was a choice between maximising and satisficing alternatives.[41] General rules of thumb do seem to be applied in organisations and adjustments in price, etc., do not occur whenever demand conditions change, but are more likely to take place where the changed conditions threaten the attainment of some target or another. The growth in practical use of management by objectives which aims particularly at the 'integration of the objectives of the business or the organisation unit with the individual manager's need to grow and develop himself',[42] seems to be a good illustration of the fact that the relationships discussed in behavioural theories do exist and this practice will in fact help reinforce them. Again, the frequent practice of management by exception, acting only when a target is not achieved, further supports the behavioural approach.

In an interesting paper Baumol and Stewart showed how they confirmed the mark-up model used by Cyert and March in modelling a department store's price policy and agreed that many routine decisions do follow a rule of thumb as predicted.[43] But they found that the particular model was too simple since it did not allow the rules of thumb to change as economic conditions changed, and the model gave no clue as to the response in the values of its parameters to exogenous changes in the economic data, such as the price level or the rate of interest.

While the behavioural approach has much to commend it as a description of the way in which decisions are made, it is still in a relatively undeveloped state. At present it is of limited value since it does not help in indicating the way in which the rules of thumb are determined in the first place or, as Baumol and Stewart pointed out, in indicating the relationship between the parameters in the rules of thumb and the exogenous economic variables in the company's environment.

While there is undoubtedly scope for further development of these theories and of explanatory simulation models it should also be noted that there are features of some organisations that appear to deny the heart of the behavioural approach. Of particular importance is the fact that even in some large public companies there is still a single person, maybe the chairman, maybe the managing director, who keeps a tight rein on the decisions and the overall performance of the firm.[44] Frequently one finds that investors, including the now defunct Industrial Reorganisation Corporation, will (rightly or wrongly) back an individual rather than a management team. Also relevant is the growth in the use of stock option and other performance-related schemes which aim to increase the identification of managers with the company and with the interests of the shareholders. Finally, it seems that some firms breed or develop a particular form of corporation man. It may be that this at least helps to reduce the variation in the goals that individuals would choose to pursue and therefore reduces both the importance of bargaining and the need for side payments.

Conclusions

The literature on the question of the goals and organisation of the firm is vast and continually increasing. Unfortunately formal economic analysis has tended not to add to our ability to understand or to explain the behaviour of firms and much of the controversy about the theory of the firm, and in particular the assumption of profit maximisation, has been obscured by an apparent failure to comprehend exactly the function that was to be expected of that particular approach. We now have a range of alternative models from which to choose but they are in no sense perfect substitutes for each other. In general, however, it may be helpful to attempt to reach some conclusions on the complex situation as it stands at present.

(1)   It is necessary to move well away from the idea of a small, holistic

firm operating in a perfectly competitive market. Interest is primarily in the decisions of large, complex organisations, operating in markets where they have some degree at least of managerial discretion.

(2) In many cases, decisions are either made or adapted by collectivities of people in an organisation. Decisions are therefore to be seen as a sociological process rather than a 'single-minded codification of rationalism'.[45] Attention to questions of organisation structure and processes is relevant. Organisations, however, are not homogeneous and different patterns of control, etc., emerge in different companies.

(3) Profits are certainly important to all firms and should be present in all decision-making theories. If they are not recognised explicitly they are present implicitly in a security motivation. It is probably easier now for firms using modern management techniques to get nearer to an optimising solution than ever before. The use of capital budgeting techniques suggests that in some areas of resource allocation firms are thinking as maximisers. Certain types of market and organisation structure, the intervention of institutional shareholders and the general fear of takeover raids may well reduce the element of discretion in reducing the status of profit in the overall objectives of the firm.

(4) A distinction can usefully be drawn between objectives and goals. Subject to some profit constraint a firm may have a number of other primary and secondary objectives. These are not in themselves normally defined in operational terms and therefore a number of operational goals subsequently have to be specified. These take the form of target or aspiration levels and are very much influenced by previous achievements as well as an assessment of what is possible in present market situations. The testing of hypotheses about the behaviour of firms needs to have regard to the question of the effect of the attainment or non-attainment of operational goals rather than a specific consideration of over-riding objectives.

(5) Behavioural theories offer an important understanding of the nature of the internal decision process, the importance of learning, bargaining, the role of rules of thumb in the attempts by firms to deal with uncertainty. There is some doubt at present as to the extent to which they can be used to describe and predict general situations rather than specific cases.

(6) Both behavioural and managerial theories tend to contribute to the discussion about the reconciliation of multiple objectives in the organisation, and behavioural theories then offer some understanding of the effect on goal formation. They do not, however, make much contribution to a discussion of the price behaviour of firms. Indeed, probably the most significant feature of the current discussion of the objectives and goals of the firm is that it is no longer easy to relate this to a discussion of price formation. Consequently the theory of the firm and the theory of value have tended to diverge. This may, however, in time prove to be of benefit since current discussions of the theory of the firm are tending to emphasise that the firm is a system in itself rather

than part of a market paradigm[46] and the key to further developments appears to lie in the dropping of the rigid assumption that the decision-making of the firm can be analysed in a static, equilibrium framework.

CHAPTER 7
GROWTH AND THE FIRM

The growth of the firm

The pursuit of its own growth may be a major objective for a firm. Indeed in some modern discussions of the objectives of the firm, especially those emphasising the implications of the separation between ownership and control for decision-making within the firm, the maximisation of the growth rate, possibly subject to some constraint such that the valuation ratio should not fall so much that it invites a takeover raid, is considered to be the primary objective of the firm.[1] The question of the objectives of the firm has been discussed in Chapter 6. In this chapter we shall be concerned with the causes and implications of different forms of firm growth and in the following chapter we shall consider the anti-trust aspects of growth through merger.

Firms have a choice of two alternative fundamental methods of growth – internal expansion or external expansion through merger. They each have their advantages and disadvantages and the overall growth experience of a firm is likely to contain elements of both. Whichever is selected firms also have to decide between alternative directions of expansion. They may grow by increasing their scale of activity in existing product markets or they may choose to diversify by moving into new markets or offering new types of product or service. In later sections of this chapter we shall pay particular attention to the role of mergers in the growth of the firm and to the role of diversification in the strategy of the firm. To start with, however, we will look at some more general aspects of the growth of the firm.

We have already noted that the pursuit of growth is treated in some theories of the firm as an important objective in its own right. Some commentators have, however, chosen to emphasise that the decision to grow is a response to particular opportunities or pressures rather than simply a managerial objective. In many cases these can be seen to relate ultimately to a desire to increase profits, either through the exploitation of new market and investment opportunities, or to obtain the cost reducing benefits of larger scale operations. Considerable emphasis has also been placed on the importance of growth as a means of using more extensively or more effectively existing productive resources. Thus Mrs Penrose mentions the availability of unused productive resources, the ability to utilise labour more extensively and the availability of new productive services as the internal inducements to expand.[2] Barna, in his study of the growth performance of firms in the British food manufacturing and electrical industries, concluded that the effects of technological change leading to rising productive efficiency meant there was an increase in the real capacity of firms, including management, and that there were therefore pressures in the firm to find ways of using this surplus capacity. In particular he found that as management looked to maintain its area of control, the spare managerial capacity of the firm found ways of using itself.[3] A series of interviews conducted by Richardson and Leyland with 16 British firms with good growth records also indicated that a primary reason for the pursuit of growth was the desire to preserve and occupy an existing management team.[4] These explanations of the reasons for the pursuit of growth in the firm are in no sense in contradiction to the formulation provided by Marris but they do suggest that even if growth was not an important element in a managerial utility function there would still be other pressures and inducements upon the firm to grow.

Whichever interpretation one selects of the reasons why firms seek to grow, it is clear that the planning of growth, identification of growth opportunities and the successful execution of the growth process are important functions and responsibilities for top management. The next question that we should ask therefore is whether there is any evidence that might allow us to identify factors influencing the success of firm growth. Amongst the limited number of studies of this question there is considerable agreement that the quality of management is important. Mrs Penrose emphasised the importance of the quality of entrepreneurial resources especially in terms of versatility in outlook, ambition, judgement and fund-raising ability. Barna found that the variation in growth rates between the firms in his sample was largely explained by the personal characteristics and attitudes of management in the different firms and the speed and energy with which they adjusted to, and exploited, the new situation. This, he concluded, was more important than economic factors. Barna's emphasis on the ability and readiness of management to precipitate change, the importance of foresight and the disadvantages of conservatism is particularly important and extends the analysis of Mrs Penrose especially through the emphasis placed on the importance of the personal characteristics and attitudes of entrepreneurs.

In Mrs Penrose's analysis, even if continued expansion in existing product markets would be unprofitable, the firm that wishes to grow can always expand by diversifying into other products. The main limit to the growth of the firm in her view is set within the firm itself and is particularly dependent upon managerial ability. Richardson also found that the shortage of managerial capacity and the risks in recruiting new management from outside the organisation were the main limitations on the growth of the 16 firms that formed his sample.[5] However, as both Penrose and Richardson have noted there are other hindrances to the growth of firms particularly in the form of shortages of other factor inputs or of capital.

Not only do some firms fail to make the most of their growth opportunities, some others grow too fast and subsequently falter. Often it seems that firms founded and controlled by a perceptive entrepreneur are particularly prone to disaster. This may be because the firm had not yet grown sufficiently large and diversified to be able to spread its risks through several different products or markets. But all too often the primary cause seems to have been a lack of effective managerial control, especially in the financial area. Clearly it is possible not only to grow too slowly but also to grow faster than existing managerial resources and the cash flow will be able to stand. In this area it is undoubtedly the case that managerial quality exercises an important influence on the performance of firms, but difficulties of comparing management qualities between firms on any reliable basis render statistical investigations of the relation between management quality and firm performance impracticable. Statistical analysis has however been carried out by some commentators in an attempt to identify whether there are any measurable variables that are associated with high or low rates of growth of firms.

The majority of such statistical investigations in both Britain and the USA have concentrated on the question as to whether there is any evidence that the rates of growth of firms are systematically associated with the sizes of those firms. Gibrat's Law, the law of proportionate effect, suggests that there would not be such an association and that the probability of a firm growing at a given rate during any specified period of time is independent of the size of that firm at the beginning of the period concerned. Of course, growth rates of individual firms will vary as a result of other factors but the observed rates of growth for a group of firms will not differ systematically with the sizes of those firms. If this law is to be confirmed, two different statistical tests would need to be satisfied. First, we would need to confirm that firms of different size classes did have the same average growth rates. Secondly, we would also need to find that firms of different size classes had the same dispersion of growth rates about the common mean growth rate. If the law was confirmed this would have some interesting implications. It would indicate that in general the rate of growth of a firm in one time period had no influence on its rate of growth in later periods. It would suggest that there was no optimum size of firm from the point of view of growth since all sizes of firm were equally likely to benefit from growth. As we saw in Chapter 1 such equal proportionate growth would lead to increasing concentration over time since the dispersion of firm sizes will continue to increase. Finally, if the law of proportionate effect is confirmed, this would suggest that explanations of the growth of firms must emphasise the important stochastic component in the forces determining the growth of firms that arise from the cumulative effects of the chance operation of a large number of random disturbances acting independently of each other. Consequently it would be very difficult to adopt a deterministic explanation of the growth of firms.

Actual empirical testing of the law is a difficult operation. The law itself assumes that over the period of time for which growth rates are being measured the population of firms is constant. In practice this is not the case and both births and deaths of firms occur. There are problems concerning the quality of the statistical information to be used. How is a reliable measure of growth to be found, especially to overcome the problem of the differential propensity of firms to revalue their assets? In practice most studies tend only to use data relating to public companies (that is those with a stock exchange quotation) since relevant information is most readily available on these. This does, however, mean that the 'small' firms referred to in such studies are not at all small by most standards. Some investigations have, for example, used only the one thousand largest firms in the USA as the basis of their analysis,[6] so 'small' is very much a relative rather than absolute concept. By using only public companies it is also likely that the analysis concentrates on firms where the separation of ownership and control is most advanced and concentrates on those firms where the maximisation of a managerial utility function including growth as an important element is most likely to be relevant. A further problem is that testing the hypotheses in Gibrat's Law must involve the assumption that the environment in which firms are operating is neutral, that is there is no evidence of discrimination in favour of one size of firm to the detriment of others. In fact, as we shall observe later in this chapter, it is often the case that fiscal, monetary or anti-trust policies do operate in such a way that they favour one size of firm rather than another and this must have an important influence on the confidence with which we can interpret the results of tests of the law of proportionate effect.

The statistical findings partially but not completely support Gibrat's Law. A number of studies have indeed demonstrated that the average rate of growth of different size classes of firm is independent of the opening size of the firm.[7] However, the second element in the law, that the dispersion of growth rates is the same for firms of all sizes, is less readily demonstrated. Although Simon and Bonini found in a study of the 500 largest American firms that the dispersion of growth rates over a short period was the same for all size groups,[8] a number of other investigators have reported that small firms have a more variable growth experience than larger firms.[9] Other studies have reported, as exceptions to the law, some slight evidence that size in one period tends to breed growth in the next period,[10] that large firms tend to grow faster than small firms,[11] (although other studies have reported the reverse[12]) and that the relative growth experience of large and small firms tends to vary over different periods of time.[13] Several studies have also emphasised that small firms had much lower chances of survival than large firms.[14]

Bearing in mind the reservations regarding the variable quality of the data used in these studies and their different data inputs, it seems reasonable to conclude that in general there is quite strong evidence that the initial sizes of firms do not have a marked influence on their average rate of growth over a succeeding period of time. However, the full implications of Gibrat's Law are not sustained as there is considerable evidence that the dispersion of growth rates within a size group of firms is negatively associated with the actual size of firms. This is consistent with the view that there are other pressures which impose a greater threat to the survival or ability to grow of the small firm but indicates that those small firms that do grow have a particularly favourable growth experience, allowing them to sustain the mean growth rate for all small firms at a level comparable to that for larger firms.

Studies relating growth to other variables are less numerous. Singh and Whittington[15] investigated the relation with 14 financial indicators – firm size, rate of growth, profitability, liquidity, all measured in various ways, trade credit, stocks and the valuation ratio. They found that the rate of return was positively related to the rate of growth and this was the only variable that had much explanatory power. Even so the relationship was not stable over time or across the four industries for which data was collected. Barna[16] and Marcus[17] also found a positive correlation between growth and profitability. Marcus further found a negative correlation between the firm's market share and its growth rate and suggested that this was because large firms would be more cautious in their growth plans since their growth would be more likely to have an adverse effect on prices and would be more likely to provoke a retaliation by other firms. This explanation obviously applies more to growth within existing product markets than to growth through major diversification programmes.

Neither Singh and Whittington nor Barna found any evidence of a strong association between liquidity and growth. Barna concluded, 'All in all it appears that firms that wanted to grow and had the ability to make profit also had the ability or opportunity to raise finance'.[18] The only other variable that seems to have been found to have much explanatory power is innovative activity. Looking at the American steel and petroleum industries, Mansfield found that successful innovators grew more than twice as fast as non-innovators of initial equal size. He found that small firms in particular gained greatly in terms of growth from their innovations.[19]

This review of the growth process of firms does not lead to any simple conclusion. It seems that on average small firms as a group are just as likely to grow at a particular rate as larger firms. Larger organisations individually seem better able to preserve their independent existence and to ensure that their own growth rate approaches near to the mean for the group as a whole. Stochastic processes should not be ruled out as important influences on rates of growth but the growth performance of individual firms seems also to be dependent on their past profitability, their innovative performance and especially the quality of their management.

Mergers and the firm

Firms have been involved in mergers of one form or another for many decades. The type of merger has varied through time and early merger movements in the late nineteenth and early twentieth centuries frequently involved the consolidation of a large number of firms into a single unit. The involvement of just two firms in a merger has of late become the more important phenomenon, as has also the tendency for one firm to be clearly recognisable as the acquirer and one as the acquired or victim firm, rather than a merger of two firms on an equal basis. In this chapter the term merger will be used to refer to all forms of consolidation, merger and acquisition, though as our primary interest will be with present industrial structure and practices we shall frequently be dealing with situations that are more of the nature of acquisitions.

It is also helpful at the outset to deal with the terminology that describes the direction of particular mergers. Three main types of merger are most frequently referred to in the literature; horizontal, vertical and conglomerate. Horizontal mergers occur between firms engaged in the same levels of economic activity in the same industry. These are normally considered to have potentially the most serious consequences for market concentration. Vertical mergers are those between a supplier and his customer or vice versa. While this does not directly affect market concentration in the industry concerned it is often considered to pose a threat to competition in the industry because of the possibility that 'squeeze' activities will ensue that will hinder competition from other, independent, firms. This problem was discussed in Chapter 3. By a process of elimination we can see that conglomerate mergers may be loosely described as those that are neither horizontal nor vertical. Wherever a firm acquires another that is neither its direct competitor nor its supplier or customer, that merger would be classed as a conglomerate. In practice, however, this distinction is too crude and analysis tends normally to make a distinction between concentric mergers and the pure conglomerate merger. Concentric mergers take place between firms that are not at the time direct competitors but have a common element in their activities – a common production technology or major raw material input or that use similar marketing techniques or distribution channels.[20] 'Pure' conglomerate mergers tend to relate to mergers between firms with quite disparate activities and are often acquisitions made by financial holding companies.

Of course, many modern mergers do not fit into one single type category at all. This is especially true of mergers between the larger public companies that often have a diverse range of activities and there may well be horizontal, vertical, concentric and pure conglomerate elements within a single such merger. Even in the case of a horizontal merger between two firms in the same industry there may in fact be no increase in market concentration. The industry as identified on a standard industrial classification basis may be too broadly defined and the items produced by the firms may be quite different and uncompetitive. Even if they produced the same items the firms might prove to be operating in quite different market segments – either in terms of geographical location or product quality. On the other hand, firms that are not directly competitive at the present moment may be potential competitors if it is likely that even if a merger does not take place one firm, by its own internal expansion, would invade the market of the other. Again it may well be that firms that are classified into different industries are in fact producing products that are directly substitutable for each other and so a merger that is shown as having taken place between firms from different industries may actually tend to reduce competition in a particular product market. These comments should indicate that the categorisation of mergers by the direction of merger activity is not an easy matter and requires considerable information about the actual product markets served and that might potentially be served by the firms concerned.

Public discussion and economic attention in recent years has focused increasingly on the role and consequences of mergers and it seems appropriate and highly desirable that this should be so, both from the point of view of those concerned with managerial decision-making within the firm and on the part of those concerned with public policy issues of industrial structure and performance. In recent years it appears that the economic significance of mergers has been increasing, though whether this is a temporary phenomenon or not is difficult to say. A high proportion of public companies have gone out of existence as a result of mergers, though these tend to be concentrated in a limited number of industries which are therefore also likely to have experienced a considerable increase in concentration. Thus Kuehn[21] found that between 1957 and 1969 over 43 per cent of the publicly quoted companies on UK stock exchanges were taken over and in a number of industries – soft drinks, breweries, chemists goods, food, hosiery, medical equipment, cotton textiles – the proportion was over 50 per cent. A high proportion of the leading companies are involved in mergers; Newbould estimated that in 1967–8 70 of the hundred largest British companies were involved in mergers.[22] Expenditure on mergers has also increased, when measured in terms of the total value of outlays on acquisitions, in the average size of outlays and as a proportion of total expenditure by firms. This suggests that acquisitions represent an important investment decision to the firm and the evidence from many firms that mergers are often unsuccessful indicates that a merger can be a very risky investment.

Numerous empirical investigations of different aspects of the causes and consequences of mergers have been undertaken, some using various forms of statistical tests and others based upon case study investigations that allow some comment to be made on the influence of non-quantifiable variables such as the history of an industry, actual managerial motivations and qualities etc. Neither technique alone offers a complete picture and we shall refer to evidence obtained from both types of study to try to build up an overall picture.

(1) Why Do Firms Merge?

Many commentators have provided long lists of possible reasons why mergers occur.[23] The one that follows here will no doubt be equally long. This suggests that there are numerous explanations of mergers that have been found to contain some empirical validity. It also warns that a search for a general theory of the causes of mergers may well be meaningless. While some firms have a clearly thought-out acquisition strategy[24] the behaviour of many firms is reactive rather than active and purposive. We will look at explanations for acquiring and acquired firms separately and then note attempts to explain variations through time in the aggregate incidence of mergers in terms of more general economic variables.

The range of possible explanations as to why firms make acquisitions is very extensive and it is significant that one observer has pointed out that acquirers may be at either end of the spectrum: they may have been doing well or badly; they may have surplus management or be seriously lacking in management; they may have excess productive capacity or no capacity at all; they may have been successful in research or unsuccessful.[25]

Some commentators see decisions to acquire another company as motivated purely by financial considerations. They argue that an acquisition will take place if the valuation placed on a company by a potential acquirer is greater than the value placed on it by the existing owners and if the discounted stream of expected profits satisfies normal investment appraisal criteria. Undoubtedly in some cases an acquirer does find a company that, because of capital market imperfections, is substantially undervalued, but this does not seem to explain the decision process underlying many mergers. The reasons for acquisition and the hopes that it raises may not be readily amenable to quantification and it may not be easy to make accurate forecasts of the true earnings potential of a firm until it has been acquired and thoroughly appraised. It appears that very little formal investment appraisal is undertaken by firms before making an acquisition and often the price they pay for a company commits them to requiring an almost impossibly high compound rate of growth of profits from the acquired firm to satisfy normal rate of return criteria.[26] One finance director once commented on this question, 'you can't do a DCF [discounted cash flow] for faith'! In fact it seems that a few mergers can yield very high profits but the chances of this occurring are sufficiently low as to render merging a speculative activity.[27]

In rare cases it may be that high liquidity on the part of an acquirer is an important stimulus to a merger. For example, it was suggested that one reason for the bid by GKN for Birfield was GKN's high liquidity at the time as a result of the compensation it had recently received on the re-nationalisation of its steel interests. The possibility of increasing profits might be particularly relevant in mergers where there is scope for rationalisation and the achievement of cost reductions or where, as a result of vertically integrating, costs of using the market are avoided.

Many mergers have as a primary objective the benefits of expansion. This may be in order to improve the market coverage, to round out existing product lines or to challenge an existing market leader. Expansion may hinge upon the successful acquisition of a company with customer goodwill, well established brand names, a good sales performance and high margins. Alternatively it may be that the firm considers acquisition the quickest or least risky form of growth and may be under pressure to achieve this in order to meet the personal aspirations of its senior executives or to expand the range of opportunities for its existing management team.

The implicit assumption has been that the firms with the motives discussed so far are reasonably successful and looking for profitable expansion opportunities. In a large number of cases this is obviously appropriate. It does not, however, follow that all acquiring firms are in this position. Indeed it has seemed that many firms resort to merger in an effort to defend themselves or to solve one problem or another. Some are concerned that unless they expand in size they will be subject to a takeover bid themselves and so a merger may be to increase the security and chance of independence of the acquiring firm. This may often be a motive when the economy is experiencing a high general level of merger activity and one merger leads to others and indeed to expectations of yet more. The desire for security may also encourage vertical acquisitions in order to ensure continuity of supplies or of outlets. Sometimes an acquisition may be prompted by fear on the part of the acquirer that another bidder may take over an important customer or supplier. The bid by British Motor Corporation for Pressed Steel was, for example, considered to have been prompted by the fear that if BMC did not acquire Pressed Steel, Rootes, which by then had access to greater financial resources as a result of its link with Chrysler, would do so.

In the minds of some firms competition may call for defensive mergers. Firms are often concerned about the market-spoiling activities of weak sellers and may attempt to take them over. This was an important reason for the bid by British Sidac for Transparent Paper which was ultimately rejected by the Monopolies Commission. However, the line between controlling weak sellers and closing down excess capacity on the one hand and the attempt to create a monopoly position on the other is very difficult to draw. Some companies might, if unconstrained, use mergers simply as a means of controlling or even stopping competition. Wallpaper Manufacturers Ltd. preserved its substantial market dominance in the supply of wallpaper by acquiring 22 other wallpaper manufacturers between 1906 and 1934.[28] It has been suggested that the early merger, or more accurately, consolidation movements both in Britain and America were motivated primarily by a desire to establish a substantial monopoly position,[29] but effective anti-trust action in the USA at least reduced somewhat the aspirations of merging companies and encouraged them to be satisfied with mergers involving smaller market shares which thereby created oligopoly.[30]

Mergers may also be used as a means of helping the firm to solve some pressing internal problem. It may be concerned about its performance and may make a reverse takeover bid in an attempt to acquire management to run its activities in general or a particular loss-making subsidiary. It may use merger to obtain access to know-how or patents for new products or processes that will allow it to extend its range of products to offset unfavourable growth prospects or to keep up with the rate of technological progress in its industry. Alternatively it may wish to acquire other succcessful companies to enable it to maintain its profit levels when its existing patents expire. This was alleged to be an important reason why Rank (whose xerox patents were shortly to expire) bid for De La Rue and also why Beecham was anxious to acquire Glaxo. In the brewing industry the operation of the tied house system and the licensing system has made it difficult for brewing firms to expand other than by acquiring other brewers. Their prime purpose in making acquisitions has been to gain access to further outlets for their own production.

Some firms are happy to be acquired while others strongly oppose a bid. It seems that often it is difficult to resist a takeover bid successfully, especially where the shareholding is widely dispersed. It may be possible by mounting a spirited defence to raise the price paid for the company and even on occasions a bid-for firm will arrange for a third party with whom a merger would be preferred to make a bid. Opposition to a bid may not always occur where it would be appropriate. The decision to recommend acceptance of a bid is made by the board of directors some of whom may be hoping for senior executive positions in the acquiring company. Other members of the management team may also favour a merger on the grounds that their job opportunities will be enhanced in a larger organisation. In the interests of their future job prospects they are unlikely to wish to involve themselves in strong opposition to the bid. Under such circumstances the behaviour of the board and senior management may not reflect due consideration of the interests of shareholders.

Managements may agree to a takeover if they consider their organisation was suffering from a lack of profit or liquidity or capital raising ability or if there was no apparent managerial succession. In some cases a management may simply feel that as a relatively small company in a giant's world it is fighting a losing battle in its attempt to keep up with the leaders. The board of Martins Bank felt like this:

> Martins told us that over the years it had received several inquiries from other banks about the possibility of amalgamation but its Board was unreceptive, wishing to remain independent. However, in 1967 the Board felt

it was necessary to reconsider its attitude; the increasing cost of opening new branches and impending heavy expenditure on tranferring branch accounting to computers were making an amalgamation more attractive, possibly even inevitable.[31]

Shareholders may also have some influence. Dissatisfaction with the performance of their investments may lead shareholders to sell out thereby lowering the share price and hence the valuation ratio and leaving the firm exposed to a takeover bid. Institutional shareholders are becoming increasingly important owners of equity in major companies and rather than sell out through the market they have been known to try to find a bidder for a company with a poor performance under its existing management. The actions of shareholders may even provoke acquisitions when they least expect them. ICI held a trading investment in Pyrotenax, manufacturers of certain forms of insulated cables. Having decided to sell off this investment, ICI offered it to Yorkshire Imperial Metals who decided they did not want to acquire it. So it was offered to British Insulated Callenders' Cables (BICC) who accepted but decided it did not want a minority holding so made a bid for the whole of the equity of Pyrotenax.[32] It was only ICI's decision to sell off its holding that encouraged BICC to consider the possibility of such a merger at all.

Much of the published explanation of the motivations of the acquired companies in selling out seems to centre upon the experiences of smaller, owner-managed firms. Here a number of different reasons for a 'death wish' are apparent. The owner may wish to retire and have no family members or others who are willing or considered able to assume control of the company. Tax reasons figure large for the small firm: these were found to be an important cause of acquisitions in the USA[33] and are particularly relevant where there is likely to be a death duties problem or where income is taxed at a higher rate than capital gains.

While there is always a certain amount of merger activity, occasional peaks and troughs are identifiable. Is there any possible explanation of the timing of merger waves? Various commentators have attempted to deal with this question[34] but have produced conflicting results. The independent variable most frequently used in attempts to explain intertemporal variation in the level of merger activity is the movement in share prices. Some commentators have found a close positive correlation between the two but others, for different countries and different periods of time, have found a negative correlation. A priori, a reasonable explanation could probably be offered for either result. A positive correlation would be consistent with the influence of psychological considerations – the market expects takeovers so bids up the share prices and relative price/earnings ratios of likely acquirers and in so doing makes acquisitions cheaper in real terms, especially where they are financed by share issues and other loan stock. On the other hand falling share prices may increase the incentive to shareholders to sell out and make acquisitions for cash cheaper. Declining industrial production or a slowing down of economic growth may imply growing excess capacity, and a desire to avoid the severities of competition will increase the incidence of merger activity.

Other environmental features may also be important. Major changes in patterns of communication and technology may give rise to substantial changes in industrial structure. The activities of merger promoters maybe important.[35] These may include merchant banks, specialist merger brokers, economic development councils, or a body like the Industrial Reorganisation Corporation. The government's own attitude to mergers may also influence the general climate of opinion and hence the level of merger activity while other aspects of anti-trust policy, especially attempts to control restrictive trading agreements, may encourage mergers. In both the USA[36] and Britain[37] it has been shown that the introduction of anti-cartel measures encouraged firms to turn to mergers as a means of continuing to obtain the same degree of restraint on competition. Last, but by no means least, we must note the influence of the general fiscal and financial situation. Changes that give relative advantages to one type of organisation or another can influence the level of merger activity. For example, Leyland pointed out that the introduction of penal clauses relating to close companies in the 1965 Finance Act made the financial position of a large number of small and medium sized firms at the very least uncertain and increased markedly the supply of companies willing to be taken over.[38]

(2)   The Financial Characteristics of Acquiring and Acquired Firms

We have noted so far particular reasons why firms may wish to acquire or be acquired and possible environmental influences on the incidence of merger activity. The next question we must ask is whether there is any evidence that the characteristics of acquired and acquiring firms differ significantly or whether acquired firms or acquiring firms tend to come from a relatively homogenous group. A certain amount of empirical testing in this area undoubtedly arises as a result of interest in the validity of the newer managerial theories of the firm. The statistical tests most frequently used for this purpose are the tests of significance of the differences of mean values between the two groups of firms. In some cases this involves comparisons between acquired firms and acquiring firms and in other studies the characteristics of acquired firms have been compared against a control group that is a sample of all non-acquired firms whether they have made an acquisition or not. Tests of the significance of differences in mean values between groups of firms will only consider possible explanatory variables singly. It is possible, however, to consider the significance of variables in combination with each other and thereby reflect the multivariate nature of the influences on merger decisions by using a binary regression or, more usually, discriminant analysis. The two are formally similar.[39] Where a multivariate analysis is employed the likelihood that a particular variable will be found to be significant is less than on a univariate test. However, in the discussion of the characteristics of acquired and acquiring firms we shall not distinguish between results from univariate and multivariate tests, neither shall we comment separately on results from tests that compared acquired and acquiring firms from those that compared acquiring firms against a control group of all other firms.

Four main groups of variables have been used in attempts to identify the characteristics of acquired and acquiring firms: size and growth; profits; stock market rating and liquidity. The results are not in all cases entirely in agreement with each other. Acquired firms have been found to be more likely to have lower growth rates and to be smaller. There does not, however, appear to be a linear relation between size of firm and the chances of being acquired. Singh found that above a certain size the probability of acquisition fell much more rapidly. The evidence on the influence of profitability is also not unanimous. Several studies have indicated that acquired firms tend to have lower rates of return and a slower rate of growth of earnings. Newbould, however, found no difference in rates of return between acquired firms and others, while in a Canadian study Reuber and Roseman found that acquired firms have higher median profit rates although as a group they were also more likely to be making losses. Tzoannos and Samuels on the other hand found to their surprise that on average acquired firms had less volatile profits. Studies have variously shown that acquired firms have low retention rates, low dividend pay-out rates, more variable dividends and a higher dividend yield. Other studies have shown that stock market ratings of acquired firms tend to be poorer with lower price/earnings ratios and, in some cases, a lower and even a falling valuation ratio. Evidence on the liquidity position of acquired firms is inconsistent. Some investigators have found that acquired firms have lower or equal liquidity positions but the majority of studies seem to indicate that acquired firms have higher levels of liquidity. Tzoannos and Samuels also paid attention to the question of capital gearing and found that acquired companies tended to have higher absolute levels of capital gearing, a stronger upward trend but also greater variability in their gearing. From this they concluded that acquired firms had already used their borrowing possibilities and that such firms were not being purchased to allow the acquirer access to new loan funds.

Less attention has been paid to the characteristics of acquiring firms, though Kuehn, Newbould and Singh have provided some information on this question. Acquiring firms tend to be larger and to have shown faster growth. The evidence on profitability is mixed. Kuehn indicated that acquiring firms have lower rates of return and lower retention ratios while Singh found the opposite. There is some evidence that acquiring firms have a favourable stock market rating through a higher price/earnings ratio and a higher valuation ratio though not all investigations are unanimous on this. Acquiring firms have also been found to be less liquid and to have a higher gearing.

In his study Singh also paid considerable attention to the overall classificatory performance of his discriminant analysis. It is one thing to be able to identify variables which distinguish significantly between two groups of firms when the groupings are known, but is it possible knowing only the financial variables to classify correctly the individual firms to their appropriate group – acquiring or acquired? Singh found that on this criterion his results were disappointing. Only size of firm and, to a lesser extent, pre-tax profits were good discriminators and the overall discriminatory power as indicated by the proportion of firms correctly classified was in most cases not much better than that which would have been obtained from a random allocative process. This indicated that the characteristics of the two groups overlapped considerably and that the two groups of firms could be considered as having been drawn from the same, homogeneous, population of firms. The fact that the valuation ratio was not a significant variable in the discriminant analysis led Singh to conclude that there is not a level of the valuation ratio that will guarantee a firm's security against a takeover bid and therefore the stock market does not in his opinion appear to exercise the restraining influence over the activities of firms that Marris's model imputes to it.

We are therefore some way from having an entirely clear and consistent set of empirical observations of the nature of the characteristics of acquired and acquiring firms. Some pointers regarding size, rate of growth, stock market rating, liquidity, profit levels and pay-out experiences can be identified but even they do not all point unequivocally in one direction. The diversity of results and poor overall explanatory performance of these variables are however interesting in their own right. They emphasise that there is no guarantee that a firm that attains or fails to attain a particular performance level will be involved in merger activities and therefore suggest that explanations of the causes of mergers based purely on financial considerations are not sufficient. They also serve to reinforce the view that there are many other managerial and market considerations, often specific to the firms involved or that reflect particular environmental phenomena, that are equally relevant, if not more so, to actual merger decisions.

(3)   The Success or Failure of Mergers

Different commentators have offered their assessments on the proportion of mergers that are 'successes'. All have been to a greater or lesser degree pessimistic regarding the proportion of mergers that are successful. Many estimates of the proportion of successful mergers indicate that well under 50 per cent fall into that category. It would seem that any merger has therefore at least an even chance of not being judged a success. Clearly therefore it is necessary to pay some attention not only to the causes and nature of the merger process but also to what happens after the merger has taken place.

Our first task must be to attempt to establish some reasonable indication of what is meant by 'success'. Are we interested in success to management or to shareholders or in the achievement of benefits that enhance a more broadly conceived public interest? Can success be measured objectively and if so how? A number of criteria have been used to assess success. Some of these are essentially quantitative and normally involve comparison of the financial performance of merging firms with that of a control group of non-merging firms. Other criteria are more qualitative but often place considerable emphasis on the extent to which synergy has been obtained from the combination of the two firms. Synergy is often described as the $2 + 2 = 5$ effect – the attainment of a greater output at the same costs from the two units in combination than would be possible if they continued to operate independently. Alternatively, synergy will allow the same output to be achieved for lower costs. This concept seems to contain elements akin to both the economist's view of a downward shift in the cost function and the attainment of economies of scale, that is, a move along a downward sloping cost curve. Synergy may be obtained or at least hoped for in most areas of an organisation's activities but particularly in the combination of production facilities; through the exchange of technological know-how and R and D results; through rationalisation of marketing activities; in managerial and organisational functions – especially through increased specialisation and a reduction of duplication in overheads; and in finance as a result of the larger buying and bargaining power of the merged organisation.[40]

There is no doubt that mergers can be found which have been highly successful, at least in meeting the objectives of the acquiring company's management: unprofitable operations have been turned round; the quality of products raised; production specialised in different plants and scale economies obtained and the opportunity to automate seized; the marketing network rationalised; the process of adjustment to change in declining industries advanced; small uneconomic plants closed; cheaper buying prices obtained as a result of vertical acquisition; duplication of overhead expenses especially in the central administration of the organisation reduced and management stimulated.[41] But even on a qualitative assessment the results are often considered disappointing. The failures seem to arise for one of two main groups of reason. Either the acquiring firm has simply made a bad purchase through inadequate appraisal or a merger has failed to produce the benefits that were hoped for and indeed introduced other costs and disadvantages as well. Either way this does serve to emphasise that if, as is widely held, mergers are a higher risk activity with a long delay before a pay-off should be expected [42] then firms ought to consider carefully the opportunity costs of committing resources – financial and managerial – to acquisitions rather than devoting their efforts to internal expansion.

The experience of firms suggests that synergy is very difficult to release and the main areas of gain are in pecuniary advantages – improved buying terms and cheaper access to capital. Economies tend to occur at head office level rather than in operating functions and divisions.[43] Newbould's investigation of 38 mergers in Britain revealed that there had been little evidence of synergistic gains and indeed in many cases little attempt to reorganise to gain synergy at all.[44] Some mergers have simply produced benefits that the recruitment of an experienced senior executive could have obtained without the heavy expense of a merger.[45] Others have been used as an opportunity for internal reorganisation that was not necessarily dependent on the merger at all or have produced benefits that are benefits of size *per se* rather than of merger.[46]

Not only do mergers fail to release benefits that would otherwise be unobtainable but they appear on occasions to produce new problems and costs. Extensive drains on managerial resources and capital, problems of integration of plants with different styles, incompatibilities of accounting and computer systems, the high costs of moving staff and arranging early retirements, the effect of uncertainties about post-merger arrangements in delaying new product development, have all been emphasised by different researchers as reasons why acquiring firms found that their mergers were unsuccessful.

Several studies have also attempted to assess the quantitative effects of mergers on the financial performance of the acquiring firms.[47] Many of the financial variables used in this sort of investigation are similar to those used in comparisons of the characteristics of acquired and acquiring firms – return on capital, growth in share prices, earnings per share, etc. Some recent writers have suggested that it is appropriate to look at the performance of those ratios (profits, growth of firm) which reflect the interest of management separately from those that reflect more closely the interest of shareholders (share price movements, earnings per share). In view of current thinking on the divorce between ownership and control this is clearly appropriate. In all cases we really need to know how the firm would have performed had it not been involved in mergers. This, of course, is not something about which we can ever have reliable evidence so the procedure often adopted is again to use the performance of a control group of non-acquiring firms as an indicator of how the acquiring firms might otherwise have been expected to perform had a merger not taken place.

The early American studies of the effects of mergers were really concerned with the effects of consolidations and the performance of the large firms that arose from the consolidation movement. Their findings were not encouraging. The National Industrial Conference Board found that the consolidations did not achieve their promised increase in the rate of return, the share values of the merged companies did not perform any better than those of other companies and there was no evidence of superior efficiency, though some of the consolidated companies did lead in technical progress. Many of the consolidated organisations proved to be weak and subsequently had to be reorganised. Dewing also found that many consolidated companies failed to meet their profit forecasts and Livermore concluded that while some of these were financially successful others were not and many collapsed shortly after their formation.

More recent studies have been concerned with the current phenomenon of an acquisition or the merger of just two firms. While the results are not entirely in agreement with each other the pattern of results indicates that merging firms as a group do not improve their performance compared with non-merging firms. This is particularly the case where variables reflecting shareholder interests are concerned. Reid found that while firms that had been involved in mergers expanded faster than non-merging companies they returned a worse performance when measured in terms of share price or profits per share. Ansoff found that acquiring firms had lower growth rates on most financial variables and had lower rates of return on capital employed than non-acquiring firms. Kelly reported that merging companies were slightly less effective performers than non-merging companies. As we would expect, the merging companies obtained higher price/earnings ratios but mergers seemed to have no effect on the profit margin. Hogarty found that mergers did not raise profitability and that the investment performance of the heavily merging firms was generally significantly worse than that of the average investment performance of firms in their respective industries. Singh found that two years after a merger the average profitability of the firms concerned had not increased and he suggested that the mergers had generally not given rise to a more profitable utilisation of resources. He thought that it might have been the case that firms were sacrificing profits to growth. Newbould also conducted a small experiment comparing the performance of 24 merging companies with that of 24 comparable non-merging companies. The merging companies showed a faster increase in size but he also concluded that, if anything, shareholder interests and general economic efficiency interests were better served by the non-merging firms.

The results taken together with our discussion of the qualitative assessment of the performance of mergers suggests that many mergers are not successful as far as the firm is concerned, and even less so from the point of view of shareholders. The risks of failure are high and greater attention might profitably be paid to growth through internal expansion. No doubt a large number of mergers will continue to take place, partly because managements always feel that their merger will be one of the few that is highly profitable and also because other reasons not directly dependent upon considerations of subsequent financial performance may encourage firms to merge. This being so, is there any guidance that might help to reduce the chance that mergers will prove unsuccessful from the point of view of the acquirer? There is not complete agreement on all aspects of this but some pointers are possible. The first emphasis must be on the place of a merger as part of a planned programme rather than simply an opportunistic purchase. Ansoff has shown that firms that carefully planned their mergers showed a much better and more consistent performance than firms that did not plan.[48] In view of the frequent failure to use appropriate appraisal techniques and the tendency for prices to be paid in acquisitions that committed the acquiring company to very high compound rates of growth of profits if the purchase was to be economically justifiable,[49] emphasis should also be placed on a more realistic investment appraisal before a company is acquired.

In the last resort, however, the key to success or failure depends upon the success of the internal organisation of the acquisition. The pursuit of synergy must inevitably involve a much closer integration of the two firms, and hence the likelihood of rationalisation and redeployment of personnel, than if synergy is not sought. So the pursuit of greater benefits involves greater risks. The need to allay anxieties amongst the staff of both firms about proposed future developments must be a very high priority and reporting relations must be clearly established. Some authorities would argue that it is important to introduce a senior manager from the acquiring company into the acquired organisation to assist the integration process. It is also most important not to underestimate the demands that an acquired company can impose on the managerial and capital resources of the acquirer. It is necessary to be sure that these resources can be made available to the subsidiary, and if they cannot be spared perhaps the merger ought not to proceed.

Diversification and the firm

Much of the growth of the firm, both internal and especially external, is to a greater or lesser degree through diversification and it is this particular phenomenon that we shall consider in this section. We shall consider both diversification that is 'concentric' in the sense that there is a common technological or marketing base in the firm's existing products and that which is conglomerate where the diversification is into quite disparate activities. Much diversification does have a strong concentric element.

A diversification strategy may make much good sense to the firm for a number of different reasons. It is an important means of growth especially where further expansion within the firm's existing market is limited by a low rate of growth of that market; where the market structure is such that an attempt to increase market share would precipitate severe competition that the firm is anxious to avoid; where further expansion by horizontal merger is precluded by lack of suitable firms to acquire; or where such mergers would be prohibited by anti-trust action. Diversification may be a prudent move offering security against possible adverse effects of a decline in sales and profits in the primary area of activity or the adverse effects of increasing competition. It may help to stabilise the flow of earnings or the level of activity if the existing products of the firm are subject to seasonal or cyclical fluctuations or as a result of the shortening of product cycles. It will also reduce excessive dependence on just one customer or just one line of activity. The benefit from a pooling of risks across a number of activities is often held to be a major benefit of diversificatory and conglomerate activities. Diversification may be a consequence of successful research and development which has provided expertise and sometimes a patentable new product to encourage the addition of a new product line. It has been argued that it becomes easier to pursue a diversificatory strategy where the firm has adopted a multi-division organisational structure and successful diversification is therefore considered to be very closely dependent upon the internal organisation of the firm.[50]

According to an American study of the diversification pattern of large firms, the firms that are most likely to diversify are those that are relatively large, are in more concentrated industries and employ a high proportion of qualified technical personnel.[51] It was found that firms tended to diversify into industries that were young and fast growing and where there was a high rate of technical change as indicated by heavy capital requirements, a high level of employment of technical and scientific personnel and a fast increasing labour productivity. This is not unduly surprising since new entry is likely to be much easier and will cause less disturbance when an industry is experiencing rapid growth and technological change. It is also presumably wise for a firm wishing to diversify to choose an industry where the growth prospects are good and the prospective return on investment is high.

Gort also found that diversification tended to take place within the same two-digit industry group. This strongly suggests that firms did choose to diversify into areas where there was either a common technological or marketing base. It is also likely that many diversifications outside the original two-digit industry group still had a substantial concentric element. Thus Gort showed as an exception to the general diversification pattern the fact that several petroleum firms diversified into chemicals which constitute a separate two-digit industry. However this diversification is based on a very closely related technology and serves merely to emphasise that it can sometimes be misleading to assume that simply because two industries are allocated to different classifications there are low cross-elasticities of demand or supply between them. The British experience is similar. Mergers between firms from different industrial sectors still appear to have concentric elements. Thus it has been found that electrical engineering firms acquired firms in the non-electrical engineering sector, textile firms acquired those in clothing and footwear, and chemical manufacturers acquired textile firms.[52]

Qualitative British evidence also indicates that much diversification is closely related to the existing activity of the firm. Thus Unilever described its proposed merger with Allied Breweries as a product extension merger: 'a consolidation of two companies whose activities are related functionally at either the production or marketing level but where the products are different'.[53] Much of Unilever's own diversification in common with that of some other British companies has been based on a common raw material. In Unilever's case the common element was the technology used in processing oils and fats.[54] This had led it into three quite disparate product areas – soap and from that washing products; margarine and then on to the production of animal feeding stuffs; chemical products for industrial use. But Unilever had also used its expertise in marketing consumer goods to diversify on the basis of concentric marketing and distribution and added to its margarine sales through grocers' shops, ice-cream, frozen foods, jam, tea, coffee, soups, cake mixes and cheese. Its detergent and other washing products sales also benefited from the same marketing and distribution expertise. The Rank Organisation is another example of a diversified firm, with its diversification based on different leisure activities, the concentric element in this case being in the end use for the goods and services produced rather than the internal production or marketing activities involved.[55]

The organisation that is prepared to make pure conglomerate acquisitions will not be as constrained as the firm looking for concentric diversification. Its concern will be rather more with the discovery of favourable financial opportunities in firms with under-utilised or undervalued assets which can be turned to a more profitable use. Here too the original motivations for diversification may well have been concern about the future growth prospects of the original markets. De La Rue for example added formica and Potterton central heating boilers to its product range because it feared that the market for its banknote printing activities would grow more slowly as more countries decided to become self-sufficient in this area.

While some diversification moves are highly successful others run into considerable difficulties. To the normal problems of managing any sort of merger we have to add some extra problems that are a direct consequence of the process of diversification. Some companies have found that the firms they purchased have major problems of their own and poor growth prospects and that acquired subsidiaries present a constant drain of resources upon the parent company without ever making a contribution to profitability.[56] Possible synergies in concentric acquisitions may have been overestimated and companies have found that their managerial expertise is not as readily applied to other industries as they had hopefully imagined. British Match told the Monopolies Commission that the non-match activities into which it had diversified before its bid for Wilkinson Sword 'had, taken as a whole, achieved unsatisfactory profits, exhibited only variable growth potential and possible difficulties of satisfactory management'. In 1972–3 its non-match activities accounted for about 47 per cent of sales but only 26 per cent of group profits.[57] It seems that concentric and pure conglomerate acquisitions both involve above average degrees of risk and some authorities have argued that the financial performance of conglomerate organisations has been unimpressive [58] though this has been challenged by others.[59] But there is evidence that the variability of profits of large diversified firms is lower than for other organisations and this is an indication that one of the prime reasons for diversifying – the pooling of risks – is being achieved.

CHAPTER 8
GOVERNMENT AND MERGERS

Mergers and concentration

In most industrialised societies governments are not prepared to leave all developments in market structure to the free play of market forces. Among other policies they may attempt to exercise some influence through controls on mergers, either by making certain types of merger a legal offence to be enforced by the courts or by operating a more pragmatic administrative policy working on a more or less *ad hoc* basis to investigate those cases where a merger may not serve the public interest.[1] The reason for a specific concern with mergers is because they are assumed to be a particularly important influence on industry structure and hence on likely market conduct and economic performance. Not only does government have a policy interest in the efficient performance of industries as such and in the possible benefits of competition, but the efficient performance of industry in general is likely to influence the ability to attain macro-economic policy objectives such as economic growth, full employment, stable prices, an equitable income distribution and a healthy balance of payments, etc.

When a merger 'boom' is in progress it may appear that industrial concentration is increasing rapidly and the growth in the scale of expenditures on acquisitions may give rise to considerable public concern. Experience in Britain over the last fifteen years or more has certainly heightened interest and concern regarding the implications of mergers. Table 8.1 indicates the trend in the number of larger mergers based on information collected in recent years by the Board of Trade and the Department of Trade and Industry. This suggests that while there is some cyclical fluctuation in the number of mergers there is no evidence of an upward trend through time. It is difficult to estimate the trend in the real level of expenditure on mergers as it is necessary to allow for inflation and for share price fluctuations, especially as such a high proportion of acquisition outlays now take the form of exchanges of share capital.

Nevertheless these figures do indicate that a substantial number of the larger firms in the British economy are each year losing their independence and the chances are that they are not being replaced in sufficiently large numbers by up and coming firms to leave the level of concentration unchanged. This trend was emphasised in an analysis carried out by the staff of the Monopolies

Table 8.1 *Expenditure on acquisitions and mergers of industrial and commercial companies*

	Number		Value £m	
1964	940		505	
1965	1000		517	
1966	807		500	
1967	763		822	
1968	946		1946	
1969 [1,2]	906	846	935	1069
1970		793		1122
1971		884		911
1972		1210		2532
1973		1184		1291

Notes:

[1] From 1964 the series was based on information derived from company accounts of quoted companies.

[2] Since 1969 the series has been based on press reports relating to all industrial and commercial companies. The right-hand figures for 1969 are those relating to information based on press reports.

Source: *Business Monitor M.7 Acquisition and Mergers of Companies,* HMSO *passim*

Commission.[2] They showed that in 1957 there were 2,024 companies which by 1961 had assets of £1½ million or more and had their shares quoted on a stock exchange. By the end of 1968 as a result of mergers this number had been reduced to 1,253, a reduction of 38 per cent. The pattern of reduction was unevenly distributed between industries but some industries experienced a very heavy reduction in the number of large firms from the survey population. The largest reductions were in drink (63 per cent), food (54 per cent), chemicals (45 per cent), vehicles (44 per cent), bricks (43 per cent), electrical engineering (42 per cent), textiles (41 per cent). This suggests a substantial increase in industrial concentration and this was also borne out by other evidence in the same survey. Taking as a criterion the number of firms required to account for 50 per cent of the net assets of an industry, it was found that there had been a marked reduction in the number of firms responsible for 50 per cent of net assets in several important industries, including drink, textiles, food and vehicles (see Table 8.2). There was also evidence that large firms were taking an increasingly major share of the total value of assets acquired in mergers and were increasing markedly their share of the total assets.[3] Between 1961 and 1968 the 28 largest firms had increased their shares of total UK assets from 31 per cent to 40 per cent.

This sort of evidence raises fears about trends in industrial concentration both within individual industries and in aggregate. Past experience and some

Table 8.2 Number of firms required to account for 50 per cent of net assets in different industries. Industries with a marked increase in concentration.

Industry	End 1957	End 1967
Drink	12	4
Textiles	8	3
Food	7	4
Vehicles	5	2
Clothing and footwear	3	1
Paper, printing and publicity	6	3
Wholesale distribution	21	14

Note: This analysis is based only on the sample population of 2,024 firms studied and does not therefore offer an entirely reliable guide to the actual extent of concentration in those industries.

Source: *A Survey of Mergers* 1958–1968 HMSO (1970), Appendix 10.

forecasts of future trends have been discussed in Chapter 1. The question that has to be asked is whether mergers have a major influence on the level of concentration and if so whether it is likely that concentration increase will continue. There is little doubt that towards the end of the 1960s the government considered that there was a close association between merger activity and the level of concentration [4] and this view was also held for an earlier period by Eveley and Little.[5] However, other commentators have doubted whether this is the case. From a series of 32 industry case studies where concentration was high, Walshe found that mergers had promoted high concentration in one-third of the trades investigated and had some influence in a further third, in other cases relatively faster (internal) growth by smaller firms had reduced the level of concentration that had been built up by merger. Walshe commented, 'in effect, however, we may conclude that internal and external expansion had been equally responsible for the promotion of high concentration'.[6] Two American investigations have also argued that mergers do not exert an unduly powerful influence on concentration.[7]

However, in a review of the evidence used in *A Survey of Mergers 1958 to 1968* Utton argued that the relatively greater rate of growth by the large firms shown was overstated by the fact that firm sizes at the end of the period under investigation had been used to determine the rank order of firms by size rather than sizes at the start of the period. He showed that had ranking by size at the start of the period been used no correlation between the ranking by size and the rate of growth would have been found. Consequently the published figures overstated the rate at which concentration had been increasing in the United Kingdom. Utton also showed that the largest firms ranked by size in 1954 had, by 1965, achieved a lower proportion of their growth through merger than had relatively smaller companies and consequently the effect of mergers on concentration had also been overstated.[8] This does not mean that the impact of mergers on concentration levels is unimportant. Rather, it serves to emphasise that care has to be taken in using appropriate statistical measures and that concentration increases may come about for reasons unconnected with mergers. Equally the long-run effects of mergers will depend upon other factors such as the rate of growth of the market, relative rates of growth of different sized firms, new entry, rates of product innovation and technical change and competition from imports.

But is there any justification for government intervention in mergers at all? Some economists and indeed some firms have argued that there should be no official interference with the normal processes of the market where mergers are concerned. They argue that there exists a market for corporate control through takeovers and general stock market activities and this is a more appropriate means of obtaining the right mergers rather than direct official intervention either to promote or restrain mergers.[9] As might be expected neither the Board of Trade nor the Monopolies Commission have accepted this argument. The Board of Trade argued that official intervention is necessary where a divergence between private and social interests may occur especially over questions concerning likely factory closures, the distribution of wealth and the concentration of economic power.[10] It was also pointed out at that time that the Industrial Reorganisation Corporation (IRC) existed to promote desirable mergers that the market had not achieved, presumably there too the market and the IRC had different opinions as to what mergers were desirable. Indeed this was reflected in the government's own justification for setting up the IRC: 'there is no evidence that we can rely on market forces alone to produce the necessary structural change at the pace required. Some of the industries most in need of rationalisation have an inbuilt tendency to stay as they are'.[11] The Monopolies Commission also rejected the argument that the stock market is the best arbiter of the efficiency aspects of a merger,[12] claiming that the Commission has more information than the market and is therefore better able to assess the issues. Further, the Commission claimed that shareholders are interested in personal financial gains rather than efficiency and the two are not directly related. On balance there does seem to be a case for government involvement in merger policy since the private interest of the firms concerned may not be identical with the public interest however defined.

Economic analysis and mergers

Economic analysis of the likely effects of mergers tends to concentrate mainly on situations where large firms with some degree of market dominance are involved. In Chapter 7 we considered the effects of mergers from the point of view of the constituent elements in the firms concerned. Here we shall pay attention to the public interest issues of the sorts most likely to be considered by government and policy-makers in their desire to maximise the welfare derived by the community from its use of scarce productive resources. In this respect it is convenient to bear in mind the three concepts of economic efficiency that are normally discussed by welfare economists. The first is allocative efficiency which, loosely speaking, concerns whether the right products are produced in the right quantity. The second is technical efficiency which is concerned to achieve production of the right quantities at least cost. The third is distributive efficiency which is concerned with the way in which the aggregate output is allocated among members of the community. All three are relevant to discussions of public policy towards mergers.[13]

Present-day thinking on the economic consequences of major mergers tends to emphasise that there may be either benefits or disadvantages from a merger or, most probably, a mixture of the two. In the USA, however, governmental policy and the attitude of some economists is less inclined to accept that there may be economic advantages. Analysis of the likely consequences will therefore need to be concerned with prediction and a balancing of the likely benefits and detriments. Two predictions are, strictly speaking, required. Not only must the consequences of the merger proceeding be predicted but this should then be contrasted with a prediction of the way the situation would develop if the merger did not take place.

While certain general principles that would be applicable to most situations can be identified it is likely that the nature of the outcome in each case will be influenced by features that are unique to the industry concerned – the relative sizes, market positions and competitive relationships of the firms concerned, the history of the industry, the role of the firms involved within the industry, the quality of their respective managements, their managerial and competitive philosophies, the rate of change of technology in the industry and the state of demand for the products of the industry. In addition prediction of the market consequences of a merger involves a correct identification of the relevant market on which the analysis should be based, whether it should be narrowly or broadly defined and the role that should be attributed to potential competition through the threat of new entry. This listing of relevant factors that ought to be considered should serve to emphasise the complexity of the analysis that is required. Unfortunately policy-making is not helped by the almost total absence of any follow-up investigation on the effects of mergers viewed from any standpoint other than the private interests of the firm, whether defined as managers or shareholders. Investigation of the total public interest consequences of major mergers that have proceeded would seem to be a high priority.

Benefits from mergers may be hoped for from the advantages of larger scales of activities, better co-ordination and rationalisation and the injection of more aggressive management. The opportunity to achieve greater economies of scale or other synergistic benefits should appeal both to the firms concerned to whom this may be a source of increased profits and to government to whom the opportunity to obtain a given output from a smaller total of factor inputs would indicate a real resource saving. Rationalisation and specialisation of production and marketing activities could be important benefits. Mergers may be seen as a highly desirable means of restructuring an industry to reduce excess capacity, to achieve the operating advantages of large size, or an increased ability to provide funds to finance modernisation and new investments, or to undertake more effective research and development and to introduce important process or product innovation. An acquisition by a more successful or efficient firm which probably implies a superior management team should be beneficial because the existing level of assets should be more profitably and efficiently utilised. Better management may mean a more aggressive outlook in terms of both domestic and international competition and so a reduction in the number of firms as a result of merger may lead to increased competition and an improved export performance.

But mergers may give rise to detriments, particularly in respect of their effects on competition and efficiency. The traditional case against mergers emphasises that a merger (especially, but not solely, a horizontal merger) will lead to increased market dominance, a reduction in competition and hence an increase in prices and a reduction in output. This has some validity but does not tell the whole story. Some commentators would argue that the fear of an increase in prices and profits was not necessarily an important detriment to be considered, since extra profits may be used to finance new investment and research and development and are anyway subject to high rates of taxation. They also suggest that price controls and the threat of investigation by the Monopolies Commission can be used to deal with the possibility of an adverse performance by a dominant firm.[14] There are also those who argue that the welfare loss due to monopoly in a society is small [15] and consequently that there is less reason to fear adverse effects from mergers that generate increased market power.

However, there are still considerable grounds for fears concerning the effects of mergers on competition. In many industries increasing concentration is likely to mean tighter oligopoly and greater emphasis on price leading and forms of non-price competition that may be considered socially less desirable. If a merger does change the balance of power in an industry it may encourage further mergers as other firms seek to re-establish their own positions. This is the problem of incipiency and seems to be highly relevant in some important industries. Again, a merger may, by creating a powerful leader in a market, force other firms to acquiesce in its leadership and discourage attempts to compete with it for fear that the greater over-all strength of the leader would enable it to drive the others out of existence. Any merger involves the loss of an independent decision-making unit and may have the effect of removing a fast growing and successful company which might have successfully challenged its acquirer had it been allowed to remain independent. Reduction of choice to consumers as a result of a merger is one problem, reduction of the number of decision-makers who may have taken a different view of market prospects and the type of innovations to back may be an equally important disadvantage and may mean that the merger leads in the long run to a loss of allocative efficiency.

The possibility that mergers lead to a reduction in the quality of performance and hence to a decline in technical efficiency is also sometimes feared. The firm may find that it has grown too large for its existing managerial resources and so experiences an increase in control problems and hence incurs diseconomies. Again it may be that increased market power associated with many mergers increases the ability of firms to pursue non-profit objectives and allows greater opportunity for them to pursue objectives that seek to satisfy the aspirations of managers rather than shareholders. Even if cost savings are potentially available the firm that is protected from competitive pressures may allow its liking for the quiet life or its desire to satisfy managerial objectives to allow costs to creep up and return to the level that would have existed without the merger, or even to above that level. In other words it is possible that the increased protection from competitive pressures that additional firm size and/or market power resulting from mergers will often allow will create a situation in which actual costs are allowed to rise above the minimum level that could be attained. The difference between minimum attainable costs and actual costs for a given level of output was described by Leibenstein as X-inefficiency[16] and recent writings on the question of mergers have placed considerable emphasis on the importance of this influence.[17]

Finally we should note that the possibility that a merger may lead to rationalisation of production or distribution activities and hence cause redundancies has been considered an important detriment to be taken into account.[18] Whether this should really be a relevant consideration in anti-trust policy is a matter that others have challenged. Certainly government has an important responsibility in relation to the creation and maintenance of employment opportunities but is anti-trust policy the right way to adminster it? The danger is that desirable increases in efficiency through merger or in competition through the abandonment of restrictive practices may be hindered if government is concerned that there will be a consequential short-term increase in unemployment. It might be more appropriate that the action which is correct in economic efficiency terms should be taken but at the same time appropriate social policies should be introduced to deal with the important human issues that arise.

So far we have concentrated mainly on issues that are most likely to be applicable to substantial horizontal or vertical mergers and in which the trading-off of potential cost savings against market power increases is most obviously meaningful. But some mergers seem to raise different types of issues. This certainly applies to conglomerate and, to a lesser extent, concentric mergers[19] and indeed in some respects to all cases where firms of 'large' absolute size are either involved or created.

The objections to such mergers centre on two main issues – the effect on market power and the financial behaviour of such firms. While, by definition, a conglomerate or concentric merger does not increase market concentration, it does increase aggregate concentration and hence the concentration of economic wealth and power in a society. It may also affect market conduct in a number of ways. By entering through merger a market in which it was obviously interested in making an investment, the acquiring firm has removed the possible benefit of new entry through the creation of new capacity and thereby of adding to the number of independent decision-making units. In this way a conglomerate or concentric merger reduces the potential competition that might have come from new entry through internal expansion. Some aspects of the market behaviour of large, diversified firms of all sorts may be detrimental to the public interest. They may have 'deep pocket' advantages, where the benefits of their substantial financial resources may be used to influence the pattern of conduct in any particular market. It may be that they will use their aggregate financial strength to subsidise the activities in one particular market either through predatory behaviour using severe short-run price competition to weaken other competitors in order to enhance the long-run market position, or they may use their resources to spend heavily on advertising and other pro-motional activities, thereby raising entry barriers against new competition. The use of a 'deep pocket' advantage means that a firm's power in that market is greater than that represented by its market share alone and so the controlling impact of market forces is weakened where diversified firms have freedom in redistributing their resources between activities. A further fear is that as firms grow in size and spread of interests they come increasingly into contact with other similarly large firms and are likely to recognise their own mutual inter-dependence and adopt a live and let live attitude to each other, taking care not to compete strongly in, and indeed not even to enter, each other's markets. Large firms may also tend to make less use of the normal processes of the market in acquiring supplies but may increase their reliance on reciprocal dealing both between subsidiaries within the same organisation and possibly between giant firms in general.

The second main type of objection to conglomerates is based on aspects of their financial operations. It is argued that they lack a sound capital structure, base their acquisition activities on the issue of paper that is not backed by real assets and that their limited disclosure of the performance of operating sub-sidiaries makes a realistic appraisal of their activities difficult.

Some at least of the objections to the consequences of conglomerate mergers mentioned in the previous paragraphs seem to be based on reasonable fears rather than observed practice though other objections are clearly justified in individual cases if not in relation to the performance of all such organisations. The firms themselves would argue that they do not like reciprocal trading and that divisions anxious to obtain funds for new developments are not likely to be happy if scarce resources are used to subsidise a loss-making activity in another division. It has been suggested [20] that the allocation of investment funds is more efficient when undertaken within a conglomerate organisation, at least one that is organised on a multi-divisional basis, since the firm operates as its own capital market. It is also claimed that because of its large resources, a conglomerate organisation may be better able and more willing to undertake projects with a high risk but offering a high social pay-off than smaller organisations. New entry through merger by large firms may offer increased competition in an industry when the firm it acquires would not have had the financial or managerial strength to maintain strong competitive pressure on the other firms in the industry. Some synergies or scale economies may be attained especially in the financial area but also possibly, depending on the degree of concentricity involved, in the fields of production, marketing and research and development. Leyland has argued that if the acquired firm is one with a poor stock market performance due to the failure of its management to maximise the potential of its resources then an acquisition, even if subsequently followed by a resale of all or some of its assets, could represent economic benefit since the utilisation of resources should be improved.[21]

The problem for policy-making is that, in all major mergers at least, many different economic issues and possibilities arise. Thus public policy decision-making on a merger involves not only forecasting future developments but weighting the significance of the different factors considered and then trying to assess the relative overall balance of advantages and disadvantages. One problem is that both benefits and detriments may occur from the same action. The rationalisation of production may lead to cost savings but also to re-dundancies, increased market power may lead to higher prices and profits but possibly also to a better export performance or higher investment. A merger where little or no action is taken to integrate may have far less impact one way or the other than one where post-merger activity gives rise to both benefits and detriments. How then do we decide whether a merger should be allowed and how do we attempt to weight the different influences and interests that must be taken into account?

Many economists would probably agree that policy-making on mergers is amenable to a form of cost-benefit appraisal in which the advantages and disadvantages of a particular merger are traded off against each other.[22] The most explicit formulation of a trade-off model has been advanced by Oliver Williamson.[23] His concern was with the occasional cases of mergers where both efficiency and market power consequences were important and therefore needed to be balanced in order to assess the allocative implications of a merger. The background to his paper is clearly to be found in the fact that the American courts would not allow economies of scale as a defence in cases where the legality of a merger was under investigation and he was concerned to show that in certain cases it would be appropriate to allow such an argument in the courts.

He was however at pains to emphasise that, as set out, his model was a naive one and based on the assumption that before the merger took place the market was more or less perfectly competitive with price equal to average cost. The model is shown in Figure 8.1. It is assumed that the merger creates some monopoly power and so price rises from P_1 to P_2 but some efficiency gains are achieved which allow costs to fall from AC_1 to AC_2. Consequently the price-cost margin has also increased. Consumers have suffered an increase in prices and have therefore incurred a deadweight loss represented by the triangle X Y Z, but resource savings have been made approximating to the rectangle U V W X. The net allocative effects are determined by the difference between the rectangle and the triangle. If U V W X is greater than X Y Z the merger has resulted in a net efficiency gain.

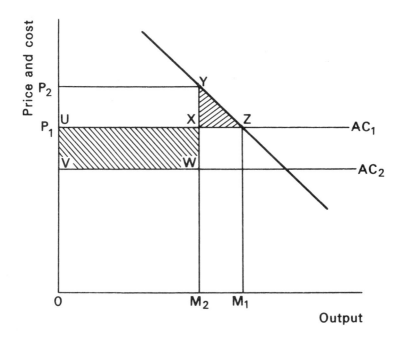

Fig 8.1 A trade-off model for assessing the net effect of a merger

Williamson then proceeded to show that the size of cost reduction required to offset even a sizeable price increase, given alternative values of the elasticity of demand, is quite small. For example he showed that if a reduction in unit costs of 5 to 10 per cent is available as a result of the merger, then the merger must give rise to price increases in excess of 20 per cent if the value of the elasticity of demand is -2, or more than 40 per cent if the elasticity of demand is $-\frac{1}{2}$ before the net allocative effects become negative. He concluded that his naive model indicated that if non-trivial real economies are obtained from the merger then there would have to be a substantial market power increase and relatively large price increases for the net allocative effects to be negative. The model is a formal statement of the analysis which has underlain British merger policy since 1965 though there is no evidence that British policy has in any sense taken into account consideration of the sorts of orders of magnitude that would be involved for mergers to offer the net benefits or net detriments that Williamson suggested in his paper.

However, Williamson's actual numerical conclusions may be of very limited practical significance and he himself emphasised many of the qualifications to the applicability of his results. Nevertheless, in view of the value of the model as a tool of analysis it is worth mentioning here some of the limitations.

The model assumes perfect competition before the merger. The results have therefore little to offer where judgements are involved on a merger that involves an increase in the degree of oligopoly that already exists in an industry. It does not necessarily follow that a merger will leave unchanged the elasticity of the industry demand curve. A merger might, by allowing increased profits, permit the firm concerned to increase the differentiation of the product and so make new entry more difficult and consumer attachment to a particular brand stronger. The analysis tends to concentrate only on the performance of the merged firm and does not allow for the possibility that non-merging firms may also raise their prices, perhaps following a price leader, or that one merger will generate other mergers and hence higher prices in the same industry. The model has no time dimensions. It is quite likely that cost savings will ultimately be achieved through internal expansion, particularly as a result of the natural growth of the market, without necessarily incurring any adverse market power consequences. Effective analysis should really consider the alternative time paths of the efficiency gains through mergers compared with natural growth before trading these off against the deadweight loss. It may be that other disadvantages may be introduced as a result of the merger, through adverse effects on the rate of technical progress and through the possibility that the pressure to maintain full operating efficiency, and hence minimum costs, may be reduced.

Williamson also assumed that income distribution effects can be ignored although the model indicates that there is a transfer of benefits away from consumers who pay higher prices and in favour of producers (managers, employees and shareholders, he does not distinguish between them) who benefit directly or indirectly from the greater profits. Again there would be considerable support for the view that anti-trust policy is not the place to deal with distributional questions[24] though we shall later suggest that there may be reasons for taking a stronger line in favour of the consumer and for the adoption of a presumption in favour of pressure to pass on cost savings in the form of price reductions.

British merger policy

(1)   *Ministerial Action*

Until 1965 there had been in Britain no provision for direct governmental controls on the merger activities of firms. The opportunity to refer to the Monopolies Commission any dominant firms that had been created by merger, as in any other manner, had existed since 1948 but there is little evidence that concern about their merger activities had been an important reason for references of firms.[25] In 1965 legislation was passed which allowed references to the Monopolies Commission of mergers where, as the result of the merger, at least one-third of the market was in the hands of a single supplier or where the value of the assets acquired exceeded £5m.[26] The key provisions have been incorporated in the Fair Trading Act 1973, although the market share criterion for reference has been reduced from 33 to 25 per cent. Where the Commission found in the case of a merger referred to it that either of these criteria were satisfied it was then required to report whether the merger operated or might be expected to operate against the public interest. In addition, newspaper mergers normally had to be investigated by the Monopolies Commission.

The arrangements for administration of merger policy have normally been located in the Board of Trade, now the Department of Trade and Industry (DTI). References are made by the Secretary of State upon the advice of an inter-departmental committee of civil servants but the vast majority of mergers have been allowed to proceed. Since the Fair Trading Act 1973 the formal administration of the policy has been the responsibility of staff in the Office of Fair Trading but references to the Commission are still the responsibility of the Secretary of State for Consumer Affairs. As our concern here is mainly with actions taken before the passing of the Fair Trading Act, our discussion will refer to actions by the Board of Trade and the DTI. There is no formal registration procedure for mergers but it appears that the merger panel readily acquires details of all the major mergers. It then sets in motion an investigation to establish whether there are any reasons why a merger which qualifies for reference to the Commission under either or both of the criteria should in fact be referred. In reviewing the need for a reference the staff of the panel will see the parties concerned and often receive representations from other interested parties.

The factors considered in these investigations are set out in the Board of Trade *Handbook on Mergers*[27] but the weighting attached to the different considerations is not quantified and appears to vary from merger to merger. The general objective which merger policy seeks to advance is 'to increase industrial efficiency and international competitiveness'. The panel makes its own balancing of possible detriments and expected benefits. Its function is clearly predictive and it attempts to assess not only the potential benefits but also the chances that the management of the acquiring firm will actually realise the available gains. It also takes into account the relative strengths of the acquiring and acquired firm, the implication being that it would be less enthusiastic about a weak firm acquiring a strong firm. Besides the economic consequences normally considered in merger policy such as the effects on competition and efficiency, the panel also considers the likely impact of the merger on the balance of payments, on regional policy and the likely amount of redundancy. It seems that the government is particularly anxious about the effects of mergers on employment levels in assisted areas and this is likely to be a matter on which the government would attempt to obtain assurances from the firm concerned before permitting a merger.[28] The handbook emphasises that a decision to refer a proposed merger to the Monopolies Commission does not indicate that the merger is necessarily contrary to the public interest.

Since the legislation was passed over 800 proposed or actual mergers have been investigated which seemed to satisfy at least one of the criteria for reference to the Monopolies Commission. The yearly pattern of examinations, references and the numbers of mergers abandoned after references were made are set out in Table 8.3. Only 27 mergers have been the subject of a reference to the Commission, and this represents just about 3 per cent of all qualifying mergers. References have normally been on the assets and market share criteria or on the assets criterion alone. Undoubtedly this is a much easier basis for reference and overcomes the possibility that references may be made on the basis of information about market shares alone which subsequently proves to be inaccurate or where the definition of the market has been inappropriate. The small proportion of references made has been criticised[29] but this seems to reflect the fact that for a large part of the time during which the legislation has been in existence the government has taken the view that industrial reorganisation and increasing concentration was desirable and so the balance has probably been in favour of not hindering most mergers. Nevertheless this does have the disadvantage that there have been few precedents to allow firms to deduce the key criteria on which decisions whether or not to refer are made. It also means that the majority of decisions on the public interest issues, even in the case of major mergers, are taken by government, and this effectively means the civil service, rather than by the Monopolies Commission. Towards the end of 1972 there was, however, a hint of change of policy. The Secretary of State commented:

> If there is a doubt about whether a reference is desirable the balance is likely in future to be struck in favour of referring rather than not referring. Certainly we expect to refer mergers where the sole aim is quick short-term gains from asset stripping. Although conglomerate mergers do not necessarily diminish competition where such conglomerate mergers raise doubts we shall not hesitate to refer them to the Commission.[30]

Certainly in 1973 there seems to have been a marked increase in the number

Table 8.3   Action taken on mergers since 1965

Year	Number of mergers examined	References made excluding newspaper mergers	Newspaper mergers referred	Mergers abandoned after reference made
1965	50[1]	1	–	–
1966	60	5[2]	1	–
1967	90	1	1	–
1968	130	2	–	–
1969	110	3	1	1
1970	90	2	–	1
1971	110	1	–	1
1972	120	3[2]	1	1
1973	85	9	1	4

Notes: [1] 10 months only.
  [2] Counting the bids for the Amalgamated Dental Co. Ltd. as two references and counting the bids for Glaxo as two references.

Sources: *Board of Trade Journal; Trade and Industry; Annual Reports on the working of the Monopolies Commission.* See also J. D. Gribbin 'The operation of the Merger Panel since 1965' *Trade and Industry* (17 January 1974) p. 70.

of references made to the Commission and the reduction in the Fair Trading Act in the market share criterion for reference from one-third to one-quarter may increase still further the proportion of proposed mergers that are referred.

From the last column in Table 8.3 it seems that the mere fact of a reference may have the effect of stopping a merger. It is surprising that such a high proportion of the proposed mergers recently referred to the Commission have been abandoned. The actual cases concerned have been Marley/Redland; Burmah/Laporte; Reed/Bowater; Timpson/Sears; Whessoe/Capper Neil; Tarmac/Wolsley Hughes; Armitage Shanks/Glynwed; Bowater/Hanson Trust. In some other cases a decision to refer a merger to the Monopolies Commission had been taken but before the formal references could be made the merger plans had been abandoned. Cases in this category included Imperial Tobacco/Smith's Crisps; Valor/Rippingilles.[31] Even where the Monopolies Commission has conducted an investigation and approved a proposed merger it does not necessarily follow that it will proceed. Both the proposed dental goods mergers and that between Unilever and Allied Breweries failed to take place in the end. It seems that there are often too many of these instances for them all to be due to random influences and their relatively high incidence suggests that an explanation ought to be sought. In some cases it seems the firms concerned may have thought their chances of success before the Commission were slim and preferred to use their management's time and resources on other activities. Or it may be that there were some facets of their activities that they wished to keep from public scrutiny. It may be that in the intervening period relative movements in the share prices of the companies concerned moved adversely. If this is the explanation it indicates that the market did not think much of the proposed acquisitions at least on the terms proposed or it points to 'the melancholy conclusion that share price considerations were more important than economic and business factors'.[32]

The most likely explanation, however, is the more simple one that the managements of the firms concerned realised on further reflection that perhaps their plans to merge were not such a good idea after all. If this is so, it is arguable that the mere fact of a reference to the Monopolies Commission may have a desirable effect in encouraging firms to reappraise their intentions and consider again the desirability of the particular merger. If so high a proportion of firms involved in referred mergers decide not to proceed one wonders how high is the level of regret after other mergers that were not referred have been completed. Certainly the evidence reviewed in Chapter 7 suggests that many firms may have cause to regret particular acquisitions. The question therefore arises whether it might not be desirable to enforce a compulsory 'cooling-off' or 'engagement' period before any large merger is allowed to proceed. During this period firms would have the opportunity to assess more extensively their chances of gaining synergies, to establish their reorganisation and integration proposals and, if they do think there is little chance of the merger proving successful on their own criteria, to withdraw without loss of face.

Other mergers that have been allowed to proceed without reference to the Monopolies Commission have been the subject of assurances extracted from the firms by the ministry concerned. The sorts of assurances given include undertakings by the firms that they will not discriminate in price or over supply arrangements; they will consult with government and trade unions regarding the implications of the merger for their employees and will take into account government regional and redundancy policies; they will not misuse the market power that the merger produces; they will maintain or increase exports; they will maintain and expand the acquired company's business; they will buy British; they will preserve the separate identity of the acquired company and/or maintain separate accounts for it.[33] This use of assurances is open to criticism. Many of the assurances are vague and non-operational. Some impinge directly on the acquiring firm's use of its own commercial judgement – what supplies it buys, not to integrate but to preserve a company's separate identity, etc. They would be very difficult to enforce and indeed there are no formal powers to enforce assurances unless they follow from a Monopolies Commission report. The ability of the civil servants, in a quick investigation, to identify all relevant issues and to frame appropriate assurances is doubtful. The over-all effect must be to reduce the number of cases sent to the Commission and hence increase the probability that only particularly doubtful mergers may be referred.

In making a merger reference the minister may indicate some considerations that the Commission should particularly take into account. Normally, however, no particular matters are specified. The minister also has the power to hold up a merger while an investigation is in progress. In some cases, however, (BMC/Pressed Steel; GKN/Birfield; BICC/Pyrotenax) the merger has been allowed to proceed while the Commission's investigation was in progress. This has been defended on the grounds that otherwise it allows a bid-for company to organise its defences against the bid, even to the extent of undertaking a capital reconstruction in order to make it harder for it to be acquired.[34] However, there seems to be a strong practical reason for holding up any merger that is referred. Even though there are now powers to order divestiture after a merger has been completed it seems likely that the Monopolies Commission would apply less stringent criteria in deciding whether a merger would be contrary to the public interest if it has already been completed than if the firms' actions in this respect have been stayed until the Commission has reported. It seems as though a reference while the merger is allowed to proceed is intended to do little more than ask the Commission to place on record what particular dangers might be guarded against and what undertakings should be sought to protect the public interest. However, the chances of an adverse finding on the public interest question must be much reduced.

In concluding this review of direct ministerial action on mergers we should comment on the action taken after a report has been received by the Monopolies Commission. Normally where the Commission decides against a merger the firms concerned agree to drop their proposals. In the case of Rank's bid for De La Rue, after receipt of the Commission's adverse report, the government made an order prohibiting the merger. In the case of the proposed merger between Barclays and Lloyds Banks, the Commission was divided with six members opposed and four in favour. There was not therefore the two-thirds majority opinion necessary for the government to act upon the report. In its review of the issues the government then decided that such a merger would be against the public interest and stated that it considered the danger that such a merger would lead to the creation of a duopoly was greater than either the majority or the minority members of the Commission had anticipated.[35] The parties concerned then abandoned their merger plans.

(2) *The Industrial Reorganisation Corporation*

Although the Industrial Reorganisation Corporation (IRC) is no longer in existence its activities are highly relevant to a consideration of merger policy in Britain over the last few years. It was set up in the latter part of 1966 and wound up in 1971. It was established because the government felt there was a need for concentration and rationalisation to promote greater efficiency and international competitiveness in British industry. The government had no confidence that market forces alone would bring about desired structural changes at the right pace and so created the IRC to provide the initiative and sponsorship that was considered to be lacking.[36]

It had two main roles, first, to encourage structural reorganisation, eliminating duplication and gaining scale economies through mergers and the hiving-off of subsidiaries, and secondly, to assist an individual company in an expansion or modernisation scheme by making available to it financial assistance. Our interest here is with the former role. Its efforts were concentrated particularly in industries where structural reorganisation had been slow or non-existent and where rapid technological change and/or intense competition made rationalisation particularly desirable. While size per se was not considered to be the solution, the IRC argued that size could provide the essential base for the large scale of effort needed to prosper in world markets.[37] It paid particular attention to the quality of management in deciding which mergers to support and looked for a merger that would have wide repercussions throughout an industry and would lay the basis for far-reaching changes in the structure of that industry. This philosophy is most revealing, especially as it was announced at a time when to some extent the Monopolies Commission and the government were expressing concern about the dangers of incipiency when assessing the likely consequences of mergers in other industries. No doubt different industries and different problems demand varying responses. But this does serve to indicate the potential difficulties that can arise where two pieces of legislation are apparently at cross-purposes with each other. The situation was made to appear from the outside even more remarkable since one ministry (Ministry of Technology) was responsible for the work of the IRC while a different one (Board of Trade, then Department of Employment, then Department of Trade and Industry) was responsible for administering the Monopolies and Mergers Act. It was rumoured that conflicts had arisen between the two ministries that had had to be settled at cabinet level. We do, however, know that none of the mergers sponsored by the IRC was referred to the Monopolies Commission even though some of them were very large in size and had substantial market power implications. On the other hand some of these mergers were the subject of assurances given, by the parties concerned, to the Board of Trade.

Much of the IRC's work was conducted in secret but its annual reports indicate the extent of the impact it claimed to have. It had been involved in 90 projects (not all of which were mergers) of which it reported that at least 75 were turning out as expected.[38] It had sponsored or contributed to major reorganisation in numerous key industries including motor vehicles, computers, the electrical industry, electronics, ball bearings, mechanical engineering, mining machinery, trawling, paper and scientific instruments and therefore had exerted an important influence on the structure of many British industries. Sometimes its tactics did not endear it to all sides of industry. It supported a bidding company (GEC) when the management of the company to be acquired (AEI) was resisting the merger. It bought shares in the open market in an attempt to ensure that George Kent gained control of Cambridge Instruments rather than Rank in a major merger in the scientific instrument industry.

Hopefully the activities of the IRC in restructuring British industries have been advantageous. No systematic attempt seems to have been made to assess whether this has been the case. The danger, however, is that excessive enthusiasm for the promotion of mergers may have been achieved at the cost of detriments which the IRC had not considered.

(3) The Monopolies Commission on Mergers

Where it receives a merger reference the Monopolies Commission is required to do two things. It has to report whether the grounds for investigation (market share or size of assets to be acquired) specified in the reference are satisfied and if so whether the merger would be expected to operate against the public interest. Note that the Commission is not required to be satisfied that a merger would be in the public interest and a neutral balance of advantages and disadvantages would be sufficient to allow the merger to proceed.

As we have already noted, only a very small proportion of mergers that qualified for reference to the Monopolies Commission have been so referred. The pressure for industrial reorganisation, the acceptance of assurances in place of a reference and the abandonment of mergers that were referred have all helped to reduce the number of reports by the Commission. At the time of writing 13 reports have been published (excluding those on newspaper mergers). In two reports (on mergers in the dental goods and pharmaceutical industries) two different merger proposals have been considered and the report on the banks merger rejected the major merger between Barclays and Lloyds but was prepared to sanction the acquisition of Martins by either of the other two parties. The broad features of each of the Commission's merger reports are set out in Table 8.4.

An important issue especially in the case of horizontal mergers is the correct definition of the market.[39] If it is widely drawn then it is likely that the impact upon it of any given merger will not be as large as if it is narrowly defined. The crucial question is not whether there is *any* substitution between alternative products but *how much* substitutability there is. The Commission has often gone carefully into this issue and considered relevant information such as the pattern of buyer behaviour and the pricing relationships between the firms supplying different but possibly substitutable products in reaching a conclusion. In several important cases it has indicated that the relevant market is to be narrowly defined as there is only a low degree of substitutability between the products in the narrowly defined market and those that would constitute a more broadly defined market. Thus in Ross/Associated Fisheries the appropriate market for analysis of the effects of the merger was not that for all fish but only cod landed at the Humber ports of Hull and Grimsby. In BICC/Pyrotenax it was mineral insulated cables, not all cables; in UDS/Montague Burton it was cheap men's

Table 8.4   Analysis of mergers reported on by the Monopolies Commission

Merger	Date of Report	Type of merger	Relevant market	Market shares (a) acquiring company (b) acquired company in relevant market	Size of net assets acquired
BMC/ Pressed Steel	1966	vertical	—	—	£33m
Ross/ Associated Fisheries	1966	mainly horizontal but some vertical elements	Distant water cod landed at the Humber Ports	(a) 19 per cent (b) 32 per cent (of white fish landed at Humber ports)	£16.8m
Dental Mfg./ Amalgamated Dental	1966	Horizontal and some product extension	Dental goods	(a) 17 per cent (b) 33 per cent (of total home trade in dental goods)	£9.3m

| Commission findings | | | Other influences on decisions |
Benefits	Detriments	Public interest	
1) some savings from increased specialisation and co-ordinated production planning 2) gains in overseas operations and exports by Pressed Steel 3) Avoids waste of resources in long run from BMC establishing its own body production facilities	Risk that Pressed Steel would not maintain its supply of car bodies for independent customers	Not against the public interest Unanimous	1) Pressed Steel's position precarious 2) Advantages in Pressed Steel being owned by a British company 3) Commission said assurances that Pressed Steel would continue to supply their other customers on fair and reasonable terms were an important influence on the decision
Small savings from raising trawling efficiency of Ross and amalgamating transport facilities. But these not significant, would not result in lower retail prices and would not significantly improve the financial position of the two companies	1) Would give the combined firm very great and growing power over the market 2) Competition between the two companies needed to bring about efficiency improvements	Against the public interest 2 dissentients	1) No prospect of other mergers to counterbalance the combined size of Ross/AF 2) Merger would not contribute significantly to strengthening of the fishing industry
Some savings, especially in production and distribution	1) No detriments to competition 2) Some doubt whether Dental Mfg. would successfully integrate into one firm 3) Risk of loss of overseas sales	Not against public interest Unanimous	1) Dental Manufacturing had good record in dental goods and efficient management 2) Countervailing buying power from Ministry of Health 3) Competition from imports

Table 8.4—continued

Merger	Date of Report	Type of merger	Relevant market	Market shares (a) acquiring company (b) acquired company in relevant market	Size of net assets acquired
Dentists' Supply Co./ Amalgamated Dental	1966	Geographic market extension	Dental goods	(a) 0 per cent (b) 33 per cent (of total home trade in dental goods but some Dentists' Supply Co. products sold in UK by Amalgamated Dental	£9.3m
GKN/ Birfield	1967	Horizontal	(i) propellor shafts and constant velocity joints (ii) drop forgings	(i) (a) 27 per cent (b) 73 per cent (ii) (a) 39 per cent (b) 5 per cent	£18.8m
BICC/ Pyrotenax	1967	Horizontal some vertical aspects	mineral insulated cable	(a) approx. 47 per cent (b) approx. 48 per cent (of home and export sales of m.i.c. assuming Glynwed has 5 per cent of total sales)	N/A

Commission findings			Other influences
Benefits	Detriments	Public interest	on decisions
Immediate gains of currency for UK -	1) No detriments to competition 2) Loss of remission to UK of export earnings 3) Small risk that Dentists' Supply would reduce production in UK	Not against public interest 1 dissentient	1) Countervailing buying power from Ministry of Health 2) Competition from imports
1) Scope for some saving by concentrating manufacture in specialised plant 2) Possibility of gain in export sales	1) Loss of possibility that GKN would enter the constant velocity joint market independently 2) Monopoly supplier may be more cautious in production planning but not a significant risk to security of supply 3) Ability to use market power in one line to influence demand for other products but no serious abuse likely	Not against the public interest Unanimous	Birfield unlikely to remain independent. No other potential merger that would offer greater advantages. Fear of foreign takeover. Countervailing power of motor car assemblers will keep initial equipment prices down
1) Possible gains from rapid increase in exports 2) Small savings from better production planning and exchange of technical experience 3) Lower price of copper tubes to Pyrotenax but not solely dependent on merger 4) More rapid increase in exports, avoidance of duplication overseas and therefore resource saving	1) Sharp reduction in competition, higher prices, less good service 2) Reduced incentive to expand sales of m.i.c. 3) Fear that BICC would squeeze customers that were also competitors 4) Possibility that BICC would use m.i.c. as a loss leader to gain sales of other cables or to drive Glynwed out of the m.i.c. market	Not against the public interest Unanimous	Assurances were important in avoiding the danger of unfair competition or discrimination against BICC's customers

Table 8.4—continued

Merger	Date of Report	Type of merger	Relevant market	Market shares (a) acquiring company (b) acquired company in relevant market	Size of net assets acquired
UDS/ Montague Burton	1967	Horizontal	retailing of men's suits costing up to £20	(a) and (b) combined 45–50 per cent	£640m
Banks The two mergers were Barclays/ Lloyds and Barclays or Lloyds/ Martins	1968	Horizontal	Banking services	Barclays 24 per cent Lloyds 18 per cent Martins 5 per cent	Gross Assets Barclays £4534m Lloyds £2639m Martins £573m
Thorn/ Radio Rentals	1968	Horizontal some vertical aspects	mainly specialist television rental	(a) 18 per cent (b) 27 per cent	£36.8m

Commission findings			Other influences on decisions
Benefits	Detriments	Public interest	
Negligible efficiency gains	1) Reduced competition in sale of men's suits 2) fear of further mergers leading to oligopoly 3) Some concern about increased power in buying wool cloth supplies	Against the public interest 1 dissentient	
1) Some saving from rationalisation of outlets and on computerisation but would take some time to achieve 2) Trivial balance of payments advantage	1) Loss of source of finance would be serious to small and medium sized firms 2) Some inconvenience to public from closing of branches 3) Reduction in the number of decision - making u n i t s would lessen the chances of desirable competition and innovation. Might be a decrease in operating efficiency	6 members said Lloyds / Barclays merger would be against the public interest, 4 said would not be against the public interest No objection to merger between either Barclays or Lloyds and Martins	Competition and innovation would be keener with four banks of equal size
1) Savings in production of television sets 2) Savings in rental activities in accounting administration, servicing, distribution	Some danger that competition between manufacturers would lead to increased vertical integration and rigidity in market shares and an artificial division of the market. But this largely discounted	Not against the public interest 1 dissentient	Competition between manufacturers would remain strong and competition from imports increasing

Table 8.4—continued

Merger	Date of Report	Type of merger	Relevant market	Market shares (a) acquiring company (b) acquired company in relevant market	Size of net assets acquired
Unilever/ Allied Breweries	1969	Product extension/ concentric marketing	—	—	£307.3m
Rank/ De La Rue	1969	con- glomerate	—	—	£39.2m

Commission findings			Other influences on decisions
Benefits	Detriments	Public interest	
1) Some greater efficiency in the use of resources especially in technology and marketing 2) Merger may stimulate other brewers to greater efficiency and competition 3) Some gains in R and D effort and in process innovation and rising productivity in Allied 4) Some benefits though cross fertilisation of ideas 5) Small balance of payments advantage	1) Loss of potential competition that would result from Unilever's separate entry into the drinks industry 2) Some slight pressure for exclusive intra-firm trading 3) Small risk of anti - competitive consequences of heavy advertising	Not against the public interest Unanimous	
1) Possibility that in the longer term Rank might be able to market some of De La Rue's products more efficiently	1) Danger of creation of exclusive intra-firm trading in some products but insignificant in size 2) Technological exchange would be less easy and opportunities might be lost 3) Merger would adversely affect the present efficient De La Rue management This could lead to a loss of efficiency and of business	Against the public interest Unanimous	

Table 8.4—continued

Merger	Date of Report	Type of merger	Relevant market	Market shares (a) acquiring company (b) acquired company in relevant market	Size of net assets acquired
British Sidac/ Transparent Paper	1970	Horizontal some vertical aspects	Cellophane	(a) 35 per cent (b) 11 per cent	N/A
Beecham/ Glaxo	1972	Horizontal	Research based sector of the British Pharmaceutical Industry	(a) 19 per cent (b) 31 per cent (percentage of prescription medicines supplied by British-owned companies)	£109.1m

Commission findings			Other influences on decisions
Benefits	Detriments	Public interest	
Some savings in administration, selling and overhead expenses but these were speculative	1) Prices of cellophane film expected to increase 2) Reduction in competition that was already weak 3) Slight possibility of higher prices of polypropylene film too	Against the public interest Unanimous	
1) Some benefit in overseas marketing and production through avoidance of duplication. Profits from this would provide more finance for R and D 2) Some benefit in R and D from greater ability to engage in more costly and risky R and D 3) Domestic cost savings from avoidance of duplication of facilities	1) Removal of incentive to Beecham to broaden the base of its research 2) Removal of important independent centre for decision - making on the allocation of funds to research areas could impair chances of continued British success in R and D 3) Damage to morale of Glaxo staff and lower quality and output of work 4) Loss of competition would mean fewer new R and D ideas and loss of a separate source of innovation	Against the public interest Unanimous	Commission clearly anxious to keep a number of separate British pharmaceutical firms to increase the chances of success in the discovery and development of new products

Table 8.4—continued

Merger	Date of Report	Type of merger	Relevant market	Market shares (a) acquiring company (b) acquired company in relevant market	Size of net assets acquired
Boots/ Glaxo	1972	Horizontal and vertical	Research based sector of the British Pharmaceutical Industry	(a) 9 per cent (b) 31 per cent (percentage of prescription medicines supplied by British-owned companies	£109.1m
British Match Corporation/ Wilkinson Sword	1973	Conglomerate with elements of concentric marketing	—	—	£10m

Commission findings			Other influences on decisions
Benefits	Detriments	Public interest	
1) Avoidance of duplication of effort in R and D 2) Financial strength of merged company 3) Ability to engage in R and D projects that would be too costly for either company alone 4) Benefit to exports and balance of payments through better facilities for overseas marketing of Boots products 5) Increased profits from overseas marketing would provide more finance for R and D	1) Removal of incentive to Boots to broaden the base of its research 2) Removal of independent decision-maker on the allocation of funds to research areas	Against the public interest Unanimous	Commission clearly anxious to keep a number of separate British pharmaceutical firms to increase the chances of success in the discovery and development of new products
1) Provision of management to assist British Match in its attempt to diversify 2) The possibility that Wilkinson Products would penetrate new overseas markets more easily and more quickly 3) Greater size and stability of earnings would allow acceptance of a higher degree of investment planning than was possible for Wilkinson alone	—	Not against the public interest Unanimous	Commission did not think British Match and Wilkinson were likely potential entrants into each others' markets. Predatory behaviour not expected. No likelihood that other mergers would be encouraged. Key question was whether the merger would be a success or whether it would waste resources. No adverse effects expected on efficiency

suits not all men's clothing; in British Sidac/Transparent Paper it was cellulose film, not all packaging;[40] in Thorn/Radio Rentals the most relevant market was the specialist television rental market and not all television set supply activities.

One important consequence of this approach to the identification of the appropriate market for analysis is that in terms of its share in the relevant market the firm to be acquired was often larger than the firm proposing to make the acquisition. This was certainly the case in Ross/Associated Fisheries, both the proposed dental mergers, GKN/Birfield (for propellor shafts and constant velocity joints), Thorn/Radio Rentals, Beecham/Glaxo and Boots/Glaxo. In addition BICC and Pyrotenax both had about the same market shares. It may well be that such mergers are particularly likely to be referred to the Commission though there is no clear evidence that this has a bearing on the likelihood that the Commission will disapprove the merger. One other feature that is quite noticeable from the reports, though not shown in Table 8.4, is the number of cases in which the firm to be acquired or at least some of its officers were less than enthusiastic and in some cases hostile about the merger. Victim firms that seem to have had some reservations about the merger included Amalgamated Dental (in respect of the bid from Dental Manufacturing), Transparent Paper, De La Rue and Glaxo (in respect of the bid from Beecham). When faced with opposition from the firm to be acquired it does seem that perhaps the Monopolies Commission is more likely to conclude that such a merger would be contrary to the public interest.

Although information on the benefits and detriments considered by the Commission can be readily identified from the reports, it is often more difficult to be clear just what weight each carried in influencing the overall public interest conclusion reached by the Commission. There are two reasons relating to the Commission's procedure why this should be so. The first difficulty in interpretation arises because the Commission usually has a different role in appraising benefits as compared with detriments. The benefits to be expected will be claimed by one or both of the parties to the merger and the Commission has simply to decide whether these are realistic claims. Not that this is a simple task! In the case of detriments, however, the Commission has to identify the likely detriments itself (unless it receives evidence from witnesses hostile to the merger) and then decide whether these are likely to be serious. Hence in some cases the Commission seems to be raising the spectre of a detriment in one sentence and writing it off in the next. Secondly, because the Commission ultimately has to present a firm conclusion as to whether a merger would be contrary to the public interest it tends to present the report in such a way that detriments are often heavily discounted if a merger is to be approved and benefits are discounted if a merger is to be opposed. It is not always clear whether the Commission is saying the benefit or detriment has been considered but found not to exist or whether it is really indicating that the benefit or detriment is there but is not sufficient to outweigh the public interest decision taken in the light of other considerations. Although both benefits and detriments are discussed in each report there has been no case so far where the Commission has indicated both the likelihood of substantial benefits and substantial detriments.

The main benefits normally claimed for a merger are cost savings in one form or another. These may arise from specialisation or rationalisation of production, distribution or overhead services, or from better production planning. Generally speaking, however, the Commission has considered the size of the likely savings to be small and it has often rejected such claims altogether. In other cases it has decided that the cost savings could have been obtained without the necessity for a merger or that they would not materially affect the public interest. Often it has not been possible for the Commission to do more than offer a qualitative assessment whether it thinks the savings claimed are reasonable but in the case of the proposed banks mergers it was able to compare the claims made by Barclays, Lloyds and Martins against the plans and estimated savings of National Provincial and Westminster who had been allowed to merge without reference to the Commission. It also had access to information on cost savings achieved through the large Scottish banking merger in 1959 between the National Bank of Scotland and the Commercial Bank of Scotland.

Benefits to the balance of payments have often been claimed and have been considered to have some validity by the Commission in several cases and to be particularly important in BMC/Pressed Steel and BICC/Pyrotenax. The size and significance of the gains has not always been thought to be large and, as with cost savings, it does not follow that just because the possibility of some benefit is established the merger will be allowed to proceed. Other benefits accepted by the Commission tend to have less general applicability. Some gains in research and development as a result of a merger have been accepted but do not necessarily guarantee approval of the merger. Unilever's acquisition of Allied Breweries was thought likely to stimulate competition in brewing and the cross-fertilisation of new ideas. The merger of BMC and Pressed Steel was thought to offer a saving on the resources that would have to be committed if BMC decided to build its own body plant. The advantage of keeping a firm in British control was a benefit of the particular proposals to acquire Pressed Steel and Birfield. The distribution of the likely benefits from a merger does not seem to have concerned the Commission unduly. In several cases it has stated that it is unlikely that consumers would receive any of the benefits and in the Thorn/Radio Rentals and Unilever/Allied Breweries cases the Commission did not raise any objections to the merger even though it specifically commented that it did not anticipate that prices would be reduced as a result.

The detriments identified are rather more wide ranging. The classic fears of higher prices were considered relevant in Ross/Associated Fisheries, BICC/Pyrotenax and British Sidac/Transparent Paper and a general weakening of competition or choice as a result of the merger in Ross/Associated Fisheries, UDS/Montague Burton, Barclays/Lloyds, British Sidac/Transparent Paper, Beecham/Glaxo. The Commission has often paid particularly close attention to the degree of competition between the two firms proposing to merge and if this has been direct and keen and if the merger is thought likely to weaken competition in general there is a high probability that the merger will be found to be contrary to the public interest. In at least some cases, however, prediction of the effect of a merger on the degree of competition in the industry depends on the conduct and performance of the other firms which are not involved in the merger and about whom the Monopolies Commission may have only limited information. Assessments of the effects on competition may therefore require a study of the industry as a whole and this is not practicable granted the time constraints on the Commission's investigation. This problem was emphasised in the case of the British Sidac/Transparent Paper investigation where the role of British Cellophane, the market leader, was crucial to predictions about the likely effects of the merger on competition. Countervailing buying power or growing competitive pressure from imports may encourage the Commission to permit a merger to proceed while the lack of other strong competitive firms in the industry and fears of further mergers may cause the Commission to feel that this is a particularly serious detriment.

The possibility has also been considered that increasing vertical integration or a broadening of the range of products handled may give rise to competitive abuses. Customers that are also competitors may be squeezed and over-all strength in a product range may allow a firm to engage in full-line forcing or price discrimination or in other ways to influence adversely the pattern of competition. In the cases of BMC/Pressed Steel and BICC/Pyrotenax it is clear that assurances given about the subsequent conduct of the firms concerned in these respects were important in encouraging the Commission not to raise objections to the merger. Adverse effects on research and development were feared in the case of the GKN/Birfield merger and the two proposed pharmaceutical mergers. The proposed acquisitions by GKN (in relation to constant velocity joints) and Unilever were thought to raise the detriment that this removed the possibility that the firms concerned might make their own independent entries into the markets in which the firms to be acquired were operating. Adverse effects on morale and managerial efficiency and performance were feared in the cases of the proposed acquisitions by Dental Manufacturing Company, Rank and Beecham.

The case of the bid by Dentists' Supply Company of New York is interesting as it is the only merger that the Commission has been asked to consider where the bidding firm was controlled from abroad. The Commission thought that there might be detriments from a loss of remission of overseas earnings to the United Kingdom and also that there was some danger of a reduction in the level of production in the United Kingdom, but this did not stop the majority of the Commission from concluding that the merger would not be contrary to the public interest.

The only general pointer that can be derived from this review of the benefits and detriments identified by the Monopolies Commission and their bearing on the public interest conclusions is that a merger is most likely to be opposed if it is thought that it will have an adverse effect on the type and degree of competition in the industry. Otherwise the same benefits and detriments seem to be identified equally in cases where the merger is approved and those where it is not. This suggests not unreasonably that the implicit weighting given by the Commission to the same considerations varies markedly from case to case.

Considerable interest was shown in the simultaneous references and reports in 1969 on two 'conglomerate' mergers — Unilever/Allied Breweries and Rank/De La Rue, although on our own criteria (see Chapter 7) the former was really a concentric marketing merger and the latter a pure conglomerate. In the Unilever/Allied Breweries case the Commission decided that the benefits claimed by the companies were somewhat vague and overstated. However, the Commission decided that there was likely to be some gain from greater efficiency in the use of resources, especially in research and development, increased technical efficiency and productivity on the part of Allied and some minor gains in the opportunity for Allied to use some of Unilever's central services and, in the take-home drinks market, from access to Unilever's skills and expertise in market research, presentation and packaging. The Commission found little ground for thinking that there would be significant marketing benefits overseas as a result of the merger and the benefits to the balance of payments appeared to be uncertain and small. It also thought that there was little prospect that any increase in efficiency in Allied Breweries would be reflected in lower prices to the trade or to the consumer. There was, however, thought to be a chance that the exploitation of the efficiencies the merger might produce could cause other brewers to seek greater efficiency themselves, and that the resulting stimulation of competition in the industry might eventually bring benefits to the public.

A number of possible detriments were also considered. The Commission recognised that Unilever was a potential entrant into the drinks industry but the Commission decided the loss of competition that might have ensued if Unilever entered the industry other than by acquiring Allied would be less significant because Unilever was more interested in the international drinks market than the domestic market. The traditional arguments that conglomerates would use their financial power to cross-subsidise an unprofitable activity or that it would increase exclusivity in trading or that there would be a heavy growth of sales expenditure, were all considered and rejected. The Commission also considered the possibility that such a merger might encourage more mergers among the large brewers but decided that it could not say whether this would lead to more competition or less and consoled itself with the observation that such mergers could also be referred to the Commission. The possibility that the merger would produce managerial difficulties was also considered but the Commission thought that Unilever's experience in takeovers would enable it to overcome these problems more easily. The Commission decided that there was no clear indication of likely damage to the public interest and did not therefore oppose the merger although it pointed out that as Unilever's price/earnings ratio at the time of the report was lower than that of Allied, a very large increase in profits would be required for a merger to show a profitable return for Unilever.

The issues considered in the Rank/De La Rue merger were rather less extensive. The tone of the report was set by the Commission's insistence that it was an appropriate body to consider the effect on the efficiency with which resources would be used as a result of the merger. As a 'pure' conglomerate merger there were no market power effects to be considered, so the matter resolved itself into a consideration of the effects on the efficiency of resource use. As the bid was a contested one Rank had no access to information on which to base its claims that there would be benefits, though the Commission was prepared to accept that the greater marketing orientation of Rank would lead to greater efficiency. The Commission did, however, also feel that Rank had underestimated the difficulties involved in trying to raise the efficiency and profitability of De La Rue. Normally in merger investigations efficiency considerations are assessed as likely benefits. Here, however, the Commission decided that the merger would lead to a loss of efficiency and hence this would be a detriment. The Commission feared that the merger would create a serious risk that the efficiency and trading volume of De La Rue would be impaired and that there would be adverse effects on management, personnel and overseas trading and technical exchange connections. Consequently the Commission decided this merger would operate against the public interest.

A pure conglomerate merger such as Rank/De La Rue has negligible competitive consequences and, though a concentric merger may often reduce potential competition, in the case of Unilever/Allied Breweries the Commission chose not to pay much attention to this aspect. Presumably it felt that while competition may be needed in domestic markets, effective export performance may not be so dependent on competition. Overall it seems the Commission did not feel that there would be any significant benefits to the public interest and the approval for the Unilever/Allied merger was very much dependent on the legal formulation of the Commission's responsibilities which merely required it to be satisfied that the merger would not be contrary to the public interest. Had the requirement been that a merger should be *in* the public interest it seems unlikely that the Commission would have reported favourably upon it. In both cases the Commission placed greater emphasis on the management difficulties that might be encountered than it normally did in other merger investigations. In the Rank/De La Rue case management considerations and the attendant fear of loss of efficiency were the main reasons for the rejection of the merger, though it is likely that the opposition by the De La Rue management was also a major contributory reason for the Commission's decision.

More recently the Commission has also considered a third conglomerate merger, between British Match Corporation and Wilkinson Sword Ltd. In this case there was no overlap between products or product markets and there was little ground for thinking that either company was a potential entrant into the other's markets. Both companies had been through difficult phases. British Match had found that its non-match activities were unprofitable and was attempting to reorganise its management structure in order to achieve a greater degree of control over its operations. Wilkinson had been suffering declining profits as a consequence of a straining of resources and severe competition following its introduction of a coated razor blade. The emphasis in the merger was on the advantages to British Match of increasing its stake in the consumer disposable product field and the access to Wilkinson's management resources.

Wilkinson expected some benefits as a result of the larger sized organisation that would be created which should mean that more risky investment projects could be considered and the size of the central organisation and the presence of British Match in overseas markets would allow it to penetrate new markets more rapidly.

The Commission did not consider that on balance there would be any adverse effects on competition or on employment. The main potential drawback and the key issue discussed was the possibility that allowing British Match with an unsuccessful management record to diversify by acquiring Wilkinson could lead to a failure to utilise resources as efficiently as would have happened had the merger not been allowed to proceed. On balance the Commission pronounced itself hopeful on this score: '. . . while there might well be other methods of reaching the same objectives, the merger is more likely than not to lead to more efficient utilisation of the total resources of both companies'.[41]

This report seems to be a model of a concise, clear discussion of the key issues, although the quotation just cited does indicate that the Commission breached a desirable precedent established in earlier reports by not considering any alternative arrangements that might have produced the same benefits without the need for a merger. Since both companies had, for different reasons, been facing difficulties before the merger, it will be particularly interesting to observe whether, in combination, they do help each other out of their problems into a more profitable situation, or whether the combination of their difficulties submerges them still further.

It is not really possible to obtain a general guide to British attitudes to conglomerate mergers from these three reports. The circumstances surrounding each of them were different and the degree of 'conglomeration' implied in each case was variable. However the Commission has demonstrated that a modified form of cost-benefit analysis is appropriate to deal with such cases. Instead of the comparison of gains from greater efficiency against the losses from increased market power as is broadly the approach for horizontal mergers, the analysis for conglomerates is primarily concerned with estimating both the likely gains and the likely losses in the efficiency of organisational control and resource utilisation. The emphasis seems therefore to be much more directly concerned with an appraisal of management quality in investigating the public interest aspects of conglomerate mergers.

Where an institution, be it a court or a commission, has been charged with reaching economic decisions it is unlikely that everyone will agree with its conclusions. This is particularly likely to be the case where different, conflicting considerations may need to be given implicit weight and where decision-making has to be based on predictions of likely outcomes from alternative market structures or patterns of market conduct. Predictably therefore, the Monopolies Commission has come in for criticism from economists and others over some of its reports.[42]

The report on the BICC/Pyrotenax merger which the Commission did not oppose has been the most widely criticised [43] and certainly does not seem easy to defend. The benefits claimed for the merger did not appear to amount to much. Some would have been obtainable without the necessity of the merger and there was no intention to integrate the two firms' activities in order to obtain synergistic benefits. The Commission recognised that there was unlikely to be much benefit in the UK from the merger, though it thought there might be important possible gains in exports. However, any reduction in competition might increase the risk of a loss of efficiency and anyway the size of the benefits to BICC's overseas activities and hence to the balance of payments were likely to be small in relation to the total activities of the organisation.

Of course as the law is framed it was not necessary for the Commission to be satisfied that there would be net benefits as a result of the merger, only that there would be no net detriments. The Commission saw some dangers of possible detriments in the form of higher prices and profits, loss of service and of failure to exploit to the full the potentialities of mineral insulated cable. The Commission felt that this would not in fact be a detriment because it had received certain assurances from BICC [44] and because BICC's decentralised management policy would help to retain competition. Neither reason is very convincing. The assurances were imprecise and if the need arose to enforce them would leave a considerable scope for interpretation. It is also strange that a lack of intention to integrate the operations of two merging companies should be considered a means of avoiding a detriment that might otherwise ensue. In its conclusions the Commission seemed to imply that there was not much to be said either for or against the merger. The critics of the report have, however, suggested it was too lenient and that the merger might have been opposed had it not been for the fact that the government had already allowed the merger to proceed before awaiting the Commission's report. The possibility that the Commission's judgement in this case was materially influenced by the governmental action that had already been taken emphasises the need to hold up all mergers while a Monopolies Commission investigation is in progress.

The Thorn/Radio Rentals merger report also raises some doubts as to the appropriateness of the Commission's conclusion not to oppose the merger.[45] There were certain similarities between this merger and that between UDS and Montague Burton which the Commission had rejected. In the Thorn/Radio Rentals case the criticism turned on the question of the likely effects of the merger on competition. The Commission had chosen to emphasise that the relevant market for analysis was the narrowly defined specialist television rental market but in justifying their view that there would be no detrimental effect on competition the majority of the members seemed to go against this evidence by emphasising the strength of competitive forces in the general supply of television sets. In so doing they discounted factors that were likely to increase the insulation of the specialist rental market, failed to consider the possibility of incipiency and to analyse adequately the likely effects on the future price policy of the merged organisation.

The question of the correct definition of the market has proved important in many merger investigations and the subsequent appraisal of the Commission's reports. Ellis has criticised the Commission's vagueness in not justifying more explicitly its choice of a particular market [46] and Rowley has taken issue with several of the early reports over the Commission's emphasis upon a narrow definition of the market and what he considered to be the Commission's apparent failure to understand the realities of modern competition.[47] The handling of quantitative benefits, especially the likely size of cost savings, has also been criticised as cursory and unconvincing [48] and it has been suggested that the Commission should make more use of quantitative assessment of economies of scale.[49]

Sutherland has claimed that the Commission has taken a less severe attitude towards dominant positions created by mergers than towards existing positions of market dominance, and in particular where a merger has been allowed to proceed in advance of the submission of the Commission's report he concluded that the Commission had required a lower standard of net benefit. He inferred that the Commission had tended to take the view that if there was no probability of fairly tangible and immediate detriment, then the longer term and more general detriments that might arise from the reduction in competition may be given minimal weight and the benefits claimed by the company would not be probed severely.[50]

Appraisal

In this chapter we have paid particular attention to recent British policy towards mergers. The policy is highly pragmatic or discretionary and in consequence it is not easy for firms to assess, in advance of the announcement of a proposed merger, the chances of a reference to the Monopolies Commission

172 Industrial Structure & Market Conduct

and there is even less on which they can base a prediction whether the Commission would be likely to approve or oppose the merger. While such a policy offers advantages of flexibility it offers the disadvantages of uncertainty. Whether it should be dignified with the term 'policy' is perhaps open to debate. One commentator has had doubts on this score: 'We have no anti-merger policy; merely an emergency procedure for preventing those [mergers] thought to be harmful'.[51] In the early years after the introduction of powers to prevent mergers in 1965 there seems to have been the further difficulty that different government departments were working at cross purposes, one attempting to encourage greater rationalisation, the other attempting to maintain competition. During that period it is arguable that too much encouragement was provided to firms to merge and it has been argued persuasively that the emphasis placed on the benefits that larger organisations might offer was unjustified.[52]

By lowering the market share criterion for a merger reference, the Fair Trading Act has increased the proportion of mergers that will qualify for investigation.[53] Whether it has any practical effect will depend upon the way in which the government uses its discretion, although there are some signs that greater use will be made of these powers in the future. One possible approach that might be worth considering in deciding on merger references would be to distinguish between those cases concerned with the supply of consumer goods and services as compared with those in producer goods industries and to make greater use of investigations of mergers in consumer goods industries. As we have seen in Chapter 1 a concentration measure offers only one indication of market structure and it is therefore only a limited predictor of economic performance. While other influences are no doubt taken into account in deciding whether to make a reference, one that seems particularly relevant is the existence of countervailing power. This is normally much stronger in producer goods markets than in markets to supply consumer goods and services and so under normal circumstances the economic performance implications of a given degree of concentration will be more serious on consumer goods than on producer goods.

The approach of the Monopolies Commission is based upon a simple, largely qualitative, cost-benefit approach. In a small number of cases the Commission's reasoning has seemed open to objection, though it is often difficult from the reports alone to ascertain just how much weight was to be placed on a particular benefit or detriment or indeed how far the Commission may have been influenced by other considerations – its view of the qualities of the respective managements, for example – that for obvious reasons it has not made public. The Commission's task is not made easier if a merger is allowed to proceed while the investigation is still in progress or if it only receives for investigation those cases that are most likely to be found contrary to the public interest.

The main suggestion for revision of the approach adopted by the Commission has centred around the public interest criteria to be applied. It has been suggested that instead of asking the Commission to report whether a merger would be likely to be *contrary* to the public interest, the requirement should be changed to ask whether a merger would be likely to be *in* the public interest. This might apply generally or simply in relation to, say, mergers in which the hundred largest companies are involved. This suggestion was not, unfortunately, incorporated in the Fair Trading Act and the concept of the public interest set out in Section 84 of the Act is still nebulous. It does not give any guidance to the Commission about the emphasis or relative weightings to be given where different public interests conflict. It simply requires the Commission to take into account all matters which appear to be relevant and to have regard to the desirability of promoting effective competition; and for promoting the interests of consumers, purchasers and other users in respect of the prices and quality and variety of goods and services; of promoting through competition cost reduction and innovation and of facilitating the entry of new competitors to existing markets; of maintaining and promoting the balanced distribution of industry and employment; of maintaining and promoting competitive activity in export markets.

A case could be made out for the view that high priority should be given to the passing on of cost savings in the form of lower prices. This would imply that merger policy would have a slight income distribution emphasis but it would be a way of attempting to ensure that the creation of additional market power did not allow the benefits of resource savings to be lost through an increase in X-inefficiency. It is also arguable that the Commission should be encouraged to make it much clearer in future that it would only take into account cost savings that could not be achieved in any other way – through better management or as a result of the natural growth of the market and of the internal growth of the firm. It has been pointed out by several writers that growth may obviate much of the case for horizontal mergers as a source of additional scale economies.[54] Assuming that technology remains unchanged a merger may only slightly speed up the attainment of scale economies that growth would ultimately produce and after taking into account the possibility that a merger also imposes detriments it may be preferable to wait for internal growth. If this were considered important the Commission would need to take a view of the time path over which the benefits claimed for a merger were likely to be achieved. It would imply a lesser willingness to approve mergers in growth sectors and more tolerance of mergers in static or declining sectors.

The lack of effective *ex post* investigation of the consequences of merger decisions – those that proceeded and those that did not proceed – must constitute a hindrance to effective decision-making in merger policy. The evidence reviewed in Chapter 7 indicated that often mergers had not been successful at least when seen from the point of view of the owners of the firm. This suggests that economies in resource utilisation had not been achieved but there has been remarkably little investigation of the public interest consequences of major mergers. This lack of information must surely affect the quality of public policy-making.

The British policy that we have been describing is only one of a number of alternative approaches that might be adopted to deal with mergers.[55] At one extreme there may be no attempt to deal directly with mergers, although other provisions may be introduced to adjust the relative balance of advantage between different types of industrial investment or to deal *ex post* with adverse economic performance by a dominant firm. At the other extreme a non-discretionary policy may be adopted in which rules of varying degrees of severity are laid down and decisions on the desirability or legality of particular mergers are taken in relation to the predetermined rules based solely upon structural considerations. This is largely the present situation regarding merger policy in the USA.

Assuming that a country is to adopt a policy towards mergers, there has been discussion whether it should be essentially discretionary, relying on a cost-benefit approach, or whether a more rigorous, non-discretionary approach would be more appropriate. Williamson has argued for a liberalisation of American merger policy, advocating that structural, non-discretionary rules should be applied where a merger is above a specified minimum size but that below that size, though where the market share was still significant, a discretionary or cost-benefit approach would be more appropriate.[56]

In Britain the question is whether a less pragmatic policy might not be preferable.[57] It is argued that a structural, non-discretionary approach would cause firms less uncertainty regarding the way policy is to be applied, it would avoid the high costs involved in a series of case by case investigations and would not run into the difficulties of predicting performance *ex ante* and quantifying the different costs and benefits that are implicit in a discretionary, pragmatic policy. This might be the only way to deal with a substantial increase in the number of important mergers during a merger boom and in view of the reluctance to undo a merger that subsequently proves undesirable it might be better to err on the side of allowing too few rather than too many mergers.

The pragmatists would, however, argue that a structural approach is too dogmatic and inflexible, that we do not know at what level of concentration mergers bring net detriments and that it is wrong to assume that a given degree of concentration will have the same market power and performance consequences in all situations.[58] The definition of the market is of crucial importance in any merger policy but a structural policy makes it more difficult to ensure that the appropriate market has been correctly identified.

CHAPTER 9
THE MULTINATIONAL COMPANY

The nature and extent of multinational operations

The multinational company (MNC) is becoming an increasingly important form of industrial enterprise, yet it is still not completely recognised as a matter for consideration in texts on industrial economics. Instead, early analysis was normally based upon the tools and approaches of international trade theory. Credit for emphasising the industrial organisation aspects is usually given to Stephen Hymer and there is little doubt that much of the behaviour and implications of MNCs is amenable to analysis within the framework of industrial economics. The MNC should be of particular interest and importance to the industrial economist because of the additional managerial implications that arise in multinational operations, because an MNC can have a major impact upon individual domestic markets and also because of the normative problems that MNCs present for both governments in the home country and in host countries where they establish their operations.

It is as well to define here some of the terms that will be used in this chapter. The 'home country' refers to that country in which the parent organisation or head office of the MNC is based. A 'host country' is any country which has an MNC subsidiary operating within it. 'Foreign direct investment' refers to the decision by an MNC to establish production facilities abroad and 'inward investment' relates to the direction of the flow of the investment funds. Thus inward investment takes place into a host country.

There are several alternative ways of obtaining an interest in overseas activities. A firm may simply export capital in the form of portfolio investments; it may export finished goods and services; it may license the domestic producers of other countries to use its processes and know-how; it may undertake what are known as turnkey projects – establishing an operation and then handing it over to a local firm or host government when the project is fully operational; or it may decide to go for production abroad. The true multinational company is one that is actually engaged in productive activities outside its home country. But this is not really a sufficient definition of an MNC, although opinions vary about other characteristics of the true MNC. Some commentators would insist that an MNC should be deriving at least 25 per cent of its revenues from overseas activities and some would argue that only

175

companies with annual sales of more than $100 million would really qualify. Others suggest that a true MNC would have production facilities in at least six host countries.

The key to the overseas operations of an MNC is to be found in the resources that it transfers abroad. Whereas a firm making a portfolio investment transfers only capital, a genuine MNC transfers a package of resources that includes not only capital but also enterprise and managerial skills; organisational scale and ability; technological know-how, goodwill, access to supplies or markets and the ability to feed back and appraise the information gleaned from these activities. It is particularly relevant to emphasise the importance of the transfer of knowledge in its various forms as this is a key element in the MNC's activities and is a major basis of the comparative advantage which justifies its overseas investment at all.

Organisational structure is of particular interest in the MNC since, although the various subsidiaries are operating under different national sovereignties, their operations are co-ordinated and controlled in varying degrees by the parent. The parent is also a major source of various factor inputs for its subsidiaries. It is the degree of co-ordination and control exercised by a foreign, parent MNC over its subsidiaries that is a potential source of difficulty with national host governments. While all industrial organisations are to some extent affected by their relationships with government and while all governments must have some regard to the performance of domestic firms and industries, the relationship between MNCs and host governments constitutes a particularly important political as well as economic phenomenon. Although to consider the political issues in detail would substantially extend the scope of this chapter it is an important practical element in any complete analysis of the performance and consequences of MNCs. [1]

MNCs are predominantly American in origin, though some originate from Britain, Canada, several European countries and Japan.[2] The recipients of inward investment through MNCs are also mainly industrialised societies – especially Britain, Canada and America – though about one-third of the activities of MNCs are based in less developed countries. Their current size and relative importance in particular countries is a clear indication as to why so much attention is now being paid to the economic implications of the MNC. For example, in Canada foreign owned MNCs are estimated to be responsible for 60 per cent of that country's manufacturing output. The share in the United Kingdom is lower at 13 per cent but MNCs are responsible for 20 per cent of all UK exports. In individual industries the share of MNCs is greater still. In Britain, for example, Dunning has shown that MNCs have over 40 per cent of UK production in many industries including cars, office machinery, sewing machines, breakfast cereals, cosmetics and toilet preparations, pens and pencils, razor blades, foundation garments, petrol, drugs, domestic boilers, detergents, telephones, management consultancy, films, advertising agencies.[3] MNCs tend to be very large in absolute terms. Taking the ten largest MNCs together, their value added in 1971 was more than three billion dollars and this was estimated to be greater than the GNP of more than eighty countries. At the present time the MNCs are continuing to grow in importance. Each MNC is tending to increase the number of subsidiaries operating in other countries, foreign direct investment is growing at twice the pace of world output and trade between MNCs is constituting an increasingly important element in overall international trade. These figures should be sufficient to indicate that in relation to particular industries and economies and as a global force MNCs represent an important phenomenon. Whereas twenty years ago they were welcomed unquestioningly in most countries there is now much greater concern about their activities on the part of nation-state governments who have been slow to respond to these and other global developments.

There seem to be three reasons for the recent growth in importance of MNCs: better communications, improved organisation and control within the firm, and rising incomes. Communications have always been held to exercise a marked influence on the rate of industrialisation and of concentration in a society. Now jet aircraft and the development of the telex make for much quicker and easier international communications and therefore allow increasing international concentration of productive activities as a firm is enabled to extend its range of influence without foregoing the opportunities of control. New organisational structures have been developed to cope with large, complex and more far flung operations and control has been assisted not only by communication improvements but also by new technologies in office machinery and data processing, including of course the computer. Rising incomes increase the proportion of expenditures on high technology and luxury items supplied by MNCs and the tendency for tastes and cultures to be standardised between countries increases the scale advantages of such organisations.

MNCs tend not to be evenly distributed across industrial sectors but are concentrated in a limited range of activities.[4] In general it seems that they are most likely to be found in industries with at least some of the following characteristics: they are science based; effective research and development and technological skills are important; operations are capital intensive and substantial scale economies are available; the products are highly differentiated and marketing skills play a major part; or the operations are in extractive industries where overseas activities are undertaken to obtain access to raw material supplies. In addition we find that industries in which MNCs are particularly important are often those where the income elasticity of demand for the product is or has been high and where, in consequence, American firms have benefited from the early development and growth of their domestic markets and now have sufficient advantages of scale and leads in know-how to encourage them to exploit similar market opportunities as they arise abroad. There is also some evidence to suggest that MNCs are most likely to come from oligopolistically structured industries in their home countries and to be located in oligopolistic industries in host countries.[5] There is room for doubt as to whether a causal relationship exists between the level of foreign direct investment and the degree of industry concentration. It is likely that the nature of the product or the production process is both most likely to necessitate a concentrated industrial structure and to be such that inward investment by, say, an American MNC is most likely in view of its know-how and scale advantages. If this is a plausible explanation it would be wrong to conclude that MNCs deliberately seek out oligopolistic industries as such for new entry activities.[6]

The overseas investment decision

Whether or not to establish a production subsidiary abroad, either for the first time or as an extension to an existing network of subsidiaries, is a major decision for any firm. It is major both in relation to the size of the capital outflow likely to be involved and also in relation to the possible risks and uncertainties that are associated with such a decision. The overseas investment decision involves three main steps: the decision to produce abroad rather than export or license a domestic producer; the choice of the countries in which to make the investment; and the form that the investment should take – whether by joint venture, through acquisition of existing capacity or through establishment of a wholly owned new subsidiary.

There is no general theory of the overseas direct investment decision though many relevant considerations have been identified and discussed in the literature. Some distinction has been made between the relative contribution of financial and economic influences on the one hand and organisational and behavioural considerations on the other. The respective emphases given by various commentators tend to vary, with some stressing financial and economic motivations while others argue that financial appraisal is rarely the determining basis on which a foreign investment decision is taken but that the availability of markets, political appraisals, the desire to defend an established position and internal pressures for growth are more important.[7] As with any other study of motivation of business behaviour it is likely that they will all have some applicability to different firms and to different situations facing the same firm. It is also likely that some distinction can be made between aggressive and defensive motives [8] and between those that represent a 'pull' influence from the host country and those representing a 'push' influence from the home country.

Much interest has been shown in the product cycle explanation of the overseas investment decision.[9] According to this, after the firm has successfully established its domestic production it will begin diffusion of the product abroad through overseas trade by means of exports and possibly then by licensing an indigenous producer. Later the firm will make some direct outlays abroad, maybe starting with a distributing organisation and moving on to the packaging and finishing of products before engaging in full manufacture abroad. After this the product may be imitated by local producers. This explanation has much to commend it but it says nothing regarding the speed at which the different stages occur. It would also be wrong to conclude from this that there are not occasions or products where a direct choice has to be made between exporting and producing abroad or between licensing and overseas production.

A very simplified explanation would suggest that one strategy rather than another will be selected where the capitalised values of that strategy after allowing for risk are greater than the projected returns from the alternative. In practice the outcome is less predictable as less quantifiable considerations such as political and economic uncertainties, management preferences, the nature of the product and its production processes and the over-all strategy of the firm all have to be taken into account.[10] Nevertheless some general principles can be identified. Production in the host country may be preferred to exporting where the market is large enough to justify local production and where the transport and other costs of exporting goods to the market or the perishability of the product makes exporting unprofitable. Production on the spot may increase customer confidence in the quality of the product or in the availability of spares and may offer the producer greater opportunity to meet a profitable increase in demand. Local production may also be important for a supply industry where the ability to supply at short notice from adequate inventories or to provide a specific servicing facility is of the essence.

On the other hand, exporting or licensing may be preferable to production in the host country if the firm feels unable to bear the costs, risks and uncertainties involved in transferring and utilising its knowledge abroad, if it is doubtful of its ability to cope with the greater problems of co-ordination or motivating management operating abroad, or if it has doubts about the financial and political climate in the host country. A firm may prefer to license rather than produce abroad where the life cycle of the product is short and licensing is the quickest way of exploiting the product and the firm's know-how in production or where reciprocal licensing offers some benefit in exchange. Conversely, licensing may be inappropriate where the firm has a technological lead to exploit, where sophisticated technology requires high quality control over the production process, where licensing would entail disclosing important secrets or where the firm has a particular wish to control future developments in that market. Some limited evidence that licensing and direct production overseas are alternatives is to be found in the apparent preference of firms in the plastics industry to license others to produce. This seems to be because heavy capital requirements would be involved in creating a production facility. In computers there is a preference for overseas production rather than licensing, presumably because of the profits available and the desire to preserve secrecy about techniques.[11]

The actual decision to establish production operations in a particular country is influenced by a range of other considerations, some directly economic, some not; some aggressive, some defensive. Undoubtedly firms expect their operations to be profitable but this does not necessarily mean that MNCs compare the rate of return after allowing for risk on a prospective marginal foreign direct investment in one country with the similar return on an alternative use of the same funds. DCF techniques are considered to be difficult to apply in relation to the operation of MNCs and seldom seem to be used. It is often claimed that the prospective rate of return is not the main reason for undertaking a particular foreign investment project. An investment may be approved by an MNC because it will enable it to increase its global profits rather than maximise the profits of the individual subsidiary or may, rather than leading to an actual increase in profits, help the organisation to protect and defend its position in some particular market.

The main reasons for foreign direct investment may be categorised as the pursuit of growth, the exploitation of advantages and the protection of market opportunities. Internal pressures for growth are a general feature of modern industrial organisation and multinational expansion is one way in which this pressure can be satisfied and spare managerial capacity used. To some extent geographical diversification and product diversification may be alternatives. There does, for example, appear to be evidence that American MNCs are less diversified than similar domestic firms. Multinational growth may well be a response to a slow rate of growth or low level of profit in the home market or to particular anti-trust or fiscal policies at home that hinder further domestic expansion. Inward investment is most likely to occur in a market that is growing and where the profit prospects are good. Following the product cycle hypothesis, it may be a natural development from an export activity when the level of sales becomes so large that an import agent could not handle the distribution effectively.

It has been pointed out that foreign direct investment will only take place where there are market imperfections which allow the potential foreign direct investor the opportunity to exploit his advantages. These may be in the form of technical know-how or in marketing or managerial skills and they may arise from economies of scale in research and development or in risk bearing. Inward investment may alternatively be a reflection of the relative advantages of a host country in its factor endowments or in the value and security of its currency vis-à-vis those of other nations.

Defensive reasons for establishing overseas production can, it seems, be generally described as the protection of market opportunities. This does, however, cover a diverse range of motivations. Firms may move abroad to protect their access to raw material supplies. In oligopoly there tends to be a considerable element of 'follow my leader' and this seems to apply in overseas investment decisions as well as in domestic production and marketing activities. If one MNC opens a production facility in a particular country others will follow in order to preserve their own interests and attempt to prevent a loss of market. A decision to commence production in a country may be a response to concern that the host government will insist on domestic production and possibly raise tariff barriers or other forms of import control to enforce this policy.[12] It may alternatively be a response to rising transport costs and delays that make exporting an ineffective way of supplying that particular market.

Decisions on which countries will be recipients of the new investment outlays are also dependent upon a mixture of economic and political considerations. Size and rate of growth of market and expected profitability of the operations and/or their ability to contribute to the global profit of the organisation will all be relevant. So too may be the value of incentives in the form of investment allowances, tax holidays, willingness to grant tariff protection and the quality of the public utilities and other elements in the infra-structure including the stability of law and order that a prospective host government is able and willing to offer. The level of perceived risk will also have an important bearing on a location decision. Rates of inflation, currency stability, the risk of nationalisation, attitudes to foreign ownership and the repatriation of funds will all be considered in deciding whether an investment should be undertaken.

Even if a firm decides to make a particular foreign direct investment, it still has to decide whether to make this in the form of a joint venture in partnership with another, probably local, firm or whether to establish a wholly owned subsidiary. If it chooses the latter it must then decide whether to attempt to acquire an existing local firm or to set up an entirely new production facility. Where new processes or products are being introduced through inward investment there is rather less advantage in acquiring an existing local firm as the basis for the operation. Under other circumstances, the ability to utilise an existing firm's goodwill, local market knowledge and skilled staff and management may be important advantages, especially to a firm making its first investment in a particular country.

The choice between a joint venture and a wholly owned subsidiary is a difficult one as both forms of operation have advantages and disadvantages. There are two main advantages to the MNC of a joint venture. First, as with an acquisition, it may allow quicker and easier entry by offering access to capital, local market knowledge and goodwill, scarce skills and domestic know-how. These are essentially short-term advantages but depending on the importance of a quick entry into the market may be very valuable. Secondly, a joint venture may be politically more acceptable to the host government. It may be the only way of entering some countries where governments (as in India and Japan) insist upon such a method of operation if an MNC is to be represented at all. It also reduces the risk to the MNC that its assets will be seized or that it will be discriminated against by the host country government in some other way. These are more durable benefits. The advantages of a wholly owned subsidiary are primarily concerned with the operating strategy of the subsidiary and would be expected to persist indefinitely. A wholly owned subsidiary is able to retain more secrecy as it has to disclose less about its activities in the host country. It gains considerable additional flexibility and ability to determine its activities solely in the light of the needs and interests of itself and its parent company. The opportunity it has to control the level of dividend payment according to the needs of the organisation rather than the interests of local shareholders may be a particular advantage. It avoids conflicts over the determination of priorities, in the pricing of products, on decisions regarding the source of supplies, and over recruiting and staff promotion. It seems clear from this that MNCs will normally find it in their own long-term interests to use wholly owned subsidiaries and some of the major MNCs will not agree to participate in joint ventures. However, there may be sound pragmatic reasons why joint ventures should be adopted if this is the only effective way to enter, or retain security in, an important market.

Organisation and operation in MNCs

Any organisation with subsidiaries faces additional control problems and decisions regarding transfer pricing on intra-company sales, the allocation of scarce resources between subsidiaries and the allocation of central overhead charges. These issues as such are not unique to MNCs. However, in contrast with domestic companies, MNCs do face a more extensive set of problems and opportunities about which decisions have to be taken. The additional problems faced by MNCs relate primarily to the variety of cultural, political, economic and legal environments in which they are operating. The variation in cultural, educational and linguistic backgrounds means that production and marketing techniques may not be equally applicable to all countries and adaptation may be required. Control arrangements may be made more difficult as a result of differing cultural attitudes to authority.

On the other hand MNCs have opportunities to further their own interests in ways that do not present themselves to domestic firms. By virtue of its size and accumulated resources and experience an MNC is better able to overcome entry barriers, achieve scale advantages and share information between subsidiaries and to obtain quicker and easier access to managerial resources and to raise capital more readily and cheaply. As a result of the geographical spread of its activities an MNC derives numerous benefits. These include access to a wider range of sources of capital; a greater ability to avoid the impact of credit controls or other monetary policies in any individual market; the opportunity to lessen its global tax liability through transfer pricing arrangements; greater flexibility in controlling its own money flows and asset holdings; and it is better able to exploit for its advantage differences in tariff structure which might encourage it to manufacture in one country and assemble in another. It may also be able to exercise some bargaining powers with host governments or unions by threatening to withdraw its investment and locate it in another country. The extent to which an MNC is able to benefit from these opportunities is largely dependent upon the degree of control and co-ordination that it is able to exercise over the decision-making of its subsidiaries.

There seems to be fairly general agreement that while the extent to which the parent controls its subsidiaries varies, the trend is for the degree of control to be increased. In other words MNCs are increasingly operating less like holding companies and more like integrated organisations.[13] At the same time attempts are being made to increase the degree of responsibility delegated to individual managers but within a more circumscribed decision-making area. Clearly if an MNC is to take advantage of its particular breadth of experience and geographical diversification of activities it is necessary that it should think globally and should attempt to integrate its various operations. The growing tendency for MNCs to look for specialisation of production with the different subsidiaries in different countries each contributing a different stage in the overall production process for a given product, does necessitate a much closer degree of integration than would be required if subsidiaries were simply concerned with supplying their own domestic markets. This represents an important development in the activities of MNCs. Before this it was perhaps legitimate to view MNCs as organisations that, for one reason or another, had chosen to produce in a particular country to satisfy the demand for its products there instead of by exporting or licensing another producer. Now decisions to locate only part of a production process in one country indicate that some MNC location decisions are no longer motivated so much by the level of demand in that market as by factor cost differentials that encourage the practice of an international specialisation of functions in production.

Even if the opportunity for close co-ordination and control is present it does not necessarily follow that in all cases it should be pursued to the fullest degree possible. Co-ordination and control that is too close may prove very expensive and give rise to excessive bureaucracy while losing the benefits of the initiative of the staff of the local subsidiary. It may give rise to conflicts between subsidiaries or between a subsidiary and its parent over questions of resource allocation, transfer pricing, ability to develop new product lines or over staffing and career development. On the other hand, too little control from the centre may cause a loss of opportunity and a waste of resources. In practice it seems that the closest control is exercised by the larger MNCs over younger subsidiaries and especially those that are operating in high technology sectors or have a product range similar to that of the parent. To some extent the degree of control is likely to vary according to the management philosophy of the parent, its taste for decision-making, its risk aversion preferences and concern about the economic or political environment in which the subsidiary is operating, the performance of the subsidiary and the extent to which its processes are self sufficient and within the range of competence of the parent.

MNCs also vary in respect of the areas in which controls are exercised. Direct and close controls are most likely to be imposed as a result of the centralisation of financial decision-making – through the budget, setting performance targets, through controls on capital expenditure through standardised accounting procedures throughout the organisation, through centralisation of policy on transfer pricing and the flows of funds back to the parent. In some cases parents also exercise control over production line decisions, dictating the location of production, approving subsidiary proposals to change the product line or attempting to ensure that all subsidiaries produce an identical product in all markets.[14] Personnel decisions tend to necessitate a higher degree of local autonomy though appointments of board members and key executives are likely to be made by the parent. The degree of influence over pricing and marketing decisions tends to be variable. Subsidiaries of some MNCs seem to experience little independence here and are even subject to controls on the type of package design to be adopted. In other cases a much greater degree of freedom and hence local flexibility in pricing and marketing decisions is allowed. Limitations on the markets to which subsidiaries may export seem to occur frequently. This territorial allocation may be intended to avoid unnecessary competition between different subsidiaries within the same organisation or it may be to ensure that subsidiaries abide by the home country government's requirements regarding trading arrangements (not trading with the enemy etc.). Again, it may be a means of ensuring that subsidiaries keep to the terms of international market sharing agreements reached between different MNC parent organisations. It is also likely that MNCs may find it profitable to co-ordinate their worldwide purchasing activities, though some companies avoid this on the grounds that the exercise of such purchasing power might create political difficulties. Control over subsidiaries may be exercised with equal effect simply as a result of the presence of senior executives of the parent on the board of each subsidiary, through the discipline imposed by the need to make regular financial and other reports to the parent, by encouraging or requiring the adoption of common management and accounting methods or through general liaison, visits and exchanges of information.

Once a subsidiary is successfully established it seems that it is more likely to be on balance a net remitter of funds to the parent rather than a net receiver of funds from the parent. Most MNCs encourage their subsidiaries to meet their capital expenditures out of retained earnings. This will normally meet a high proportion of a subsidiary's needs. The balance is likely to be made up of local funds obtained through borrowing, trade credit, unpaid taxes and occasionally through inviting local shareholdings or from foreign funds external to the company such as overseas borrowings and credits and borrowings on the Eurobond market.

In an integrated or centralised MNC the performance of the subsidiary can only be understood in terms of the objectives of its parent. The purpose of the co-ordinating role exercised by the parent is to attempt to ensure that each subsidiary makes its required contribution to the global objectives of the organisation as a whole. The broad objectives (satisfactory profits, growth etc.)

are unlikely to differ much from those of a domestic company. But in its decision-taking an MNC will also have to take into account other influences, such as the desire to reduce the risk of the loss of its capital either through exchange rate fluctuations or appropriation and differing government policies on trade, investment and taxation which offer an MNC a greater opportunity and incentive to minimise its total (global) tax burdens.

One of the ways in which it might achieve this is through the use of transfer pricing techniques which, by adjusting the prices paid and received by sub-sidiaries in sales with each other, offer an opportunity to adjust the level of profit earned in different countries to reflect different tax levels and exchange risks in those locations. There is a division of opinion as to just how important a trading practice this is in multinational operations. It may be an important means of reducing the level of reported profits in countries where the level of taxes on distributed profits is very high but in general it seems unlikely that the tax authorities would allow gross distortions of market prices by MNCs. It is, of course, also a practice that brings with it particular internal control problems for the firm, and our discussion of this phenomenon in Chapter 3 applies as much to the vertically integrated MNC as to the vertically integrated domestic company. There it will be recalled we argued that the establishment of artificial transfer prices would lead to an internal misallocation of resources and production effort and would cause additional difficulties in control and appraisal of the performance of subsidiaries.

Transfer pricing is, however, only one of the means by which an MNC is able to transfer funds between subsidiaries and between a subsidiary and the parent. Funds may be transferred as dividends, loans or trade credits or as charges against income in the form of interest or royalty payments or as fees for central services provided by the parent. The exact form in which funds are remitted will depend upon tax and exchange conditions in the host and home country markets. The level of remission of funds from a subsidiary to its parent will also be influenced by economic conditions in the two countries, the degree of autonomy allowed to the subsidiary and the respective needs for funds of the parent and the subsidiary. Generally speaking subsidiaries are often required to remit quite high proportions of their profits to the parent and this is especially so where there is thought to be a risk of devaluation or other threat to the parent's holdings in its subsidiary. Dividend payments by subsidiaries to parents appear to be closely related to profits in each year.[15] This means that they are likely to be more volatile than the payment of dividends by a public company to its external shareholders.

The impact of the MNC on host countries

Much attention has been focused on the effect of inward investment upon host governments. A number of major economic issues can be identified, which suggest that inward investment offers both benefits and detriments. By and large, these tend not to lend themselves to quantitative appraisal. In some cases they also have important political and sociological implications which may mean that an overall judgement of the value of the existence of MNC subsidiaries in a host country may not be based solely upon economic considerations. Our discussion here will deal separately with the effects of inward investment by MNCs on the supply of factor inputs; on efficiency; on market conditions; and on domestic economic policy. We will then identify potential points of conflict between MNCs and host governments.

(1)   The Supply of Factor Inputs

The supply of three main types of factor input may be influenced by the activities of MNCs: capital, technological know-how and manpower. The initial inflow of capital may be most welcome to a host, especially where the domestic level of savings is low or the absence of a well organised domestic capital market or reluctance of local businessmen to invest is depressing the level of economic activity. On the other hand capital inflows may be inflationary in an economy working at or near full capacity and capital received at one point in time implies a commitment to future outflows of funds in servicing that debt. As we have already observed, after an initial investment has taken place, future capital movements are most likely to represent net outflows of funds away from the host country as the successful subsidiary repatriates some of its profits. There is also a fear that MNC subsidiaries will deprive domestic firms of access to local sources of capital or otherwise raise the supply price of capital.

Access to technical know-how and especially the embodiment of research and development expertise is often held to be an important benefit to a host country. This may mean speedier, better and cheaper access to recent product and process developments than reliance upon domestic firms alone would allow. On the other hand, the technology that is transferred may not be appropriate to the host country. This is perhaps particularly important in the context of discussions on the choice of techniques in developing countries. It is sometimes claimed that the use of the MNC parent company's research and development will stifle research in the host country and that much of the research that brings benefits to the host country is government financed and sponsored and that all the MNCs are really doing is transferring the benefits of their development work rather than research as such. American firms normally spend only a small proportion of their total research and development budget abroad but because of their much greater overall size it appears that they are likely to be spending as much on research and development in a host country as their domestic competitors.[16] On balance there seems to be a feeling that host countries do gain a small net benefit from the transfer of technology and know-how and this is undoubtedly associated with the view that it is much cheaper to import technology from the United States or the home country of some other MNC than to try to produce it in the host country using only domestic resources.

MNCs are normally held to have superior managements and skills. While this is also related to the question of efficiency it is a benefit of the transfer of particular types of factor input. The emphasis on training and improved management and production techniques can undoubtedly have benefits in the local economy as these advantages are demonstrated to domestic firms and as staff trained by MNCs leave to join host country firms. The consequences are, however, not entirely advantageous if the entry of MNCs means that they merely attract the better trained staff away from domestic firms. Similarly the introduction of nationals from the home country of the parent organisation to the host country may have less desirable consequences in terms of the style of life in the local culture of an area, the effect on the price of housing, etc.

(2) The Effect on Efficiency

Studies of the performance of MNCs compared with control groups of domestic firms have shown that MNCs, especially American organisations, tend to be more efficient – they have higher productivity, higher profits, and export a greater proportion of their output.[17] This indicates that MNCs are likely to be more efficient in their use of resources. They may also contribute to a favourable balance of payments position, though this is also dependent upon the level of import demand they generate and the pattern of capital flows. The causes of the superior performance by MNCs are generally thought to be due to better quality and less conservative management, the use of superior technological and managerial techniques and a greater willingness to innovate in managerial or marketing policies.[18] As a result of their competitive impact and of demonstration and spillover effects this should lead to increased efficiency on the part of domestic firms. It is also likely that MNCs help to raise standards of efficiency in their customers or suppliers by insisting on a high and consistent quality of products, by providing the opportunity of longer production runs as a result of larger orders, and by providing training and access to new developments available in the MNC's home market.

The disadvantages here seem not to be very great. It may be objected that because of transfer pricing and other arrangements for the transfer of capital sums measures of rates of return achieved by a subsidiary in a host country are not reliable indicators of actual performance. It is true that quite a high proportion of MNC exports are sales to other subsidiaries within the same organisation and so once more the recorded value of imports or exports may well be influenced by transfer price decisions. It is also possible that while subsidiaries of MNCs seem to be flexible and adaptable in their management techniques and decision making, excessive emphasis by some on the application of American styles and ways of doing things may be less geared to local market needs and opportunities and may create difficulties.

(3) Market Consequences

The existence of an MNC in a market may have highly beneficial effects especially where, as tends to be the case, it is more efficient than domestic firms. Its management may be more likely to adopt a competitive stance and there certainly seems to be some ground for believing that American MNCs are less likely to participate in cartels or other formal restrictive practices in host country markets.

However, there are a number of possible disadvantages that should also be considered. First, the existence of a powerful MNC subsidiary may encourage rationalisation among domestic producers. This may be advantageous if it yields further scale economies or makes for more effective competition. It may on the other hand help to tighten the degree of oligopoly that already existed and hence change the pattern of competition. It is at least arguable that a reduction in the degree of price competition and increasing emphasis on marketing competition – through advertising and other forms of product differentiation might not be altogether advantageous.

The second objection relates to the nature of the products that an MNC makes available. If the product cycle explanation of the stages in the move to overseas manufacture is to be accepted, does it not imply that overseas subsidiaries are always producing older styles of products and not those more recently developed by the parent company? Again, it may be objected that an MNC does not really produce items that are appropriate for the host country market but places too much emphasis on trying to sell luxury items developed for the home market. The attempt to sell western luxury items in developing countries has been criticised on the grounds that it not only attempts to create inappropriate wants but also that it undesirably reduces cultural diversity between countries.

Major MNCs may also be part of a worldwide oligopolistic structure in which they recognise their mutual interdependence with each other and allow this to affect their behaviour in international and individual host country markets.[19] It is possible that the entry of one MNC into a particular host country will encourage others to follow suit in order to preserve their own interests and position. The danger of such 'follow-my-leader' entry is that this may cause a situation of excess capacity to exist in the industry with less chance of rationalisation through merger. This will mean that firms are working below their technical optima, costs will be higher and efficiency of resource utilisation lower than is necessary. This seems to be a particular problem in the motor industries of some Latin American countries.[20] If this problem is to be avoided it may be at the expense of some form of international market sharing arrangement, possibly supported by patent exchanges or cross licensing. Either way the outcome may not prove to the benefit of the host country.

One of the key tests of the benefits of the operations of MNCs in a host country is to enquire whether it is likely that prices are lower as a result. It may be that an MNC subsidiary does generate increased efficiency or stimulate competition on price that is to the benefit of the consumer. It may be that supplies are cheaper in the host country as a result of production there by an MNC than if the alternative was to pay transport costs and duties in importing the item. Existing domestic firms may react vigorously when new entry occurs or access to an MNC parent's know-how and expertise may be necessary to generate effective competition in a market that would otherwise tend to be a single firm monopoly.[21] It may be, however, that oligopoly conditions generate non-price rather than price competition and that heavy marketing outlays create barriers to new competition and allow the firms concerned to enjoy very high profits.

It is not altogether clear just how much freedom individual MNC subsidiaries are able to exercise in pricing their products in a particular host market. It appears that several American MNCs operating in Britain attempt to set prices that are closely in line with prices for similar items prevailing in the United States. This certainly seems to apply to prices of butyl rubber,[22] hearing aid batteries,[23] colour film[24] and Polaroid cameras. The implication of this is clear. Prices in a particular host market may bear no relation to actual production costs in that market if it is the American costs that dictate a common international price. This may mean that prices are higher than they need be in Britain or any other host country if wage and other costs are lower there than in the home country of the MNC. It may alternatively mean, if the size of the market is smaller in Britain, that shorter production runs or the use of a less economical technology will make British costs higher than American, but a common international price will mean the British price is lower than it would otherwise be. Either way a failure to relate prices to costs will lead to a misallocation of resources in the host country. Under these circumstances and taking into account also transfer pricing and other accounting difficulties, it becomes very difficult for a host country's anti-trust or price control policies to take a meaningful view on the reasonableness of prices and profits of an MNC subsidiary's activities in a host country.[25]

(4)   Impact on Domestic Economic Policy

A powerful MNC may have a significant impact on the success or otherwise of the domestic economic policies of the host government while the MNC may, by virtue of the international nature of its operations, be able to render itself relatively immune from the impact of those policies upon its own activities.

A major prospective benefit from an MNC is the contribution to the achievement of economic growth as a result of the MNC's access to international supplies of capital and its location in growth sectors of the economy. There will be further gains if the MNC subsidiary increases the domestic content in the production process and stimulates further investment by supplying firms or firms producing complementary products. But there may be disadvantages by virtue of its ease of access to capital outside the host economy and its propensity to rely heavily on self financing. An MNC's subsidiary may be better able to ignore domestic monetary restraints in the host country and may therefore exacerbate inflationary pressures at a time when the host government is attempting to take some of the steam out of the economy. Again, if it simply increases the demand for fully utilised resources and bids up factor costs it will be inflationary. Some consideration has been given to the question whether MNCs are likely to be more prone or less prone to bid up wage levels than domestic firms. MNCs may be weak wage bargainers and therefore prone to bid up wages if the integrated nature of their international operations means that production must be kept going at almost any price. On the other hand their greater ability to transfer production to a plant in another host country may make them tough wage bargainers and less likely to concede inflationary wage increases.

One major benefit that MNCs are normally considered to offer to a host country's employment and regional policy is a greater willingness to establish plants in areas of high unemployment. Such new investment may be expected to have a beneficial regional multiplier effect. However, it appears that the initial effect is that MNC subsidiaries tend to hire skilled and better equipped workers who are already in employment and they do not make much direct contribution to a lowering of the unemployment level in that region.[26] This is no doubt related to the propensity of MNCs to adopt capital intensive rather than labour intensive techniques, but does indicate that the regional benefits may not be as large and immediate as is often assumed. While an increase in the level of economic activity will raise the level of tax revenue a government will expect to obtain, the international operations of an MNC will provide some opportunity at least to reduce its tax burden in a high tax country as a result of the adoption of transfer prices and other payments for services rendered, royalties and fees for licences and know-how. Hence the direct fiscal benefits to the host may be less than they should be.

The potential influence of an MNC on a host country's balance of payments is also important. The general impression is that an MNC subsidiary tends to have a better export record than an equivalent domestic firm and this will also have the effect of helping to improve the terms of trade and strengthen the currency. Some worries have, however, been expressed that territorial arrangements between the different subsidiaries of an MNC, or international market sharing agreements between parent MNCs, or parent adherence to a home country government's restrictions on trading with the enemy, may weaken the export performance of a subsidiary in a particular host market. While this could no doubt be a problem it does not seem to have been of much quantitative significance. These fears have been most widely expressed in relation to the effect on Canada as a host country but at least one study has shown that MNC subsidiaries did not appear to be unduly circumscribed and that MNCs had little adverse effects on either imports or exports.[27] Under normal circumstances it seems that the worldwide contacts and market intelligence of an MNC organisation are likely to be put at the disposal of its subsidiaries and would therefore be to the benefit of a host country. The balance of trade effects should therefore be favourable to a host country. Whether the balance of payments effects are also favourable depends on capital movements as well as other considerations and we have already seen that in the long term there may well be net capital outflows from a host country.[28] Short-term capital movements are also a source of potential difficulty for a host country. International access, through the standing of the parent, to the Eurobond market and other sources of international lending allows MNCs quick convertibility between currencies and may intensify any instability in a host country's currency.

(5) Points of Conflict

By and large it seems that the points of conflict between host country governments and MNCs and between host and home governments are more concerned with potential than actual difficulties at the present time. Host governments, however, do appear to have some justifiable grounds for concern about a possible loss of control and of sovereignty. A large and important sector[29] of the economy may be in the hands of companies whose control is located outside the sphere of influence of the host government. This implies increasing technological dependence upon another country and a loss of control in key industrial sectors. Decisions taken by the subsidiary are not necessarily to maximise its performance in the host country but are to fit in with the global strategy of its parent. Thus it is argued that with an MNC there is scope for a much wider divergence between the private interest of the organisation and the social interests of the host than would be the case with a domestic company.

Host governments also react strongly against the possibility that home country governments may intervene in their affairs either using the MNC as its agent or by restricting the freedom of the MNC to pursue the policies it chooses. This is the problem of extra-territoriality and arises when home governments seek to dictate to subsidiaries in other countries in respect of their trading arrangements or the application of home country anti-trust policies to subsidiaries based overseas. Difficulties can also arise if home countries attempt to control capital outflows to countries that are heavily dependent on inward foreign direct investment.

Relations between host governments and the management of MNC subsidiaries and between managers in MNC subsidiaries and their parent organisations may also be potential points of conflict. Especially in less developed countries, the management of an MNC subsidiary may have a high social and economic status and the host government may be anxious to liaise with it on policy matters. Often, however, the standing of the subsidiary's management may be higher in the host country than in the MNC parent organisation. Where this is so the ability of the local management to co-operate with the host government or to give some indication about the subsidiary's future operations in that host country may be circumscribed. There may also be a role conflict problem for local managers of MNC subsidiaries. Many are nationals of the host country. As they are also employees of an organisation based in another country, where should their loyalties lie should the interests of the two diverge?

In general it seems that MNCs are anxious to be good corporate citizens of the countries in which they are operating subsidiaries. However, difficulties and suspicions may arise if it is thought that tax avoidance or transfer price policies are working to the disadvantage of the host country. These will be magnified if the MNC refuses to allow the host government and its agencies access to information it would need to assess this issue. The British experience in dealings with Roche, an MNC based in Switzerland, gives some indication of the sort of difficulties that can arise. The Department of Health and Social Security had to use its statutory powers to obtain financial returns from the company and the Monopolies Commission was unable to obtain information that it considered necessary to assist its own investigations.[30] The suggestion from the now defunct Prices and Incomes Board that proper appraisal of the performance of a subsidiary in a host country would require access to the books of the parent organisation involves a much wider issue of principle altogether. If a host country demanded to have at least some information about the activities of an MNC in its home country it would reverse the normal debate on extra-territoriality.

(6) Appraisal

The government or economist appraising the effects on a host country of inward investment either generally or in a particular case should relate benefits and detriments of the existing situation to all the feasible alternatives. These would include: no action and a loss of the production and products concerned; reliance on imports; reliance on production by a domestic firm rather than an MNC subsidiary; some form of turnkey project or perhaps a joint venture. Unfortunately not only are costs and benefits difficult to quantify but it is very difficult if not impossible to appraise alternatives that have not been experienced. Assessment therefore of the impact of MNCs on host countries tends primarily to answer the simple but relevant question: 'do the benefits of MNCs exceed the costs they impose?' The general conclusion reached by most commentators[31] is that although there are some problems and fears, on balance MNCs have had favourable effects. For example Dunning concluded that 'international direct investment has almost certainly added to the level and quality of the world's real capital stock and hence world output'.[32] Steuer produced a cautious estimate that inward investment contributes about two per cent to real income in the United Kingdom.

The issues discussed here would not contradict a cautious judgement in favour of MNCs. In terms of the effects on the availability and utilisation of factor inputs, efficiency and economic policy, there are some possible drawbacks and problems but it seems the gains outweigh the disadvantages. The balance is, however, probably negative when the market effects are considered. Although potential conflicts between host governments and MNCs or home governments are perhaps not very likely, one of the main problem areas is again the question of competition policies and the control of dominant firm behaviour. This suggests that the greatest practical need is for an effective domestic and international competition policy to ensure that the efficiency gains that MNCs produce are in fact passed on to consumers.

There must, however, remain some room for consideration whether there is not a more fundamental ground for questions about the net benefits to be derived from inward investment through MNCs. This relates to the timing of the benefits and detriments. It does seem that the gains from inward investment appear to come from a speeding up of a process of change and improvement that would take place anyway, though maybe at a slower rate, or that could be obtained in others ways. The detriments on the other hand appear to be more likely to be longer term and permanent. If this is so then the balance of advantage to a host country depends not only upon the actual performance outcomes but also on its rate of time preference.

The impact on the home economy

While most attention has been focused on the effects on host countries there has also been some investigation of the impact of the flows of direct investments from the home countries of the MNCs. The American and the United Kingdom governments have shown some interest in this issue with special reference to the question of whether such capital outflows have favourable or unfavourable effects upon the balance of payments. Reports have been published in both countries on this question[33] and while we shall not attempt to offer a critical review of these studies[34] we can note the broad issues and the most likely sources of gains and losses.

The main costs of overseas direct investment are the inevitable capital outflows; a loss of tax revenues as firms take their profits abroad; a reduction in the level of domestic economic activity at home because firms have chosen to invest abroad rather than at home (it is assumed the supply of capital is not perfectly elastic). The balance of trade will suffer since some exports from the home country will be displaced by production in the host market and, because the overseas subsidiary may have a cost advantage in producing, there may be an increase in the level of imports replacing domestic production in the home economy. In addition there may be a loss of income if a firm could otherwise have obtained royalties from licensing an overseas firm to produce instead. All these costs involve a loss of economic benefit and a possible worsening of the home country's foreign exchange and currency position.

On the other hand, a country will receive benefits from its overseas investment activities. There will be initial exports of equipment as the investment is made and a new market for sales of components and semi-finished products would be created. Not only would the MNC parent be likely to export to its overseas subsidiary but other home country organisations also would be likely to gain export sales. Home country services – banking, shipping and consultancy – may gain extra business. The parent organisation and so the home country will gain from profits remitted to it (though these will now be net of local tax) and earnings in the form of interest payments, royalties and fees for services and know-how will all represent inflows to the home country. The parent company may also gain from an increase in the scale of its activities, the opportunity to keep up with its major international competitors and from access to new technologies and market information. These will bring benefits in the form of tax revenues and increases in economic activity to the home country.

While it is not difficult to identify the major sources of gain and loss to the home country, it is less easy to reach a definitive conclusion on the net balance of advantage and disadvantage. So much depends once again upon the view that is taken of the most likely alternative outcome if the outflow of funds had not taken place. The actual result is often very sensitive to the assumptions used in the analysis. The general opinion seems to be that there is a fair chance that although the short term effects on the balance of payments capital account are unfavourable or negative as a result of the initial capital outflows, in the long run there is likely to be a favourable balance on the current account. It should, however, be emphasised that this is by no means a unanimous view and further investigation of this question could be informative.

Proposals for control

Although it is possible to identify the sources of possible benefits and detriments from the operations of MNCs to various interest groups, we have found it much more difficult to indicate the relative magnitude or even the direction of the net balance of these outcomes. Equally it seems that there is very little agreement on the form that control policies might take, assuming that any controls are required either generally or in particular circumstances. This debate is only really just beginning and will probably need to proceed quickly if nation states are to regain the ground they consider they have already lost to the MNCs.

Three broad areas might be noted in which policy changes could prove helpful as a means of increasing effective control over MNCs and the chances that the benefits are passed on to citizens in the countries in which they operate. First, an attempt might be made to increase the degree of participation by the host country in ownership and control of an MNC subsidiary or through purchase of shares on the Eurobond market in the MNC parent company itself. Local shareholdings would be the most obvious development here and there is, of course, some experience of such arrangements already. However, it might prove disadvantageous to host countries if, as a result, some MNCs did not proceed with a new inward investment, or if they restricted the subsidiary's access to the know-how of the parent or charged higher royalties and fees for the know-how, patents and services of the parent. The purchase of an equity share in an MNC subsidiary may, where capital is scarce, deprive a domestic firm in the host country of access to capital for its own development.

The second area would involve changes in domestic policies within a host country. Governments might be more selective in allowing only inward investments that they estimated would produce significant net benefits. They should aim to maximise the speed of diffusion of the know-how and skills that an MNC brings throughout the economy and, by effective competition policy, should aim to ensure that the benefits of superior MNC efficiency are passed on to citizens of the host country. Consistency in domestic economic policies towards industry is also important if benefits are to be obtained, but some countries are open to criticism on this score. Safarian was very critical of Canadian policies and particularly of the effects of high tariffs in reducing competitive pressures; he commented, 'tariffs continue . . . to play an important role in raising costs, in preserving an inefficient number of firms and products and in limiting market horizons'.[35] A host government should also be prepared to do everything it can to reduce the MNC's fear of expropriation. If the perceived risk is high it may mean that desirable foreign investment is lost or if it is already in a country the risk will cause MNCs to limit their capital inflows and to try to repatriate as large an amount of funds as possible. This is therefore likely to raise prices in the host country market and reduce the host's tax revenue.

The third area concerns suggestions for international harmonization of the policies of national governments towards MNCs. This would deal with the problem of extra-territoriality and might cover international anti-trust provisions, the imposition of a single international corporation tax on MNCs or common exchange control arrangements and a common patent system. All MNCs might be incorporated under international law and made subject to the control of an international agency. There might also be an advantage in investigating the possibility of establishing an international agency to assist the transfer of resources from donor firms to recipient countries in such a way that an MNC only supplied that part of the package of resources normally involved in foreign direct investment that a host country really required and without therefore the necessity for the MNC to assume complete control over its activities in that country.

CHAPTER 10

THE FIRM AND ITS MARKET

A large and important area of price theory in economics emphasises the question of the behaviour of firms (and individuals) in different types of market. Unfortunately, even where the firm is assumed to be free of the immediate constraints on its actions that a perfectly competitive market is assumed to impose, many formulations emphasise that decisions are taken in relation to consideration of price and outputs alone. In consequence economists do not always take into account the breadth of marketing activities available to the firm that may have an important bearing on market conduct and performance. The outcome is a failure to recognise the important relation that ought to exist between economic and marketing studies and all too often it is claimed that economists fail to understand the nature and implications of competition within a modern economy.

It would require a whole textbook to deal at length with areas where the links between economics and marketing could usefully be explored in depth.[1] Let us however just briefly note a few areas in which both economists and marketers would be interested. These would include:

Pricing decisions The influence of different market structures; price discrimination; channel pricing and the problems of recommended and maintained resale prices; the inter-relationships between prices, economies of scale and investment decisions.

Product decisions The nature of the competitive process; the role of research and development; innovation studies; branding and other forms of product differentiation and own brand decisions..

The marketing mix Forms of promotion: price and non-price; the choice between different forms of promotion and appraisal of their effects; the implications of treating advertising as a capital good; the economic and social effects of advertising.

Conduct in particular types of market The concept of a market and its effective identification; games playing and questions of strategy; the problems of bilateral monopoly and countervailing power.

Consumer behaviour This is probably the area where formal economic analysis is at present furthest removed from economic reality.[2] Yet understanding and prediction of consumer responses to changes in prices and other elements in the marketing mix is crucial both to analysis, forecasting and decision-taking by policy-makers whether in a firm or in government.

Demand forecasting Again this is crucial for decision-making within the firm since over-production will cause a costly build-up of stocks and possible loss of distributor goodwill, while the technology may be such that to work at less than full capacity could be prohibitive in cost terms. Under-production on the other hand will mean a lost opportunity, market share gains by a rival and a loss of distributor and customer goodwill.

Channels of distribution The distributive sector is an important group of industries in its own right. The interface between manufacturer and distributor has become increasingly important and selection of appropriate channels of distribution, decisions on the correct margin and distributor back-up arrangements are all of crucial importance to a manufacturer.

The social control of industry This is again an important area in most industrialised societies and there is often friction and disagreement between businessmen and those concerned with the framing and execution of anti-trust policy. The charge is often made that the policy-maker's understanding of the nature of competition is deficient and consequently the policy is ill-conceived or undesirable.

Undoubtedly more examples could be found of areas in which economics and marketing both have a contribution to make to the resolution of policy questions for both the firm and government. But this review should have indicated that a text on industrial economics must have due regard to some of the central issues referred to here and in subsequent chapters on advertising, pricing, price discrimination, oligopoly and the control of restrictive practices, an attempt has been made to offer a treatment that is both true to economic analysis but also realistic within a marketing framework. In this chapter it will, however, be convenient to deal with one or two further issues that relate to the way in which firms perceive their market and the challenges it presents. We shall pay particular attention here to questions of the identification of the market, the nature of the competitive process and the choice of the marketing mix.

Identification of the market

Firms are often criticised for taking too narrow a view of their market and consequently failing to respond sufficiently quickly to competition. In a well-known paper on this question Levitt argued that firms that viewed their markets too narrowly tended to be slow to make innovations. He particularly pointed to evidence in the United States that important innovations in motor fuel marketing had not come from the major oil companies who were pre-occupied with production and refining. Similarly, although the oil companies owned substantial natural gas deposits in the United States, they were only exploited by former oil company executives who had left the oil companies.[3]

Numerous examples could be given of cases where a firm or industry has lost ground because it considered its range of potential competition too narrowly. The failure of the film companies to recognise that their competition was from all branches of the entertainment industry rather than just from other film companies is perhaps 'a classic'. Other providers of entertainment and leisure activities including professional sport are also becoming aware that they are all competing with each other to supply the household's need for entertainment and hence to obtain the same portion of consumer spending power and leisure time. They are consequently attempting to improve the amenities they offer and change their image to respond to this competition. Transport is another area where major sectors failed to appreciate that their competition was, to a greater or lesser degree, from all other sectors. Thus for example the railways and internal airlines are part of an internal transport network and not pure monopolies in their own right.

Development of new products and changes in consumer tastes will influence and alter the extent of competition faced by firms outside their narrowly defined, product based, industry. Competition between wallpaper and paint, between bricks and new industrialised building forms and concrete, between banks and other financial institutions for savings, between traditional retailers and more recent self-service stores, supermarkets, discount stores and hyper-markets are only a few of the examples that come readily to mind. Even margarine has been made to present more of a challenge to butter. This is the result of considerable market research effort to identify the way consumers contrasted the two products and then the use of marketing skills, especially in packaging and promotion, to emphasise the differences between the two and especially the apparent advantages which margarine has in terms of softness and easier spreading powers when it is cold.[4]

Effective market identification is therefore based on the recognition of other products and other suppliers that can meet consumer demands for a particular set of characteristics. The key is clearly first to determine the relevant characteristics that are required by consumers and then to identify the various forms in which those characteristics can be supplied. Any producer who can provide items which are accepted as having those characteristics is a competitor. Part of the persuasive function in marketing is exercised where suppliers convince consumers that their products do offer the relevant characteristics in greater quantity than their competitors or that their product had a relevant characteristic that the others do not possess at all. But the relevant market may not only refer to existing suppliers; it may be necessary to take into account the role of potential competition. Limit price theories assume that firms already in a market will set a price for their product sufficiently low to minimise the risks of new entry but, subject to that constraint, sufficiently high to maximise their profits, (see Chapter 4 for a discussion of this question). But practical experience indicates that firms often either ignore the threat of new entry altogether or overestimate the height of the entry barriers protecting them.

But the scope of the market is also influenced by demand considerations. The successful identification of actual or potential customers and customer needs is therefore an important marketing activity. The development of new products to meet customer requirements is, however, a risky undertaking and many new products prove unsuccessful. There are considerable difficulties in obtaining reliable research information on customer needs and in assessing the chances that consumers would use a particular product if it was developed. Consequently a careful stepwise procedure of product trials, test markets and so on before national launches is often needed to try to minimise the chances that a product will prove unsuccessful.

Even with an established product there is still considerable scope for the provision of further market information by identifying the types of people that do (and do not) use a particular product and brand and the apparent reasons why this might be so. Not only should investigation of this question deal with the socio-economic characteristics of buyers and non-buyers but it may also be the case that the psychological perceptions, drives and values of consumers might be relevant in establishing clearly the key characteristics of the market that is being served.[5] Effective classification of different types of customers is the key to successful market segmentation and a more efficient total production and marketing effort. This may lead to a decision to adopt a policy of price discrimination, charging different types of customer, where they are clearly separable, different prices. Or it may encourage the development of product differences to meet more effectively the needs of different market segments. Cadbury's decision to attempt to segment the instant tea market was a result of the discovery that different members of many families preferred different flavours of tea and that in many cases a single cup of tea was all that was required. This encouraged the attempt to develop the market for tea bags. The identification of different types of people that are not users of a particular product may encourage particular efforts to develop this market segment. Perhaps the best known of all such attempts was the decision by John Bloom to direct his washing machine marketing efforts at council house tenants, where the market was less saturated. But other attempts to identify different classes of consumer, either in objective terms or on the basis of their psychological characteristics and perceptions may also help to make for a more realistic and appropriate marketing policy geared towards a particular relevant segment of the market.

Correct identification of the market is therefore important to the firm not only from the point of view of its ability to meet competition more effectively, but also as a key to successful new product development and to more effective pricing and promotional strategies based upon the successful identification of different market segments. But the correct identification of the relevant market is also a necessary prerequisite for effective government control of industry. We have already discussed this to some extent in Chapters 1 and 8 and so will not dwell unduly on this aspect now. We might just note in passing one or two general conclusions. In Chapter 1 we saw that a structural approach, using measures of the structure of an industry was unlikely to offer completely reliable predictions of behaviour or performance in individual markets. In Chapter 8 we showed that the Monopolies Commission tends to adopt a pragmatic approach, identifying the relevant market as it thought most appropriate. It is likely that for anti-trust purposes the market will be narrowly defined to reflect only situations where there is high substitutability, while a firm should view its market more broadly as it searches for new opportunities and seeks to meet competitive challenges. Short-sightedness may be indefensible in a firm but quite appropriate for anti-trust policy!

The competitive process

What do we mean by competition? At first sight this may seem a simple and straightforward question but failure to offer a satisfactory answer has been one of the main causes of misunderstanding and dispute between economists and businessmen. The businessman argues that the economist thinks only in terms of price as the medium of competition and that by basing his analysis on the deviation of actual market situations from a perfectly competitive norm he overlooks important elements of competition that arise in other market structures. We shall see in this section that this is not, or should not be, a valid criticism of the economist's appoach. In return the economist might argue that what the businessman or marketer understands by competition may indeed have short-run value but the outcome of such practices in the longer term may sometimes be anti-competitive when seen in a dynamic framework.

Several writers, including Abbott, Andrews, J. M. Clark, Downie, Fellner and Schumpeter,[6] have chosen to emphasise the dynamic nature of competition in an effort to move away from the twentieth-century neo-classical analysis and the misunderstandings that have arisen from this. In their approach the key elements of competition are innovation, promotion and the threat of new entry. In Schumpeter's view the kind of competition that is decisive is that which comes from 'the new commodity, the new technology, the new source of supply, the new type of organisation'[7] since it is these that in the long run strike at the very survival of the organisation. Clark's emphasis is more on the role of product differentiation and he argues that 'the differentiated product has become an economic variable at least as important as price along with the methods of selling effort and demand creation that necessarily go with product differentiation'.[8] The essential points about this form of competition are that it can bring about marked shifts in the market shares of the various firms, it can be effective with fewer firms than would be required for effective price competition and it emphasises entrepreneurial skills in a way that does not arise with price competition.

The analytical implication of these contributions is that competition is compatible with only a few firms in an industry. Clark described this as workable and then as effective competition and argued that it was compatible with a downward sloping demand curve. Andrews, without going into the same depth of analysis of the different nature of marketing activities, argued that in the long run after allowing for quality and service differences between products, prices would be competitive even under product differentiation.[9] He appeared to base his analysis mainly on firms supplying producer goods and stressed that prices would be forced to be competitive as a result of the threat of potential competition, the search for cost savings and the range of information available to the buyer. It is, however, not altogether clear that the same incentive to search for cost savings or access to expert information about alternative products is available to the individual purchaser of consumer goods.

But non-price behaviour may be interpreted in a different light as uncompetitive. Certainly this was one of the issues that arose out of Galbraith's discussion in the *New Industrial State*. He argued that the complexity, time and capital involved in modern production processes meant that a firm could not afford to have unstable demand and fluctuating prices. The firm needed a predictable market and this it obtained through 'planning' the market. Marketing techniques were important aids to this planning.[10] Whereas in what he called the 'accepted sequence' the consumer acted through the market to determine what the firm produced and the quantity it supplied, now in the 'revised sequence' the firm was able to determine what was bought and at what prices through its planning of the market. As a consequence, he argued, the American economy was no longer competitive or even a market economy since consumer preferences, profit incentives and the price mechanism had all been swept away by the large corporations and the market had been subordinated to the goals of the firm's planning. The malleability of consumers with incomes above the subsistence level was considered an important reason for the success of marketing activities in helping to control the market.

While Galbraith's comments were considered seriously and the US Senate

Sub-Committee on Small Businesses held a seminar on the 'question whether planning and regulation are replacing competition in the industrial state', others took issue with his arguments. Without reviewing the whole range of the controversy we may note that it was pointed out that firms do not always succeed in selling what they want to the consumer. Many products fail despite the most careful monitoring of test market experiments and heavy market research outlays. The failure of the Ford Edsel which Galbraith treated rather as the exception that proves the rule may perhaps be an example that holds all too frequently. The development of cheaper communications, greater numbers of substitutes as a result of innovation and the threat of potential competition as larger firms diversify and come into closer market contact with each other through their innovations are all indicative of a possibility that competition might in some respects at least be increasing.[11]

An interesting formulation of the process of competition that takes place in industries is to be found in Downie's description based upon the concept of two tranformation mechanisms, the transfer and the innovation mechanism. He argued that the dispersion of efficiency and progress is the key indicator of the economic performance of an industry. Efficiency differences exist between firms as a result of the ability of some firms to work nearer full capacity and to gain greater pecuniary economies than others and as a result of changing practices and technologies in firms. Now the relative efficiencies of previous periods are reflected in present-day market shares and the operation of the transfer mechanism will mean that the more efficient will tend to gain sales at the expense of their rivals. But concentration will not increase indefinitely because the threat of a loss of sales will be sufficient to induce the less efficient to innovate in order to survive. He called this the innovation mechanism. Thus, in Downie's formulation, the pressure to innovate comes from relative inefficiency and the operation of the two transformation mechanisms together ensures that the average efficiency of the industry is continually rising through time. The process will be hindered where high concentration, restrictive practices or other disincentives to competition exist or where heavy capital investment has to be amortised or an industry is in secular decline. Downie claimed empirical validity for his explanation as he found that changes in the relative sizes of firms did occur over time and that the firms that had increased their productivity the most had grown the fastest, thus supporting the concept of a transfer mechanism. He claimed that the causal relation was such that the increase in efficiency led to the increase in size rather than *vice versa*. He also found that the rankings of firms by productivity do change through time and this is consistent with an innovation mechanism. He did not, however, find strong evidence that industries that were highly concentrated or had restrictive agreements tended to impair the transfer mechanism.

Competition through innovation

Considerable emphasis has been placed at a macro-level on the importance of technical progress for economic growth. But the level of technical progress in an economy is a function of the innovative process of individual firms, possibly motivated by quite different considerations. By and large, firms will make a product innovation for one or more of three main reasons. First, they may do so in order to exploit a particular market opportunity that they have identified and in so doing would expect to achieve the benefits of growth and higher profits. Where this is concerned with a newly identified need the effect on other firms' market shares may be negligible. Where the innovation represents a superior product offered in an existing market segment this will have an effect on the market shares of all firms in the industry and will be highly competitive. Secondly, firms may innovate in order to defend themselves against the competition of other firms. This is a key element in Downie's explanation of the competitive process and it does appear to have practical validity from other investigations of innovations. It is interesting that Mansfield reported that a leader with one innovation was likely to be relatively slow with the next innovation [12] and this is again entirely consistent with Downie's formulation. A third motive is as a response to low margins and/or static or declining markets on existing products. This may be a consequence of competition. It may also serve to emphasise that innovation is a key to continuing success for the firm. Thus we have both aggressive and defensive considerations for innovative activity in a firm. Some firms may be sufficiently committed to innovation that they are constantly on the look-out for new products, others may be forced to be innovators by market conditions.

A successful innovation can yield a very high return indeed and may lead to a marked change in the level and distribution of an organisation's income. Where a firm does rely heavily on a highly successful product, especially if it is protected from competition for a period of time by patents, as the effective life of the product or of its patent protection draws to a close the firm may become particularly anxious to find a new winner to replace it or otherwise face a marked fall in earnings. Where the firm's own R and D has not come up with such a replacement innovation this may be a signal for a search to acquire other companies that might have a suitable product. In some industries the chances of finding a winner may be very low and this may generate very intensive research effort and may be a reason for attempted mergers. In the pharmaceutical industry for example it has been estimated that only one compound in every 5,000 that are synthesised ultimately reaches the market. This means that each major drug company will on average make a major product development only rarely and will be under pressure to exploit fully the advantages it has from those that are successful.

In Chapter 1 we discussed the question of whether one form of market structure was any more or any less likely to encourage innovation than another and concluded that there was little to support the view that concentration and innovation were closely associated, though there was some evidence that too much concentration in an industry might hinder innovation. Similarly, we found that large firms did not appear to have major advantages in invention though they might have in innovation. Various studies have also paid attention to the question of whether particular types of firm are more or less likely to be successful innovators.[13] This is a most important issue since many products that are test marketed do not reach the point of a national launch and even of those that are made generally available a large number fail to attain the market that had been predicted for them and subsequently have to be withdrawn.

It is unlikely that a single common influence would be identified and it is again unlikely that identical considerations would necessarily apply in all situations. Some of the conditions for success that have been most frequently mentioned are:

(1)   Effective market research and test marketing should have been undertaken in order to reduce the level of risk by predicting more accurately how the consumer will respond. Close understanding of the market and the needs of customers is required for success.

(2)   The product should be right first time. It is not clear that in all cases a firm has to be first with an innovation to be successful but speed is clearly important where two more or less identical products are being developed by rival producers. This seems to have been the problem that faced Lever Bros. in its competition with Procter and Gamble in the launch of a biological detergent. The Lever product, Radiant, was launched on the test market nine months before Procter and Gamble's rival Ariel. However, Radiant was found to have only limited consumer acceptance, due primarily it seems to deficiencies in its whitening powers. Even a second, improved, version was found on test marketing to require further changes and it was not until 21 months after the initial test market programme started that Radiant was launched nationally. Ariel on the other hand was found to be right first time and moved to a national launch within nine months of its test market. Ariel was nationally available three months ahead of Radiant despite Ariel's initial nine months lag.[14]

(3)   The product should fit effectively into the firm's existing product lines and use the same channels of distribution.

(4)   There should be close and effective liaison between the various functional areas – R and D, production, sales, marketing – within the firm. Innovation should not be seen as merely the responsibility of an R and D department, it is a corporate task for the whole organisation. Often a strong, senior manager may be needed to take responsibility for the outcome of the project and to ensure it receives the attention and resources it requires to assist its progress.

(5)   All elements of the marketing mix – price, packaging, advertising – should be carefully determined. An innovation will normally need to be backed by heavy marketing effort. Distributors should be happy to accept the product. This is one of the major difficulties that has recently faced

manufacturers of grocery products and other consumable goods. Large retailers are often unwilling to give new products the shelf space they need for effective display. For their part, the distributors argue that they are being asked to handle increasing numbers of new products, many of which they judge have little chance of success.

(6) In the case of producer goods, close contact between supplier and user will often be necessary.

It is also possible to distinguish the characteristics of successful innovators when compared with unsuccessful innovators. The SAPPHO project in the Science Policy Research Unit at the University of Sussex was based on a study of 29 paired successful and unsuccessful innovations in the chemical and scientific instrument industries. The analysis showed that there were five key considerations which distinguished between successful and unsuccessful innovators. It was found that successful innovators had a much better understanding of user needs; paid much more attention to marketing; performed their development work more efficiently, eliminating technical defects before the launch, though not necessarily more quickly; made more effective use of outside technology and scientific advice; had a key individual, with responsibility for the project, who had greater seniority and authority than in an unsuccessful firm.[15] The information from this and similar studies is important since it indicates that developments that might be profitable to the firm and beneficial to the consumer may be wasted and lost if the firm fails to adopt appropriate strategies in its development and marketing of the innovation.

Much product and process innovation undoubtedly adds to economic welfare. It may increase competition, new products may be made available that satisfy a particular need or a new process may lead to savings in production costs and therefore in resources. It is less likely that such innovations will lead to reductions in absolute prices though if a hedonic price were calculated reflecting the price paid for a particular 'basket of characteristics' the price might be found to have declined.

So far, however, we have made little attempt to establish just what is an innovation and whether all innovations are equally desirable. A major new product or a major new process is clearly an innovation. But is it also correct to describe as an innovation minor modifications to an existing product introduced in an attempt to get round a patent or to convince consumers that their existing units are now obsolete and should be replaced? Exactly where is the line to be drawn? Often competition may tend to emphasise such minor modifications and styling changes. Here it might be more strongly argued that such competition, which often includes built-in obsolescence, is wasteful. Inventing around a drug or some other patented product may offer little ultimate benefit but will have used up resources in the process. Frequent style changes especially in the motor car industry have also been criticised on the grounds that they are costly and do not really improve the product. Such competition also makes it difficult for smaller firms to stay in the industry since they will not have fully amortised their existing overhead equipment before it is necessary to incur the tooling and other costs of new style changes.

An American investigation attempted to look at the costs of model changes by asking the question: 'What costs would have been saved had the cars available in 1949 continued to be made available, but using developing technology, at later dates?'[16] The additional costs that were identified as occurring as a result of model changes were the costs of increasing the size and horse-power of the cars and the effects on petrol consumption of the 'horsepower race'; the costs of automatic transmission, power steering and power brakes (though some of these could be avoided by consumers as they could be bought separately); the retooling costs and the increase in advertising costs. By the late 1950s the authors estimated that the annual cost of model changes was running at $4,843 millions, in other words an average of an extra $700 had been added to the price of each car. In addition account had to be taken of future petrol costs that had already been committed as a result of the changes. By 1959 these were 20 per cent up on the equivalent for 1949 cars. In 1961 it was estimated that the present value of the future petrol cost already committed amounted to $7,110 millions. It was recognised that some monetary benefits had been gained, such as the savings from faster average speeds of travel, which had not been taken into account but against this we should probably need to set certain external costs such as the higher cost of accidents occurring at faster speeds and the pressure for faster, better quality roads. The authors of the study emphasised that they did not seek to blame the manu-facturers for this state of affairs but rather assumed that consumer sovereignty existed. Whether this was a justifiable assumption is perhaps debatable. Whatever the cause, this study indicates that the functioning of the market may well have produced an undesirable consequence, causing motorists to incur heavy extra costs and probably weakening the few remaining smaller motor manufac-turers in the United States.

Competition through the marketing mix

Although various writers have emphasised that it is innovation that is at the heart of the competitive process, much competition takes place through variations in the level and skill of use of different elements in the marketing mix available to the firm. Indeed, whereas decisions on innovations will only be taken occasionally by a firm, decisions on variations in the marketing mix will need to be taken very frequently indeed. If we define marketing as the creation and satisfaction of wants it is clear that all functions within a firm should to a greater or lesser degree be considered to be part of the marketing activity and indeed it is often the firms that lack a market orientation that are most prone to run into difficulties.

The range of variables on which the firm has to take decisions really constitute the marketing mix of the firm. These will include price and margin decisions, the use of a brand name, packaging and appearance, delivery arrangements, the role of the sales force, the choice of channels of distribution, the number of brands to offer in the same market, promotions above the line through media advertising or below the line through other forms of promotional activity. Some of the decisions will be constrained by legal requirements such as the Trade Descriptions Act or the Resale Prices Act. Many decisions on one variable will influence a decision on another. It is, for example, unlikely that a firm could afford to have both a low price and an expensive promotional policy for the same product. The objective of the firm therefore must be so to allocate its promotional budget, including price, that it obtains the best return at the least total cost. In fact, it seems that there is evidence that firms appear to allocate a fixed quantum to marketing outlays and seek to distribute this between the different elements in the mix in such a way as to try to achieve the best possible return. In this section we shall offer some brief comments on the implications of some of the main elements in the marketing mix and in the following chapter will discuss in rather greater depth the issues concerning the role of advertising.

Although we have indicated that much competition tends not to be based on price this is not to say that price is unimportant or that it no longer has a part to play. A product that is priced markedly out of line from its rivals and without compensating non-price advantages will normally fail to sell and so price acts at least as a constraint. Firms often prefer to avoid price competition because of the fear that this will generate price wars or that price changes are easy to copy whereas competition using other marketing strategies is less easy to copy. However, there may be occasions where price reductions or the shading of prices constitute a very important form of competition. Where the unit value of a product is low as with a bar of chocolate and small adjustments to prices are not always possible a weight reduction may be used as an effective alternative.

The role of branding is well established in many product areas. A well established brand name is often considered to be to the advantage of the manufacturer as it may reduce the amount that has to be spent on product advertising and may assist the introduction of new products. This advantage may also extend to a well established and respected company name where a company's reputation for high quality products may make consumers more willing to try a new product offered by the same manufacturer. If a manufacturer has successfully undertaken a market segmentation exercise he may find it profitable to offer for sale two brands of the same product but aimed at different types of consumer in each segment. They may well be in essence the same product but the addition at low marginal cost of an extra ingredient or a variation in the package may make it possible to serve two quite different types of customer more effectively than if only one brand was on offer. Product design, appearance and packaging can also be important influences on the success of the brand though only infrequent changes can normally be made in view of the relatively high costs of changing production and printing equipment.

Many facets of the distribution policy of the firm contribute to the success or failure of a product. A firm may have a choice between different types of channel of distribution – whether to use wholesalers or to undertake the wholesaling function for itself, what sort of retail outlet to use, whether to go for exclusivity in distribution by offering a limited number of franchises or mass distribution, and so on. Decisions on the sort of distribution channel to use will influence decisions about the size of retail margins that need to be built into a retail price. For example, grocery outlets work on a lower gross margin than chemists, hardware shops, electrical retailers, etc. Attempts to sell the same product in different types of outlet can cause difficulty as an appropriate margin for one type of retailer may be either too high or too low for another. Margins that are too high may cause severe price cutting. Margins that are too low will discourage retailers from stocking the item. Effective representation and display in the outlets selected is crucial. Demand and supply are interdependent since stocks have an important demand-creating role. A manufacturer must therefore pay careful attention to his distributive outlets and he will often be encouraged to provide additional incentives to distributors in the hope of obtaining improved display. Similarly, since it is known that many consumers select an alternative when a preferred brand is not in the shop, a manufacturer will try to ensure that retailers are not out of stock of his brands.

Brands with low sales face extra difficulties. There is often a critical minimum threshold level of sales below which it becomes very difficult to stay in the market at all. Large retail chains may be unwilling to stock products on which the value of sales is less than a specified minimum level. Brand choice may be influenced by a demonstration effect so the larger the volume of a brand already in use the easier it will be to achieve further sales. This seemed to have been the problem facing British and other foreign car producers attempting to sell in the American market, at least some years ago. The number of foreign cars seen on American roads was small and in consequence there was little demonstration effect and second-hand prices were depressed. Very few dealers found it worthwhile to accept franchises for foreign cars. Volkswagen met this problem by buying a large number of garages from coast to coast in the United States and so gave itself a much better opportunity to attain the critical threshold level of sales beyond which it was able to become a force in the market. Other manufacturers, especially those whose products are retailed through specialist outlets that concentrate on only one or a few products, may also find that expenditure on the acquisition and improvement of outlets is an important and profitable form of competitive behaviour and a major use of the total marketing resources of the organisation.

Of course, not all suppliers will choose to use normal distributive outlets. Direct selling may prove for some firms to be a more effective way of using the total marketing mix. Others may also choose to deal direct with the customer through mail order sales.

The range of promotional activities available to a firm is considerable and seems to have increased rapidly in the last ten years or so. The forms of promotional effort actually adopted will depend upon the nature of the product and of the market that is being served. Two examples might perhaps indicate some of the range of promotional activities available to a supplier. Kelloggs were reported to use the following forms of promotion: advertising through the media, television, press and posters; competitions requiring the sending in of cereal packet tops in order to enter; free mail-in offers of specially obtained items again in return for packet tops; premium items inserted in the packet; self-liquidating premium offers where other goods are obtained at a bargain price and offered for sale in return also for a specified number of packet tops (they are termed self-liquidating because the revenue from the sale of the goods together with the boost to cereal sales exceeds the cost of the goods and of the administration of the offer); related tie-ups where, for example, a free packet of tea is offered in return for a cereal packet top; free samples; money-off coupons; cash incentives and other improved terms for short periods of time offered to retailers to encourage them to promote the product with an in-store price reduction and special display.[17] In this case some part of the marketing effort has to be directed at retailers and part at consumers as the final purchasers of the product. In contrast in the pharmaceutical industry, which is another industry where promotional expenditures tend to be high, the nature of the product and its marketing arrangements means that the main objective of the drug companies is to promote to those whose job it is to prescribe particular drugs – general practitioners and hospital doctors. Consequently nearly 50 per cent of the total promotional outlay of the drug companies is on sales representation. Nearly one-fifth is on the provision of literature on drugs and the costs of sending it through the post. Advertising in professional journals and the provision of samples are other major forms of promotional expenditure in this industry.[18]

Marketers tend to make a distinction between 'above the line' and 'below the line' promotion. Above the line promotions comprise all forms of media advertising and are particularly concerned with building up an image and establishing continuing brand loyalty. Below the line promotions consist of all other forms of promotional expenditure – reduced price offers, competitions, free samples, money-off coupons, self-liquidating premium offers, etc. Their purpose is the rather more immediate one of trying to persuade consumers to try a particular brand. During the latter part of the 1960s below the line promotions claimed a rising share of the manufacturer's total promotional budget especially on products sold through supermarkets and such outlets. This development was probably associated with the shift in the balance of power away from manufacturers and towards the large retailers and the greater ability of the leading retailing groups to influence the forms of promotion adopted. Many manufacturers appear to regret this trend and have attempted to reverse it. They argue that, by emphasising price reductions, below the line promotions have heightened consumer price consciousness at the expense of brand loyalty and have therefore made their overall marketing task more difficult.

Even if it helps to increase the firm's sales or market share, not all market behaviour is necessarily desirable from a public interest point of view. Some marketing strategies – full-line forcing, aggregated rebates, price discrimination, the maintenance of lists of approved dealers or suppliers – may hinder competition and have, for this reason, frequently been criticised by investigatory authorities. Branding and excessive and spurious product differentiation may constitute a barrier to entry and so may help to weaken competition. Innovations may not represent major product improvements and may cause a waste of scarce economic resources. Promotions are often very expensive. The question is whether they are unreasonably so and whether the same benefits could be obtained with lower or different forms of promotional outlay. Opinions are, of course, divided on this.

It is clear that the array of marketing techniques that can be deployed has been expanded quite markedly in recent years. This means that suppliers need to be increasingly skilful in establishing the most effective marketing mix. It also means that there is a continually growing need for effective guidance and protection for the consumer to counteract the marketing pressures from both manufacturer and distributor.

CHAPTER 11

ADVERTISING AND THE COMPETITIVE PROCESS

We have argued in Chapter 10 that advertising is only one among a number of alternative promotional forms and often does not even represent an unduly large proportion of total marketing outlays. Yet a disproportionate amount of critical attention has focused upon advertising in isolation. Why should this be so? It may be that advertising exercises particular economic influences that other marketing strategies, no matter how important, do not, or that advertising raises social and ethical issues that are not apparent with other forms of marketing strategy. In this chapter we shall investigate some of the main controversies surrounding the economic implications of advertising while bearing in mind that there is much more to marketing, and indeed to promotion, than advertising alone.

The incidence of advertising

In 1972 total expenditure on advertising in the United Kingdom amounted to £708 million. This is equivalent to about 1.8 per cent of consumer expenditure or about 1.3 per cent of GNP. These ratios have remained more or less stable through the 1960s.[1] In global terms £84 million was spent on food advertising, £69 million on household and leisure goods, £55 million on drink and tobacco, £41 million on toiletries and medical products and just under £80 million was spent by retail organisations. About 25 per cent of advertising expenditure went on television, 27 per cent on regional newspapers, 18 per cent on national newspapers and 9 per cent on magazines and periodicals. If we exclude classified advertising and the placing of company reports and other financial details, it seems that about 75 per cent of total advertising expenditure is explicitly for the purpose of gaining a market or expanding sales. Undoubtedly the distribution of such 'marketing oriented' advertising is such that television and magazines received proportionately more marketing oriented advertising, while newspapers were proportionately more important recipients of classified advertising. Television advertising revenues seem to be heavily dependent upon a limited number of product areas. The PIB reported that nearly 50 per cent came from food, drink and tobacco advertising, 20 per cent from household equipment suppliers and 11 per cent from pharmaceuticals, toileteries and cosmetics.[2]

While a measure of total outlays on advertising will give an indication of the contribution of a particular sector to total advertising revenues it is less useful as a basis for deciding whether the incidence of advertising is particularly high or low. A more appropriate measure for this purpose would be the ratio of advertising outlays to total sales for the relevant product group. However, even the advertising/sales ratio has its limitations. It is unable to take into account the differential importance of economies of scale in the advertising of different products. Excessive reliance upon advertising/sales ratios by those concerned with the economic implications of marketing outlays may lead them to give tacit approval to other firms and industries where this ratio is low but where other forms of promotional outlay are high. For example, heavy advertising may be inappropriate in producer goods industries but a low advertising/sales ratio would not necessarily justify a commentator in concluding that there was no problem of excess promotional activity there. It may well be that equally heavy outlays are incurred through direct selling or in providing business lunches, which it has been suggested are the equivalent in producer goods industries of advertising on consumer products.[3]

It seems that the intensity of advertising as measured by advertising/sales ratios tends to be at similar levels for the same product in different countries. This suggests that the incidence of advertising is not determined simply by random influences but that it is meaningful to look for specific conditions under which advertising intensity is expected to be high.

It has been observed that highly advertised products tend to have certain common characteristics. They are often items with low price elasticities of demand; they offer good opportunities for product differentiation; the costs of shopping around tend to be high in relation to the likely benefits (this is especially likely to be the case with low price consumer products); the product may have hidden qualities that cannot be assessed at the time of purchase; new products or brands are frequently introduced; the identity of purchasers is changing rapidly; consumer tastes and loyalties are fickle. In some cases it is not easy to be certain whether some of these characteristics are the cause or the effect of advertising. It has, however, been strongly argued that the intensity of advertising on such products is a reflection of a high level of consumer demand for information from advertisers about these items.[4] It may alternatively be argued that these are the characteristics that give the manufacturer the greatest opportunity to appeal direct to the consumer, the greatest opportunity to exploit the existence of existing market imperfections arising from consumer ignorance or inertia, or the greatest need to attempt to mould consumer choice so that the level of demand is rather more predictable.

Other explanations of the incidence of heavy advertising on certain types of product are also to be found. It has been pointed out that heavily advertised products are often those where demand is, or may be, subject to psychological motivations associated with considerations of status, health, children, sex, etc.[5] It is also arguable that manufacturer production conditions and market relationships are important influences upon the intensity of advertising. Capital intensive production conditions and the possibility of scale economies will provide an incentive to firms to maintain a high and predictable level of production, and advertising may offer some opportunity to attain this. Such production conditions are likely to limit the number of firms in an industry and emphasise the extent of oligopolistic interdependence between manufacturers. This form of market structure tends to encourage the use of advertising rather than price reductions as a means of sales promotion. Here too, the direction of causality is open to discussion. For the moment we can simply note that heavy advertising is likely under such circumstances. Oligopoly is discussed in depth in Chapter 14.

The role of advertising

Effective advertising has both an informative and persuasive role and it is not really helpful to attempt to make an operational distinction between the two functions, although the normative implications may be quite different. It is useful in informing potential consumers of the availability of a product and of changes in prices, qualities, etc. In this respect it heightens competition by making choice more informed. In its persuasive role, advertising restructures preferences encouraging consumers to accept as desirable the characteristics of the advertised brand. Several likely consequences of the persuasive role of advertising may be identified. First, the elasticity of demand facing the individual supplier is reduced as brand loyalty is strengthened. If this is accompanied by the successful differentiation of the product and establishment of a distinctive brand image it may be possible for a manufacturer to establish a premium price for his brand. Secondly, it is quite likely that the demand curve facing the brand (and possibly the product group as well) will be shifted outwards as more consumers are persuaded to commit some of their resources to this particular product. Thirdly, advertising may assist new entry, both of new brands by existing producers [6] and also of new suppliers. Fourthly, the effect of advertising is long lasting and is cumulative. In this way advertising acts as a capital or investment good, building up future sales through the continued exposure of the consumer to an advertising message.

There does not seem to be much helpful guidance available to manufacturers in deciding how much to allocate to advertising. Doyle has shown that the optimum level of advertising will be found to exist where the marginal value product of the advertising is equal to the price elasticity of demand for the product.[7] But if advertising is treated as an investment good then effective allocation of resources also requires the consideration of the resultant flows of income over time, probably using some form of discounted cash flow analysis. Appraisal is also made more difficult by the likelihood that a decision by one manufacturer to increase advertising will be matched by his competitors and so, as with pricing decisions in oligopoly, the effect of advertising on sales is not uniquely determined for that manufacturer alone but is dependent upon the reactions of his rivals.

Whether because of the difficulties of establishing a meaningful advertising appropriation policy or because of the lack of scientific management, many firms use only a basic rule of thumb technique for determining their advertising appropriations. While trading conditions remain unchanged they will tend to allocate a set proportion of the previous year's sales or of the current year's anticipated sales or a fixed proportion of profits or of the firm's liquid resources.[8] Alternatively they may allow the previous year's advertising budget to serve as a guide to the level for the following year. When demand falls or business conditions generally become worse, it is often advertising expenditure that is the first to be cut back. It is not difficult to understand why firms take such a step since it is much easier to cancel reasonably quickly a particular promotional campaign and so improve the firm's cash flow position than to initiate many other cost-saving activities. However, if advertising is effective it must be doubted whether this is the most opportune action to take. It is sometimes argued that advertising can be an important counter-cyclical force but the evidence shows that advertising outlays and the business cycle are positively correlated. This means that any stabilising functions advertising may have are not effectively utilised.

Advertising has, like other products and processes, economic features which the decision-maker needs to take into account in deciding on his most appropriate policy. We have already noted that it is best viewed as a capital good with cumulative effects spread through time. This has a bearing on the way the return to advertising should be assessed. Advertising is subject to increasing returns to scale to the firm since it is cheaper to buy advertising space or time if larger quantities are purchased; there is greater opportunity to achieve an optimum mix of different media and there are gains from a greater total exposure of potential purchasers to an advertising message. Kelloggs for example had a lower advertising/sales ratio than two of its three main rivals but this was not an indication of less advertising effort by Kelloggs but rather of the high threshold level for effective advertising and promotion in its product areas and of the scale advantages in buying advertising time and premium goods that accrued to the large firm.[9] The advertising elasticity of demand is normally held to be less than unity. This indicates that to obtain a given percentage increase in sales will require a more than proportionate increase in advertising expenditure.

The advertiser should however always remember that advertising is but one element in the marketing mix and is by its relatively unselective nature likely to be wasteful in terms of the amount of money spent on disinterested and unresponsive people. There is therefore a need for advertisers constantly to appraise the benefits they receive from advertising against the likely returns from using the same funds on an alternative promotion or form of marketing expenditure. Often, however, despite its apparent wastes, advertising may be the most cost-effective form of marketing technique. An equivalent price reduction may be insignificant to consumers. It has been argued that firms with higher advertising costs tend to have lower total marketing costs which suggests that they are in fact achieving an efficient marketing mix. Equally, advertising (like other forms of promotion) if skilfully used will be difficult to copy and is therefore more valuable to a firm than a price reduction or a margin increase. But in other cases it may be that firms have failed to monitor the effects of their advertising and are showing a negative return to advertising. In a review of petrol marketing in several countries Lambin argued that the petrol companies would be better advised to place greater emphasis on increasing their shares of outlets and improving the overall performance of their distribution networks than to maintain present levels of advertising expenditure.[10] It may be that the companies recognise this but are afraid that if they take such action their rivals will not follow suit and that they would consequently lose out. Once again we are therefore faced with the problem of the interdependence in decision-making between firms and the difficulties that this creates for any individual firm wishing to make a radical change in the status quo in an industry.

The economic consequences of advertising

The economic consequences of advertising have been discussed at length by numerous commentators some of whom have reached favourable conclusions and others unfavourable. Such studies have been marked by problems of the unavailability of much relevant data and the poor quality of the statistical information that is available. There has often been subsequent debate over the validity of the data and/or the techniques used in arriving at different conclusions. A number of different areas have been noticed where advertising might have some impact, including the effects upon concentration, barriers to entry, prices, profits, etc. Instead of considering these facets separately we shall consider the implications of advertising for industry structure, market conduct and economic performance.

(1) Advertising and Industry Structure

The relationship between advertising and concentration levels either generally or for selected product groups or industrial sectors has received extensive investigation. It might be argued a priori that advertising is likely to increase concentration by giving advantages to larger firms and that the lagged effects of advertising create long-standing monopoly power and so discourage new entry. Alternatively it may be that by improving information flows advertising helps to increase the likelihood that new entrant firms could establish their position in an industry. The direction of causality might also be debated. While advertising might be a cause of concentration, concentration might also be a cause of high advertising, at least in oligopolies where fears of price wars encourage firms to look for alternative forms of competition. A similar inducement to advertise would not be expected either in more competitive or in monopolistic industries. This suggests that the relation between advertising intensity and concentration may well not be linear but may take the form of an inverse U, peaking at levels of concentration consistent with oligopoly. Some case might, however, also be made for the view that so many other influences besides market structure affect the decision to advertise that there is little reason for expecting a close relation between advertising and concentration and that it is only for mass-produced goods with similar marketing characteristics that such a relationship would be expected.[11]

Some empirical investigations have found a positive relationship between advertising and concentration,[12] and in some cases the tendency has been noted for advertising intensity to be high in oligopolies. A recent investigation [13] for 26 consumable products in the United Kingdom found a strong inverse U-shaped relationship between advertising intensity and the Herfindahl index (H) measure of concentration. Advertising intensity was highest where the H value was .4 and this is consistent with high advertising in duopoly. The estimated advertising/sales ratio rose from 4 per cent for products in competitive market structures to 15 per cent in a duopoly. Other investigations have, however, found no association between a high advertising intensity and high market concentration.[14]

The conditions of entry are of course an important influence upon market structure. Bain's investigation showed that product differentiation was often a major barrier to competition.[15] Certainly the existence of scale advantages both in the current period and through the effect of past advertising activities may constitute a major barrier to competition from smaller and new entrant firms. This view has been given qualitative support by the Monopolies Commission in its report on detergents where it decided that the advertising and promotional activities of the two leading firms constituted a barrier to entry [16] and on cigarettes where the Commission reported that advertising had helped to preserve the power of a few firms.[17]

On balance it seems that, while there are exceptions, there is good reason for thinking that advertising is more likely than not to create a barrier to competition and to be at its peak in tight oligopoly situations. However, the nature of the product will be an important influence on the sort of relation that is found to exist. The implication of this is that results of regression analysis covering a disparate variety of products may be quite misleading as

218 Industrial Structure & Market Conduct

to the true role of advertising in influencing market structure. The key question to ask is whether the level of concentration is higher as a result of heavy advertising than it would otherwise have been. One commentator has offered the opinion that if there were no advertising there would not be any less concentration [18] but this view is unlikely to meet with unqualified agreement from all economists.

(2) Advertising and Market Conduct

We have seen in Chapter 1 that market structure is not necessarily a good proxy for either market conduct or performance and it may be that the impact of advertising on conduct and performance is different from its impact on structure. If we accept that competition has a meaning much more extensive than price competition and covers all forms of rivalry between producers, changing market shares, innovation, etc., then advertising and competitive behaviour may be quite compatible. Indeed in certain circumstances advertising may be of crucial importance to competition. This is so where it facilitates the introduction of new brands or products and where it provides the consumer with information on prices, suppliers, etc. That advertising is associated with competition and especially product innovation has been demonstrated in several studies dealing with cigarettes, pharmaceuticals and electrical goods.[19]

It does not, however, necessarily follow that all forms of competition are equally desirable and some (though not all [20]) would still hold that price competition is normally to be preferred. Certainly, emphasis on advertising may weaken price competition, may encourage the public to pay attention to spurious novelty elements in a product and so may lead to wasteful expenditures in developing new and improved products where the changes are of little intrinsic value to the consumer. The problem is that many of the areas where advertising is most likely to be a useful competitive element are also most likely to be those where the charge of wasteful innovation is most likely to apply.

(3) Advertising and Economic Performance

The welfare aspects of economic performance have three main dimensions concerned with allocative, technical and distributive efficiency. All three are relevant here. The question of allocative efficiency is concerned with whether the effects of advertising are to lead to the most desirable allocation of resources. Although information is sometimes a commodity that can be purchased direct – through for example subscriptions to *Which?* or other consumer test journals – advertising is supplied in association with a particular product. The price of the product really incorporates also the price of the information supplied through advertising but as the information is not separately charged for this means that the direct price of the advertising to the consumer is zero.

This suggests that more advertising is supplied than people really want and would be willing to pay for if an economic charge were to be made for it direct.[21] The effect of including the cost of advertising in with the price of the product means that consumers have no opportunity to exercise their sovereignty to indicate whether they wish to receive advertising messages or not and the public has ultimately to pay the costs of an activity from which it may derive little or no benefit. These objections turn not only on the fact that advertising is supplied at zero price but also on the assumption that advertising is not a valuable source of information. Either view is sufficient to indicate some misallocation of resources but the combination of the two may cause a more serious loss of welfare. The effects on resource allocation may also be adverse where the effect of advertising is to change the distribution of consumer expenditure towards advertised items and where it changes the relative prices of goods (raising prices) and of the media – press and television (lowering prices here through the element of subsidy).

The implications for technical efficiency arise from the effects of advertising on the total costs of a firm's operations. It is arguable that advertising is cost effective because it allows the attainment of economies of scale and may facilitate a reduction in other marketing costs through, for example, the ability to offer lower retail margins to distributors where the product is heavily pre-sold through advertising. It may also be that there are scale advantages in supplying a joint package of the product plus its associated advertising, thereby avoiding the transaction costs of supplying advertising separately for individual customers [22] so that any separate informational substitute for advertising might be more expensive. But it is also arguable that some advertising is prone to bid up total costs. Advertising competition in static markets and between oligopolists is liable to have a ratchet effect, continually bidding up the stakes with no firm being willing to run the risk of lowering its outlay. It may be costly because its blanket coverage means that advertisers are unable to be selective in providing information only to those that seek it. It may bid up the cost of new entry by increasing consumer attachment to existing products and because the existence of a low advertising elasticity of demand necessitates particularly heavy outlays for any gain in sales volume. If the effect of advertising is to shorten brand life and increase the rate of product obsolescence this will also have the effect of hindering the minimisation of costs and so will harm economic performance.

Distributive efficiency considerations are concerned with the effect on market power, and hence on prices and profits, of advertising. It is possible that if the cost savings already discussed are attained the effect of advertising might be to lower prices. On the other hand it is arguable that advertising is more likely to raise prices and profits by acting as a force that weakens competition, increases barriers to entry and heightens the monopoly power of existing large firms. The Monopolies Commission found that the detergent manufacturers had undertaken heavy advertising and promotion as a means of preserving their respective monopolies. The excessive advertising had kept up prices and margins, had weakened price competition and had not resulted in the attainment of extra economies elsewhere.[23] In the case of breakfast cereals the Commission found that Kelloggs' advertising had reduced the price elasticity of demand, had helped to create manufacturer independence of the market and had given increased freedom in pricing. The Commission found that the effect on prices and profits was substantial though it did not consider that at the time of the investigation it was excessive.[24]

Increased market power would be expected to lead not only to higher prices but also to higher profits and on both counts a redistribution of income away from the consumer and towards the producer. Various studies have investigated the relationship between advertising intensity and profits or price-cost margins and have found in varying degrees that high advertising intensity and high profits are correlated.[25] In one case it was found that heavy advertisers tended to have profit rates that were 50 per cent above those in other industries and much of this was attributed to the effect of advertising in creating entry barriers. It was not thought likely that the explanation was due to a reverse direction of causation in which high profits generated heavy advertising.[26] Statistical testing of this relationship, however, also has its problems. Not only may advertising/sales ratios be an inappropriate measure but the rate of return on capital employed is also subject to limitations as a reliable indicator of profit. Of particular relevance in this context is the possibility that firms in advertising intensive industries overstate their rate of return because their accounting conventions encourage them to treat advertising as a current expense whereas if it was treated more realistically as an investment the reported level of capital employed in the company would be raised and the rate of return reduced.[27]

The social implications of advertising

Much has been made of the social and ethical consequences of advertising [28] and there are aspects of this that bear a close relation to specific economic considerations. The main objections can perhaps be grouped together under the allegation that 'advertising provides too little information and lays too much stress on persuasion'. Within this umbrella objection we find criticisms that advertisers make meaningless and even misleading claims;[29] that by playing on the emotions they encourage irrational motivations and give rise to moral and physical danger; that advertising emphasises spurious novelty elements in the product; that it encourages inter-personal comparisons of utility and creates consumer dissatisfaction. Clearly if these criticisms are justified one of the social consequences of advertising is to encourage a maldistribution of consumer spending power through a shift in consumer preferences. It would not, however, be justifiable to assume that all advertisers and all advertising were equally subject to these criticisms and it would also be incorrect to assume that the various protection agencies, such as the Advertising Standards Authority, were ineffective in controlling the quality of advertising copy even if sometimes their standards seem not to be sufficiently rigorous.

A second issue that combines social and economic considerations is the question of the subsidy that advertising brings to the press and television. The revenues of the independent television companies are almost entirely dependent upon their advertising income and on average 70 per cent of the revenue of the quality daily and Sunday newspapers is from advertising while the equivalent portion for the popular papers is about 40 per cent.[30] This indicates that even after making allowances for the production costs of the media in transmitting the advertisements, advertising represents a very substantial subsidy to the media. Whether or not this is desirable is a matter of opinion. Heavy dependence upon a major advertiser may weaken editorial freedom. Receipt of such advertising revenues may help to increase the number of different sources of information available to the public but may make the economic position of the press more unstable since the level of advertising is closely related to economic fluctuations. The existence of a subsidy from advertising to the media also has welfare implications. It distorts resource allocation by encouraging an over-production of mass-communication services unless the media produce useful externalities or are subject to falling long-run marginal costs. To the extent that the purchasers of advertised goods are not identical to television viewers and newspaper readers there is an element of income redistribution away from purchasers of goods who have to pay higher prices and towards the recipients of mass communication services who pay less than they would otherwise be required to. However, the magnitude of these problems in relation to press advertising is reduced when it is recognised that at least 50 per cent of the advertising revenue of the quality newspapers comes from classified advertising which is less open to objection on other economic and social grounds.

Appraisal

The position of advertising within the competitive process is a complicated one and it is perhaps right to emphasise that not all advertising is subject to the objections that have been levelled at the apparent economic abuses that arise from heavy promotional expenditures on a limited number of well-known products. The problem is that there is a paradox in the relationship between advertising and competition. Up to a point advertising may indeed have a positive role to play but beyond this point its effects appear more likely to be less favourable. The practical problem is to attempt to decide where that point is reached and whether the chances of going beyond that point are more likely to be dependent upon the nature of the product or of the competitive market relations between suppliers. This question does not seem to be satisfactorily resolved at the moment.

Any effectively competitive market needs adequate flows of information to buyers and sellers. At the moment advertising has a major role in the provision of information to consumers, although with the growth of consumerism other sources of information are also becoming available. Questions of the quality and quantity of information supplied in this way are important and there are grounds for concern that advertising is not providing sufficient relevant information. There are also reasons for thinking that the distribution of advertising expenditures is sub-optimal. There is evidence that consumers subscribe to consumer test magazines primarily for information to guide them in purchasing consumer durables. This is presumably because the infrequency of purchase and the high outlay involved on each purchase means that consumers have less confidence in their own judgement and experience in buying these products than in purchasing consumable goods where frequent repeat purchases and low unit prices mean that the risks to the consumer of a bad purchase are much lower and the learning effect much faster. Yet advertising intensity tends to be highest on consumable products and is low on consumer durables. This suggests that in terms of its role as a provider of information the distribution of advertising expenditures is misallocated. It also does not support the attempts of some economists to explain the incidence of advertising in terms of the level of consumer demand for information.

Even assuming that there was any desire to introduce controls either generally or in specific cases it is not easy to suggest suitable policy measures. Oligopolistic reluctance to cut back on promotional expenditures may necessitate direct action to encourage or force firms to reduce their outlays. This was the policy that the Monopolies Commission had in mind in making recommendations in the report on detergents for at least a 40 per cent reduction in selling expenses and a 20 per cent reduction in retail prices and the introduction of an automatic sanction possibly by disallowing selling expenses above a certain level as an expense for tax purposes.[31] After discussions between the Board of Trade and the manufacturers concerned these recommendations were not implemented. The possibility of discriminating against advertising through the system of tax allowances has, however, been more extensively discussed.[32] There could be problems if the price elasticity of demand facing the advertiser for his product was sufficiently low that he was able to shift the extra tax burden incurred on to the consumer in the form of higher prices. If such tax discrimination were not to hinder smaller competitors and so the growth of competition, it might be necessary to impose the restriction only on firms above a particular size.

The question still arises, however, as to whether there is any reason for adopting a more restrictive attitude towards advertising than to other forms of promotional and marketing expenditure. Although advertising might have some detrimental consequences that are more readily identifiable, care should be taken before adopting a policy which encourages a shift to another form of promotion or marketing effort which may prove to be equally unacceptable. Similarly, merely because a particular type of product lends itself to some form of marketing outlay other than advertising, it should not be assumed that it is necessarily acceptable. Excesses in any form of marketing activity may impose economic disadvantages.

In practice the real issue is not between all or no advertising but, at the margin, between a greater or lesser degree of a particular form of marketing expenditure. In distributive efficiency terms there is often a case to be made for preferring price competition to advertising competition. The role of own-brand products which are largely unadvertised and sold under the retailer's private label, often at lower prices than the alternative manufacturer advertised brand, may be an important competitive constraint upon the monopoly power of leading advertisers. Other ways of increasing the cross-elasticity of demand facing individual suppliers and so weakening the hold that their product differentiation activities gives them are also appropriate. In particular cases this may involve selling a product not under a brand name but under a generic description[33] or it may involve other attempts to promote more objective information and protection to the consumer, maybe through countervailing advertising and tighter controls on trading standards and practices generally. These controls seem to be required because of the paradox that while advertising may at first sight appear to be a competitive mode of market conduct, it may have effects on market structure and performance that are not consistent with a competitive norm.

CHAPTER 12
PRICE FORMATION BY FIRMS

Discussions of pricing are of central importance in economics and the neo-classical theory of the firm offers a coherent predictive model of the effects upon the level of prices of different production and market conditions. As with other optimising models it is, however, less useful as an explanation or description of the decision-making process. Just how much emphasis should be placed on the predictive performance of a model irrespective of the reality of its assumptions and of the quality of its explanatory properties has been a matter of major debate in economics.[1] This issue has already been touched on in Chapter 6 in the context of the discussion of the profit maximising assumption.

In this chapter we shall pay particular attention to the factors that firms take into account in setting their prices. It is, however, helpful to note briefly those respects in which the neo-classical models are deficient as behavioural descriptions of the price formation process.

There may be neither the desire nor the ability on the part of those responsible to maximise profits and decisions are more likely to be based upon rules of thumb rather than optimising techniques. The actual prices set will be a consequence of the reconciliation of divergent views about the correct price on the part of different functional groups within the firm. For example, whereas a marketing department may seek low prices for a product and may be supported in its wishes by the production department, pressures for larger distributive margins and hence higher prices may come from the sales force, pressures for higher prices in order to yield larger returns on investment may be emphasised by the accountants, while members of the legal department may be particularly anxious about the structure of prices and possible dangers of reference under anti-trust laws.

The neo-classical pricing model is a single product model and ignores not only the financial strength of the firm but also all other decision variables apart from price and output. A multi-product firm may have greater freedom in pricing any individual product, may choose to subsidise losses on one product from gains on another and may face considerable difficulties in allocating its indirect costs between individual items. By ignoring all other elements in the marketing mix the model ignores many of the important decision variables associated with the product. In practice decisions may also have to be made on product size, design, packaging, advertising and other marketing outlays, not to mention delivery time, distributor margins, etc.

With differentiated products price may not be the key equilibrating mechanism at all and it is probably true to say that choice is influenced by the consumer's perception of the sum of a number of characteristics of competing brands of which price is but one. If we are going to produce simple two-dimensional diagrams in discussing the theory of value, we should probably be prepared to describe our y axis not simply as a price axis but as some sort of 'value for money' or even 'psychic value for money' variable. This would include price and non-price variables together. Not only would this appear to be relevant from the demand analysis point of view,[2] it would also be appropriate as a description of the simultaneous decision-making that is required regarding price, cost and product characteristics in multi-product organisations.[3]

As a short-run static model the neo-classical approach is also unhelpful since it ignores the dynamic facets of the decision-making process and the attendant interdependencies between variables and decisions. As the limit price and other dynamic discussions have emphasised, a policy that is simply based on short-run adjustments is hardly likely to prove appropriate in the long run. From the point of view of the life of a product it is not possible to divide time into separate discrete independent short periods. Instead decisions taken at one point in time will not only influence other variables on which decisions are made at the same time but they will also influence subsequent decisions in later periods. Thus a decision on a given level of prices will influence the level of sales achieved and hence the length of production run and the degree of accumulated learning which will itself affect prices both now and in the next period. The role of stocks is an important influence on demand, especially for consumer goods, and so the production and demand sides of the equation cannot be kept separate but are, in fact, interdependent.[4] There is also a close link between investment and pricing decisions, since an investment decision presupposes a price in the first instance and the required rate of return will influence the level of prices that need to be established.

Alternative explanations of price formation

(1) *Some Analytical Considerations*

When we move away from reliance on simple maximising models we have nothing that is as explicit and straightforward to put in their place. In a discussion of pricing that emphasises the importance of the descriptive or explanatory powers of the model we must begin from a recognition that organisations may have different objectives and varying procedures. They do not all behave in the same way when faced with similar conditions and in fact their pricing decisions may be made under widely varying internal and external circumstances. As we observed in the previous paragraph, it is necessary to take into account many other facets of the firm's production, marketing and investment strategies which are inter-related with the pricing decision.

The link between objectives and price formation policies is important and the nature of the objectives of the organisation will have a considerable influence on the sort of pricing and marketing policy that a firm may seek to pursue.[5] But the mode of determination of prices or the actual price arrived at will not be predictable from a simple knowledge of the firm's objectives. Even if the objective is clear, too little information may be available with which to reach an optimal price. Where multiple objectives are specified it is not at all easy to identify the price that best satisfies these. Where decisions are taken in a bureaucratic management structure there may be less chance of agreeing on an optimum price.

Discussions of pricing all too frequently tend to assume that a single price can be identified in which the economist is interested. This is not always justified and it is often necessary to make a clear distinction between a number of alternative prices. For example, it may be necessary to specify clearly the distinction between list and achieved prices, recognising the effects of price shading or the practice of granting discounts on large orders and surcharges on small orders; or to distinguish between c.i.f. (carriage, insurance, freight) and ex works pricing thereby recognising the importance of transport charges and questions of freight averaging; or between the pricing of consumer goods where list prices are published and observable and the pricing of producer goods where negotiation is more often the order of the day; or between questions of manufacturer prices and prices to the final consumer. If prices to the final consumer are of particular interest the whole question of channel pricing, that is margins to distributors, and the question of the likely effects of distributor pricing decisions (especially in the absence of resale price maintenance) are as important as simple discussions of the manufacturer ex works price.

A further important distinction may often need to be made between the pricing of new products and the alteration of prices on existing goods. Quite different procedures are implied in each case. A more extensive pricing routine is clearly involved in the pricing of new products than is normally required in the adjustment of prices on existing products which are often simply to reflect cost changes. The nature of the motivations may differ in the two cases. With an established product it is reasonable to assume that the majority of price changes will aim to re-establish a profit level that has been eroded by rising costs. In the case of a new product it is not justifiable to assume that a supplier expects to make any profit for some time to come. For example, when the Prices and Incomes Board looked at confectionery prices it reported that all brands failed to yield a profit when initially introduced and that only some of the new brands succeeded even in making a contribution to overheads in the initial stages.[6]

(2) *Some Managerial Considerations*

In setting or changing prices the decision-makers within the firm also have many considerations to take into account, some of which are identical with those already covered in the analytical considerations just discussed. But there are many other issues as well which are perhaps best discussed in terms of a series of questions that the manager must ask himself:

(a) *How does the price I am intending to charge relate to my objectives regarding capacity utilisation, market share, profit, possible stability of prices and margins, relations with competitors? Are my pricing decisions compatible with all of these objectives, and if not, how may they be reconciled or resolved?*

(b) *Are my prices compatible with the decisions I have to take simultaneously regarding cost levels, product characteristics, and on my investment decision? What price level is assumed in my investment decision-making, is it compatible with that which I would set for other reasons, is my time rate of discount appropriate?*

(c) *What are the dynamic implications of my pricing decision? What effect will today's prices have on tomorrow's sales and therefore on costs and prices? What effect will today's prices have on the likelihood of new entry and therefore on my long-term share of the market? What effect will today's prices have on the growth of the market? If allowed to do so by law, should we build-in future anticipated cost changes in our current pricing decision?*

(d) *Are there conventions in my industry regarding the level of prices to be charged or the mode of altering prices?* Frequently pricing conventions exist in an industry which it is often in the interests of manufacturers to continue to follow rather than run the risk of alienating distributors or losing the confidence of customers. Thus, for example, in industries such as confectionery, footwear and hosiery, round or conventional prices have traditionally been important. In brewing there tends to be a convention that frequent small changes in prices are made rather than less frequent larger changes, and it is also the custom that retail prices are charged in whole pence per pint in order that the price of a half pint can be adjusted accordingly without difficulty.[7]

(e) *What is to be my pricing structure? Should every product make an identical contribution to overheads (if the costings can be meaningfully calculated), or should an attempt be made to simplify the pricing structure?* Although the cost of producing different colours of paints varied, it was ICI's policy to set identical prices for most colours (other than brilliant white) in an attempt to simplify the pricing structure.[8] In some cases manufacturers may choose to price joint products in such a way that one serves as a 'loss leader' to another. This is of course an important technique open to supermarket companies, but can also apply in relation to the pricing of goods by manufacturers as well. Again it may occur that in order to obtain a target overall return a larger margin may need to be taken on non-standard lines than for standard lines.[9]

(f) *What are my expectations regarding the market and cross elasticities of demand facing my product over the relevant range of alternative prices?* Likely competitor reactions are of course highly relevant here, but so too are responses by customers. Some interesting work carried out in recent years at the University of Nottingham indicates that it is possible with the use of simply survey techniques to collect information about the sort of 'message' that a given price conveys to possible purchasers of a product and to estimate the slope of the subjective demand curve facing the producer through the responses of potential consumers when interviewed. In particular this work indicates that prices can be too low as well as too high where price is taken as an indicator of quality.[10]

(g) *What sort of a discount structure am I proposing to set; am I simply going to follow existing practice in the industry or is it worth attempting to adjust the margins to distributors, up or down? Further, how far am I prepared to allow my salesmen discretion in negotiating individual prices to individual customers? Am I therefore going to specify a list price which shall not be deviated from or will there be a set of clearly determined discounts in relation to the size of purchase, or am I simply going to have a series of guidelines regarding prices to be sought and then to allow more discretion to my sales force?* The more discretion that is allowed to other members of the marketing team the less easy it is to maintain effective control over the performance of the firm and the sales force.

(h) *Are there any ethical underpinnings which will influence my pricing decision? Have I traditionally operated on some sort of a just price basis and do I intend to do so in the future?* Interestingly, there does appear to be a certain amount of ethical influence on price decision-making in a number of firms. Barback found this in some of his case studies,[11] so too did the Monopolies Commission when they looked at the supplies of flat glass,[12] and Silberston placed considerable emphasis on this aspect in his discussion of the price behaviour of firms.[13]

(i) *Are there any legal or other public constraints on my pricing behaviour which I should take into account?* For example in some countries price agreements, maintenance of resale prices, price discrimination and even parallel pricing may be disapproved and even prohibited by law. In some instances a firm may have to consider the possibility that if it lowers prices it may be accused of attempting to monopolise while if it makes high margins it may be accused of being a monopolist. Even in Britain, which does not have the most stringent anti-trust laws in this respect, it does appear that at least some large firms have tended to have considerable regard to their desire to avoid reference to the Monopolies Commission or to the Prices and Incomes Board in their determination of prices.[14] From time to time firm pricing decisions may also be substantially constrained by the nature of voluntary or compulsory price control policies.

(3) *Alternative Pricing Procedures*

The initial empirical attack on the marginalist formulation of price formation by firms was rooted in the full cost approach. This derived from the Oxford studies on the price mechanism and is particularly associated with the work of Hall and Hitch,[15] although much of the work of other economists, including Andrews, Barback and Hague, is largely in agreement with the full cost approach. Hall and Hitch conducted their investigations amongst 'monopolistically competitive' firms which had wide margins of discretion. In most of these they found that prices were determined by (1) prime or direct costs per unit plus (2) a percentage for overheads plus (3) a conventional addition, frequently 10 per cent, for profit. The last two elements were subsequently grouped together by Andrews as the 'costing margin'.[16] Hall and Hitch reported that the firms they surveyed had no data on elasticities of demand, no information on the relation of marginal costs to prices and made no attempt to maximise profits in either the short or the long run.

Barback's researches amongst small firms led him to similar conclusions. He found that firms sought comfortable and increasing rather than maximum profits, they had short-time horizons and were more concerned with survival, loss avoidance and other non-pecuniary objectives, and they had little knowledge of elasticities of demand. He found that prices tended not to adjust automatically to demand increases but were more responsive to cost changes. Although he observed some tendency for firms to take higher costing margins when the opportunity arose this did not affect his general conclusion that the costing margin was more a function of indirect costs and the size of output. He also found that when sales fell off the costing margin was not increased to cover the consequent higher unit overhead costs from lower output.

Undoubtedly it is true that much pricing starts from the identification of average costs and some of it probably ends there, especially amongst firms where management, marketing or costing techniques are unsophisticated. Often, however, the identification of a full cost price is but a first step in a pricing process in which subsequent adjustment to that price is made by the exercise of discretion in a pricing committee.[17] In many firms, however, it is likely that the full cost explanation is not a good description of the procedures adopted by those firms for the pricing of their products and indeed Hall and Hitch themselves identified a number of exceptions to the full cost approach which are often not remembered in criticisms of their work. In particular, they found examples of price leading, some situations in which prices responded directly to shifts in demand and other cases where quality adjustments were important alternatives to price changes.

An interesting variant on the cost-plus explanation is that described as price-minus.[18] In this a firm may know, from market research, the behaviour of competitors or experience, that there is a certain price which it must not exceed. This would encourage firms to pay more attention to cost minimisation arrangements, or even to accept lower profits in order to avoid exceeding the critical price. This explanation seems consistent with Silberston's observation that while firms in the motor industry had widely differing costs, competition forced them to set more or less identical prices. The costing margins taken by each firm varied widely in inverse proportion to the relative efficiency of the firms concerned.[19] The desire to forestall entry may also indicate to firms that a given maximum price ought not to be exceeded,[20] while setting a low price may facilitate a faster expansion of the market.

Two further procedures which are also primarily cost based are the use of standard costs and the use of incremental or marginal costs. Under standard costing, prices are set on the basis of the expected average costs of an assumed standard output level. This procedure is helpful where production processes are long and prices need to be set well in advance. It means that the profits arising from the particular production process will, depending on the slope of the cost curve around the assumed standard output level, be very sensitive to the under- or over-achievement of the predicted standard output level. Incremental or marginal costing is not as much used in the private sector as it is in the public sector but it has been argued that it is an appropriate technique even in the private sector. An implication of the use of incremental costing is that certain costs such as research and development costs and market testing would be excluded from the identification of costs on the basis of which prices would be set.[21]

There is a certain amount of circularity in the relationship between investment decisions and pricing decisions. Pricing to achieve a target return on investment appears to be an increasingly used technique and is probably best seen as a mode of pricing which is more cost related than demand related. The PIB found many instances of firms pricing for a target return on their investment or at least justifying their need for price increases on the grounds that their return on investment had now fallen below that which they formerly required. In later price control policies this was recognised as a criterion for a price increase.[22] It is a particularly useful technique where capital budgeting decisions are also involved or where it is desired to compare the performance of different parts of an organisation. However, it is appropriate to point out that in his studies of pricing Hague found little evidence that rates of return on capital were calculated for individual products and argued that this should not be expected where there are considerable problems in apportioning joint costs.[23] In some cases where demand had fallen the PIB also found that firms were anxious to raise their costing margin and hence their prices, because the effects of the fall-off in demand had been to raise average fixed costs quite substantially and hence average total costs had also risen.[24] Again this indicates that many firms allow costs to dictate the timing of price adjustments. However, this case does not fit the full cost explanation since the price change here is a reflection of changes in average fixed costs rather than in variable or direct costs.

Other pricing techniques (as with the price-minus and limit price approaches discussed earlier) are more responsive to existing or predicted demand conditions. Perhaps the easiest pricing strategy is simply to be a price taker, following a particular price leader. This seems particularly important as a means of avoiding a price war where products are homogeneous. It may be easier to pursue such a policy without the necessity for formal collusion in consumer goods markets where manufacturer price changes are more easily observed than in producer goods markets. It may also be considered appropriate to follow a price leader where prices are raised as a result of some rise in a factor cost that is common to all the firms in a particular industry. But such a strategy may not be appropriate or desirable where the mix of factor inputs, or the efficiency with which they are used varies widely. In that case, the failure of a lower cost firm to make an independent pricing decision may hinder competition and fail to restrain cost increases. Price leaders are recognisable in many industries, and in some cases there is a tendency for the major domestic producer of a product to be accepted by foreign manufacturers as the price leader for that particular market.[25] In other cases there is a clearly existing price structure either of other brands or other substitute goods which tends to limit the range of choice of alternative prices available. Such price matching seems to apply in relation to tea,[26] bricks,[27] fish,[28] wrapping materials,[29] insulated cables[30] and detergents[31] amongst others.

In some cases co-operative or collusive pricing may occur, especially where the anti-trust laws of the country do not prohibit it. In others dominant firms may deliberately decide to set high prices in order to offer an 'umbrella' that helps to preserve the existence of smaller firms and so reduces the possibility that the causes and consequences of their dominant position will be called into question.

It is not necessarily to be expected that one pricing strategy will be the most appropriate throughout the life of a product. Elasticities of demand will change and the degree of competition, actual and potential, that the firm faces will vary through time. In launching a new product a manufacturer may have the opportunity to choose between a penetration or a skimming pricing strategy.[32] If a firm chooses to adopt a penetration pricing policy this means it sets a low price deliberately to allow rapid expansion of the market. This is most likely to be appropriate where there is no elite market to be appealed to, where sales are only responsive to price variations, where scale economies are important and where there is a threat of strong competition arising quickly from new entrants. Such a policy implies that short-run profits are sacrificed for longer term gains. The risks arising from the consequences of over-production as a result of an over-optimistic assessment of likely market demand at the determined price are quite considerable under such a policy. In contrast a skimming price policy means that the firm will choose to set a high price initially and then lower price through time as demand increases and costs of production are reduced through the achievement of scale economies. This policy may have much to commend it where demand for the new product may not be very price elastic but may be more responsive to promotional outlays which have to be financed out of revenue and where the market can be segmented, gradually bringing other segments with higher price elasticities of demand into the market as prices are lowered. Vintage pricing or cascading pricing are simply variants of a skimming price policy. The formulation of the concept of vintage pricing may relate, however, as much to a new plant as to a new product and is particularly likely to be appropriate where heavy investment expenditures have been incurred and, due to uncertainty or some other reason, there is a high rate of time preference on the part of decision-makers in the firm.

The impression that is left by this review of the methods of price formation is that a wide variety of techniques are in use, though in all cases a substantial element of judgement is also involved in a procedure that appears to be a mixture of art and science. Frequently however, it appears from the reports of the PIB and also from Hague's case studies that too little strategic pricing is undertaken and that price policies in British firms are often irrational, crude, ineffectual and based on too little information. Hague's view is that firms are too tied in their pricing to accounting information, and that consequently instead of looking at dynamic influences such as the product cycle, dynamic cost reductions, prediction of costs, profits, volumes and market share, firms are relying too much on static cost plus pricing.[33] Where a genuine strategy does exist it is more helpful to talk in terms of an overall marketing approach rather than simply a pricing strategy.

The material discussed in this chapter has tended to discount the role of marginal analysis in pricing. In general it seems reasonable to conclude that other explanations have greater descriptive power although we would not dissent from Silberston's conclusion that marginal considerations are important in the pricing of monopolists, in vintage pricing, in price discrimination and in considerations of pricing to forestall entry.[34]

Public control of prices and profits

The concept of the just price has a long-standing history. In its medieval treatment the essence of the principle was that equity stood above economic forces and a just price was one that was fair to both seller and buyer. Individual necessity or opportunity should not be exploited by charging unreasonably high prices or beating prices down to an unreasonable level. In some cases the state fixed the just price and in others where a free market operated the market price was accepted as just. Where there was neither government intervention nor a free market opinions varied. Some suggested that costs of production would determine the just price and others emphasised the importance of considerations of utility or value in use as a guide. One Puritan divine warned, perhaps prophetically in the light of present-day product differentiation, against 'doctoring' the product in order to gain a better price.[35]

These could hardly be considered to constitute operational criteria for determining whether or not a particular price was just and it is likely that attempts to set fair prices were not uppermost in the minds of many businessmen. Nevertheless the concept did not disappear altogether and instances can be found where attempts were made by firms to set a just price.[36] It is also interesting that the recent discussions of the price behaviour of firms by Barback and Silberston have both placed quite considerable emphasis on the role of ethical considerations.[37] It may, of course, be argued that good ethics is good business and the limit price discussions emphasise that it will pay a firm not to seek to maximise short-run profits where the threat of new entry is strong. Fears of anti-trust investigation or a loss of public goodwill may also act as control mechanisms.

On the other hand it is arguable that frequently the control mechanisms are weak and that ethical conduct is often not to be observed.[38] Allegations of profiteering have been made and the prices set by some companies have been considered excessive. A former member of the Monopolies Commission has commented that trade associations, whose price fixing activities had been investigated by the Commission before 1956, were prone to be strongly influenced by considerations of what the market would bear. He suspected that the elaborate cost-estimating procedures put to the Commission were merely a facade to give an appearance of respectability to monopoly pricing.[39] There is also the possibility that firms that act ethically might suffer at the hands of their less ethical rivals especially when returns to shareholders are compared. The Sainsbury Committee on the pharmaceutical industry was concerned with this. It argued,

. . . if [price competition] is not present there is nothing but the conscience of companies or the authority of government to ensure that prices are reasonable. The British public and Committees of Public Accounts have shown a certain unwillingness to rely for their protection on the sense of social responsibility of companies; we share this feeling if for no other reason than that in such circumstances the most responsible companies would be the least well rewarded.[40]

The debate on the social responsibility of companies which is now gathering pace is going to be of considerable importance. Here we can only consider the policies and attitudes of government and its agencies regarding pricing questions. Governments may well be interested in both the level and rate of change of prices and may find measures of the level of profit an acceptable indicator of the reasonableness of prices. Levels of prices and profits are relevant to considerations of the performance of firms and industries and also have a bearing on questions of income distribution – the allocation of benefits between shareholders, employees and customers. Attempts to control the rate of change of prices constitute a major element in the anti-inflationary policies of many economies.

The level of profit is not, however, an entirely reliable and unambiguous indicator of the reasonableness of prices. While it may be the case that high profits arise as a result of charging excessively high prices through the exploitation of market power, they may also arise from superior efficiency or from the opportunity to use the organisation's capital assets more intensively. Equally, it may well be the case that a dominant position has been abused and unreasonably high prices charged but excessive costs through a lack of efficiency or the pursuit of managerial objectives that involved heavy expenditures may mean that the recorded level of profitability is low. 'Prices enhanced by unnecessarily high costs are as injurious to the public as those enhanced by high profits.'[41]

There is often considered to be a potential conflict between the accounting information on profits and capital employed and the use which the economist would wish to make of such data. For example, the accounting measure of capital employed is normally based on an historic valuation of assets, adjusted by means of straight line depreciation provisions. The economist would be more interested in the present value of assets and an appraisal of the opportunity costs of retaining them in their present use rather than some other form. The chances are therefore that the accounting measure would indicate higher profits than the economic measure. This need not be a problem if the relation between the two was stable but unfortunately this is not the case and it is made more difficult by the fact that organisations have differing policies regarding rates of depreciation and the revaluation of assets.

Evidence of profiteering is more likely to be reliably obtained from a study of price-cost margins rather than of rates of return on capital employed. Excessive margins will not produce high rates of return if volume is low and low margins with high volume may prove highly profitable. Historically it seems that too much attention may have been paid by traditional businesses to the size of the margin on each transaction without regard to overall profit-ability. Public interest appraisals, however, often tend to be based upon considerations of the rate of return because price-cost information is not available. It might be argued that ideally a dominant firm in a strong market position should have the reasonableness of its prices assessed in relation to the minimum level of costs that could reasonably be expected of an efficient firm, given some assumed volume of production.

A final caveat which should be noted is that an appropriate level of profit for one firm or in one industry may not be equally appropriate for another. The degree of risk involved may vary and high risk activities may justify higher profit margins, although persistently high rates of return would not seem consistent with a high risk activity. The need of the organisation for investment funds to be ploughed back to finance further growth may also be a relevant consideration – an acceptable level of profit may therefore be at a higher level in a growing industry than in a static or declining one. Where this is a relevant consideration it has been argued that investigatory agencies should pay attention to the level of prices and profits necessary to induce desirable new investment. That is, a DCF approach may be more appropriate than consideration of the rate of return on capital.[42]

The Monopolies Commission has tended to appraise the reasonableness of firms' prices and profits in terms of the rate of return on capital employed, often compared against a yardstick of the average profitability of all manufacturing industry. It has used this information flexibly before deciding whether the level of profits was or was not too high.[43] On occasion it has considered low profits an indication of a lack of efficiency. Some dominant firms, however, have not had high profits criticised. In the case of Metal Box the Commission commented that their profits, substantially above the average for manufacturing industry, were not surprising or a matter for criticism 'for an efficient manufacturer in a growth industry'.[44] There have however been a number of cases where the Commission has concluded that profits have been excessive and have been indicative that unreasonably high prices have been charged as a result of the firm's market dominance. There does not, however, appear to be any general criterion on the basis of which acceptable or unacceptable rates of profit can be identified. This will vary according to the Commission's view of the efficiency of the firm, the competitive pressures it faces, prevailing price levels in overseas markets, etc. The Commission has proved unwilling to consider the overall profitability of a company rather than the profitability of the supply of reference goods alone, which is normally much higher.

Interventionist policies to control inflation tend to be more concerned with the justification for proposed price *changes* rather than with approving actual *levels* of prices and profits. While the level of profit is relevant to such considerations, attention is also paid to the level and rate of change of costs and the possibility of encouraging firms to absorb some of the costs. Actual policy measures to control inflation have tended to be of rather shorter term impact and it is less easy to select issues that might remain relevant over the prospective life of a book.

Although the National Board for Prices and Incomes lasted for only a few years its work did offer some general principles that might have more general application in discussions of price control policies and also of the welfare economics of the price formation behaviour of firms. An analysis of the reports by the NBPI on its price references identified 12 principles that were relevant in assessing the reasonableness of particular price levels or proposed price increases.[45] These were:

(1) Price rises should occur only where there have been unavoidable and unabsorbable cost changes and where the resulting rate of return would be too low to maintain capacity in its present use or provide for future investment needs.

(2) Where possible, market forces should control prices. Prices should not be based on collusive arrangements between firms. Less competitive markets will require closer attention to questions of costs and efficiency; countervailing power or the imposition of direct price controls may be necessary. A price leader should be the firm best able to absorb price increases, not the least efficient. 'Umbrella' pricing should be avoided.

(3) Flexible price structures are necessary to reflect varying rates of technological progress, relative efficiencies and changes in input costs.

(4) The benefits of cost savings should be shared with consumers.

(5) Costs should be minimised through improved working methods and the use of modern management tools.

(6) A price rise is not justified where increased costs are a result of commercial misjudgements or short-run production difficulties. Cost increases that are not certain to occur may not be anticipated in price rises. Temporary cost changes should not be passed on in the form of permanent price increases.

(7) Where unit costs have risen due to a fall in capacity utilisation a price rise may be justified if prices are also reduced when capacity utilisation rises. Efforts should be made to improve capacity utilisation by improved marketing and understanding of customers' needs.

(8) Individual prices should be related to individual costs. Each customer should be charged a price which relates directly to the costs of meeting his order. Prices should offer an incentive to the purchase of standard lines in large quantities in order to allow the minimisation of manufacturer costs.

(9) Cross-subsidisation should normally be avoided. Each part of an enterprise should make a satisfactory profit in order to ensure the optimum allocation of resources. Some averaging of price rises in multi-product

organisations to take account of varying elasticities of demand is allowable but should not be such as to exploit consumers.

(10) The rate of return that is appropriate will vary from case to case according to the degree of risk involved in the industry, the cost of capital for new investment and the method of raising capital. Calculations of the rate of return should normally be on a discounted cash flow basis.

(11) Distributors' cash margins should be directly related to the cost of distribution. Distributive margins should not therefore always bear a fixed percentage relationship to manufacturer selling prices. The benefits of large discounts should be reflected in lower retail prices.

(12) Multinational companies present some problems which may ultimately need settlement on an international basis. Each part of a company's activities should be considered separately and the domestic policies of the host country should be taken into account in the firm's pricing decisions.

The conclusion of this particular analysis was that these criteria considerably extended the medieval concept of a just price, especially through consideration of the relevance of rates of return on new investment and by the application of the criteria of the welfare economist concerned with problems of resource allocation and broader questions of economic efficiency. An unjust price is as likely to be one that protects inefficiency or fails to reflect the true costs of supplying a particular item or customer as one that earns excessive profits. One of the disturbing features that seemed to be emphasised in the NBPI reports was the frequency with which firms were found to be adopting inappropriate price policies, as a result of inefficient pricing techniques and inadequate cost accounting procedures. Where this was the case, it was likely that by its work the NBPI helped to advance both the private interest of the firms concerned and the wider public interest. It is certainly not to be assumed that even the larger firms adopt pricing policies that are optimal from their own points of view.

The price control policy in 1973-4 was based upon the enforcement of specific criteria regarding the conditions for both price increases and price reductions. The largest manufacturing firms were required to obtain prior approval for price increases and smaller organisations and those in distribution were required to keep records so that the justification for their price increases might be retrospectively considered. Changes in unit costs were the main reason for accepting price increases but price rises might also be approved in order to secure new investment or to allow a firm to move out of a loss-making situation. Price reductions could be required in cases where the ratio of net profit (after tax and depreciation) to turnover had increased or where unit cost reductions had been obtained.

This policy certainly did not prevent inflation though the Price Commission claimed that rejected applications for price increases had saved the consumer many millions of £s. It is perhaps a pity that the discretion allowed to the Price Commission was very limited and it therefore had less opportunity to make as effective a contribution to pricing in British industry as the NBPI had achieved. There is always a danger that in approving a particular price rise this weakens competitive pressures in an industry. By attempting to control the level of profits the policy gave some effect to attempts to ensure that the benefits of greater efficiency are shared with the consumer. However, the absence of provisions for investigation of the efficiency of firms weakens possible constraints on the propensity for costs to increase. While action to control the overall level of profitability may have desirable income distribution implications, it does not necessarily follow that this is the best way to ensure technical efficiency.

One important point which the Price Commission has brought out is the significance of the relationship between costs and the volume of output. While output is expanding, the structure of costs in firms where fixed costs represent a high proportion of the total means that unit costs will decline and profitability will be increasing. This means that some increases in costs of factor inputs can be absorbed without the need for price increases. On the other hand, a declining level of economic activity will cause unit costs for the output that is produced to increase markedly and to constitute further pressure for higher prices.[46] General equilibrium models of price formation in particular markets would indicate that increasing demand, other things being equal, would cause prices to rise and vice versa. The evidence on price formation policies of firms with market discretion and heavy fixed costs suggests that prices are less likely to rise when demand and output are growing and more likely to rise in response to shortfalls of demand.

CHAPTER 13
PRICE DISCRIMINATION

Price discrimination is an important feature of the pricing policies of many firms in both the public and private sectors. As such it should be seen as an integral element of the price behaviour of firms. In some countries, notably the United States, it has been the subject of restraining legislation and its normative implications are also therefore worthy of some consideration.

Price discrimination may be defined as 'the sale of the same kind of product or service at different prices to different purchasers' or better still as 'the sale of products at prices disproportionate to their marginal costs'.[1] It is therefore concerned with the provision of goods or services by an individual supplier at differing profit margins in different markets and by implication this is assumed to reflect the relative strengths and weaknesses of the supplier's position in those markets. Since the essence of the practice is that the price actually charged for a given unit or to a particular customer does not bear the same relation to the costs of supplying as for another customer or a different unit, this means that strictly speaking price discrimination may not only occur where prices are different, it may also exist where prices are the same but costs are different. In many instances the setting of a discriminatory price represents a positive element in a firm's marketing policy, but in others it may arise by chance as a result of the firm's ignorance of its cost structures or inefficiency in its pricing. It may also reflect an attempt to minimise the costs and complexity of setting prices for many different products and in this situation some averaging may be entirely rational. As we observed with other aspects of price formation the actual decision-making procedure may not be based on explicit optimising principles. However, the underlying rationale is very closely dependent upon marginalist concepts and it is in these terms that the analysis is best handled.

The conditions for price discrimination

The key to successful price discrimination is the ability to divide the total market for an item into two or more segments in which the elasticities of demand are different and in such a way that consumers in one segment are unable to move into a different segment. Segments are perhaps most frequently identified in terms of the geographic, demographic or socio-economic circumstances of the consumers. They may, however, also be established in terms of the different subjective perceptions and attitudes of individuals. For example, it may be possible to identify different types of attitudes to price and the value of the product, different style preferences, different views on the relative importance of purchasing something that is going to give pleasure as opposed to being functional, etc.[2] Such information may not only allow different prices or price-cost margins to be set in the various segments, it may also suggest that the product line could profitably be extended in order to introduce different brands of what are essentially the same product to sell at different prices in order to tap successfully the different segments. In some cases separate segments are readily available. Personal services cannot be resold. Tariff barriers and high transport costs in international trade have traditionally been viewed as likely to make for the possibility of price discrimination between a less competitive domestic market and a more competitive world market. In others, product differentiation activities, consumer intertia or ignorance are the keys to successful market segmentation and hence to price discrimination.

While varying elasticities of demand in different markets are a necessary condition for successful price discrimination, it is particularly likely to occur as a response to specific cost or market conditions. Where fixed costs represent a high proportion of the total costs of production and/or where a low level of capacity utilisation is being achieved price discrimination may contribute to an expansion of sales and of capacity utilisation while making some contribution to overheads. Price discrimination may also be used for special orders and where products are being priced that are complementary with each other For example, in the sale of goods in supermarkets, staple products may be set to yield a much lower margin in order to attract customers into the shop in the anticipation that they will then purchase the more profitable non-staple goods.[3] Competitive conditions are also likely to influence the incidence of price discrimination. Shading of prices may be used to gain sales in a difficult market. Competitive conditions in international markets may encourage price discrimination in favour of buyers in those markets. The exercise of countervailing power by substantial buyers may appear to necessitate the existence of discriminatory pricing policies. This seems to be a feature of the supply of motor accessories to the motor car assemblers which we shall discuss later in this chapter. In other cases still price discrimination may be required by law or other statutory authority as for example in relation to the supply of public utility services to people in rural parts of the country at prices which do not reflect the true costs of supply to them.

Types of price discrimination

Following Pigou, three types of price discrimination have traditionally been identified.[4] First degree price discrimination occurs where each customer is charged the highest price he would be prepared to pay. There may therefore be as many prices as there are customers. This is illustrated in Figure 13.1. The demand curve in this case is identical to the marginal revenue curve since output is sold at varying prices along the demand curve reflecting the highest price that the individual purchaser is willing to pay. The profit maximising output is OQ where the marginal cost curve cuts the demand curve. Total revenue is ODYQ and with total costs OCEQ, total profits are CDYE. There is no consumer surplus. While this is ideal to the producer it is normally not practicable because perfect market segmentation and knowledge of the maximum price each consumer would be prepared to pay is normally not available to the seller. Second degree discrimination recognises this and postulates instead the setting of blocks of prices, charging consumers the highest of those prices which the consumer is prepared to pay. In this case also the producer gains a larger volume of producer surplus than under a single profit maximising strategy but his surplus under second degree discrimination is less than under first degree discrimination.

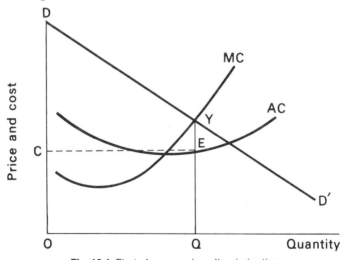

Fig 13.1 First degree price discrimination

Both first and second degree price discrimination pose considerable operational difficulties and are unlikely to be found to exist in practice. Third degree price discrimination is more likely to be a viable operational technique since it requires less detailed information of actual market conditions. It is based on the assumption that buyers can be divided into a small number of groups. Although the individual members of each group may have different elasticities and each group will therefore have a continuous demand function, the demand functions for each group may well have different elasticities at the same price. Where this is so it pays to discriminate in price between the groups, raising price to the group with the less elastic demand function and lowering price to the group with the more elastic demand function.

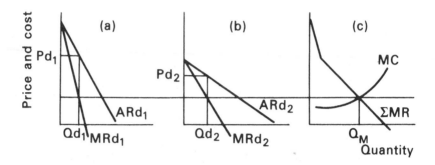

Fig 13.2 Third degree price discrimination

The model indicating the determination of price and output under third degree price discrimination between two markets is shown in Figure 13.2. The profit maximising condition is of course that aggregate output should proceed up to the point at which marginal cost equals marginal revenue and this is shown in part (c) of the figure where the individual marginal revenue curves are summed to produce an aggregate marginal revenue curve. Whereas in a non-price discriminating situation the profit maximising output would be sold at a single profit maximising price, where price discrimination is possible sales are allocated between the markets under consideration so that a higher price P_{d1} is charged in the less elastic market and P_{d2} is the price in the more elastic market. The allocation of the total profit maximising output Q_m between the two markets is based on the rule that marginal revenues in all markets should be equalised. Thus the essence of a third degree price discrimination policy is that marginal revenues are equalised between markets.

The tendency for discussions of price discrimination to be forced into a limited framework of optimising behaviour that assumes price and quantity to be the only decision variables has been criticised by Stephen Enke. He suggested that the traditional description of price discrimination is insufficiently comprehensive and ignores forms of discrimination that are commercially important.[5] In particular he stressed the importance of discrimination between units of the same product through the offer of quantity discounts and the segregation of buyers through product differentiation. These are important practical criticisms and need to be taken into account in discussions of the different methods of price discrimination that are found to exist in practice.

Methods of price discrimination[6]

Four modes of price discrimination by suppliers may be identified: discrimination between consumers of the same product; between consumers of different products; between different units of the same product; discrimination through time. There is inevitably some overlap between these categories but the central features of the practice and the motivations differ in each case.

(1) Between Consumers

This is the form that is commonly most applicable to the three degrees of discrimination discussed above. Where personal services are being priced or each particular order is quoted an independent price the outcome might approach towards first or second degree discrimination, the more so if the supplier has detailed knowledge of his customers and his competitors.

Much price discrimination arises as a result of the exercise of countervailing buying power whereby large buyers negotiate for substantial price savings, leaving the supplier to balance up his overall profitability by taking a larger profit margin through higher prices on supplies to less powerful customers. A good example of this seems to exist in relation to products which are supplied both as initial equipment parts in the assembly of a larger product and also as replacement parts where they are sold individually. This is particularly important in the supply of many accessories and items of equipment that go into the final production of a motor car. The motor car assemblers, BLMC, Ford, Chrysler, Vauxhall, etc., are particularly powerful purchasers since they each acquire a substantial proportion of the total production of each of the accessory manufacturers and furthermore have in most cases the technical competence to produce these accessories for themselves and know very closely at what costs they could produce if the need arose. The individual motorist who buys in the replacement market is, however, in a very much weaker position. Each individual's purchases are insignificant in the overall total and he is unable to bargain with the threat of producing his own goods. Consequently there is often a wide disparity in the prices charged and profits earned in supplying the two markets. For example, Automotive Products Ltd. were reported to be making a 25 per cent profit on sales of replacement clutches, whereas on initial equipment sales to the major car assemblers they only made around 7 per cent.[7] An even more striking situation was found to exist in the case of electrical equipment used in motor vehicles where some initial equipment was sold at prices which yielded a loss to the producers while very high margins indeed were achieved at the expense of the individual motorist buying a replacement part.[8] Overall, the profitability of the supplying companies may still be substantial as the high profits on replacement sales are more than sufficient to offset low or even negative profits on initial equipment sales.

Price discrimination may also be an important means of responding to differing intensities of competition between suppliers. Thus supermarket companies may lower prices in some branches to meet the challenge of a new competitor in a local market, fighting companies have on occasion been used to force prices down in one area in order to exclude a small competitor [9] and the brewers charge higher prices on the supply of beer to tied houses than to free houses where they face greater competition in supply.[10] Price shading – the reduction of prices to particular purchasers below those published in price lists – in industrial goods markets will reflect the outcome of bargaining and the state of the market. With consumer products, the practice of varying dealer discounts as part of the manufacturer's below-the-line promotional activity would appear to be the equivalent of price shading on producer goods, both in terms of its cause (through differential bargaining power) and its effect (weakening a general price structure).

The treatment of transport and other delivery costs on some products offers considerable scope for price discrimination. Freight absorption may well be used as a means of offering a competitive price reduction to some customers but it may also exist because suppliers have failed to see the need to relate prices to the costs of meeting individual orders. When the Prices and Incomes Board investigated prices charged for fletton bricks by the London Brick Company it found that the difference between ex-works and delivered prices was insufficient to cover transport costs and that, as a result of a two-part tariff method of pricing, customers located near the plant were charged more than the actual costs of supplying them, while more distant customers were undercharged on this basis.[11]

In some trades, especially those dealing with homogeneous goods and where delivery charges are particularly important elements in the total costs of a product, competition through freight absorption has threatened to create serious instability in the industry. In order to avoid this, various forms of basing point system have been developed which are in fact important forms of price discrimination. Under such a system all producers, irrespective of their location, set a delivered price which reflects the cost of supplying from a specified basing point. There may be only one such basing point in a market in which case there is a substantial degree of price discrimination against customers situated close to the supplier and in favour of those further away. Or there may be a number of basing points where the relevant one is that nearest to the customer and this has of course the effect of reducing the extent of the price discrimination.

(2)   In Multi-product Organisations

Clearly a multi-product firm has more scope for price discrimination than a firm that is dependent upon a single product. To take varying levels of profit on different goods may be entirely justified by the degree of risk in the supply of each product. However it appears that many organisations do practise a substantial degree of price discrimination by taking higher margins on products for which there is less elastic demand and taking lower margins on products where demand is more price elastic. Some retail outlets, particularly supermarkets, sell different products at different margins, with some products being used as 'loss leaders' to attract custom to the store. This is therefore a particularly marked form of price discrimination [12] but is likely only to be available as a strategy for retailers selling a basket of goods to each customer. Price discrimination of this sort would hardly be available to traders such as electrical goods retailers who normally would only expect to sell one product to each consumer. This is of course also the reason why supermarkets have traditionally been very anxious to discourage the habit of consumers simply 'cherry-picking' that is buying only the loss leading special offers. In other situations it may be that a firm would choose, for reasons of convenience, to set a number of products at the same price even though costs of production are different. Thus ICI, in effect, price discriminated by charging the same price for all its paints (other than white paints) even though the costs of production differed for different colours. [13]

Manufacturers have also found that the development of branding and other product differentiation techniques allows them to segment their market by introducing more than one brand to sell in the same product market. Different prices and price-cost margins are taken on the different brands. The electric lamp manufacturers, for example, sold two different brands of lamps – a main brand and a secondary brand. These were of largely identical quality and were often made on the same machines. But they were sold at widely differing prices that were not justified by the respective manufacturing and distribution costs. In this case it was explained that the reason why the main brands could sell at higher prices was due not so much to manufacturer restraints on competition between the major and secondary brands but to customer inertia. [14]

(3) Discrimination between Units Sold

The offer of succeeding units of a good for sale at varying prices to the same customer is another form of price discrimination that is sometimes found to exist. Again it is unlikely that prices generally would be set in such a way that consumers' surplus is fully removed. The offer of some form of quantity incentive as, for example, where one unit of a commodity may be offered for £1 but three may be on offer for £2.50 will be an effective technique of price discrimination if the customer is not willing to pay £1 for a third unit but is prepared to pay between 50p and £1 for it. [15]

(4) Discrimination through Time

Price discrimination may also reflect temporal considerations in pricing policy.

As we have seen in Chapter 12, some new products may be introduced initially at a high price and margin aimed at that section of the market that is least price elastic. As the market expands the price will be lowered, bringing in market segments where demand for the product is more elastic. In some cases this lowering or cascading of prices may simply reflect changing costs of production in which case it is cost related and is not therefore discriminatory. In other cases the size of the profit margin achieved will also vary and this is therefore a genuine example of price discrimination.

A supplier may wish to attract a particular group of customers in the anticipation of retaining their loyalty for a period of time. This may induce him to offer more favourable terms initially to attract the custom in the anticipation that as the customer's income increases his demand will become less price elastic and the profits foregone by the supplier in the early stages will be more than compensated later on. This seems to be the reasoning that influences banks in their willingness to grant more favourable terms to young customers such as students [16] and is also an explanation of the fact that in the men's clothing trade cheap suits were found to make little contribution to shop overheads and profits but the contribution per unit sold rose rapidly as more expensive suits were purchased.[17]

A further form of temporal price discrimination may be held to exist where prices vary according to the time at which particular goods or services are required. The difference between peak and off-peak prices may be an example of this. Retailers have less flexibility due to the difficulties of frequent price adjustments but the offer of bonus trading stamps on slack trading days does help in this respect. Such variations are primarily responses to market conditions and are therefore evidence of price discrimination, but if operating costs are lower at off-peak times and the ratio of prices to marginal costs is the same at the different time periods this is not, strictly speaking, an example of price discrimination.

Practical difficulties of price discrimination

The pursuit of a discriminatory pricing strategy may pose difficulties. Perfect, or first degree, discrimination is highly unlikely because a knowledge of individual customers' elasticities of demand is not normally possible. Even where markets can be broadly segmented as required in the concept of third degree discrimination and in the extensions of this approach to the role of branding as suggested by Enke [18] difficulties may still arise. It may not be possible to keep the markets separate because resale is still practicable, as Mallory Batteries discovered to their cost when the higher prices they set in the United States were undercut by wholesalers buying in the lower priced British market and then reselling in the American market.[19] Strictly speaking, this is not a pure example of price discrimination by the manufacturer since the cost of producing batteries differed between the two countries. However, to the wholesaler and consequently to the purchaser it was an example of attempted price discrimination in a situation where the markets were not completely separated. In this case Mallory wanted to remove the price differential by raising the price in Britain but this would be an example of price discrimination since the ratio of prices to marginal costs would then not be the same in the two markets. Manufacturers who produce identical items in and for two different domestic markets where costs of production differ run the risk of resale occurring between the two markets and undercutting the higher cost production. Thus where production takes place in different locations a manufacturer may not be price discriminating from his own point of view because he charges the same mark-up on his production from his different plants, but the different prices do constitute price discrimination from the point of view of the purchaser. If resale between the markets is possible the key condition of separability of the markets is not satisfied and the price differential cannot be sustained. If manufacturers continue to produce in different locations almost irrespective of the differing costs of production and in a time in which tariff barriers generally are falling then it is likely that the problems that such price variations pose to manufacturers in regulating their marketing arrangements will increase.

Where price shading occurs there may be problems of keeping the information about the reduced prices away from other customers and competitors. The possibility of having to lower prices to all other customers is a cost that will have to be taken into account in deciding whether to offer a favourable price on a particular order or contract. Discrimination through product differentiation is likely to cause changes in output techniques and levels that may weaken the ability to achieve economies of scale and hence may reduce the profitability of such activities. Finally, it may well be that price discrimination creates administrative control problems and costs to the firms since fewer standard operating rules can be laid down, checks on the performance of the sales force are more difficult to achieve, or where as a result the organisation is continually involved in repricing its products. Clearly in the light of these possible difficulties the costs to the firm of discriminating may outweigh the benefits to be obtained.

The effects of price discrimination

In certain situations price discrimination may have beneficial consequences. It may help to increase competition by facilitating price shading in oligopolies which may lead to a more general loosening up of price structures, it may encourage firms to experiment more in their pricing and may reduce profits as

competition encroaches on the markets of some firms.[20] In these respects it has
an important role in the strategy of the firm and must be accorded an appropriate place in discussions of market conduct.[21] It may be the only means of
obtaining any output if, with an undiscriminated price, costs could not be
covered at any level of output. It is clear that, when compared with the profit
maximising output of an undiscriminating monopolist, first and second degree
price discrimination does lead to increased output. Whether the more normal
third degree discrimination increases or reduces output is not amenable to a
general answer; the effect here depends upon the respective elasticities of
demand in the different markets. Some manufacturers faced with the problem
of justifying price discrimination between initial and replacement markets have
argued that low initial equipment prices could be seen as a form of marketing
outlay which helped reduce the costs of marketing in replacement markets.[22]
Up to a point this may have some validity but it appears that not all firms are
happy to operate such a dual price system since there is always a chance that a
decline in the relative importance of the replacement market would reduce
overall profits to the manufacturer.[23]

The two major criticisms of price discrimination are that it hinders competition and that it may lead to a misallocation of resources. When used by a
firm in a dominant market position it is likely that price discrimination will
reduce competition. There is a danger that selected price cuts may be used to
discourage competitors and therefore to protect a monopoly position.[24] In this
manner price discrimination may become a serious form of predatory
behaviour.[25] It may rigidify the pattern of buyer/seller relations and may
therefore hinder both new entry and changing market shares. In income distribution terms price discrimination may prove undesirable if it leads to excessively
high profits overall. From an allocative efficiency point of view the possibility
that the link between prices and costs is broken, with, in multi-product
organisations, a considerable scope for cross subsidisation of activities in the
long run,[26] may lead to a misallocation of scarce productive resources.[27]

The basing point system is, as we have seen, a rather special case of price
discrimination but has the same disadvantages that it reduces the incentive to
compete on price and may encourage wasteful competition on services and
selling costs and on cross-haulage activities.

Public policy on price discrimination

Whereas in the United States price discrimination is subjected to legal control,
primarily through the Robinson-Patman Act,[28] there has been no legislative
attempt to control it in Britain. As a paradigm for legislation in other countries
it seems to be generally agreed that the Robinson-Patman Act is unhelpful.
Under it price discrimination is illegal where it harms competition *and* where

it injures competitors. Any price difference is prohibited on a sale to another purchaser unless it can be shown to be directly related to cost differences or is to meet competition from another supplier. The purpose of the legislation was to control powerful buyers who were suspected of obtaining their favourable terms through coercion. As such it is to be seen as a piece of explicit small business legislation rather than general legislation concerning price discrimination.

Some commentators, however, would argue that it has hindered rather than promoted competition.[29] Certainly a number of anomalies and unsatisfactory features are apparent from the working of the Act. Co-operative buying groups set up to improve the competitive strength of small traders are hindered and a vertically integrated distributor cannot, it seems, receive a wholesaler's as well as a retailer's margin even though he is responsible for the wholesaling activity. Although the Act was intended to control coercion by buyers, in practice the main provisions appear to strike against suppliers rather than buyers. For example since it is difficult to demonstrate the size of economies available from a large order, arbitrary quantity discounts tend to be imposed and any special reduction offered by a supplier to distributors as part of a special promotional campaign has to be offered to all purchasers *at the same time*. This means that limited promotional activity which is a frequent form of manufacturer marketing strategy is made very much more difficult. In consequence the legislation appears to have reduced price flexibility. We have seen that not only may price discrimination exist where prices differ but, in economic terms, price discrimination may also exist where prices fail to differ to reflect cost variations. In the United States, however, the courts do not concern themselves at all with situations of identical prices where costs differ even though the economic implications of this form of price discrimination in terms of adverse effects on resource allocation may be important.

In Britain both the Monopolies Commission and the PIB faced individual examples of price discrimination and have been unhappy about the practice where either competition has been hindered or where it has constituted an inefficient form of pricing and therefore a waste of resources. Considerably less attention has hitherto been paid in Britain to the question of the effect of price discrimination on competition from small traders. There are signs, however, that this is now changing as small traders become increasingly concerned about the concentration of retail buying power and as manufacturers feel the effects of the squeeze that is exercised by powerful retail purchasers. Undoubtedly the opportunity costs to a manufacturer of losing an important retail outlet are high and bargaining and the use of threats by distributors to purchase supplies elsewhere has been increasing. The Bolton Committee on small firms made some reference to these problems and indicated its concern that discounts given to large buyers are often concessionary and not cost justified, that the practice of giving favourable discounts would force out of existence independent traders and furthermore might result in less manufacturer competition. The Committee considered that price discrimination in favour of large purchasers was of only transitory benefit to the public and recommended that the Department of Trade and Industry should consider referring to the Monopolies Commission 'the question of the market power exercised by large firms through their buying policies and the possible damage to the competitive structure of industry, through discrimination against small firms, which results from it'.[30]

Appraisal

Price discrimination can generally be defined as a situation in which there is a failure to maintain a consistent relationship between prices and marginal costs on different products or in different markets and in which the circumstances for successful price discrimination are to be found in differing elasticities in separable markets. It is, however, clear that in terms both of its origins and consequences a number of different types of price discrimination have to be noted and analysed separately. Price discrimination may arise simply from the exploitation of different market elasticities; it may come about through the use of squeeze activities aimed at hindering competition; it may take the form of price shading for competitive advantage; it may be the reflection of the existence of effective countervailing buying power or it may simply come about as a result of inefficient pricing techniques on the part of firms. Much price discrimination is clearly dependent on marketing strategy – segmentation, product diversity, decisions to add extra lines, etc., and it is therefore necessary not only to accord price discrimination a place at the heart of price theory but it is also necessary to recognise its importance in the overall marketing strategy of the firm.

Some of the facets of price discrimination are likely to be open to objection in terms of their effects on competition or the efficiency of resource allocation but not all would fall into this category. Price discrimination that generates increased competition is desirable, especially if the benefits are sustained in the long run. It is often not possible to determine what price differences are cost justified and what are not and this would make general legislation difficult. Clearly price discrimination that is used to hinder competition or to exploit excessively particular market inelasticities is serious and needs controlling.

The causes of comparative imbalance in competitive strengths in markets may need closer investigation. This may not rest simply on differences in supply relationships in the two markets but may also be a consequence of differing demand conditions as well, especially where in one market strong countervailing power is brought to bear which is absent in the other market. This particularly seems to apply in relation to those goods which are sold both to producers of finished products and to individual consumers whose individual countervailing power is minimal. The implications of the changing balance of bargaining power between manufacturers and retailers needs further investigation and the Bolton Committee was right to draw attention to this. However, if effective legislation is to be introduced to control price discrimination and to enhance the public interest it will need to be very carefully thought out and to take greater cognizance both of the varying forms which it may take and also of the role of price discrimination in manufacturer marketing strategy.

CHAPTER 14

OLIGOPOLY

Although it now has a central position in conventional price theory, oligopoly is also of considerable importance to the industrial economist. It is normally considered to be a particularly pervasive feature of modern industrialised societies, with an estimated 70 per cent or more of the output of manufacturing industries produced by industries that are oligopolistic in structure.[1] Oligopoly theory, at the moment, tends to be less deterministic than some other areas of price theory and so offers greater opportunity to relate empirical observation to analytical interpretation. Here the extensive role of non-price behaviour becomes of crucial importance and so much of the economic analysis of marketing and of the competitive process is particularly relevant. Oligopoly behaviour is not easily handled by normal anti-trust procedures and so it raises important policy and control issues.

The features of oligopoly

The normal starting point in the definition of an oligopoly is to be found in the emphasis on fewness. In fact this alone is an inadequate definition and it is unlikely that a simple count of heads in an industry would be sufficient to identify an oligopoly situation. Nevertheless, oligopoly is a situation in which there is a high level of firm concentration and where the distribution of the size of the firms concerned is such that several (two or more) firms each have significant market shares and in consequence their behaviour is likely to impinge directly on each other. It is therefore more accurate and meaningful to emphasise the pattern of behaviour that arises in an oligopoly and to recognise that it is the *interdependence* between firms that is the key. Because the behaviour of rivals in oligopoly needs to be predicted, but is unpredictable, we may say that the key is really conjectural interdependence. This emphasises that oligopoly is a situation where the outcome depends not only on the actions of the firm itself, and of chance, but also on the actions of other firms who sometimes oppose, sometimes fortify, those of the firm concerned. That is, firms are not in control of all the variables on which the result of a particular decision depends.[2] Conjectural interdependence will be particularly important where homogeneous goods are produced and the cross-elasticities of demand facing each supplier are consequently high. It is also likely to be very significant where overhead costs are high as a proportion of total costs, where there are barriers to entry (though it must be recognised that behaviour in oligopolies may *cause* the barriers), where there are relatively low market elasticities of demand (that is, the industry demand curve is price inelastic) and where there is a static or slowly growing market.

The consequence of oligopoly is that firms respond not to impersonal market forces but personally and directly to their rivals. Consequently, since the quantity sold by each firm at a pre-determined price will depend on the prices and other elements in the marketing mix of his competitors as well as his own decisions, it is not possible to define a single firm demand function from information on buyer preferences alone. Competition in this situation tends to take place not only between products, but also between producers and there is a considerable emphasis on entrepreneurial skills in identifying and devising new and effective forms of competition. Product and marketing competition is therefore particularly important. There is, however, not necessarily all-out competition in all dimensions and at all times in an oligopoly. Often there will be attempts to generate co-operation between firms, firms will bargain with each other and side payments may often be made.

The analysis of the behaviour of firms in oligopoly will normally place considerable emphasis on questions of the strategy of the firms and it should take cognisance, not only of this, but also of the organisational structure of the firms concerned and of the history of the industry. Oligopoly may be as much an international as a domestic phenomenon and interdependence between international producers may often influence the outcome in individual domestic markets.

Economic theory and oligopoly

There is no single and generally acceptable model available to explain and predict the behaviour of oligopolists. Numerous theories have been put forward over the years. Some have attempted to offer deterministic solutions using the traditional economic variables of price and quantity, while others have emphasised the importance of also introducing behavioural or psychological aspects into the analysis. Some have focused on the co-operative nature of decision-taking and others have emphasised that while firms inevitably take each others' likely reactions into account in formulating their own strategies, they remain independent of each other and do not collude. Even if firms co-operate in setting prices, it still does not necessarily mean that all forms of competition are avoided.

One further distinction that may be analytically relevant is that between producer goods and consumer goods. Different forms of product differentiation activity take place in the two cases. It is much easier for the final purchaser to find out about competitor price moves in a consumer goods market than a producer goods market. In the case of producer goods, secret price reductions are more likely to persist unmatched and where supply contracts are the subject of tenders the price adjustment cannot be immediate, but must wait for the next round of tenders. Here, too, the relative value of each order is much greater than for consumer goods. It is therefore likely that a greater incentive may be felt on the part of producer goods manufacturers to find means of formally colluding in order to maintain a stable situation, whereas a similar non-competitive outcome may be maintained in consumer goods markets simply through recognising a price leader.

Early approaches to the economic analysis of oligopoly are to be found in the treatment of duopoly by Cournot and Bertrand. Cournot assumed that each firm set a profit maximising output on the assumption that its rival did not change output. Thus the strategy in Cournot's model was based upon quantity variations. Bertrand's model in contrast was concerned with price variations. He hypothesised that each firm would assume that its rivals would keep prices unchanged, so in order to maximise profits the first firm would set a price just below that of its rival. The other firm would then set its own price slightly below its rival and so the prices would fall continuously down to the level of zero profits. Both these formulations are seemingly unrealistic in that they ignored the possibility that firms learn through time that their assumptions about the responses of their rivals were wrong and consequently the possibility was overlooked that firms either change their own assumptions and strategies or indeed that a leader is identified in the industry. These early explanations therefore ignored the importance of conjectural interdependence which is now considered to be a central feature of oligopoly and of more modern explanations of oligopoly behaviour. Alternative theories of oligopoly may perhaps be grouped into those theories which emphasise the competitive aspects of the behaviour of oligopolists and those that have as a central assumption the view that oligopoly behaviour tends to lead to some form of co-operation or collusion. In between these two it seems helpful to place the kinked demand theory which really emphasises neither competition nor co-operation and collusion, but rather a sticky price outcome or a stalemate.

(1)   Theories Emphasising Competitive Aspects

The least complicated form of explanation of competitive oligopoly behaviour is that which assumes that firms seek the maximisation of their own profits in an entirely independent, non-co-operative, manner. The implication of this as with Bertrand's explanation of the behaviour of duopolists is that firms will cut prices until they reach the level where further cuts would reduce individual profits. With homogeneous products this means that prices would eventually end up at the level of marginal costs. This form of explanation is open to the same sort of objections that were raised against the views of Cournot and Bertrand. In particular it ignores the possibility that learning effects will cause firms to realise that their own independent strategies are not in fact optimal. This is not, however, to rule out the possibility that price competition does occur under other circumstances especially as a test of strength between companies and where some firms consider that they have a cost advantage, perhaps through some improvement in production efforts which they are anxious to turn into an increase in market share.

One particular extension of this approach which has received much attention in recent years has been in terms of the development of tactics to discourage new entry, especially by setting a limit price. This has been discussed in Chapter 4. In this formulation the assumption is that firms are particularly concerned to avoid the threat of potential competition and consequently set a price which is sufficiently low that potential competitors do not think it worth their while to enter the market.[3] The conjectural element is very important here, since the potential entrant must consider not only existing market prices but the likely nature of the responses of existing firms if entry did occur. For example, it would need to decide whether it expected existing firms to adopt a belligerent policy, possibly holding output constant and allowing prices to fall or whether existing firms would be expected to be more concerned with keeping prices stable and consequently would be prepared to accept a reduction in their output and sales. Clearly a game of bluff is to some extent involved in such considerations.

Even in those formulations which assume a lack of price competition in oligopoly we often find the expectation of keen product competition. The main considerations underlying product competition have been considered in Chapter 10. However, it is important to investigate the extent to which many of the effects, and possibly the benefits, of the competitive process can be obtained through non-price competition. Consideration of actual empirical cases later in this chapter will indicate the practical importance of this form of behaviour. The availability of product variation, selling costs, innovation, style changes, etc., expands considerably the oligopolist's 'strategy space' to use Shubik's description.[4] They also have the advantage to the firm that it is less easy for rivals to initiate a direct response. In Abbott's view this may even be conducive to a situation of greater price flexibility since 'quality differences can ease such a situation [where price differences are very noticeable] by creating a mist of uncertainty behind which moderate price differences may arise and be varied'.[5] Emphasis on product differentiation is also consistent with Baumol's sales revenue maximisation hypothesis to explain oligopoly behaviour since it may well be that advertising and other forms of non-price competition are more effective in building sales than an equivalent outlay on a price reduction.[6]

The use of game theory in the explanation of oligopoly behaviour has been attempted by several writers, most notably Shubik. This seems particularly relevant since it recognises the actual inter-personal relations implicit in oligopoly through the introduction of such concepts as the rules of the game, players, strategies, learning, pay-offs, information flows, perception, co-operation, speed of response, toughness, etc. The emphasis here is on the tendency for the game to go on through time and consequently for learning to take place. Hence a given action may meet different responses from rivals at different points in time depending upon the amount they have learned about each other. While the approach seems to be highly appropriate, as with other attempts to use behavioural concepts in the explanation of actual behaviour, it has not so far proved possible to construct a model that has general predictive value. A further problem arises since the easiest form of game in which to derive a solution is the two-person, zero-sum game, in which case a minimaxing strategy is the most appropriate. In practice, however, oligopoly 'games' are not zero-sum and are normally played by more than two players. Consequently while in conception the approach has much to commend it, especially with its emphasis on the strategic aspects of behaviour, in practice it has not produced particularly helpful results so far.

An alternative formulation that has some similarities with game theory is that of Rothschild, whose framework was based on concepts of warfare.[7] Here, although firms seek secure profits and price rigidity is the norm, from time to time price wars break out and 'their probability really dominates the situation'.[8] In order to prepare for such wars firms need to increase their total size and their reserves and to strengthen their security through advertising and vertical integration.

(2)   The Kinked Demand Theory and Sticky Prices

The kinked demand approach to the explanation of oligopoly now has a long history in economic theory, the approach having been developed initially by Hall and Hitch[9] and also, perhaps more extensively, by Sweezy.[10] Indeed, some tend to imply that the kinked demand approach is *the* theory of oligopoly. This is not justified, but for some time it has been widely accepted as having considerable empirical validity.

This approach is based on the assumptions of one firm about the likely responses of its rivals to a change in its price. The firm assumes that the conjectural demand curve facing it is such that in whichever direction it changes price the outcome, as a result of the responses of competitors, is unfavourable and its total revenue will fall since its rivals will not allow it to benefit from its actions. Thus, if the firm were to raise the price its rivals would not follow and since in an oligopoly the cross-elasticity of demand is high, then sales and hence sales revenue would fall off markedly. Equally, if it lowers price its rivals will feel obliged to match any price reduction and so no firm will gain an increase in sales sufficient to prevent total revenue falling (it being assumed that the total market for the product is not in any significant degree price elastic). The consequence of this is, therefore, that prices remain highly sticky and output also does not change even when costs change.

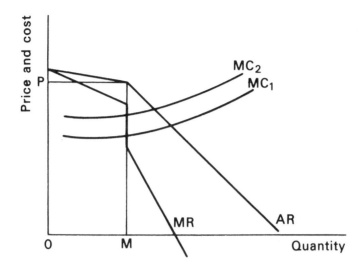

Fig 14.1 Price and output of a firm under the kinked demand curve assumptions

This situation is illustrated in Figure 14.1. It will be observed that the demand curve is kinked at the point of the existing profit maximising price and output. The demand curve facing the firm for a price increase is highly elastic and it is inelastic for a price reduction. Consequently the marginal revenue curve is also discontinuous at the output level existing at the kink. This model predicts that cost changes which cause the marginal cost curve to shift, say from MC_1 to MC_2 but still to pass through the discontinuity in the marginal revenue curve, will not cause any change in prices and outputs. Prices will therefore be sticky.

In this formulation the key to the extent to which prices will be sticky lies in the length of the discontinuity in the marginal revenue curve, the longer the discontinuity the more sticky will prices be. The kink is likely to be most pronounced where products are homogeneous and cross-elasticities of demand high; where there is a low level of inter-firm knowledge because new entrants have recently come into the industry, or indeed where the industry is itself new; where there are high overheads, high capitalisation, a large funded debt, small owner equity and majority shareholder control.[11] These conditions are all conducive to making firms strongly aware of their own mutual interdependence and reluctant to take any action that reduces the predictability and stability of the environment and might provoke an adverse response by a rival.

In contrast, the absence of a kink, or a reduced length of discontinuity in the marginal revenue curve, indicates a greater freedom on the part of firms to determine their own price and outputs. Where the kink does not exist at all, we are of course back with the normal demand function which is not dependent upon conjectural interdependence between firms. It is, however, possible that a non-kinked demand curve could exist in an industry which is still oligopolistic and where conjectural interdependence is also recognised. This is most likely to be found where the oligopolists are few enough in number to recognise and follow a leader, or where there is formal collusion, or substantial learning has occurred as a result of the maintenance of a stable industrial structure through time. In these cases, uncertainty about the likely effects of one firm's decision on the others is reduced and stickiness in prices is less essential. There may be confidence that all will follow a price rise and this may be reinforced in circumstances where all firms experience similar cost increases which they wish to pass on and where all firms are working at full capacity. Oligopolists may be able to anticipate that price reductions on their part will not meet the disasters that are implicit in the kinked demand explanation. They may, for example, be able as suppliers of producer goods to make secret price reductions which will not easily be discovered. Market demand may be sufficiently price elastic that sales will expand as a result of price reductions. Alternatively, a smaller firm may be able to anticipate making successful price reductions without provoking retaliation from the larger companies, either because it is too small for retaliation to be profitable, or because large firms fear the likelihood of anti-trust action against them on the grounds that they were attempting to monopolise the industry by driving out competitors.

It seems that the kinked demand theory does have value in situations where price variations can be damaging and where all firms are anxious to keep in step with each other. Conditions of high fixed costs, high cross-elasticities of demand and low learning are particularly relevant here. It may also be the case that if the theory were extended, as Shubik suggested, to take account of the structure, costs, liquidity, and financial strengths of the individual firms, it would be even more informative on the circumstances in which firms seek to avoid price competition. But there are also many exceptions. Stigler's study of price movements in seven oligopolistic industries showed that in some cases price rises were followed and in others they were not. In some, price reductions were not followed. He concluded that there was no reason for firms to assume that price rises would not be matched and so it appears that the particular conjectural assumptions about rivals' responses implicit in the kinked oligopolistic demand curve is not justified.[12]

Prices may of course be sticky on some products and in some industries for reasons that are not associated with the kinked demand curve explanation. Infrequent price changes may be necessitated in order to avoid the administrative costs of making frequent price adjustments and the problems of dealing with stock revaluations, etc. They may also be encouraged by the administrative convenience to buyers as well as to sellers of having stable prices. There may be problems in raising prices to consumers other than from one conventional price to another, so the tendency may well be to save up cost increases in order to be able to make one larger price increase. Sticky prices under these circumstances are not, however, necessarily dependent upon the kinked demand theory as a model for explaining or predicting such behaviour. While the kinked demand theory offers interesting insights into some of the circumstances in which prices may be sticky, it does not seem to merit the status of a general theory of oligopoly behaviour.

(3)   Theories Emphasising Co-operative Aspects

It is not easy to make a clear distinction between competition and co-operation, especially as there may be co-operation in respect of some decision variables but competition over others. The explanations that we shall deal with in this section are, however, those that, while not necessarily implying total collusion, place greater emphasis on the choice by firms to keep in step with each other and to co-ordinate their policies, especially in respect of the prices they charge. Whether or not a particular action or situation is considered to be collusive may vary from commentator to commentator. Some are more inclined to emphasise competitive elements and the inevitability of parallel behaviour in certain circumstances without the need for formal collusion, whilst others are prone to hold that any form of parallel behaviour is indicative of some tacit arrangement to collude, or at least to follow each other. Thus, for example, Turner has argued from his considerable experience with American anti-trust proceedings that in oligopoly there may well be agreement to agree: 'There is no reason to exclude oligopolistic behaviour from the scope of the term agreement simply because the circumstances make it possible to communicate without speech'.[13]

Parallel prices are held to constitute strong evidence of co-operative behaviour in oligopolies. They may come about as a result of formal collusion to fix prices or through some form of price leading. Normally two alternative forms of price leading are identified – dominant and barometric – though the distinction is not altogether clear.[14] A dominant price leader is one which as a result of its particular leading position in the industry (it will often have the largest market share, but may also or alternatively be the most liquid, the most efficient or the most aggressive) will be able to set a price which all firms will be forced to follow. The Monopolies Commission took the view that dominant firm price leadership is not consistent with oligopoly because the leader here is likely to have by far the largest market share. Certainly many examples of dominant firm price leading are not located in oligopolies. However, it does seem reasonable to take the view that one firm may be recognised as dominant in pricing decisions even though the distribution of market shares and other aspects of the behaviour of firms are in keeping with oligopoly. Barometric price leadership, on the other hand, occurs where a firm is unable to impose its wishes on the rest of the industry, but is followed because its own price decisions reflect market forces or the needs and aspirations of all member firms in the industry.

The assumption is that parallel prices are the outcome of a conscious (though not necessarily collective) decision by the member firms in the industry that they should keep in line with each other, based on the common recognition that their interests are best served by the co-ordinated pursuit of the interests of the group as a whole. A number of factors may contribute to this view. Threats or the experience of past warfare may be an influence. But in general the normal phenomena associated with oligipoly provide a strong reason for parallel pricing. High seller concentration, the existence of of high barriers to entry and the homogeneity of products facilitate parallelism. High cross-elasticities of demand and low market elasticities of demand, the particular distribution of costs with fixed costs representing a high proportion of the total and the fears of weak selling especially where there is excess capacity may, in the opinions of the firms concerned, render co-operative pricing behaviour desirable.

If the anti-trust laws allow, prices may be set by the firms operating as a cartel or by a trade association acting on behalf of the firms. Frequently, however, the firms will have to act less formally and it is here that price leading in one form or another becomes important. The price leader will often be the firm with the leading position in the industry, or it may be the one which historically or through the personality of its senior executives is the most obvious choice. Often, especially in a barometric pricing situation, the leader will need to exercise considerable skills in judging the most appropriate time for, and extent of, price changes. The leadership of an industry may change through time, either by consent or as the result of a previous breakdown of oligopolistic co-operation.

It is claimed that it is not likely to be difficult to find a price that will be acceptable to all firms in the industry. If price changes are made only infrequently and only after major demand or cost changes, as for example a national wage agreement in the industry, the leader can be more confident that his price will be followed. A stable industry structure allows learning to take place through time between the firms involved and the leader is thereby more likely to be aware of the needs of the group as a whole than would be the case if the major firms in the industry were changing with any rapidity. Some commentators have argued that a parallel price outcome is not therefore dependent upon any explicit collusion. Shubik emphasised the importance of cost similarities between firms as an explanation of the similarity of prices. Fellner[15] and Schelling[16] both argued that one firm has a reasonable idea of what the other firms in the industry would find acceptable and will reflect this in their pricing decisions in order to assist the pursuit of a joint profit maximisation objective. Fellner did, however, take the view that the main objective of the firms would be to maximise aggregate industry profits and although he thought this would not, for various reasons, actually be achieved, firms would attempt to influence and bargain with their rivals in order to persuade them to adopt a form of behaviour acceptable to all firms in the industry. He called this a quasi-agreement.

In other cases, however, there may be more direct additional aids to the achievement of a satisfactory co-operative solution. Social pressures may be used to persuade decision-makers not to spoil the cohesiveness of the group. The industrial convention or the trade association may have this effect. It is clear that the Gary dinners organised for senior staff in the leading American steel companies had a similar effect by helping to generate mutual respect between the firms and a reluctance to compete with each other.[17] In order to avoid the possibility that some firms may be tempted to set lower prices other policy action may also be required. The American cigarette companies, for example, tried to ensure that, by paying identical auction prices for their tobacco, no company would achieve a cost advantage which might be reflected in price competition.[18] In other cases firms may find it necessary to agree, formally or tacitly, on standard conditions of sale in order to maintain the parallelism of their prices.

It is unlikely that all industries will be equally successful in the degree of co-operation and co-ordination that they achieve. The closer is the co-ordination the nearer the outcome is likely to approach to the joint maximising position of a monopolist.[19] But it is also important to recognise that the tightness of the co-ordination may influence the extent to which all firms make a full and prompt response to a price initiative by the leader or the possibility that price parallelism may break down.[20]

Some evidences on price behaviour

Much of the discussion in the preceding section was concerned with price decisions and economic theory has traditionally been primarily concerned with this particular variable. In this section we shall note examples of actual price behaviour by oligopolists. Instances can be found where the group of firms make stable price adjustments and other examples are available where price competition has broken out. Inevitably, it is likely that the same industry will experience both types of price behaviour at different times and it is interesting to consider the circumstances under which each outcome is most likely.

As we have already noted, the most obvious way of obtaining stability in pricing is through a price fixing cartel. But in many instances this may be prohibited by law. Firms may therefore attempt to obtain the same benefits of 'orderly marketing' through the exchange of price lists, the organisation of meetings to discuss trading conditions, other forms of information exchange or by following a price leader. Where a price fixing cartel has not long been broken up it is quite likely that the firms concerned will continue to achieve the same pricing results simply by continuing to apply the same pricing rules. This seems to have been the situation in the electric lamp industry following the abandonment of the cartel as a result of the first Monopolies Commission report in 1951. Outcomes were obtained similar to those that the cartel would have produced because the experience of operating in the cartel meant that each manufacturer was able to make assumptions about the actions of its competitors. They all knew each others' discount structures, exchanged information with each other and informed each other of any changes they were contemplating.[21] In this way uncertainty about the behaviour of rivals was substantially reduced and the cohesiveness of the group sustained. Government price control policies, laying down conditions for price increases and sometimes encouraging the firms in an industry to make a joint application for permission to raise prices, are also helpful to industries in their attempts to maintain stability in their pricing decisions. Price leadership seems to exist in many oligopolies. Dominant price leadership seems most frequently to be associated with situations where the leader does have a much larger market share than its rivals and may not therefore offer particularly good examples of oligopoly price behaviour. However, at the time of the Monopolies Commission investigations it seems that Imperial Tobacco had acted as a dominant price leader in the cigarette industry which does have other characteristics of an oligopoly and Dunlop was the leader in the rubber footwear and tyre oligopolies, even though in the case of rubber footwear Dunlop was a high cost producer.[22]

Barometric price leadership seems more likely to occur where there are several firms of approximately similar size, any one of which might presume to become the price leader if the existing leader's judgement did not continue to reflect market conditions and the wishes of the other firms. The motor industry and petrol seem to be examples of barometric price leadership and in petrol the two leading companies Shell/BP and Esso seem to have allowed the leadership to rotate. In a study of price leading in a number of British industries Maunder showed that the plant-baked bread, glass bottle and the sanitary ware industries offered examples of barometric price leadership in oligopolies. The leading firms tended to have similar market shares and price changes were simultaneous and similar. National wage negotiations, similar efficiencies in the different firms and full capacity working helped to reinforce the acceptability of the leader's decisions.[23]

It is not possible to say with confidence whether such examples of oligopoly pricing that preserve the stability of price structures in the industry are examples of collusive behaviour or whether, as Shubik has argued, firms in oligopolies reach a common price policy without the need for formal co-operation.

From time to time price competition occurs in oligopolies. However, the continuous series of price reductions which, according to the kinked demand theory, firms are assumed to fear tend not to take place. Three types of price competition can be identified. First there are cases where small firms persist in setting a price below that charged by their major competitors but where the major firms do not respond. It may not be worth their while to do so since the price cutter's market share remains small or it may be undesirable for public relations for them to do so. For a number of years Jet sold higher octane petrol at lower prices than the major oil companies. Similarly Icelandic Airlines stayed outside IATA and undercut the cartel rate but was too small to justify retaliatory action.[24] However, firms indulging in such practices should not assume that they can do so indefinitely without provoking retaliation. Our second case is therefore that in which large firms *do* respond to their smaller competitors. When Esso lowered its petrol prices in 1967 on the introduction of a British Standard for petrol this was widely seen as an attempt to control the small cut-price oil companies. It appears to have had some success but at the expense of short-term losses to Esso. This is, of course, quite consistent with the view that the objective of firms in oligopolistic industries is not to maximise short-term profits but rather to establish a position from which longer term developments can be built. A similar example appears to have occurred in bread making where late in 1970, instead of raising prices by an expected 2d, Associated British Foods, the price leader, announced a rise of only 1d, which would on decimalisation be rounded down. This was also widely seen as an attempt to squeeze the independent bakers whose price cutting had been causing annoyance.[25]

The third type of price competition is that between the major companies. Here the costs and risks of losing or even of winning a long drawn out struggle are substantial and the asset structure of large rivals in an industry may well make it quite clear that should a battle occur it would be protracted. Situations can arise, however, where such price reductions do occur. Unilever initiated a price war with Procter and Gamble (or more accurately, Thomas Hedley, the company subsequently acquired by Procter and Gamble) in early 1955, apparently in an attempt to obtain a quasi-agreement (to use Fellner's term) for a reduction in the level of promotional expenditures. Hedley, however, did not respond as Unilever had expected. Whereas Unilever reduced prices on synthetic detergents in which Hedley had a considerable lead in the market, Hedley retaliated by making substantial reductions in the prices for its soap powders. Prices were quickly restored but not before Hedley's profits had suffered a serious set-back and its market shares in the synthetic powder market had fallen noticeably.[26] Price competition between major firms seems most likely where price shading has upset the confidence of firms in the conduct of their rivals, or where the gains from breaking away from the herd are too large and too tempting or where a manufacturer wishes for one reason or another to challenge the position of the established leader.[27] Such situations appear more likely to occur where industry demand is weak or where market shares have been changing, perhaps as the result of successful new entry or rapid growth by one firm in the industry.

Non-price competition in oligopoly

In the absence of regular price competition, much of the competition in oligopolies tends to take non-price forms, especially through variations in marketing effort and in new product development and product improvement such as that discussed in Chapter 10. For oligopolists concerned about the effects of price wars such competition through marketing effort may be entirely rational since there is often likely to be a delay before a response can occur to a non-price move and such responses are normally not as complete or direct as a price reduction. Non-price competition also has the advantage to the firm that it reduces the apparent homogeneity of the competing products and so reduces the cross-elasticity of demand facing it. The development of new non-price competitive ploys often involves a substantial degree of inventiveness and this is an important entrepreneurial activity, thereby giving support to the argument that in oligopoly competition is between people as much as between products.

It may be asked why, if firms find it rational to avoid price competition, they do not also find it rational to avoid non-price competition too. Fellner suggested that there was an incentive to firms to extend their quasi-agreements to cover non-price competition, but in practice he thought the nearest firms got was in placing a limit on particular varieties of competition rather than eliminating competition altogether. This is consistent with the evidence, for example, that for a number of years the detergent manufacturers had an agreement not to use bargain cut-price packages, coupons, premiums and trading stamps. In their study of the American cigarette industry Havrilsky and Barth also found that under normal conditions firms were averse to independent non-price behaviour.[28] Clark reported that all the leading car manufacturers in the United States in 1925 had in readiness a similar list of improvements to their models but delayed their adoption because each knew the others were prepared to follow suit and therefore it was doubtful if the gain to the leader would be worth the cost involved.[29] Doyle has suggested that manufacturers are really reluctant to compete by bidding up advertising expenditures since any increase in advertising has to be matched by competitors.[30] In all these cases there is the fear that competition pushes up costs and reduces profitability because other firms will follow. It is therefore likely that firms would as much prefer to avoid non-price competition as price competition, especially where the non-price competition can be readily copied.

But in practice there is rather more evidence of non-price competition than of price competition in oligopolies. This is perhaps due to the fact that some non-price competitive strategies are less easy to copy than a price reduction (consider, for example, the value of a good advertising agency in thinking up new themes for a manufacturer) and so firms may be more willing to break the discipline of a non-price quasi-agreement. In some cases non-price competition occurs in circumstances where economic analysis would predict price competition. Thus Havrilsky and Barth showed that shifts in demand were an important cause of intense non-price competition in the American cigarette industry and Alemson, in two interesting articles on Australian experience, has shown that actual new entry is likely to represent the occasion for severe non-price competition, which he describes as a 'battle royal', through marketing outlays and product differentiation and improvement.[31]

In the motor industry [32] price competition has hardly been of great significance since the decline of public interest in the Model T Ford around 1927. Since then, with the exception of some limited price cuts by Rootes in the 1960s, the motor manufacturers have tended to concentrate on model price competition in which the competition is to produce a superior car within a particular price range. Competition is therefore on quality improvements and style changes reinforced by advertising aimed at highlighting product improvements. A further element in the competitive process here is competition to improve the quality of the retail network.

The main feature of competition in petrol distribution [33] between the oil companies has been the attempt to secure tied outlets and to own profitable sites. The Solus System was initially introduced by Esso as a non-price competitive weapon and it often involves the offer of financial inducements such as interest free loans to persuade retailers to commit themselves to one supplier for a long period of time. For several years competitive promotions were also an important element in competition between suppliers and this placed considerable emphasis on the role of inventiveness and ingenuity in the development of new forms of promotion. Fears that one company might break the conventions seemed to be justified when, in response to the successful Shell 'make money' offer, Jet offered to give a price advantage on Jet petrol to consumers with Shell 'make money' coupons! Before the petrol shortages changed the marketing environment it had been suggested that such games were costly to the oil companies and not sufficiently beneficial to encourage their continuance. The emphasis in petrol competition was reported to have shifted from marketing to technological competition.

The British household detergent market [34] is to all intents and purposes a duopoly. Both firms, Unilever and Procter and Gamble, appear anxious to maintain an identical market coverage and so when one company produces for a particular type of market the other quickly follows, thus Surf followed Tide, Omo followed Daz, Fairy Snow was introduced to challenge Persil and

Radiant and Ariel were both launched as biological washing powders. The importance of maintaining a complete range of lines was emphasised when, having failed to develop its own washing-up liquid successfully, Unilever bought up Domestos Ltd. in order to have a competitive brand in that market. This emphasis on coverage has also led the manufacturers to introduce second, competing, brands into the same market.

The firms concerned claim that competition is strong on quality improvements but it is clear that the Monopolies Commission found it difficult to decide whether there were really genuine quality improvements or whether this was a case where advertising created imaginary improvements and differences between products. Advertising and premium offers are a major form of competition here and the competitive escalation of advertising and promotional costs was criticised by the Monopolies Commission not only as a major source of waste but also as a practice that considerably raised the height of entry barriers. An agreement to limit particular forms of promotional activity had been reached by the firms during the 1950s but uncertainty in the minds of the companies about the competitive intentions of the rival and the effects of new product innovations led ultimately to the breakdown of this agreement.

The cigarette industry also offers similar features of oligopolistic behaviour with price leading by Imperial Tobacco and considerable emphasis on non-price competition.[35] Now that television advertising is banned other forms of promotion and coupon trading and new product introduction are important. Coupon trading was first used in the British market by American companies entering the market around the turn of this century. It was used again in the latter 1920s by small cigarette companies in their attempts to challenge Imperial Tobacco. This proved successful for a time and as Imperial was losing its market share it too introduced coupon brands. These were ultimately stopped in 1933 and no more coupons were issued until the Tobacco Trade Association was wound up as a result of the Restrictive Trade Practices Act 1956. Coupons were then re-introduced and after 1962 in particular there was a rapid increase in the use of coupon brands. Competition then moved to variations in the values of coupons and the terms on which they could be redeemed for catalogue items. Carreras, which in terms of market share is a small firm in the industry, competed strongly on coupon values and also offered to accept coupons issued by other manufacturers provided they were matched by equal numbers of coupons from one of its own cigarette brands. Carreras has also recently experimented with the use of trading stamps on one of their newer brands.

Finally, in our review of particular oligopolies, we may note briefly the situation relating to the supply of infant milk foods.[36] Here three firms controlled over 75 per cent of the market and there was historically a considerable reluctance on the part of those firms to break with tradition in terms of the type of retailer they supplied. They concentrated particularly upon chemist shops and adopted a very conservative approach to promotional techniques. But John Wyeth, a company with a small market share in Britain, appears to have eased the nature of this oligopolistic stalemate by introducing television advertising and by being prepared to supply grocers. This led to a liberalisation of trading policy by the major infant milk food suppliers as well.

The small firm in oligopolies

Perhaps inevitably, attention normally tends to be focused on the firms with the largest market shares in an oligopoly and their interdependence. But it should also be noted that firms with small market shares may have a particularly significant effect in loosening up competitive structures and breaking an uncompetitive stalemate by changing the rules of the game and pursuing strategies that differ from those adopted by the leading companies. In some cases, as we have seen, this may ultimately provoke a response from the major competitors anxious to bring their smaller rivals into line.

Because the firms with which we are primarily concerned here have a small market share, it would not be correct to emphasise the nature of the interdependence between them and the market leaders. But it is clear that the activities of small firms may at times embarrass their larger rivals who will need to decide what action to take to deal with the situation. If the large firms react by trying to suppress competition they may run into difficulties with anti-trust authorities and lose public goodwill by laying themselves open to the charge that they are attempting to enhance their own monopoly position. Equally it may not pay a larger firm to bother since the effect of such small firm competition on the market share or profits of the large organisation may be so small relatively speaking that the costs of competing may exceed the ultimate benefits of disciplining the rival. If the competition is highly localised then there may be more likelihood of reaping a benefit by responding to the competition than if the small firm's market is more or less evenly spread over the country as a whole.

It is also often the case that the small firm in an oligopoly is in fact part of a large multinational organisation and is therefore not necessarily small in any absolute sense. Its access to considerable reserves of assets would enable it to resist effectively an attempt to drive it out of business and might allow it to sustain unprofitable activities far longer. Equally it may also be the case that in some other market (geographical or product) the roles may be reversed and so severe competition in one market to the benefit of a particular company may in fact result in equally severe competition in another market where relative market shares may be reversed.

The petrol market offers a good example of the role of competition from minor brands, many of which are supplied by subsidiaries of the large American oil companies. As mentioned earlier, the case of Jet petrol (now a part of Conoco) is a good case in point.[37] In 1960 Jet lowered retail prices *and* raised octane ratings; later it became particularly aggressive in promotional activities. In this case, as in many others, some response from the major oil companies did occur in the end and, led by Esso, they reduced their prices in an attempt to squeeze the cut-price companies. It does appear, however, that the activities of the minor brand companies encouraged innovation and a search for increased operating efficiency from the major oil companies.

A similar situation, also mentioned earlier, was noticed in the case of infant milk foods where John Wyeth is a small brand manufacturer so far as the British market is concerned but in total is a large and powerful American organisation. It appears that Wyeth breached the existing marketing conventions of the industry by choosing not to restrict distribution to exclude grocers and also by being the first company to use television advertising. Interestingly Wyeth chose to price its products *above* those of its major competitors rather than below them. Again the effect of this was, as we have seen, to change the marketing and distribution strategy of the major companies in the industry.

Similarly Carreras is a minor brand company compared with the two dominant firms in the cigarette industry, but is again part of a major international organisation. In an effort to expand its market it too innovated by increasing the value of coupons and introducing trading stamps. At one stage it also introduced an element of price competitiveness by passing on only 20 per cent of a 5d increase in taxation. Companies with small market shares in the motor industry are also normally giants by the definitions of an industry other than motor car assembly. Because style changes are so costly it is arguable that they are less able to compete in this way with the two multinational giants General Motors and Ford. Instead they therefore compete through an emphasis on advanced technology, as is the case with Volkswagen, or by introducing an element of price competition, as it is reported [38] was the case with Rootes at stages in the 1960s. Interestingly, the response to Rootes was not a parallel price reduction by the major companies but an increase in advertising.

The role of the minor brand companies is therefore an interesting one in oligopoly markets and it is perhaps unfortunate that more attention has not been directed to their position and to their effects on the conduct and performance of an industry. Because the 'small' firm in oligopolies is often part of a powerful multinational corporation its ability to withstand competition is considerable. This must influence the nature of the response by the dominant firms in the particular market. It appears that such firms do not always reach decisions in a way that recognises their interdependence with the major companies and they are often willing to innovate on price or marketing strategy in a risky but often successful manner, so increasing their own market shares and imposing ultimately an innovative reaction from major companies.

International oligopoly

As multinational companies become increasingly important, so a new form of oligopoly arises, the oligopoly of international markets. The significance of this is that entry into local markets becomes easier for multinational companies. and this has a bearing on both the role of limit price decisions and, as we have just noted, on discussions of the role of the small firm in oligopolies. As prospects in a domestic market become limited so firms may look to opportunities to export to or produce in other markets as a means of growth. This process is likely to happen to firms in the same industry in several different countries. As they look for further expansion so they come into contact with each other in international markets and oligopoly, this time on an international scale, is again a relevant concept.

Features of international oligopolies may include occasional price or product wars in local markets to drive out new entrants and some tendency for a new entrant to be more innovative than established producers in that market. Often, however, international oligopoly may also be marked by an absence of competition and by the use of international trade association activities to control behaviour and new entry in particular markets. In the man-made fibre industry there is considerable fear of weak selling and of retaliatory price wars, and so a considerable effort is made to avoid spoiling the market. International market sharing arrangements exist and are reinforced by cross-licensing arrangements.[39] International clutch manufacturers also have agreements to exchange licences, to share markets and not to manufacture in each others' territories.[40] Similar agreements also existed between the major British and American producers of metal containers. American Can covenanted with Metal Box not to operate can making plant in Britain for 21 years. Metal Box for its part had an agreement not to produce crown cork and Crown Cork would not enter the container making or container machinery making trades. This latter agreement lasted from 1950 to 1963 and then as occasionally happens in oligopoly the agreement broke down and each firm then entered the other's market.[41] The restrictions on competition in international oligopoly may often be more formal than in domestic oligopolies since international anti-trust controls do not generally exist. However, European firms in the EEC making such agreements are now likely to find them caught by Article 85 of the Treaty of Rome.

Anti-trust and oligopoly

Although it would normally be argued that many undesirable consequences of oligopolistic structure and conduct should be caught under domestic anti-trust provisions either to deal with dominant firms or with collusion, it is often agreed that oligopoly is a problem that is not yet effectively covered by the anti-trust laws. One reason for this is the difficulty of determining whether some practices are collusive or not. 'To distinguish between oligopoly and collusion as the cause of damped down price competition is the most difficult task that the [American] courts have to face in this field.'[42] One might add the further problem that since price is not the only decision variable through which competition may occur, some view may also be needed to establish which types of behaviour are likely to be competitive and which are less likely to be competitive. This is not a straightforward matter, as we shall discover in Chapter 15. There are also considerable difficulties in producing an operational description of oligopoly. An American suggestion is that it should be viewed as a 'shared monopoly'.[43] The British Fair Trading Act uses the term 'complex monopoly' to relate to situations where two or more persons conduct their affairs, whether voluntarily or by agreement, so that competition is prevented, restricted or distorted.[44]

A division of opinion exists amongst economists and lawyers as to whether parallel prices, etc., reflect collusion or simply the outcome of prudent decision-taking by the firm that recognises the advantages of keeping in line with the rest of the group. Interpretations of the American position on this question are varied. Turner, who is of the opinion that oligopolists may have 'agreements to agree' without actually needing to formalise those agreements, has suggested that presumptive evidence of collusion would be obtained if there were identical bid prices, greater price stability, and other attempts to eliminate uncertainties.[45] But Neale has concluded that the American courts would not invent collusion if it did not in fact exist and they would need to have evidence of an actual meeting of minds rather than just evidence of parallelism. In Britain there has not so far been any need for the Restrictive Practices Court to decide whether it was prepared to infer collusion from evidence on other market practices. The issue arose in the Galvanised Tank Manufacturers contempt case but an admission by the defendants that they had colluded on some counts saved the court the need to resolve this important issue.[46] The problem is that some oligopolists collude and others do not and each form of behaviour may yield the same parallel outcome, at least in terms of prices. It also appears that some firms may arrange to stagger their price changes in order to make it appear that they are responding to a price leader whereas they are in fact in collusion.[47]

It is arguable that oligopolistic structure and conduct may have adverse consequences for competition and economic efficiency. For example, it is often suggested that price leading tends on average to raise prices and to reduce the magnitude of price fluctuations, especially if it has a ratchet effect, only raising and never lowering prices. If this is so then the price system is less efficient. It is likely that oligopolies will hinder the fight against inflation since, on at least some theoretical explanations of oligopoly behaviour, it would be expected that prices would rise when cost increases were incurred but would not fall when cost reductions were achieved. Certain forms of behaviour by oligopolists may hinder entry and new competition, particularly where market sharing agreements are reached or where an escalation of the costs of non-price competition through annual style changes or heavy advertising makes it difficult for smaller firms to match the actions of the dominant firms in the industry. An example of the sort of tactic to raise barriers to effective competition was reported in the American anti-trust proceedings against the leading cigarette manufacturers there. When they were faced with competition from lower priced brands produced by smaller manufacturers they deliberately bought up supplies of the cheaper tobacco which their competitors used but which they did not, with the intention that by depriving the independent manufacturers of their essential raw material supplies they would make the production of cheap cigarettes unprofitable. Furthermore the three major companies in this industry were held to have undertaken considerable advertising expenditures which the Supreme Court described as 'a widely published warning that these companies possess and know how to use a powerful offensive and defensive weapon against new competition.'[48] As we noted in Chapter 4, it is often difficult to be certain whether barriers to entry are deliberately raised by existing firms or whether they simply arise as a result of the particular form that competition takes between existing firms in an industry.

Action to encourage new entry may, as Fellner has suggested, be a desirable form of policy measure to control the adverse effects of oligopoly. Certain less attractive modes of market conduct might be controlled by legislation. For example tax allowances for advertising expenditures might be reduced as the Monopolies Commission proposed in its report on detergents. But there is a danger that particular types of policy may as much hinder new competition as encourage it. For example, the Monopolies Commission's suggestion to limit the number of company owned petrol stations was strongly opposed by the minor brand companies who argued that it would hinder their ability to grow and so challenge the larger companies. It does not necessarily follow that because particular aspects of the structure of an industry are considered undesirable and in need of adjustment that oligopoly should be abandoned or indeed that it could be. When it investigated the supply of cinema films, the Monopolies Commission recognised that oligopoly was inevitable in that industry but was still anxious to change the existing duopoly by introducing at least one more competitor.[49]

Where collusion cannot be proved there seems little opportunity to lay down hard and fast anti-trust rules and a pragmatic approach attempting to deal with adverse practices or outcomes is perhaps the best that can be looked for. Maybe particular attention should be paid to those cases where there is no price competition and seemingly no product innovation either. The distinction made by Allen[50] between product innovation which is likely to be beneficial and market innovation which is less likely to be so is perhaps helpful in this respect. It would indicate that oligopolies that relied heavily upon non-price promotions as the main mode of competition would be strong candidates for investigation and control. Finally, it should be emphasised that there is no point in attempting with one hand to fight co-operative pricing while on the other encouraging firms to discuss prices and make common applications for price rises where direct price controls are imposed to fight inflation. The need to harmonise policy is as great here as in other aspects of economic policy.

CHAPTER 15

GOVERNMENT AND THE PROMOTION OF COMPETITION

While many firms may act independently and in competition with their rivals, there are others which for one reason or another may wish to avoid competition either altogether or may attempt to avoid the use of particular forms of competition, especially price competition. There are a number of possible reasons why this may be so. Firms may feel that competition would increase the uncertainty and unpredictability of their environment and would harm their performance; they might fear that weak selling by rivals would 'spoil' the market and make it difficult to earn a fair return; there may be an emphasis on clubmanship within an industry which encourages businessmen to adopt policies that will help to preserve the existence of their rivals. In some cases firms may attempt to preserve and secure their positions through mergers. In other cases firms choose to attempt to regulate and reduce competition through explicit or tacit arrangements between themselves. In some industries which have an oligopolistic structure and only a few firms of any consequence it may be possible to avoid particular forms of competition by recognising a price leader or by entering into tacit arrangements that do not necessitate the formalisation of explicit agreements (see Chapter 14). In other cases where there are a larger number of firms or where uncertainties and pressures for price cutting are much greater and a history of co-operation is less strongly established, firms may seek other, more formal, means of avoiding competition. Where the law allows it, they may use a trade association to regulate their behaviour and to organise and enforce an agreement. Where, as in many countries, such cartels are outlawed other practices may be introduced in an effort to obtain a similar outcome. In this chapter we shall consider the nature of government policies regarding cartels and similar activities, and the relevance and consequences of attempts to promote competition.

The economic foundations of competition policy

Governments may seek competition simply because they believe that competition offers healthy advantages and benefits that are not to be found in other forms of economic relationship. But they may also pursue such a policy because competition is considered to be the form of industrial organisation most likely to yield certain other economic benefits. From a macro-economic point of view the promotion of competition may be thought likely to help to promote growth, price stability, a more favourable income distribution and improved performance on the balance of payments. Thus a more competitive and efficient industrial sector may produce substantial and wide-ranging economic benefits. But competition policy also has an important micro-economic justification. In general, the advocates of a strong competition policy argue that restraints on competition lead to the disadvantages of high prices, low output, a lack of progressiveness and dynamism that are held to be the normal characteristics of monopoly; whereas competition would be expected to produce economic benefits of greater pressure on costs, more price flexibility and a better all-round performance in terms of progressiveness, price-cost relations, etc.

In welfare terms the objective of economic policy is often assumed to be an improvement in economic welfare up to the point of the Paretian optimum such that no further changes can be made that would improve the position of one individual without worsening it for any other. This is only achieved when all resources are used and allocated as efficiently as possible and occurs where allocative efficiency (the optimum mix of products produced), technical efficiency (the least-cost method of production) and distributive efficiency (optimum allocation of the output among members of the community) are established. This exists where the 'marginal conditions' are satisfied: where the marginal rates of substitution between commodities are the same for all individuals, all marginal rates of transformation are the same for every pair of commodities and all equivalent rates of transformation and substitution are equal to one another.[1] It has been pointed out that the only market situation that satisfies these conditions is perfect competition where the nature and working of the system is assumed to ensure that all prices equal their marginal costs, that the market is cleared, and factor and product prices are the same for all purchasers. Consequently it is assumed that any departure from perfect competition is undesirable. However, many economists would now consider that any attempt to discuss competition policy in the light of the analytical framework of perfect competition is not only unjustified but may prove positively misleading.[2]

It is arguable that perfect competition is neither perfect nor competitive. It is not a truly competitive, dynamic system and does not allow for rivalry but only a dispersion of market power[3] and in consequence considers as 'monopolistic blemishes' non-price behaviour that may have important competitive elements. The attempt to attain a market structure consistent with the concept of perfect competition would be likely to impose a number of economic costs upon society. It may mean that firms are too small to be able to innovate effectively or to gain maximum economies of scale. Unstable price and output outcomes as the industry moves from one static equilibrium position to another and the general uncertainty implicit in the system may reduce the chances that optimum investment decisions will be reached. The existence of externalities associated with a product or production process may mean that private and social costs diverge and a pricing system that reflected only marginal private costs will not in this situation produce the best social allocation of resources. There is also the problem that, on second-best grounds, if one element in perfect competition or perfect competition in one sector cannot be attained then the pursuit of a position as near as possible to perfect competition is not in fact the second-best position.[4] This suggests therefore that not only is perfect competition an unattainable objective but that it may in fact prove to be an inappropriate objective.

If the pursuit of perfect competition and the Paretian optimum does not offer any useful guide to the formulation and execution of competition policy, the question then arises as to whether there is in fact any alternative framework that might fulfil this function. Much discussion has been centred around the possibility of devising an alternative approach through the concept of workable or effective competition. Both concepts were initially discussed by Clark and it is interesting to note his reasons for preferring the term effective competition:

> I am shifting the emphasis from 'workable' to 'effective' competition . . . because 'workable' stresses mere feasibility and is consistent with the verdict that feasible forms of competition, while tolerable, are still inferior substitutes for that 'pure and perfect' competition which has been so widely accepted as a normative ideal. And I have become increasingly impressed that the kind of competition we have, with all its defects – and these are serious – is better than the 'pure and perfect' norm, because it makes for progress. Some departures from 'pure and perfect' competition are not only inseparable from progress but necessary to it. The theory of effective competition is dynamic theory.[5]

It is not, however, possible to say unequivocally that an industry is effectively competitive. Some of its characteristics and performance may support a favourable finding on this question and some may not. Some of the outcomes that might lead a commentator to conclude that an industry was effectively competitive might also be consistent with the existence of a cartel or with oligopolistic behaviour leading to common prices. It may be that a dominant firm motivated by considerations of social responsibility may produce the performance outcomes associated with effective competition but there may be in this case less ground for confidence that the same outcome would ensue in the future. There is also scope for a disparity of views as to the criteria that should be satisfied if an industry is to be considered effectively competitive. Numerous authorities have offered their suggestions.[6] It seems that considerations of structure, conduct and performance will all be relevant though the weighting to be attached to each may vary from case to case.

Recognising this we may suggest that requirements for effective competition might be specified as follows: [7]

(1) There are a sufficient number of firms either in the market or able to enter the market easily and quickly as a result of low barriers to entry that customers have a wide range of choice between alternative suppliers of the same or readily substitutable products.

(2) The market is free of collusion, price leading and predatory practices. Each firm makes its own price and output decisions without discussion or agreement with its rivals but in the awareness that failure to prevent prices rising above those of its rivals (after allowing for compensating quality differences) will lead to loss of sales revenue as a significant proportion of consumers switch to alternative suppliers. Price and cost changes in the industry are closely related to each other.

(3) Customers are sufficiently well informed and 'mobile' that they choose rationally between alternative suppliers. There is no significant tendency on the part of consumers to be attached to any particular supplier for reasons of excessive product differentiation, goodwill or inertia.

(4) A spirit of competition exists in the industry in which each firm attempts to increase its own market shares and profits through price and product changes and other forms of marketing effort.

(5) Certain consequences in terms of performance will follow from the preceding structure and conduct elements: prices will tend to be close to average costs and in the long run profits will be reasonable in relation to the degree of risk in the industry; the industry will be progressive with emphasis on product and process innovations; the enterprising and efficient firms will gain at the expense of the unenterprising and inefficient; firms will tend to be close to optimum size and situations of significant excess capacity or insufficient reserve capacity will be avoided.

Such criteria may be useful pointers to the forms of industrial structure, conduct and the performance outcomes that policy makers may bear in mind in formulating or enforcing competition policy. There is, however, still the problem that it is sometimes argued that some deviations from an effectively competitive structure or conduct standpoint may yield a more desirable or effectively competitive industry performance. Thus a policy-maker not only has the problem of deciding what are the relevant policy objectives and criteria for competition policy, granted the technological complexities and dynamic nature of modern industry, he may also be faced with the need to identify those circumstances where formal restrictions on competition may produce a more desirable industry performance. We need therefore to consider the arguments for and against the existence of some restrictions on competition.

The economics of restrictive practices

It is a long-standing notion that businessmen will often prefer to avoid rather than to generate competition. This may be because they see a greater opportunity to exploit the market and enhance their profits or to enjoy a quiet life if they collude rather than compete with each other. Or it may be that their motives are more concerned with protecting their investment and the market from marked changes in the short run which may adversely affect their interests and may even prove to the long-term disadvantage of the general public. It appears that in Britain the majority of attempts by firms to restrain competition through the making of agreements were for reasons of protection rather than exploitation.[8] Where this is the case there may be a more delicate decision to be made as to whether an action taken to enhance the private interests of the parties to an agreement is also in the social interest.

Although, as we have seen in Chapter 10, the firm has many forms of competition open to it and indeed will often use non-price modes of competition, restrictive agreements tend to be more intent on avoiding price competition and less likely to attempt to control other forms of competitive behaviour. This suggests that the existence of price restrictions may not necessarily mean that all forms of competition are foregone even though price competition may be preferred. It may also indicate that price competition is considered the most powerful and serious form of competition and the one that is to be avoided if at all possible.[9] If this is the case, and certainly the high incidence of price fixing agreements suggests it may be, the evidence of firm behaviour casts some doubt on the Schumpeterian argument that it is innovation that is the most important form of competition and the most serious in its economic implications for the firm. Much of the general debate on the advantages and disadvantages of restrictive agreements relates implicitly to agreements over prices.

The case for restrictions seems to rest on three broad types of argument:

(a) *Short-run price competition has adverse effects.* The supporters of price agreements argue that short-run price competition may be started by firms that are able thereby to disrupt an industry but would not be able to sustain their low level of prices in the long run. Thus severe short-run price competition may be most likely to occur in industries where fixed costs represent a high proportion of the total and/or where there are a number of small firms, especially firms that are extremely liquid. It is suggested that such price competition does not force prices just down to marginal costs but actually to below the level of marginal costs, though often it is not specified whether it is assumed that all firms have the same marginal costs or not. Severe price competition may lead to a misallocation of productive effort and may, by driving profits down to a low level, have the effect of reducing the level of new investment below that which would really be required in the industry. There is undoubtedly much justification in the view that short-run disruptions in a market have very little to commend themselves to the majority of firms and indeed they may not be to the longer term benefit of the wider public interest. The desire to avoid such surprise attacks by weak sellers may therefore act as a strong incentive to firms to attempt to avoid price competition.

(b) *Agreements increase the predictability and stability of the business environment.* Businessmen will be likely to attempt to avert risk and will place emphasis on the importance of a stable and predictable environment. It is argued that high levels of risk and uncertainty may have an adverse effect on the level of investment, reducing it below the optimum level, and may lead to uninformed output decisions. The adverse effects of these outcomes may be greater than the adverse effects of fixed prices. Agreements help to overcome these problems and so may lead to a better overall allocation of resources, more informed decision-taking, easier demand prediction and benefits to purchasers by avoiding extreme price fluctuations.

(c) *Agreements facilitate technical progress.* The existence of an agreement between firms may provide them with a degree of security and confidence in each other that encourages them to co-operate. This may include the pooling of technical and other knowledge which will raise the average efficiency of the industry, a sharing in joint research and development programmes and the cross-licensing of patents which will stimulate research and development and reduce the costs of technical progress.

Even the strongest advocates of restrictions do not claim that their arguments have general applicability or that all agreements between firms necessarily have net social benefits. Restrictions on competition that are normally thought most likely to be in the public interest are in industries that experience wide cyclical fluctuations in demand, that have capital intensive production techniques, or where new plant investment or research and development expenditures are high. In Richardson's view a restriction is less likely to be undesirable because the self-interest of the most efficient or the smallest firms which wanted to grow would limit the impact of the restrictions in the industry generally.[10] A stable price system will not necessarily survive for long where there is a reduction in demand or a growth of demand which allows the anticipation of future cost reductions or a major technological change in the industry.

The case against restrictive practices is broadly based on the classic objections to monopoly but is no less strong and important for that:

(a) *Agreements cause rigidity and protect the inefficient.* The effect of agreements may be to retard the differential growth of efficient firms, make profits too easy to obtain and so hinder necessary product and process innovation. They may encourage too much concentration on existing products at the expense of new ones and therefore lead to a misallocation of resources. Agreements may further emphasise the importance to firms of clubmanship and thereby reduce the willingness generally to break away from the herd. Firms in industries protected by restrictive agreements may fail to distinguish effectively between cyclical fluctuations and long-run secular trends and this may lead to the maintenance of an unacceptably high level of productive capacity.

(b) *Cartels raise prices and profits and restrict output.* The firms in a cartel may find it possible to act as a single monopolist in their price and output decision making and this may be to the disadvantage of the public. By increasing the certainty and security of profits, an agreement may discourage or hinder innovation and may prevent price flexibility when costs change. An agreement generally provides firms with a considerable degree of protection from the market and this is especially likely to be the case where a price fixing agreement is also supported by other forms of exclusionary conduct such as controls on the allocation of raw material supplies.

Early British competition policy

Traditionally it had been assumed that the common law would deal with restrictive practices and that little formal legislative interference was required.[11] The doctrines on restraint of trade and on conspiracy provided the means to control restrictions on competition. However, during the nineteenth and early part of the twentieth centuries a succession of decisions indicated that the position of the common law had shifted. In restraint of trade cases the courts would allow firms to take any action they liked without regard to the public interest so long as it was reasonable between the parties. The development of the law on conspiracy led one judge in 1925 to deduce two propositions regarding the status of that law. First, a combination of two or more persons wilfully to injure a man in his trade is unlawful and if it results in damage is actionable. Secondly, if the real purpose of a combination is not to injure another but to forward or defend the trade and those who enter it, then no wrong is committed and no action will lie although damage to another ensues.[12] Thus it was clear that the interest of the courts was in questions of fairness between the parties rather than the implications for a wider public interest and as such the common law could not any longer be relied upon to act as an agent of public policy in this area.

As the contribution of the common law declined so governments became more involved in questions of industrial organisation. During the First World War the government had encouraged the formation of trade associations to act as channels of information between government and industry and to serve as allocators and distributors of rationed supplies of raw materials. The influence of trade associations in centralising and organising industrial activities in many trades was to become of considerable importance in later years. At the end of the war inflation and fears of profiteering led to various attempts by the government to control the price formation activities of firms. Committees of inquiry such as the Committee on Commercial and Industrial Policy 1918 and the Committee on Trusts 1919 were set up and presented reports that were generally favourable to the activities of trade associations. Some attempts were made to control prices and a large number of prosecutions were taken in 1918 and 1919 against profiteering traders. A number of investigations on prices and profits in particular industries was carried out.

Then in the later 1920s came depression and a secular decline in some industries, especially in the then staple industries of coal, cotton, shipbuilding, etc., though it was not realised for some time that some industries were in fact facing a secular decline rather than simply a cyclical fluctuation. There was a general desire to avoid ruinous competition and the elimination of firms and capacity which it was expected would be needed again when the depression subsided. The means adopted to attempt to control ruinous competition was in many cases the trade association which attempted to avoid severe reductions in prices and to achieve a controlled reduction in capacity in industries where it was ultimately realised that they were in fact experiencing a secular decline. During the Second World War trade associations again had an important role to play in allocating supplies and in the fixing of prices.

These were undoubtedly important developments in the organisation of industry. It is, however, difficult to assess their effects. The number of trade associations increased between 1919 and 1944 from 500 to 2,500 and the climate of opinion undoubtedly shifted strongly to favour cartelisation and attempts to avoid severe price competition. Some rationalisation schemes had been successful but others were less so because of the opposition to rationalisation by the owners of plants to be closed down and because of the activities of a fringe of weak sellers. In investigations of the levels of efficiency and technical progress of various British industries after the Second World War compared with their counterparts in other countries, it was concluded that in many the level of industrial efficiency and technical progress was low. Comparison of the efficiency of British industries with American industries tended to suggest that the existence and operation of cartels might be an important explanation for the relative lack of efficiency in British industry.

In 1944, in its White Paper on Employment Policy, the coalition government emphasised the importance of increasing industrial efficiency. It observed the growth of combines and agreements, market sharing and price fixing and commented, 'such agreements or combines do not necessarily operate against the public interest but the power to do so is there'.[13] It proposed to take steps to inform itself of the extent and effect of restrictive agreements and to take action against those found detrimental to the interests of the country.

The first legislative move in this direction came in the passing of the Monopolies and Restrictive Practices (Inquiry and Control) Act 1948. Under the terms of this legislation the Monopolies and Restrictive Practices Commission was established as an administrative tribunal to look at situations at the request of the Board of Trade where one-third or more of an industry was in the hands of either one firm or of a cartel or where firms conducted their business in such a way as to restrict competition even if there was no formal agreement. The Act imputed no vice to monopolies and restrictive practices as such and merely required the Commission to investigate the 'things done' and then to indicate whether the position of dominance and the 'things done' were in the public interest or not. Thus the Commission had responsibility for investigating not only the position of dominant firms but also the existence and operations of cartels. In addition it could also be required to complete reports on general references of specific trading practices.

Over the following seven or eight years the Commission completed a number of reports, many of which were concerned with the operations of cartels in particular industries. The Commission's findings indicated that certain restrictive practices existed over a wide area of industry. These included common price agreements, exclusive dealing arrangements, agreements to enforce resale price maintenance (rpm), quota schemes, agreements on tendering and agreements to restrict capacity. Some practices, including exclusive dealing, loyalty rebates, collective enforcement of rpm, the rigging of tenders and the use of quota schemes, were generally condemned where they had been found by the Commission. On the other hand price agreements were sometimes tolerated where the Commission thought they were necessary to preserve co-operation in research or in the sharing of patents and if the prices fixed were considered to be reasonable and the method of setting prices was found to be satisfactory.[14] It appeared that the Commission was more likely to be favourable to price fixing where the structure of the industry was oligopolistic than under any other forms of market structure.[15]

In 1952 a reference of a group of collective discrimination practices was made to the Commission and a report was published in 1955. This report [16] proved to be the immediate precursor of the Restrictive Practices Act in 1956. The reference required the Commission to investigate and report on all collective agreements which required the parties to them to discriminate in their dealings with other persons. The Commission dealt with six practices: collective discrimination by suppliers; collective discrimination by suppliers in return for exclusive buying; collective agreements to adopt conditions of sale especially rpm; collective agreements to enforce conditions of sale especially rpm; collective discrimination by buyers; aggregated rebates. The Commission found each of these to be generally contrary to the public interest though it recognised some instances where they might have been approved. In considering the best way to deal with the problem of these practices the members of the Commission were divided between two alternatives. One group, a minority of four, suggested that all such practices should be registered and investigated and those not in the public interest should be banned. The majority, however, argued that all the agreements covered by the reference to the Commission should be prohibited though with provision for exemption in some cases. They argued that this procedure would be quicker and would involve fewer investigations. In introducing legislation in 1956 to deal with restrictive practices the government followed more closely the suggestions of the minority group and established a procedure that allowed for a case-by-case investigation of particular practices.

The restrictive practices legislation

(1) Terms of the Restrictive Trade Practices Act

The Restrictive Trade Practices Act passed in 1956 represented the next and most important step in the formation of policy to deal with restrictions on competition in Britain. In so far as restrictive trading agreements are concerned [17] it made agreements relating to the supply of goods registrable and subject to judicial investigation. A new office of Registrar of Restrictive Trading Agreements was created and agreements, oral or written, had to be registered with the Registrar. In general the agreements that were registrable were those relating to the production, supply or processing of goods or where the restrictions related to such matters as prices, conditions of sale, the type of customer to be supplied and the kind of goods to be made, sold or purchased. Some agreements relating to export sales, the maintenance of British Standard Institution standards, etc., were exempt from the need to register. Agreements were to be referred to the Restrictive Practices Court, a court with the status of the High Court but on which legal judges and laymen sat together.

It was the duty of the court to decide whether, on the balance of the probabilities, [18] a restriction was in the public interest or not. Seven criteria or 'gateways' were laid down in the Act under which the court could rule that a restriction was not contrary to the public interest. These gateways were:

(a) That the restriction was necessary to protect the public against injury;

(b) That the removal of the restriction would deny other specific and substantial benefits to the public;

(c) That the restriction was necessary to counteract the actions of another firm or group that was not party to the agreement;

(d) That the restriction .was necessary to facilitate the negotiation of fair terms with a powerful buyer or seller;

(e) That the removal of the restriction would lead to serious and persistent unemployment in any area;

(f) That removal of the restriction would lead to a substantial loss in the volume of earnings from exports;

(g) That the restriction was necessary to maintain any other restriction between the parties that had been found not to be contrary to the public interest. In addition, if the parties to an agreement had succeeded in establishing their case under one or more of the gateways, the court then had to be satisfied in the 'tailpiece' that the restriction was not unreasonable in balancing the advantages from the restriction against the detriments that arose from it. Any restriction not approved by the court would be automatically void.

This legislation contained a number of interesting provisions. The use of a judicial procedure must have reflected considerable government confidence in the ability of the judiciary to handle economic policy issues. It may also have been an attempt to meet industry criticisms of the procedures of the Monopolies Commission. It certainly removed the likelihood that the Commission's conclusions and recommendations on a particular reference would be subject to extensive negotiation between industry and government before a decision was finally taken whether to enforce a particular recommendation. With the judicial procedure the court's decision was final and an agreement found to be contrary to the public interest was automatically void from the time of the court's judgment. There was provision for appeal on matters of law but not against the court's decisions on matters of fact. While the approach was still through the investigation of individual cases, the general tone of the legislation indicated that there had been a positive move to give practical effect to a desire to reduce the incidence of cartels in British industry.

(2)   The Question of Justiciability

However, questions arise as to whether it is appropriate to ask the courts to handle such issues as the control of restrictive practices and whether the particular framing of the legislation in the Restrictive Trade Practices Act gave the court the tools to do the job. This matter, the question of justiciability, has been considered with reference to restrictive practices law by Professor R. B. Stevens.[19] He pointed out that in view of the traditional favour which the common law courts have shown to restrictive practices it was an act of faith to introduce a judicial procedure. The issue of the appropriateness of a restrictive practice in an industry is really a policy issue and although the courts are used to resolving policy issues he argued that they are not skilled in selecting between *alternative* policies, which is what the Restrictive Trade Practices Act required. Nevertheless, he concluded that it was appropriate to ask the courts to handle such questions.

Stevens was not, however, inclined to the view that the framing of the legislation provided the court with the tools to do the job. He claimed that there was insufficient precision in the wording of the gateways and that there was scope for conflicting interpretations, especially in the very broadly defined gateway (b). Further, a wide breadth of interpretation was left to the judges in deciding what were 'fair terms', a 'substantial' reduction in exports, 'serious and persistent' unemployment and there was also a variation in the burden of proof between the gateways. Consequently he considered that an unfair burden was placed on the judges and although there was nothing inherently against using the judicial process for controlling restrictive practices, in practice the appropriate tools had not been provided in this particular legislation. Interestingly, he did comment that the terms of the Resale Prices Act 1964 which were more specific in their emphasis on the interests of consumers made that legislation more readily justiciable.

(3)   *Progress under the Act*

Table 15.1 indicates the different numbers of agreements registered and disposed of at various points of time since 1956. These figures are of course cumulative. They indicate, as might have been expected, that the vast majority of agreements were registered in the early years of the operation of the Act, although the enforcement activities of the staff of the Registrar of Restrictive Trading Agreements have been responsible for quite a high proportion of the agreements subsequently registered. The Registrar reported in his first report that out of 150 industry groups in the Standard Industrial Classification, 127 had agreements registered. The number of agreements varied from industry to industry but numbers alone are not necessarily an indication of the economic importance of restrictive practices in any particular industry. The Registrar identified 970 important agreements with nationwide application and found that, of these, 81 per cent contained restrictions on selling prices and 75 per cent were agreements made by manufacturers. Considering all the agreements registered he found that two-thirds were concerned with selling prices; 50 per cent had provisions for the adoption of standard terms and conditions and about 10 per cent contained restrictions on the nature of customers or suppliers with whom the parties to the agreement would deal. Other agreements related to the extent of the market to be supplied, made provision for the grant of special terms to favoured purchasers and restricted the quantity of production. Once again therefore we find an overwhelming preponderance of price restrictions and an apparent anxiety of

Table 15.1   Progress of proceedings under the Restrictive Trade Practices Act

Date	Agreements on the Register	Agreements terminated or varied	Cases heard by the court	Cases referred to court but not defended	Removed from Register as of no economic significance[1]	Agreements in respect of which the Registrar has been discharged from bringing proceedings[2]
31/12/59	2240	780	7	34	6	—
30/6/61	2350	1065	17	60	37	—
30/6/63	2430	1610	27	79	48	—
30/6/66	2550	2110	33	169	80	—
30/6/69	2660	2370	35	235	117	41
30/6/72	2875	2620	37	317	117	108

Note   All figures are cumulative.
[1]Under Section 12 of the 1956 Act.
[2]Under Section 9(2) of the 1968 Act.
Source: *Restrictive Trading Agreements, Reports of the Registrar*

firms to avoid competition on price. Many of the restrictions relating to standard terms and conditions of sale were adjuncts to price fixing agreements in an effort to prevent the shading of prices and the offer of larger discounts.

The Registrar and his staff have worked expeditiously through the agreements, making references to the court and preparing cases and by 1966, that is within ten years of the commencement of operations under the Act, the Registrar was able to report that there was no backlog of important agreements awaiting reference to the court and that the mass of price fixing agreements had been dismantled. The vast majority of agreements have either been terminated or allowed to expire by the parties concerned or their terms have been varied so that they no longer contain registrable restrictions. A number of agreements have been removed from the Register on the grounds that they are of no substantial economic significance under the terms of Section 12 of the Act and since 1968 the Registrar has been able to announce that he has been discharged from taking proceedings in the court in respect of a number of agreements that are not of such significance as to call for an investigation even though they will remain on the Register.

Of the agreements actually referred to the court for proceedings to commence the vast majority were subsequently not defended. Of those that were heard the parties to agreements were successful in having their restrictions upheld as not contrary to the public interest either totally or in large part in 11 cases and were mainly or entirely unsuccessful in 26. Undoubtedly the apparent severity of some of the early judgments had a major influence on the decisions of parties not to defend their agreements. There were a number of instances where one agreement was treated as representative of a whole group of similar or identical agreements and so an unfavourable decision by the court in one case would have led to the abandonment of many others. Considerations of the amounts of time and money involved in preparing and fighting a case and the possibility of finding an alternative form of arrangement that would not be registrable and might achieve the same effect as an agreement were also probably important considerations leading to firms' decisions not to attempt to justify restrictions before the court.

(4)   Proceedings in the Restrictive Practices Court

Tables 15.2 and 15.3 respectively indicate details of the cases that were won and lost in the Restrictive Practices Court. Nine of the eleven cases won by industry were in fact cases where the main restriction was concerned with some form of price fixing and seven of these were concerned primarily with supplies of producer rather than consumer goods. They were mainly won under gateway (b) which has proved to be wider in its construction and more likely to permit generalised arguments about the benefits of a particular agreement. The arguments under this gateway that were most likely to find favour with the court were those that claimed that the restriction on competition either had the direct effect of keeping prices lower than they would otherwise have been or that the avoidance of price competition encouraged firms to co-operate in the exchange of technical know-how or to share in research and development activities which were of direct benefit to the public and encouraged increased efficiency.

One case (Sulphuric Acid) was won under gateway (d) on the grounds that it enabled the purchasers of sulphur to negotiate fair terms with a powerful supplier. The Water-tube Boilermakers argued successfully under gateway (f) that the opportunity to consult on market conditions would benefit exports. The more recent case over the agreement of the Scottish Daily Newspaper Society was argued successfully under a new gateway, (h), which had been introduced in the 1968 Restrictive Trade Practices Act. This provided that a restriction might be approved if it did not restrict or discourage competition. In this case the decision of the Scottish newspaper publishers that none of them would publish if the *Glasgow Herald* was unable to publish due to a strike was held by the court not to hinder competition. The parties to the agreement had argued that by avoiding competition in the very short run they were facilitating greater competition in the longer term.

In a number of these cases arguments under other gateways were not accepted by the court and some lesser restrictions, especially the use of aggregated rebates, were declared contrary to the public interest. In some cases the court used the tailpiece in balancing certain detriments, especially of higher prices, against the benefits it had accepted as having been established under one of the gateways before declaring that on balance the restriction was not contrary to the public interest.

It also seems that in at least some of the cases the court required convincing on two different matters. First it would need to be satisfied that the predicted adverse consequences from the abrogation of the agreement would be likely to occur and secondly that the industry had performed well while the agreement had been in force up to the time of the court hearing. In the cases on cement, magnets, sulphuric acid and glazed tiles, the court indicated that it considered the prices and/or profits prevailing under the agreement to be satisfactory and in the case of cement the court also commented favourably on the performance of the industry in its efficient use of capacity, its expansion of capacity to meet rising demand and the avoidance of excess capacity and wasteful transport.[21] Its proper concern with the performance of an industry under an agreement was also emphasised in its warnings that the fixing of unreasonable prices in the future would constitute a material change in the circumstances surrounding an industry which would justify the Registrar reopening the case before the court.

Table 15.2   Cases won by industry in the Restrictive Practices Court

Cases won	Nature of main restrictions	Gateways accepted	Comments
Water-tube Boilermakers (1959)	Collusive tendering	(f), benefit to exports of being able to consult on and assess market possibilities	
Black Bolts and Nuts (1960)	Price fixing	(b), price competition would raise costs of shopping around	Other restrictions held contrary to the public interest. Any fixing of unreasonable prices in the future would constitute a material change in circumstances
Cement Makers (1961)	Common delivered prices	(b), the agreement kept prices and the necessary rate of return for new investment lower	Aggregated rebates held contrary to the public interest. It was accepted that industry performance under the agreement had been efficient

Table 15.2   Cases won by industry in the Restrictive Practices Court (cont.)

Cases won	Nature of main restrictions	Gateways accepted	Comments
Permanent Magnets (1962)	Minimum price fixing	(b), benefits to research and new product introduction and diffusion	Some minor restrictions held to be contrary to the public interest. Prices and profits had been reasonable under the agreement. The fixing of unreasonable prices would constitute a material change in circumstances
Standard Metal Windows (1962)	Price fixing	(b), benefits from the exchange of detailed technical information had kept prices and costs down	If competition from Crittalls (who were outside the group) ceased, there would be a material change in circumstances
Net Books (1962)	Agreement to enforce rpm	(b), if the agreement ended there would be no rpm and fewer outlets, higher prices and fewer titles published would result	
National Sulphuric Acid (1963)	Fixing of prices on the purchase of sulphur	(d), agreement facilitated standardisation and hence cost reduction	Profits held to be reasonable
Scrap Iron (1964)	Minimum price fixing	(b), prices lower under the agreement	A change in the method of calculating prices would be a material change and might make an agreement less acceptable
Distant Water Vessels (1966)	Fixing of minimum auction prices	(b), ending of agreement would lead to a short-run fall in prices, a loss of confidence, less investment, a loss of trawling capacity and hence higher long-run prices	
Scottish Daily Newspapers (1972)	Agreement by all papers not to produce if one paper was not produced	(h), the agreement actually helped to maintain competition in the long run	

Note on Sources: All Restrictive Practices Cases are reported in the *Restrictive Practices Law Reports* published by the Incorporated Council of Law Reporting for England and Wales. The Reports of the Registrar of Restrictive Trading Agreements contain a brief summary of each case.

Table 15.3   Cases lost by industry in the Restrictive Practices Court

Case and date of judgment	Nature of main restriction	Gateways argued	Comments
Chemists Federation (1958)	Restrictions on who could sell medicines	(a), (b)	
Yarn Spinners (1959)	Minimum price scheme and standard terms and conditions of sale	(b), (e)	Case made out under gateway (e), that abrogation of agreement would lead to a rise in the level of unemployment in the area. But on balancing in the tailpiece the court decided that the benefits were outweighed by the detriments of higher prices, loss of exports and the maintenance of excess capacity under the agreement
Blanket Manufacturers (1959)	Minimum prices, standard terms and quality specification	(b)	Quality specification restriction upheld. The minimum price scheme was found to have no effect and to be harmless but this was not sufficient reason under the Act for upholding the scheme
Scottish Bread (1959)	Recommendations on costing system, prices and wholesale discounts	(b)	
Federation of Wholesale and Multiple Bakers (1959)	Recommendations on maximum retail prices and distributor margins	(b)	Costing formula used in setting prices held by the court to be inadequate to protect the consumer
Federation of British Carpet Manufacturers (1959)	Price fixing and agreements on trade discounts	(b), (f)	Prices were arbitrary
Phenol Producers (1960)	Agreement to adopt prices, terms and conditions fixed by the association	(b)	Agreement had raised prices and had operated in interests of the producers
Doncaster and Retford Co-operative Societies (1960)	Restriction on trading areas	(b)	
Wholesale Confectioners' Alliance (1960)	Recommendations on scale of prices for sales to retailers	(b)	

Table 15.3   Cases lost by industry in the Restrictive Practices Court (cont.)

Case and date of judgment	Nature of main restriction	Gateways argued	Comments
Motor Vehicle Distribution Agreement (1960)	Trade register of approved dealers required to accept certain restrictions on trading policy	(a), (b)	
Associated Transformer Manufacturers (1961)	Minimum price fixing	(b), (d), (f)	
Glass Bottle Manufacturers (1961)	Minimum prices and standard conditions of sale	(b)	
Linoleum Manufacturers Association (1961)	Common prices and discount terms	(b), (f)	
Newspaper Proprietors and Retail Newsagents (1961)	Restriction on number of outlets selling newspapers	(b)	
Birmingham Association of Building Trades Employers (1963)	Restrictions and recommendations on tendering	(b)	Was typical of a number of similar registered agreements
Jute Goods (1963)	Agreements on prices and terms of sale	(e)	
Tyre Trade Register (1963)	Restrictions on type of customer to whom trade terms were granted	(a)	The actual agreement investigated was that of the Staffordshire Motor Tyre Co. It was typical of a number of similar agreements that had been registered
British Paper and Board Makers' Association (1963)	Guarantee of minimum prices of waste paper to local authorities	(b)	
British Heavy Steel Makers (1964)	Recommended prices, effectively used as a common price	(b)	

Table 15.3   Cases lost by industry in the Restrictive Practices Court (cont.)

Case and date of judgment	Nature of main restriction	Gateways argued	Comments
Mining Rope, Wire Rope and Locked Coil Ropemakers' Associations (1964)	Recommendation of fixed common selling prices	(b), (d), (f)	
Finance Houses Association (1965)	Fixing of maximum hire purchase rates for car purchasers	(b)	
Mallaig and Northwest Fishermen's Association (1970)	Quota fixing and other attempts to restrict supply	(b)	

Note   This list does not include a number of cases dealing with contempt of court and issues relating to the registrability of particular restrictions.

Table 15.3 lists those cases where industry has had its restrictions wholly or largely declared contrary to the public interest. This lists only those cases where economic arguments under the gateways specified in Section 21 of the Act have been fought out. Consequently contempt of court and registration cases have not been included. The broadly defined gateway (b) has been argued most frequently and, comparing Tables 15.2 and 15.3, there seems to be a slightly greater chance that the court will accept restrictions argued under this gateway than under most of the other gateways. In all, the court has found a case made out in 8 of the 29 instances where an attempt has been made to justify a restriction under this gateway. This still indicates that the chances of success are not high and the court has rejected arguments under gateway (b) that the quality of the product or the number of outlets stocking a product would fall, that prices would rise, that there would be a disadvantageous loss of technical co-operation or an adverse effect on the health of the industry if some agreements were abrogated. In a number of cases it seems clear that the court has not had much sympathy with the arguments of respondents where it has found that under the agreement prices had not been kept down, that the basis on which prices were fixed was arbitrary or reflected the use of monopolistic power and that the parties had failed to take advantage of the opportunity to exchange information with each other. Clearly a poor performance under the agreement weakens the chances of convincing the court that the abrogation of the agreement is likely to prove contrary to the public interest.

The export gateway (f) was criticised at the time of the passing of the Act as a reflection of mercantilist thinking. But only in one case (Water-tube Boilermakers) out of seven in which this gateway was pleaded was it upheld. It was rejected in two cases in which the court decided in favour of a restriction under another gateway. Gateway (c) has never been pleaded and gateways (a), (d) and (e) are applicable in relation to only a limited number of industries. The court has not accepted that restrictive agreements are likely to protect the public against injury. The argument that weak sellers or buyers should be allowed to agree amongst themselves to create some countervailing power against a dominant buyer or seller has not been upheld in any of the cases where the dominant party was a government department or public utility and the only success under this gateway has been in the case of the arrangements to purchase sulphur from an American firm about which there was evidence of a previous attempt to take advantage of its market power. The danger that the ending of an agreement would lead to an increase in the level of unemployment in a particular area has only been argued in the cases concerning cotton yarn spinning and jute goods. In the cotton yarn spinners case the court accepted that an undesirable increase in the level of unemployment would result if the agreement ended but concluded on balance that the detriments from the continuation of the agreement were greater. This is the only case where the court has found that a case was established under one or other of the gateways and then rejected it under the balancing provisions in the tailpiece.[22]

It appears that initially the court interpreted the presumption in the Act against restrictive practices very strictly and adopted a firm pro-competition stance. This is perhaps best reflected in the decision against the cotton yarn spinners agreement even though the court recognised that this was likely to give rise to an increase in the level of unemployment and a reluctance to invest in modern capacity in Lancashire, a situation the government subsequently attempted to deal with in the Cotton Industry Reorganisation Act 1959. Later on, possibly as a result of changes in the personnel constituting the court, it seemed that the court's stand on the virtues of competition had weakened and, between 1962 and 1964 in particular, industry's chances of success before the court appeared to have increased noticeably. Decisions reached by the court on individual cases have not pleased every commentator. The chances are higher that economists will be dissatisfied with judgments where the court has found in favour of a restriction and a substantial literature exists criticising such decisions.[23] It has been objected that the court's judgments are inconsistent between cases and that its economic reasoning in deciding on the public interest aspects of a particular case is often insufficiently extensive and appears to contain logical inconsistencies in the development of its conclusions.

The problem seems to be a twofold one. First, it is often difficult to obtain an adequate assessment of the performance of the industry under an agreement. The Registrar has been particularly conscious of the difficulty, especially as international comparisons have not normally been allowed by the court and as experts on an industry are often closely involved in the presentation of the industry's side of the case.[24] Secondly, the key to proceedings under Section 21 of the Restrictive Trade Practices Act is that the court is required to consider and choose between alternative predictions of the future performance of the industry concerned both with and without the agreement. This is a complicated procedure and would be challenging to professional economists, especially as predicting the outcome of the abrogation of an agreement will also require the development of a number of sub-theories regarding the likely form and extent of competition, investment decision-making under uncertainty, etc. The fact of the matter is that the court has failed to give complete satisfaction to its economist examiners of its work. Its apparent unease at deciding exactly what is implied by competition and especially at understanding the nature of the competitive process under conditions of oligopolistic interdependence is most often pointed to as a major weakness of the court.

Whether or not the method adopted has proved the most satisfactory, the fact of the matter is that the vast majority of formal restrictions on the supply of goods in British industry, that had existed in many instances for 50 or more years, were quite speedily removed as a result of the Restrictive Trade Practices Act. In the following section we shall consider some of the consequences of these changes. It is, however, worthwhile to pause briefly and consider what lessons may be learnt from British experience with the control of restrictive practices that might be relevant to another country contemplating similar action or the use of a judicial procedure in another economic policy area.

A judicial procedure has offered the benefits that arise from respect for the rule of law and from the careful investigation of issues. It has also avoided the possibility of prolonged political negotiations to try to change or weaken policy decisions that tend to arise following reports by the Monopolies Commission. As the court has appeared to treat what seemed to be similar issues differently in different cases it has not offered the certainty and predictability in its judgments that lawyers and some economists claimed would be a major advantage from a judicial procedure. This suggests that the court was not given sufficient guidance to help it balance different arguments, though it may be merely a reflection of the fact that the court ran into difficulty when it appeared to lose its presumption in favour of competition. It is fair comment that the court has not always been convincing as an arbiter of economic arguments and that it has not always been consistent in framing its own economic predictions. Suggestions have been made to increase the specialist economic membership of the court and this might help. It might also be an advantage if, while retaining a judicial procedure in reaching a judgment, the emphasis on conflict and polarisation of the arguments often implicit in an adversary procedure could be modified so that the principals on each side in a case were obliged to draw up a composite document describing their own models and predictions and indicating clearly the points at which they diverged and on which the court might wish to hear evidence. In the last resort, however, the criticisms of the court's performance as an economic policy-maker are perhaps more attributable to the general inability of economists to establish more effectively their own views as to the nature of the competitive process in order that these can be used by non-economists in a policy-making function.

A more radical view might be that it would have been financially cheaper and would have released resources to be used in a more productive manner and without causing a major loss of benefits had all restrictions been declared *per se* illegal in 1956.[25] Certainly with the benefit of hindsight this seems a persuasive argument.

The effects of British policy

It is as difficult to assess *ex post* the effects of a particular policy as it is to predict *ex ante* the likely consequences of the abrogation of restrictive agreements. Nevertheless it is important to attempt to assess the effects. While the Registrar[26] has to some extent monitored developments in industries where agreements have been terminated and indeed has brought cases alleging contempt of court where it appeared that parties to an abrogated agreement had continued to give effect to the same restrictions that had been declared contrary to the public interest, only two research investigations of any substance appear to have been carried out. The first, by J. B. Heath, followed closely upon the commencement of court proceedings and dealt primarily with the short-term consequences of some early terminations of agreements.[27] More recently research has been conducted on a case study basis of the effect of the Act on a number of agreements. At the time of writing only a limited amount of information has become available about this.[28] However, a reasonable picture of the effects of the legislation can be built up from these sources.

In some industries the ending of agreements did lead to an increase in competition. In a number of cases this was mainly of the nature of short-run price cutting caused by the initial uncertainty facing firms in the new situation. Often this was quickly replaced by the recognition of a price leader or the adoption of an information agreement. In other cases price competition became, either immediately or at a later point, more pervasive. This seems to have been the experience in industries with larger numbers of firms and was often associated with conditions of falling demand or the entry of new competitors. The Registrar has consistently emphasised the importance of keen purchasing behaviour by buyers as a means of inducing competitive pressures on suppliers and has reported that large buyers in some industries have been able to secure better discount terms once an agreement had been terminated. It is also encouraging to find some evidence that the ending of agreements has contributed to an increase in efficiency and a faster rate of technical progress, especially where the abandonment of restrictions has fostered competition from new entrants.

But there still seem to be many cases where the abrogation of agreements does not seem to have had much effect on competition. This appears to be especially true in industries that are closely knit oligopolies. Here the sense of clubmanship is probably stronger, the fears of a price war greater and the chances of continuing to organise relations between firms in such a way that competition is avoided are much higher. In such cases the recognition of a price leader is a likely alternative to a formal agreement. Buoyant demand and buyer inertia have also contributed to this situation. There are instances where mergers have apparently been used to reduce the threat of competition and to acquire high cost firms that had previously been preserved by the agreement. Frequently, however, it seems that firms have chosen to replace their restrictions with information agreements, arranging to notify through a central agency information on prices, costs, investment plans, capacity utilisation and so on. Such agreements seem to be particularly closely associated with the adoption of stringent measures against cartels. They were initially devised in the United States in 1911 as a response to the vigorous enforcement of the Sherman Act and, while not unknown in Britain, they became particularly important at the end of the 1950s when firms began abandoning their restrictive agreements. The timing of these developments and the fact that they may have served as a means of continuing to provide trade associations with a role to play once they could no longer organise a cartel suggests that they are an almost inevitable successor to cartels.

Information agreements raise many of the same issues regarding their desirability that have been discussed in relation to formal restrictive agreements. Clearly some agreements have been designed to be as close to formal price fixing arrangements as the law allows and must therefore be considered to be undesirable. Others, however, may offer a finer balance of advantage by encouraging efficiency and disadvantage through hindrances on competition.[29] It is argued that the advantages of information agreements are that they reduce the area of uncertainty and ignorance facing firms in their decision-making and enable firms to make better informed investment and output decisions, thereby achieving a closer matching of supply and demand. Information exchanges may act as a spur to greater efficiency if firms see that others have lower operating costs than their own. In the last resort, however, much of the case for information agreements is that they control forms of price competition that are considered by the firms concerned to be undesirable. They may help to prevent phantom competition – the sort of behaviour where a buyer states untruthfully that he can obtain supplies at a price lower than he is in fact being quoted by another potential supplier. They may help to avoid short-run price wars and weak selling without denying the benefits of longer run competition.

The arguments against information agreements suggest that they may be used as, or develop to be, a form of coercion to discourage more efficient firms from passing on the benefits of their superior efficiency in the form of lower prices. An information agreement may therefore hinder the revival of competition and delay the growth of the more efficient firms. It will work to discourage price shading and hinder the exercise of countervailing buying power.

Various suggestions have been made as to ways whereby the benefits could be obtained from information agreements without harming the public interest. In general it seems likely that least objection would arise where the information circulated did not give details of actual prices but merely provided information on the range of prices quoted – for example the median and the upper and lower quartile values. Individual companies should not be identified and the information should be available to customers as well as suppliers. The information should be provided on an *ex post* rather than an *ex ante* basis. In the amendments to the 1956 legislation introduced in the Restrictive Trade Practices Act 1968 provision was made for the registration of the main forms of information agreement. It has been suggested that as a consequence of this legislation and of the previous cases concerning the possible contempt of court by the parties to the Galvanized Tanks and Tyre Mileage agreements, information agreements have now largely disappeared from British industry.[30] Even if this is so it seems highly likely that they will, in one form or another, again become important since firms and industries will continue to wish to regulate their activities and the role of information will continue to be crucial to the efficient working of a modern industrial system.

While the working of the 1956 Act may be considered to have been reasonably satisfactory it did leave certain loose ends. There was insufficient enforcement activity to prevent the parties to abrogated agreements making other similar agreements. There was insufficient sanction on parties for failure to register agreements and it was possible to obtain the protection and benefits of agreements for a long time before they had to be defended before the court. In this way firms were able to overcome a particular competitive threat in the short term by making an agreement and then dropping it once it had been referred. The use of information agreements as a means of hindering the onset of competition was a serious weakness in the initial impact of the 1956 Act.

In some respects the Act seemed to operate in an undesirable way. For example, it was inappropriate that separate subsidiaries within a single organisation could make an agreement that was not registrable under the terms of the Act while small, independent firms would have to register any similar agreement they might make. This was likely to hinder the ability of small firms to compete. In particular it appeared likely that the provisions in the Act would hinder the work of the retail voluntary groups in organising special promotions among their members. It seems that this has now been overcome. Further, the terms of the Act may have hindered the making of agreements over such aspects as standardisation of products, avoidance of wasteful competition and modification of discount structures. This situation was criticised by the PIB[31] and the National Economic Development Council. There is also the problem of the failure to harmonise different aspects of anti-trust policy. Is it appropriate to adopt a strong anti-cartel policy if firms are able to buy the same degree of security through mergers which are allowed to proceed unchallenged by government? What advantage is there in prohibiting price agreements if the operation of a prices and incomes policy encourages firms to consult with each other and make common cause in applying for permission to increase prices? In any anti-trust policy it is necessary to harmonise the different strands and avoid the application of double standards. The severity of British restrictive practices legislation has not always been matched by other aspects of policy towards the structure and conduct of British industry.

Probably the one area that has been least effectively dealt with is the question of oligopoly behaviour and the question of whether pricing decisions by oligopolists are collusive or not. This problem is not unique to the British situation. It also applies in the United States: 'to distinguish between informed oligopoly and collusion as the cause of damped down price competition is the most difficult task that the [American] courts have to face'.[32] In the Galvanised Tanks contempt case the British Restrictive Practices Court was faced with the prospect of deciding whether it would infer collusion from evidence of parallel price movements but in the end it did not have to give a ruling either way on this question. Some would argue that such parallel behaviour – agreements to agree – should be considered to constitute a restrictive practice: 'there is no reason to exclude oligopoly behaviour from the scope of the term agreement simply because the circumstances make it possible to communicate without speech'.[33] The problem is that it may well be rational to take account of your competitors but parallelism in pricing may suggest something more than that. Under these circumstances presumptive evidence of collusion may require other evidence besides parallel prices. D. F. Turner has suggested that identical bid prices, greater price stability and other attempts to eliminate uncertainties would be indicative.[34] These and other questions regarding oligopoly are discussed in Chapter 14.

The 1956 legislation has been amended somewhat in two later Acts, the Restrictive Trade Practices Act 1968 and the Fair Trading Act 1973. As we have already noted, in the 1968 amendments information agreements were made registrable at the discretion of the Board of Trade and subject to Restrictive Practices Court investigation. A new gateway (h) was introduced: that the restriction does not and is not likely to restrict or discourage competition to any material degree. Rather more stringent controls on the speed with which new agreements had to be registered and on the consequences of failure to register were also included in the Act. The Fair Trading Act transfers responsibility under restrictive practices legislation from the Registrar of Restrictive Trading Agreements to the newly created post of Director General of Fair Trading. The main development so far as restrictive agreements are concerned is that there are powers contained in the Act whereby the Secretary of State may, by statutory order, extend the scope of the Restrictive Trade Practices Act 1956 to agreements or information agreements relating to the supply of services. In addition agreements as to the prices to be recommended or suggested for resale have also been made registrable.

These are useful amendments to close gaps in the basic legislation. But there are still weaknesses. Enforcement procedures have not been strengthened and the position of oligopolistic conduct under the restrictive practices laws has not been clarified. Although it was widely expected, there has been no provision to prohibit the making of any further agreements without the prior permission of the Restrictive Practices Court.

Perhaps the real issue is whether having prohibited certain forms of restraint on competition between firms it is reasonable for policy makers to assume that industry is really operating competitively. As we have seen, competition is a difficult concept to define or even to identify in practice and a satisfactory competitive *performance* may appear to come from quite different forms of market *structure* and *conduct*. If it is accepted that the private interests of firms may diverge from the public interest and that firms will continue to seek ways of regulating their market relationships, an effective competition policy will always have a role in an industrial society. As firms devise new forms of competition and co-operation so government policy will need to evolve to reflect the dynamic nature of industrial organisation and market conduct.

NOTES

Chapter 1

1 A. A. Berle and G. C. Means *The Modern Corporation and Private Property* (Macmillan 1932).
2 S. J. Prais 'The growth in industrial concentration: a theoretical excursus' (NIESR mimeo 1972).
3 This question is well discussed by M. R. Conklin and H. T. Goldstein in 'Census principles of product classification in manufacturing industries' in NBER *Business Concentration and Price Policy* Princeton University Press (1955) p. 15.
4 See J. P. Miller 'Measures of monopoly power and concentration; their economic significance' in NBER *Business Concentration and Price Policy. op. cit.*
5 In practice it has been shown that similar rankings of industries in terms of their apparent degrees of concentration are obtained when a three-firm concentration ratio, a measure of the number of firms required to account for 80 per cent of employment and the H index are compared. See G. Rosenbluth 'Measures of concentration', in NBER *Business Concentration and Price Policy op. cit.* p. 57.
6 M. A. Adelman 'Comment on the "H" concentration as a numbers equivalent' *Review of Economics and Statistics* 51 (1969) p. 99
7 See for example M. A. Utton *Industrial Concentration* Penguin (1970) p. 47.
8 See P. E. Hart and S. J. Prais 'The analysis of business concentration: a statistical approach' *Journal of the Royal Statistical Society* Series A, vol. 119 (1956) p. 150.
9 A. P. Lerner 'The concept of monopoly and the measurement of monopoly power' *Review of Economics and Statistics* 1 (1934) p. 157.
10 R. Triffin *Monopolistic Competition and General Equilibrium Theory* Harvard University Press (1940).
11 K. W. Rothschild 'The degree of monopoly' *Economica* 9 (1942) p. 24.
12 W. Fellner 'Comment' in NBER *Business Concentration and Price Policy op. cit.* p. 113 ff.
13 G. J. Stigler *The Organisation of Industry* Irwin (1968) ch. 4.
14 G. J. Stigler 'Introduction' in NBER *Business Concentration and Price Policy op. cit.* p. 3 ff.
15 These are helpfully set out in an appendix to the second edition of A. D. Neale *The Anti-trust Laws of the U.S.A.* Cambridge University Press (1970) p. 493.
16 R. Eveley and I. M. D. Little *Concentration in British Industry* Cambridge University Press (1960).
17 P. Pashigian 'The effect of market size on concentration' *International Economic Review* 10 (1969) p. 291; and K. D. George 'Changes in British industrial concentration 1951–1958' *Journal of Industrial Economics* 15 (1967) p. 200.
18 On this question, see e.g. P. E. Hart and S. J. Prais *op. cit.*; P. E. Hart 'The size and growth of firms' *Economica* 29 (1962) p. 29; E. Mansfield 'Entry, Gibrat's law, innovation and the growth of firms' *American Economic Review* 52 (1962) p. 1023; H. A. Simon and C. P. Bonini 'The size distribution of business firms' *American Economic Review* 48 (1958) p. 607; J. M. Samuels and A. D. Chesher 'Growth, survival and the size of companies 1960–69' in K. Cowling ed. *Market Structure and Corporate Behaviour* Gray Mills (1972). The growth of firms is discussed in Chapter 7.

19   A. Armstrong and A. Silberston 'Size of plant, size of enterprise and concentration in British manufacturing industry 1935–1958' *Journal of the Royal Statistical Society*, Series A 128 (1965) p. 395.

20   R. L. Nelson *Concentration in the Manufacturing Industries of the United States* Yale University Press (1963).

21   See e.g. R. Caves *American Industry, Structure, Conduct, Performance* Prentice Hall (1967) ch. 2.

22   J. S. Bain *International Differences in Industrial Structure* Yale University Press (1966).

23   H. Leak and A. Maizels 'The structure of British industry' *Journal of the Royal Statistical Society* 108 (1945) p. 142.

24   A. Armstrong and A. Silberston *op. cit.*

25   W. G. Shepherd 'Changes in British industrial concentration 1951–58' *Oxford Economic Papers* 18 (1966) p. 126.

26   A. Armstrong and A. Silberston *op. cit.*

27   K. D. George 'Concentration in British industry' *op. cit.*

28   S. J. Prais *op. cit.* By way of comparison, the equivalent figure for the USA is 31 per cent.

29   This is the concept of Galtonian regression and is discussed in Prais *op. cit.*, and also in Utton *op. cit.*

30   The Monopolies Commission *Household Detergents* (HMSO, 1966).

31   J. P. Miller 'Measures of monopoly power and concentration: their economic significance' in NBER *Business Concentration and Price Policy op. cit.*

32   See N. R. Collins and L. E. Preston *Concentration and Price-Cost Margins in Manufacturing Industries* University of California Press (1970).

33   J. S. Bain 'Relation of profit rate to industry concentration: American manufacturing 1936–40' *Quarterly Journal of Economics* 65 (1951) p. 293.

34   R. A. Miller 'Market structure and industrial performance: relation of profit rates to concentration, advertising intensity and diversity' *Journal of Industrial Economics* 17 (1969) p. 104.

35   P. E. Hart (ed.) *Studies in Profit, Business Savings and Investment in the United Kingdom 1920–62*, vol. 2, Allen and Unwin (1968), also 'Competition and rate of return on capital in U.K. industry' *Business Ratios* 2 (1968) p. 3.

36   J. M. Samuels and D. J. Smyth 'Profits, variability of profits and firm size' *Economica* 35 (1968) p. 127.

37   M. Hall and L. Weiss, 'Firm size and profitability' *Review of Economics and Statistics* 49 (1967) p. 319.

38   M. Marcus, 'Profitability and size of firm: some further evidence' *Review of Economics and Statistics* 51 (1969) p. 104.

39   J. M. Samuels and D. J. Smyth *op. cit.*

40   A. Singh and G. Whittington *Growth Profitability and Valuation* Cambridge University Press (1968) ch. 6.

41   The administered price controversy is discussed and different conclusions drawn about its significance and the balance of the evidence in P. Asch, *Economic Theory and the Anti-trust Dilemma* Wiley (1970) p. 188–95 and F. M. Scherer *Industrial Market Structure and Economic Performance* Rand McNally (1971) ch. 12. See also R. Ruggles 'The nature of price flexibility and the determinants of relative price changes in the economy' in NBER *Business Concentration and Price Policy op. cit.*

42   L. W. Weiss 'Business pricing policies and inflation reconsidered' *Journal of Political Economy* 74 (1966) p. 177.

43   For some evidence on this see J. F. Pickering 'The Prices and Incomes Board and private sector prices' *Economic Journal* 81 (1971) p. 225.

44   J. Schumpeter *Capitalism, Socialism and Democracy* Allen and Unwin (1947) chs. 7, 8; see also J. K. Galbraith *The New Industrial State* Hamish Hamilton (1967).

45   R. R. Nelson 'The simple economics of basic scientific research' *Journal of Political Economy* 67 (1959) p. 297.

46 For a discussion of some of these issues see D. Hamberg 'Innovation in the industrial research laboratory' *Journal of Political Economy* 71 (1963) p. 95.

47 On the question of small firms see C. Freeman 'Size of firm, R and D and innovation' in J. B. Heath ed. *International Conference on Monopolies, Mergers and Restrictive Practices Papers and Reports* HMSO (1971), and C. Freeman *The Role of Small Firms in Innovation in the U.K. since 1945* Committee of Inquiry on Small Firms Research Report No. 6 HMSO (1972).

48 D. C. Mueller 'Patents, research and development and the measurement of inventive activity' *Journal of Industrial Economics* 15 (1966) p. 26.

49 The remainder of this section is based on evidence in a number of sources, mainly American, including: W. S. Comanor and F. M. Scherer 'Patent statistics as a measure of technical change' *Journal of Political Economy* 77 (1969) p. 392; D. Hamberg 'Invention in the industrial research laboratory' *Journal of Political Economy* 71 (1963) p. 95; C. Freeman 'Size of firm, R and D and innovation' *op. cit.;* J. Jewkes *et. al. The Sources of Invention* Macmillan (1958); C. M. Kennedy and A. P. Thirlwell 'Surveys in Applied Economics: Technical Progress' *Economic Journal* 82 (1972) p. 11; E. Mansfield *Industrial Research and Technical Innovation* Norton (1968); J. W. Markham 'Market structure, business conduct and innovation' *American Economic Review Papers and Proceedings* 53 (1965) p. 323; F. M. Scherer 'Firm size, market structure and the output of patented inventions' *American Economic Review* 55 (1965) p. 1097; *ibid* 'Market structure and the employment of scientists and engineers' *American Economic Review* 57 (1967) p. 524; D. F. Turner and O. E. Williamson 'Market structure in relation to technical and organisational innovation', in J. B. Heath (ed.) *op. cit.*

50 See also the Monopolies Commission *Beecham Group Ltd., and Glaxo Group Ltd., Boots Ltd., and Glaxo Group Ltd., a report on the proposed merger* HMSO (1972), Appendix 6 for similar conclusions regarding the relation between size of firm and research intensity and research success in the pharmaceutical industry. The Sainsbury Committee on the pharmaceutical industry did, however, take a different view. It noted that some of the larger firms in that industry did carry out much fundamental research and that there was some evidence of a correlation between money spent on research and the discovery of new drugs of major importance. See *Report of the Committee of Enquiry into the Relationshi⋅ of the Pharmaceutical Industry with the National Health Servi⋅⋅ ⋅⋅⋅⋅ ⋅* MSO (1967) Cmnd. 3410.

51 D. F. Turner and O. E. Williamson *op. cit.*

52 G. J. Stigler 'Industrial organisation and econor⋅ (ed.) *The State of the Social Sciences* Chicago (1956)

53 B. T. Allen 'Concentration and economic progr⋅ *⋅mic Review* 59 (1969) p. 600.

54 See, for example, A. Phillips 'Structure, conc⋅ and performance, conduct and structure?' in J. W. Λ nek *Industrial Organisation and Economic Development* ⋅ son Houghton Mifflin (1970).

Chapter 2

1 See J. S. Bain *Industrial Organisation* Wiley (1968).

2 The economist should be careful to note the distinction b⋅ ⋅le factors of production which are a function of the time p ⋅d direct costs which are a function of the production proce⋅ ⋅e long run all factors of production are by definition variabl⋅ ill be overheads, that is, not directly related to changes in the sc⋅

3 C. F. Pratten and R. M. Dean *The Economics of Large Scal⋅* ⋅n *British Industry* Cambridge University Press (1965).

4 C. F. Pratten *Economies of Scale in Manufacturing Indust⋅* e University Press (1971).

5   The concept of X-efficiency was coined by Leibenstein. See H. Leibenstein 'Allocative efficiency vs "X-Efficiency" ' *American Economic Review* 55 (1966) p. 392.

6   See M. Freidman 'Theory and measurement of long-run costs' in *Business Concentration and Price Policy* NBER (1955).

7   G. J. Stigler 'The economies of scale' *Journal of Law and Economics* (1958) p. 54.

8   T. R. Saving 'Estimation of optimum size of plant by the survivor technique' *Quarterly Journal of Economics* (1961) p. 569; W. G. Shepherd 'What does the survivor technique show about economies of scale' *Southern Economic Journal* (1967) p. 113; L. Weiss 'The survival technique and the extent of suboptimal capacity' *Journal of Political Economy* (1964) p. 246.

9   The Monopolies Commission *Metal Containers* HMSO (1970) para. 321.

10 A. A. Walters 'Cost and production functions' *Econometrica* (1963) p. 1.

11 H. B. Chenery 'Engineering production functions' *Quarterly Journal of Economics* 63 (1949) p. 507; J. S. Bain *Barriers to New Competition* Harvard University Press (1956); C. F. Pratten and R. M. Dean *op. cit.;* C. F. Pratten, *op. cit.*

12 N. Baloff 'The learning curve: some controversial issues' *Journal of Industrial Economics* 14 (1966) p. 275.

13 K. Hartley 'The learning curve and its application to the aircraft industry' *Journal of Industrial Economics* (1965) p. 122; S. G. Sturmey 'Cost curves and pricing in aircraft production' *Economic Journal* 74 (1964) p. 954.

14 National Board for Prices and Incomes *Payment by Results Systems* Report No. 65 Cmnd. 3627 HMSO (1968) paras. 45–7.

15 A. M. Golding *The Semi Conductor Industry in Britain and the United States* University of Sussex D. Phil. thesis (1971).

16 W. Z. Hirsch 'Firm progress ratios' *Econometrica* 24 (1956) p. 136.

17 S. G. Sturmey *op. cit.*

18 C. F. Pratten *op. cit.*

19 For a discussion of the implications of increasing numbers of hierarchical levels in a firm see O. E. Williamson 'Hierarchical control and optimum firm size' *Journal of Political Economy* (1967) p. 123.

20 See for example NBPI reports on: *Prices of Compound Fertilisers* Report No. 28 HMSO (1967) Cmnd. 3228; *Portland Cement Prices* No. 38 HMSO (1967) Cmnd. 3381; *Price of Butyl Rubber* No. 66 HMSO (1968) Cmnd. 3626; *The Price of Hoover Domestic Appliances* No. 73 HMSO (1968) Cmnd. 3671; *Synthetic Organic Dyestuffs and Organic Pigments Prices* No. 100 HMSO (1969) Cmnd. 3895.

21 *Metal Containers op. cit.,* para. 57.

22 On this, see for example evidence in The Monopolies Commission *Colour Films* HMSO (1966) para. 148; NBPI *Synthetic Organic Dyestuffs and Organic Pigments Prices op. cit.*

23 S. G. Sturmey *op. cit.*

24 The Monopolies Commission *Man-Made Cellulosic Fibres* HMSO (1968) para. 85; NBPI *Prices of Fletton and Non-Fletton Bricks* Report No. 47 Cmnd. 3480 HMSO (1967).

25 NBPI *Margarine and Compound Cooking Fats* Report No. 147 HMSO (1970) Cmnd. 4368.

26 For a useful review of much of the empirical evidence see A. A. Walters *op. cit.*

27 J. S. Bain *Barriers of New Competition op. cit.*

28 J. S. Bain *International Differences in Industrial Structure* Yale University Press (1966).

29 C. F. Pratten and R. M. Dean *op. cit.* and C. F. Pratten *op. cit.*

30 J. Haldi and D. Whitcomb 'Economies of scale in industrial plants' *Journal of Political Economy* 75 (1967) p. 373; NBPI *Prices of Fletton and Non-Fletton Bricks op. cit.*

31 A. A. Walters *op. cit.,* p. 52.

32 C. F. Pratten *op. cit.* p. 58.

33   See *Small Firms*, Report of the Committee of Enquiry on Small Firms HMSO
      (1971) Cmnd. 4811, p. 33, 35. Much of the discussion in this section is based
      on that report and the various research reports that were commissioned by the
      Committee, see particularly J. R. Davies and M. Kelly *Small Firms in the
      Manufacturing Sector* Report No. 3; C. W. Golby and G. Johns *Attitude and
      Motivation* Report No. 7; J. Hebden and R. V. F. Robinson *The Small Firm in
      the Motor Vehicle Distribution and Repair Industry* Report No. 9; P. Hillebrandt
      Small Firms in the Construction Industry Report No. 10; J. F. Pickering *et al.*
      The Small Firm in the Hotel and Catering Industry Report No. 14; Discussions
      of the role and survival of small firms are also to be found in E. T. Penrose
      The Theory of the Growth of the Firm Blackwell (1959), C. F. Pratten *op. cit.*,
      J. S. Bain 'Survival ability as a test of efficiency' *American Economic Review
      Papers and Proceedings* 59 (1969) p. 99.

34   See Economists Advisory Group *Problems of the small firm in raising external
      finance* Committee of Enquiry on Small Firms Research Report No. 5 HMSO
      (1971); J. F. Pickering *et al. op. cit.*

35   NBPI *Costs and Prices of Aluminium Semi-Manufactures* Report No. 39 HMSO
      (1967) Cmnd. 3378.

Chapter 3

1   See M. A. Adelman 'Concept and statistical measurement of vertical integration'
     in National Bureau of Economic Research, *Business Concentration and Price
     Policy* Princeton (1955) p. 281–330.

2   See A. M. Laffer 'Vertical integration by corporations 1929–1965' *Review of
     Economics and Statistics* 51 (1969) p. 91.

3   National Board for Prices and Incomes, Report No. 13, *Costs and Profits in the
     Brewing Industry* HMSO (April 1966) Cmnd. 2965.

4   Monopolies Commission *Beer* HMSO (1969) para. 171.

5   National Board for Prices and Incomes, Report No. 3, *Prices of Bread and Flour*
     HMSO (Sept. 1965) Cmnd. 2760.

6   Though this is not always the case. For example ICI and Courtaulds have
     differing views about the desirability of extensive vertical integration in the man-
     made fibre industry.

7   Monopolies Commission *Metal Containers* HMSO (1970) paras. 62, 65–6.

8   A. Silberston 'The motor industry' in D. Burn ed. *The Structure of British
     Industry* vol. 2 Cambridge University Press (1961) ch. x.

9   The Monopolies Commission *Report on the Supply of Electrical Equipment for
     Mechanically Propelled Land Vehicles* HMSO (1963).

10   See the Monopolies Commission *British Motor Corporation Ltd. and the Pressed
      Steel Company Ltd. A report on the proposed merger* HMSO (1965).

11   See for example G. J. Stigler 'The division of labour is limited by the extent of
      the market' *Journal of Political Economy* 59 (1951) p. 185.

12   *Financial Times* 31 March 1971, p. 7.

13   Monopolies Commission *Thorn Electrical Industries Ltd. and Radio Rentals Ltd.
      A report on the proposed merger* HMSO (1968) para. 76.

14   J. F. Pickering *et al The Small Firm in the Hotel and Catering Industry* HMSO
      (1971) p. 29.

15   This is apparently the policy of Courtaulds. See Monopolies Commission *Man-
      Made Cellulosic Fibres* HMSO (1968) para. 87.

16   See Monopolies Commission *Unilever Ltd. and Allied Breweries. A report on the
      proposed merger* HMSO (1969) para. 27.

17   J. R. Gould 'Internal pricing in firms where there are costs of using an outside
      market' *Journal of Business* 37 (1964) p. 61.

18   J. Hirshleifer 'On the economics of transfer pricing' *Journal of Business* 29 (1956)
      p. 172.

19 A. D. Neale *The Anti-trust Laws of the U.S.A.* Cambridge University Press (second edition 1970) pp. 143–54 and 183–5.

20 E.g. J. S. Bain *Industrial Organisation* (second edition 1968) p. 381; C. D. Edwards *Maintaining Competition* McGraw Hill (1964) pp. 97–9.

21 Federal Trades Commission *Report on Corporate Mergers and Acquisitions* Washington (1955) p. 113.

22 *Man-Made Cellulosic Fibres op. cit.* paras 184–94 and 218.

23 W. P. J. Maunder 'Price leadership: an appraisal of its character in some British industries' *The Business Economist* 4 (1972) p. 132.

24 *Beer op. cit.* paras. 216–28, 353. It did not, however, appear to hinder the distribution of specialist beers such as Guinness, Bass and Harp, see paras. 284–5.

25 National Board for Prices and Incomes, *Prices of Bread and Flour op. cit.* paras 12, 35.

26 This paragraph is largely based upon F. Machlup and M. Taber, 'Bilateral monopoly, successive monopoly and vertical integration' *Economica* 27 (1960) p. 101 and R. Crandell 'Vertical integration and the market for spare parts in the United States automobile industry' *Journal of Industrial Economics* 16 (1968) p. 212.

27 Monopolies Commission *Petrol* HMSO (1965).

28 *Petrofina (Great Britain) Ltd.* v *Martin* [1966] 1 All ER 126; *Esso Petroleum Co. Ltd.* v *Harper's Garage (Stourport) Ltd.* [1967] 1 All ER 699; *Texaco Ltd.* v *Mulberry Filling Station Ltd.* [1972] 1 All ER 513.

29 *Petrol op. cit.* para. 87 ff. D. F. Dixon 'The Monopolies Commission report on petrol: a comment' *Journal of Industrial Economics* 15 (1966) p. 128.

30 E.g. *Petrol op. cit.*, Note of dissent by Prof. T. Barna and the subsequent debate in *Economica*: H. Townsend 'Exclusive dealing in petrol: some comments' *Economica* 32 (1965) p. 410; T. Barna 'Exclusive dealing in petrol: a reply' *Economica* 33 (1966) p. 226. See also Dixon *op. cit.*

31 *Petrol op. cit.* paras. 372–5, 382, 425.

32 *Beer op. cit.*

Chapter 4

1 J. S. Bain *Barriers to New Competition* Harvard University Press (1956); P. Sylos Labini *Oligopoly and Technical Progress* Harvard University Press (first published 1957, English edition 1969). See also F. Modigliani 'New developments on the oligopoly front' *Journal of Political Economy* 66 (1958) p. 215 for a discussion of these sources.

2 See J. N. Bhagwati 'Oligopoly theory, entry prevention and growth' *Oxford Economic Papers* 22 (1970) p. 297.

3 E.g. H. H. Hines 'Effectiveness of "entry" by already established firms' *Quarterly Journal of Economics* 71 (1957) p. 132; P. W. S. Andrews *On Competition in Economic Theory* Macmillan (1964) pp. 78–80: E. Brunner 'A note on potential competition' *Journal of Industrial Economics* 9 (1961) p. 248.

4 *Op. cit.*

5 See F. G. Pyatt 'Profit maximisation and the threat of new entry' *Economic Journal* 81 (1971) p. 242 for a suggestion that aggregate profit rather than profit per unit sold is more likely to be the entry inducing factor.

6 See H. Igor Ansoff *Corporate Strategy* Penguin (1968) ch. 7.

7 The Monopolies Commission *Guest Keen and Nettlefolds Ltd. and Birfield Ltd. A report on the proposed merger* HMSO (1967) Cmnd. 3186; *British Insulated Callenders' Cables Ltd. and Pyrotenax Ltd. A report on the proposed merger* HMSO (1967).

8 H. H. Hines *op. cit.* suggests that such new entry may be part of an overall strategy of inter-firm relations involving the markets for other products too.

9 E.g. G. J. Stigler *The Organisation of Industry* Irwin (1968) ch. 2.

10   See Adrian Wood 'Economic Analysis of the Corporate Economy' in R. Marris
     and A. Wood eds., *The Corporate Economy* Macmillan (1971) p. 50. A sales
     revenue maximiser for instance may come into a market at a prospective rate of
     return that would deter a profit maximizer.
11   B. P. Pashigian 'Limit price and the market share of the leading firm' *Journal
     of Industrial Economics* 16 (1968) p. 165.
12   See J. N. Bhagwati *op. cit;* F. Modigliani *op. cit;* B. P. Pashigian *op. cit.*
13   O. E. Williamson 'Selling expense as a barrier to entry' *Quarterly Journal of
     Economics* 77 (1963) p. 112.
14   The Monopolies Commission, *British Insulated Callenders' Cables Ltd. and
     Pyrotenax Ltd. A report on the proposed merger, op. cit.*
15   P. W. S. Andrews *Manufacturing Business* Macmillan (1949) ch. 5.
16   E.g. National Board for Prices and Incomes Report No. 64, *Increase in Prices of
     Mercury Hearing-aid Batteries Manufactured by Mallory Batteries Ltd.* (May
     1968) Cmnd. 3625.
17   J. S. Bain *op. cit.* K. D. George 'Concentration, barriers to entry and rates of
     return' *Review of Economics and Statistics* 50 (1968) p. 273.
18   The Monopolies Commission *Metal Containers* HMSO (1970) para. 315.
     Another discussion of the Monopolies Commission's treatment of barriers to
     entry in its earlier reports is to be found in C. K. Rowley *The British Monopolies
     Commission* Allen and Unwin (1966) chs. 8, 9, 13.
19   A number of Monopolies Commission reports are referred to in this section. For
     convenience they are listed here: *Report on the Supply of Wallpaper* (1964);
     Report on the Supply of Cigarettes (1961); *Petrol* (1964); *The Dental Manu-
     facturing Co. Ltd. or The Dentists' Supply Co. of New York and the Amalga-
     mated Dental Co. Ltd. A Report on the Proposed Mergers* (1966); *Household
     Detergents* (1966); *Clutch Mechanisms for Road Vehicles* (1968); *Electric Lamps*
     (1968); *Man-made Cellulosic Fibres* (1967); *Metal Containers* (1970); *British
     Sidac Ltd. and Transparent Paper Ltd. A Report on the Proposed Merger* (1970);
     Chlordiazepoxide and Diazepam (1973); *Breakfast Cereals* (1973).
20   D. C. Mueller and J. E. Tilton 'Research and development costs as a barrier to
     entry' *Canadian Journal of Economics* 2 (1969) p. 570.
21   In R. Marris and A. Wood *op. cit.* p. xvii.
22   G. J. Stigler 'Monopoly and oligopoly by merger' *American Economic Review
     Papers and Proceedings* 40 (1950) p. 23.
23   National Board for Prices and Incomes *Costs, Prices and Profits in the Brewing
     Industry* HMSO (1966) Cmnd. 2965.

Chapter 5

1   See *Convention on the Unification of Certain Points of Substantive Law on
    Patents for Invention* HMSO (1964) Cmnd. 2362 (known as the Strasbourg
    Convention).
2   *The British Patent System* HMSO (1970) Cmnd. 4407 (known as the Banks
    Report).
3   K. Boehm *The British Patent System* Cambridge University Press (1967) pp.
    64–5.
4   Banks Report *op. cit.*
5   H. Steele 'Patent restrictions and price competition in the ethical drugs industry'
    Journal of Industrial Economics 12 (1964) p. 198.
6   The Monopolies Commission *Chlordiazepoxide and Diazepam* HMSO (1973).
7   *Report of the Committee of Enquiry into the Relationship of the Pharmaceutical
    Industry with the National Health Service 1965–1967*, HMSO (1967) Cmnd. 3410
    (known as the Sainsbury Committee Report).
8   Sources of information relating to individual industries are to be found particularly
    in the Reports of the Monopolies Commission on *Household Detergents* (1966);

Colour Film (1966); *Clutch Mechanisms for Road Vehicles* (1968); *Metal Containers* (1970); *Chlordiazepoxide and Diazepam* (1973).

9   The Monopolies Commission *Colour Film* HMSO (1966) para. 191.

10   D. P. O'Brien 'Patent protection and competition in polyamide and polyester fibre manufacture' *Journal of Industrial Economics* 12 (1964) p. 224.

11   H. Demsetz 'Information and efficiency: another viewpoint' *Journal of Law and Economics* 11 (1969) p. 1.

12   See A. Silberston 'The patent system' *Lloyds Bank Review* (1967) p. 32.

13   J. M. Blair *Economic Concentration* Harcourt Brace Jovanovich (1972) p. 388–91.

14   H. Steele *op. cit.*

15   C. T. Taylor 'Do we still need a patent system?' *Journal of the Chartered Institute of Patent Agents* 2 No. 7 (April 1973) p. 292.

16   Banks Report *op. cit.* p. 114.

17   *Chlordiazepoxide and Diazepam op. cit.* pp. 19–20.

18   For an illustration of the way patents were used to drive out competition in the US glass industry see G. W. Stocking and M. W. Watkins *Monopoly and Free Enterprise* Twentieth Century Fund (1951) pp. 474–84.

19   See K. J. Arrow 'Economic welfare and the allocation of resources for invention' in *The Rate and Direction of Inventive Activity* NBER (1962) p. 609; G. J. Stigler 'A note on patents' in *The Organisation of Industry* Irwin (1968) ch. 11; E. T. Penrose *The Economics of the International Patent System* Johns Hopkins Press (1951).

20   *Report of the Committee of Enquiry into the relationship of the Pharmaceutical Industry with the National Health Service op. cit.* para 201.

21   C. T. Taylor *op. cit.*

22   K. Boehm *op. cit.* p. 68.

23   H. Steele *op. cit.*

24   K. Boehm *op. cit.* pp. 64–5.

25   Banks Report, *op. cit.* p. xviii.

26   K. Boehm *op. cit.* p. 163.

27   F. Machlup, *The Political Economy of Monopoly* Johns Hopkins Press (1952) p. 282.

28   P. H. Guenault and J. M. Jackson *The Control of Monopoly in the United Kingdom* Longmans (1960) p. 52.

29   See V. L. Korah, *Monopolies and Restrictive Practices* Penguin (1968) pp. 131–5.

30   A. Plant 'The economic theory concerning patents for inventions' *Economica* 1 (1934) p. 30.

31   C. T. Taylor *op. cit.*

32   See for example the evidence on the importance of individuals and small firms in the invention of products the rights for which were subsequently sold to allow development in large organisations in J. Jewkes, D. Sawers and R. Stillerman *The Sources of Invention* 2nd edition Macmillan (1969).

33   Even most of the nineteenth century is described as an age of 'patentless invention' Boehm *op. cit.* p. 37.

34   M. Polanyi 'Patent reform' *Review of Economic Studies* 11–12 (1943–5) p. 61; G. J. Stigler *op. cit.*

35   Banks Report *op. cit.* p. xvii.

36   *Ibid* p. 99.

37   Intergovernmental Conference for the setting up of a European System for the Grant of Patents, *Second Preliminary Draft of a Convention Establishing a European System for a Grant of Patents* (1971).

Chapter 6

1   For a most important discussion of this issue see B. J. Loasby 'Hypothesis and paradigm in the theory of the firm' *Economic Journal* 81 (1971) p. 863.

2   R. M. Cyert and J. G. March *A Behavioural Theory of the Firm* Prentice Hall

(1963) p. 8.

3 H. A. Simon 'Decision making in economics and behavioural science' in A.E.A. *Surveys of Economic Theory* vol. III Macmillan (1966).

4 It may be argued (see D. C. Hague *Pricing in Business* Allen and Unwin (1971 p. 186) that the introduction of computers might allow a centralising firm to take more rational and objective decisions. This seems unlikely, however, since there would still be the problems of agreeing on the objective function with which the computer was to be programmed and of incorporating sufficient information about the environment for a satisfactory decision to be produced.

5 Cf. R. M. Cyert and J. G. March *op. cit.* and J. K. Galbraith *The New Industrial State* Hamish Hamilton (1967). The concepts are similar although Cyert and March's coalition is defined to have a much wider membership base than Galbraith's technostructure. Galbraith's emphasis on the motivation of members of the technostructure with those nearer the centre of the organisation having a more adaptive motivation and those further away having financial motivation seems useful.

6 M. Dalton *Men who Manage* Wiley (1959).

7 O. E. Williamson 'Hierarchical control and optimum firm size' *Journal of Political Economy* 75 (1967) p. 123. Williamson shows the problems of control losses in communicating across successive hierarchical levels.

8 H. A. Simon 'On the concept of organisational goal', reprinted in H. I. Ansoff ed. *Business Strategy* Penguin (1969) p. 240; J. W. Maguire *Theories of Business Behaviour* Prentice Hall (1964).

9 R. L. Hall and C. J. Hitch 'Price theory and business behaviour' reprinted in T. Wilson and P. W. S. Andrews eds. *Oxford Studies in the Price Mechanism* Oxford University Press (1951) p. 107.

10 See the review by F. Machlup 'Theories of the firm, marginalist, behavioural, managerial' *American Economic Review* 57 (1967) p. 1.

11 R. J. Monsen *et al.* 'The effect of separation of ownership and control on the performance of the large firm' *Quarterly Journal of Economics* 82 (1968) p. 435.

12 See D. M. Lamberton *The Theory of Profit* Blackwell (1965) and G. L. S. Shackle *On the Nature of Profit* Woolwich Economic Papers (1967).

13 J. Margolis 'Sequential decision-making in the firm' *American Economic Review Papers and Proceedings* 50 (1960) p. 526.

14 B. J. Loasby *op. cit.* p. 867.

15 F. Machlup *op. cit.*; J. W. Maguire *op. cit.*; W. L. Baldwin 'The motives of managers, environmental restraints and the theory of managerial enterprise' *Quarterly Journal of Economics* 78 (1964) p. 238.

16 Indeed short-run profits may well be important here, especially for a growing firm which may not have large financial reserves. A healthy cash-flow position then becomes crucial if the more desirable long-term projects are to be pursued.

17 J. G. Blease 'Institutional investors and the Stock Exchange' *District Bank Review* (Sept. 1964) p. 38.

18 For a discussion of the predictive implications of some of these theories see K. J. Cohen and R. M. Cyert *The Theory of the Firm* Prentice Hall (1965) and J. R. Wildsmith *Managerial Theories of the Firm* Martin Robertson (1973).

19 W. J. Baumol *Business Behaviour, Value and Growth* Harcourt, Brace and World (1959).

20 Cf. J. F. Pickering 'The Prices and Incomes Board and private sector prices: a survey' *Economic Journal* 81 (1971) pp. 229–30.

21 Cf. National Board for Prices and Incomes Reports: No. 19 *General Report April 1965–July 1966* (1966) Cmnd. 3087 para 76; No. 122 *Fourth General Report July 1968–July 1969* (1969) Cmnd. 4130 para. 28. In some cases fear of anti-trust action might hinder a firm in this respect, see NBPI Report No. 77 *Third General Report August 1967–July 1968* (1968) Cmnd. 3715 para. 27.

22 O. E. Williamson *The Economics of Discretionary Behaviour* Prentice Hall (1964).

23 W. G. Shepherd 'On sales maximising and oligopoly behaviour' *Economica* 29 (1962) p. 420.

24 C. J. Hawkins 'On the sales revenue maximisation hypothesis' *Journal of Industrial Economics* 18 (1970) p. 129.

25 A. Alchian 'The basis of some recent advances in the theory of the management of the firm' *Journal of Industrial Economics* 14 (1965) p. 30.

26 M. Hall 'Sales revenue maximisation: an empirical examination' *Journal of Industrial Economics* 15 (1967) p. 143.

27 E. M. Kelly *The Profitability of Growth through Merger* Pennsylvania State University (1967).

28 National Industrial Conference Board, *Mergers in Industry* NICB (1929).

29 D. C. Mueller 'The firm decision process: an econometric investigation' *Quarterly Journal of Economics* 81 (1967) p. 71.

30 R. L. Marris 'A model of the "managerial" enterprise' *Quarterly Journal of Economics* 77 (1963) p. 185; *The Economic Theory of Managerial Capitalism* Macmillan (1964); 'An introduction to theories of corporate growth' in R. L. Marris and A. Wood eds. *The Corporate Economy* Macmillan (1971).

31 O. E. Williamson *op. cit.*

32 E. T. Penrose *The Theory of the Growth of the Firm* Blackwell (1959).

33 O. E. Williamson *Corporate Control and Business Behaviour* Prentice Hall (1970) and 'Managerial discretion, organisational form and the multidivision hypothesis' in R. Marris and A. Wood *op. cit.*

34 On a day-to-day basis decisions are taken by those employed by the organisation rather than by those who set the external environment such as consumers, tax authorities and shareholders. Thus it seems that Galbraith's description of the membership of the 'technostructure' is to be preferred to Cyert and March's 'coalition'.

35 H. A. Simon 'Theories of decision-making in economics and behavioural science' in *Surveys of Economic Theory* vol. III Macmillan (1966).

36 The discussion here draws heavily on R. M. Cyert and J. G. March *op. cit.*

37 Some comment has appeared in recent years on the question of perception, the importance of the appropriate people recognising both the need for action and the possibility of success in fully accomplishing it. This is clearly central to the whole question of the receipt and processing of information in the firm and the chances of successfully overcoming a specific problem. Loasby has argued that appreciating the need for a major decision is more difficult than actually taking the decision: B. J. Loasby 'Managerial decision processes' *Scottish Journal of Political Economy* 14 (1967) p. 243. Other comments which bear on the same theme include H. Leibenstein *op. cit.* and T. Barna *Investment and Growth Policies in British Industrial Firms* Cambridge University Press (1962).

38 J. W. Maguire *op. cit.* pp. 28–9.

39 R. M. Cyert and J. G. March *op. cit.* p. 113.

40 M. C. Wells 'Professor Machlup and theories of the firm' *Economic Record* 44 (1968) p. 357.

41 D. C. Hague *op. cit.*

42 John W. Humble *Management by Objectives* Industrial Educational and Research Foundation Occasional Paper No. 2 (1967).

43 W. J. Baumol and M. Stewart in R. L. Marris and A. Wood eds. *The Corporate Economy*.

44 Cf. G. C. Allen, *Economic Fact and Fantasy* Institute of Economic Affairs (1969).

45 W. J. Baumol and M. Stewart *op. cit.*

46 B. J. Loasby 'Hypothesis and paradigm in the theory of the firm' *op. cit.*

Chapter 7

1 See, for example, R. L. Marris *The Economic Theory of Managerial Capitalism* Macmillan (1964). The valuation ratio is defined as the ratio of the stock market

value of the firm to its total assets.

2 E. T. Penrose *The Theory of the Growth of the Firm* Blackwell (1959).

3 T. Barna *Investment and Growth Policies in British Industrial Firms* (Cambridge University Press (1962).

4 N. H. Leyland 'Growth and competition' *Oxford Economic Papers* 16 (1964) p. 3.

5 G. B. Richardson 'The limits to a firm's rate of growth' *Oxford Economic Papers* 16 (1964) p. 9.

6 See, for example, S. Hymer and P. Pashigian 'Firm size and rate of growth' *Journal of Political Economy* 70 (1962) p. 556.

7 E.g. Hymer and Pashigian *op. cit.;* P. E. Hart and S. J. Prais 'The analysis of business concentration: a statistical approach' *Journal of the Royal Statistical Society Series A* 119 (1956) p. 150; J. M. Samuels and A. D. Chesher 'Growth, survival and the size of companies 1960–69' in K. Cowling ed. *Market Structure and Corporate Behaviour* Gray Mills (1972); H. A. Simon and C. P. Bonini 'The size distribution of business firms' *American Economic Review* 48 (1958) p. 607; A. Singh and G. Whittington *Growth Profitability and Valuation* Cambridge University Press (1968); M. Marcus 'A note on the determinants of the growth of firms and Gibrat's law' *Canadian Journal of Economics* 2 (1969) p. 580; J. L. Eatwell 'Growth, profitability and size: the empirical evidence', in R. L. Marris and A. Wood eds. *The Corporate Economy* Macmillan (1971).

8 Simon and Bonini *op. cit.*

9 E. Mansfield 'Entry, Gibrat's law, innovation and the growth of firms' *American Economic Review* 52 (1962) p. 1023; Hymer and Pashigian *op. cit.;* Singh and Whittington *op. cit.;* Eatwell *op. cit.*

10 Singh and Whittington *op. cit.*

11 *Ibid;* J. Samuels 'Size and the growth of firms' *Review of Economic Studies* 32 (1965) p. 105.

12 Mansfield *op. cit.*

13 Samuels and Chesher *op. cit.*

14 Mansfield *op. cit.;* Samuels and Chesher *op. cit.*

15 Singh and Whittington *op. cit.*

16 Barna *op. cit.*

17 Marcus *op. cit.*

18 Barna *op. cit.* p. 20.

19 Mansfield *op. cit.*

20 The concept of concentricity implies that the common element between the firms is necessarily the main feature of each firm's activity. This is not necessarily the case, and the term 'intersecting merger' may be a more appropriate verbal description of mergers where there is some common element between the firms.

21 D. A. Kuehn *Takeovers and the theory of the firm: an econometric analysis for the United Kingdom 1957–69* University of Warwick Ph.D. thesis 1972. See also the discussion of this question in Chapter 8.

22 G. D. Newbould *Management and Merger Activity* Guthstead (1970).

23 Lists have been provided by among others H. I. Ansoff *Corporate Strategy* Penguin (1968); P. L. Cook and R. Cohen *The Effects of Mergers* Allen and Unwin (1958); R. Eveley and I. Little *Concentration in British Industry* Cambridge University Press (1960); Federal Trade Commission *Report on Corporate Mergers and Acquisitions* US Government Printing Office, Washington (1955); P. Hart *et al. Mergers and Concentration in British Industry* Cambridge University Press (1973); Newbould *op. cit.;* G. L. Reuber and F. Roseman *The Take-over of Canadian Firms 1945–61* Economic Council of Canada Special Study No. 10 (1969).

24 See for example the description of Singer's strategy in M. H. Pryor 'Anatomy of a merger' in H. I. Ansoff ed. *Business Strategy* Penguin (1969).

25 L. D. V. Tindale 'The role of the company marriage broker' in R. V. Arnfield ed. *Company Mergers and Acquisitions* University of Strathclyde (1967).

26 Newbould *op. cit.*

27 M. Gort and T. F. Hogarty 'New evidence on mergers' *Journal of Law and Economics* 13 (1970) p. 167.

310 Industrial Structure & Market Conduct

28 The Monopolies Commission *Report on the Supply of Wallpaper* HMSO (1964).
29 G. J. Stigler 'Monopoly and oligopoly by merger' *American Economic Review Papers and Proceedings* 40 (1950) p. 23; M. Utton 'Some features of the early merger movement in British manufacturing industry' *Business History* 14 (1972) p. 50.
30 Stigler *op. cit.*
31 The Monopolies Commission *Barclays Bank Ltd., Lloyds Bank Ltd., and Martins Bank Ltd.: A Report on the Proposed Merger* HMSO (1968) para. 47.
32 The Monopolies Commission *British Insulated Callenders' Cables Ltd. and Pyrotenax Ltd.: A Report on the Proposed Merger* HMSO (1967).
33 J. K. Butters *et al. Effects of Taxation on Corporate Mergers* Harvard University Press (1957).
34 L. Dellenbarger *Common Stock Valuation in Industrial Mergers* University of Florida Press (1966); National Industrial Conference Board *Mergers in Industry* New York (1929); Reuber and Roseman *op. cit.*; H. B. Rose and G. D. Newbould 'The 1967 take-over boom' *Moorgate and Wall Street* (Autumn 1967) p. 5; C. J. Maule 'A note on mergers and the business cycle' *Journal of Industrial Economics* 16 (1968) p. 99; R. L. Nelson *Merger Movements in American Industry 1895–1956* Princeton University Press (1959); R. J. Briston and D. G. Rhys 'Problems in the analysis of statistics relating to takeovers and mergers' in J. M. Samuels ed. *Readings on Mergers and Takeovers* Elek (1972).
35 S. R. Reid *Mergers, Managers and the Economy* McGraw Hill (1968).
36 *Ibid.*
37 J. B. Heath *Still Not Enough Competition?* Institute of Economic Affairs (1963).
38 N. H. Leyland 'Monopoly control from the point of view of the firm' in J. B. Heath ed. *International Conference on Monopolies, Mergers and Restrictive Practices Papers and Reports* HMSO (1971).
39 Examples of studies using discriminant analysis are Kuehn *op. cit.*; A. Singh *Takeovers: their Relevance to the Stock Market and the Theory of the Firm* Cambridge University Press (1971); J. Tzoannos and J. M. Samuels 'Mergers and takeovers: the financial characteristics of companies involved' *Journal of Business Finance* (1972). Other studies using univariate statistical techniques include Rose and Newbould *op. cit.*; Reuber and Roseman *op. cit.*; Newbould *op. cit.*
40 See Ansoff *Corporate Strategy op. cit.* and J. Kitching 'Why do mergers miscarry' *Harvard Business Review* (Nov.–Dec. 1967) p. 84, for discussions of the sources of synergy.
41 For discussions of some instances of these see Cook and Cohen *op. cit.* and Hart *et al. op. cit.* See also the discussion of the effects of the merger between the lighting interests of Thorn and AEI to form BLI in The Monopolies Commission, *Electric Lamps* HMSO (1968) para. 133 ff.
42 Cf. Kitching *op. cit.* and Cook and Cohen *op. cit.*
43 See Kitching *op. cit.*
44 See Newbould *op. cit.*
45 The consequences of the Monopolies Commission's rejection of the proposed merger between UDS and Montague Burton are interesting in this respect. It appears that Burton had a death wish due to doubts about its managerial succession. Having been refused permission to merge with UDS, Burton sought a new chief executive and seems to have improved its performance.
46 Cf. Reuber and Roseman *op. cit.*
47 W. W. Alberts 'The profitability of growth by merger' in W. W. Alberts and J. E. Segall eds. *The Corporate Merger* University of Chicago Press (1966); H. I. Ansoff *et al. Twenty Years of Acquisition Behaviour in America* Cassell (1971); Singh *op. cit.*; Gort and Hogarty *op. cit.*; Reid *op. cit.*; G. D. Newbould 'Implications of financial analysis of takeovers' in J. M. Samuels ed. *op. cit.*; S. Livermore 'The success of industrial mergers' *Quarterly Journal of Economics* 50 (1935) p. 68; E. M. Kelly *The Profitability of Growth Through Merger* Pennsylvania State University (1967); A. S. Dewing 'A statistical test of the success of consolidating' *Quarterly Journal of Economics* 36 (1921) p. 84. As in

our discussion of the characteristics of acquired and acquiring firms it is not possible to give a detailed description of the research methodology of each investigator. The reader is referred to the actual sources for this information.

48 See Ansoff *et al. op. cit.* A good description of the planning procedure in one industrial merger is given by Pryor *op. cit.*

49 See Newbould *Management and Merger Activity op. cit.* and Gort and Hogarty *op. cit.*

50 O. E. Williamson 'Managerial discretion, organisation form and the multi-division hypothesis' in Marris and Wood eds. *op. cit.*

51 M. Gort *Diversification and Integration in American Industry* National Bureau of Economic Research, Princeton University Press (1962).

52 See *A Survey of Mergers 1953–68* HMSO (1970) Appendix 6.

53 Monopolies Commission *Unilever Ltd. and Allied Breweries Ltd. A report on the proposed merger* HMSO (1969) para. 69.

54 *Ibid.* paras. 1–11.

55 Monopolies Commission *The Rank Organisation Ltd. and the De La Rue Company Ltd. A report on the proposed merger* HMSO (1969).

56 K. Bhaskar 'Three case studies – Guinness, Spillers and Nestles' in J. M. Samuels ed. *op. cit.*

57 The Monopolies Commission *British Match Corporation Ltd. and Wilkinson Sword Ltd.: A Report on the Proposed Merger* HMSO (1973) Cmnd. 5442 para. 74.

58 Kelly *op. cit.;* Reid *op. cit.*

59 J. F. Weston and S. K. Mansinghka 'Tests of the efficiency performance of conglomerate firms' *Journal of Finance* 26 (1971) p. 919.

Chapter 8

1 For a description of several different types of national policy towards mergers see the symposium in *Texas International Law Forum* 5 (1969) pp. 1–126.

2 *A Survey of Mergers 1958–1968* HMSO (1970).

3 A few large mergers do, of course, account for a large proportion of the total expenditure on acquisitions. In 1970 for example, the 47 mergers whose expenditure exceeded £5m accounted for a total expenditure of £605m whereas the 799 mergers recorded by the Department of Trade and Industry with expenditure below £5m accounted for total expenditure of £464m. Thus just over 5 per cent of mergers accounted for over 56 per cent of total expenditures on acquisitions, see *Trade and Industry* 16 November 1972. In 1972 there were 60 acquisitions involving expenditure of £5m or more and these accounted for 5 per cent of mergers recorded. They were, however, responsible for 76 per cent of expenditure on mergers. See *Business Monitor* M7 'Acquisitions and mergers of companies' HMSO (August 1973).

4 See for example the speech by the then President of the Board of Trade reproduced in Board of Trade *Mergers* HMSO (1969) p. 63.

5 R. Eveley and I. Little, *Concentration in British Industry* Cambridge University Press (1960).

6 G. Walshe, *Recent Trends in Monopoly in Great Britain* Cambridge University Press (1974) chapter 5.

7 Y. Ijiri and H. A. Simon 'Effect of mergers and acquisitions on business firm concentration' *Journal of Policital Economy* 79 (1971) p. 314; M. Gort and T. F. Hogarty 'New evidence on mergers' *Journal of Law and Economics* 13 (1970) p. 167.

8 M. Utton 'Mergers and the growth of large firms' *Bulletin of the Oxford Institute of Statistics* 34 (1972) p. 189.

9 B. Hindley *Industrial Merger and Public Policy* Institute of Economic Affairs (1970), though Hindley would prohibit some horizontal mergers.

312 Industrial Structure & Market Conduct

10 Board of Trade *Mergers op. cit.* p. 64.
11 *Industrial Reorganisation Corporation* HMSO (1966) Cmnd. 2889 para. 4.
12 Monopolies Commission *The Rank Organisation Ltd. and the De La Rue Company Ltd. A report on the proposed acquisition of the De La Rue Company Ltd.* HMSO (1969) para. 82.
13 For a discussion of these concepts see D. E. Needham *Economic Analysis and Industrial Structure* Holt Rinehart (1969) ch. 10.
14 See C. F. Pratten 'The merger boom in manufacturing industry' *Lloyds Bank Review* No. 90 (October 1968) p. 39.
15 See C. K. Rowley *Anti-trust and Economic Efficiency* Macmillan (1973) p. 48.
16 H. Leibenstein 'Allocative efficiency vs. "X-efficiency" ' *American Economic Review* 56 (1966) p. 392.
17 E.g. Rowley *op. cit.*
18 See Board of Trade *Mergers op. cit.*
19 The distinction between concentric and conglomerate mergers is discussed in Chapter 7.
20 O. E. Williamson 'Managerial discretion, organisation form and the multi-division hypothesis' in R. Marris and A. Wood eds. *The Corporate Economy* Macmillan (1971) ch. 11.
21 N. H. Leyland 'Monopoly control from the point of view of the firm' in J. B. Heath ed. *International Conference on Monopolies, Mergers and Restrictive Practices Papers and Reports* HMSO (1971).
22 Though not all economists would favour the trade-off approach, see the comments by R. B. Heflebower on Williamson's arguments in *American Economic Review Papers and Proceedings* 59 (1969) p. 119.
23 O. E. Williamson 'Economies as an anti-trust defence' *American Economic Review* 58 (1968) p. 18.
24 C. K. Rowley *op. cit.*
25 See C. K. Rowley *The British Monopolies Commission* Allen and Unwin (1966) pp. 232–4. Only the acquisitions by British Oxygen, British Match and Wallpaper Manufacturers had been criticised in reports by the Monopolies Commission.
26 *Monopolies and Mergers Act 1965.* For a detailed discussion of this legislation see V. L. Korah *Monopolies and Mergers* Penguin (1968).
27 Board of Trade *Mergers op. cit.;* see also P. Carey 'Mergers and monopoly – the public interest' in R. V. Arnfield ed. *Company Mergers and Acquisitions* University of Strathclyde (1967).
28 As for example in the case of the mergers in 1973 between Richard Johnson and Nephew Ltd. and Thomas Firth and John Brown and between Gradon and Monotype where assurances were given about activities at the plants of the acquired firms, see *Trade and Industry* (1973) passim.
29 A. Sutherland 'The management of mergers policy' in A. Cairncross ed. *The Managed Economy* Blackwell (1970); also T. S. Ellis 'A survey of the government control of mergers in the United Kingdom Part I' *Northern Ireland Legal Quarterly* 22 (1971) p. 251.
30 Reported in *Annual Report on the Working of the Monopolies Commission, Year Ended 1972* HMSO (1973) para. 18.
31 In addition the proposed merger between Chloride and Oldham, which had been the subject of detailed assurances from Chloride about the future behaviour of the merged group, did not take place and Oldham was eventually acquired by Carlton Industry Ltd. See *Annual Report on the Working of the Monopolies Commission Year Ended 1970* HMSO (1971).
32 F. R. Jarvis *The Economics of Mergers* Routledge and Kegan Paul (1971) p. 122.
33 See Ellis *op. cit.*
34 See Carey *op. cit.*
35 *Monopolies and Mergers Acts 1948 and 1965: Annual Report by the Board of Trade for the year ended 31st December 1968* HMSO (1969).
36 Cmnd. 2889 *op. cit.*
37 *Industrial Reorganisation Corporation, Second Report* HMSO (1969).
38 *Industrial Reorganisation Corporation, Fourth Report* HMSO (1971).

39 It seems that the situation may occur where the reference to the Commission may require it to decide whether a technical monopoly is created in a market defined in one way while the Commission may decide that the appropriate market for analysis of the effects of a merger should be identified in a different way.

40 This particular decision was interesting since it differed from an American anti-trust action on the same products which had adopted a broad definition of the market. See G. W. Stocking and W. F. Mueller 'The cellophane case and the new competition' *American Economic Review* 45 (1955) p. 29, for a critique of that case.

41 The Monopolies Commission *British Match Corporation Ltd. and Wilkinson Sword Ltd.: A Report on the Proposed Merger* HMSO (1973) para. 92.

42 See, for example, T. S. Ellis 'A survey of government control of mergers in the United Kingdom Part II' *Northern Ireland Law Quarterly* 22 (1971) p. 459; V. L. Korah 'Merger regulation in the United Kingdom' *Texas International Law Forum* 5 (1969) p. 71; J. F. Pickering 'The Monopolies Commission and High Street Mergers' *Scottish Journal of Political Economy* 18 (1971) p. 69; C. K. Rowley 'Mergers and public policy in Great Britain' *Journal of Law and Economics* 11 (1968) p. 75; A. Sutherland *The Monopolies Commission in Action* Cambridge University Press (1969).

43 T. S. Ellis *op. cit.*; V. L. Korah *op. cit.*; A. Sutherland *The Monopolies Commission in Action op. cit.*

44 These assurances were that BICC would continue to supply other cable makers with mineral insulated cable (mic) at prices that would make it commercially practicable for them to participate in the sale of mic; that BICC would not give more favourable terms to its own electrical contracting organisation than to other comparable electrical contractors; that BICC would not offer especially favourable prices for mic in order to win business in other types of cable; that BICC would not offer mic at uneconomic prices calculated to drive competitors out of the market to supply mic; that BICC would publish its prices and make available to each category of customer its terms for mic appropriate to that category; that at the request of the Board of Trade BICC would grant licences under any patents relating to mic including accessories on reasonable terms.

45 J. F. Pickering *op. cit.*

46 T. S. Ellis *op. cit.* Part II.

47 C. K. Rowley 'Mergers and public policy in Great Britain' *op. cit*

48 T. S. Ellis *op. cit.* Part II.

49 C. K. Rowley 'Mergers and public policy in Great Britain' *op. cit.*

50 A. Sutherland *The Monopolies Commission in Action op. cit.*

51 V. L. Korah 'Legal regulation of corporate mergers in the United Kingdom' *Texas International Law Forum* 5 (1969) p. 111.

52 See A. Sutherland 'The management of mergers policy' in Cairncross *op. cit.* on this.

53 The reason for the change is apparently the availability of research evidence that there is a greater chance of anti-competitive behaviour in an industry where the four-firm concentration ratio exceeds 50 per cent. Lowering the market share criterion for a reference is an attempt to deal with the tendency for less competitive situations to arise. See Sir Geoffrey Howe 'Public policy on mergers and monopolies' in *Mergers, Takeovers and the Structure of Industry* Institute of Economic Affairs (1973).

54 E.g. R. M. Cyert and K. D. George 'Competition, growth and efficiency' *Economic Journal* 79 (1969) p. 23; G. L. Reuber and F. Roseman, *The Takeover of Canadian Firms 1945–61* Economic Council of Canada Special Study No. 10 (1969).

55 See C. K. Rowley *Anti-trust and Economic Efficiency op. cit.*

56 O. E. Williamson 'Economies as an anti-trust defence' *op. cit.* and 'Allocative efficiency and the limits of anti-trust' *American Economic Review Papers and Proceedings Supplement* 59 (1969) p. 105.

57 T. S. Ellis *op. cit.*; M. A. Crew and C. K. Rowley 'Anti-trust policy: economics

versus management science' *Moorgate and Wall Street* (Autumn 1970).

58 M. Howe 'Anti-trust policy: rules on discretionary intervention' *Moorgate and Wall Street* (Spring 1971) p. 59; G. J. Stigler 'Mergers and preventative anti-trust policy' in *The Organisation of Industry* Irwin (1968).

The merger reports referred to in this chapter are as follows:

The British Motor Corporation Ltd. and Pressed Steel Company Ltd. (1965).

Ross Group Ltd. and Associated Fisheries Ltd. (1966).

The Dental Manufacturing Co. Ltd. or The Dentists' Supply Co. of New York and the Amalgamated Dental Co. Ltd. (1966).

Guest Keen and Nettlefolds Ltd. and Birfield Ltd. (1967) Cmnd. 3186.

British Insulated Callenders' Cables Ltd. and Pyrotenax Ltd. (1967).

United Drapery Stores Ltd. and Montague Burton Ltd. (1967) Cmnd. 3397.

Barclays Bank Ltd., Lloyds Bank Ltd. and Martins Bank Ltd. (1968).

Thorn Electrical Industries Ltd. and Radio Rentals Ltd. (1968).

Unilever Ltd. and Allied Breweries Ltd. (1969).

The Rank Organisation Ltd. and the De La Rue Company Ltd. (1969).

British Sidac Ltd. and Transparent Paper Ltd. (1970).

Beecham Group Ltd. and Glaxo Group Ltd. The Boots Company Ltd. and Glaxo Group Ltd. (1972).

British Match Corporation Ltd. and Wilkinson Sword Ltd. (1973) Cmnd. 5442.

Chapter 9

1 There are many useful publications available on the whole question of multinational companies. The sources cited are amongst the most valuable.

2 For statistical information on the incidence of MNCs see Department of Economic and Social Affairs *Multinational Corporations in World Development* United Nations (1973).

3 J. H. Dunning *The Role of American Investment in the British Economy* PEP Broadsheet No. 507 (1969); J. H. Dunning 'Technology, United States investment and European economic growth' in C. P. Kindleberger ed. *The International Corporation* MIT (1970).

4 For a discussion of the industry distribution of MNCs see especially R. L. Caves 'International corporations: the industrial economics of foreign investment' *Economica* 38 (1971) p. 1.

5 M. D. Steuer *et al. The Impact of Foreign Direct Investment on the United Kingdom* HMSO (1973).

6 See also G. Rosenbluth 'The relation between foreign control and concentration in Canadian industry' *Canadian Journal of Economics* 3 (1970) p. 14 for a discussion of this question.

7 For some discussions of the factors underlying the foreign direct investment decision, see the introduction in J. H. Dunning ed. *International Investment* Penguin (1973); R. Z. Aliber 'A theory of direct foreign investment' in C. P. Kindleberger *American Business Abroad* Yale University Press (1969); M. Z. Brooke and H. L. Remmers *The Strategy of Multinational Enterprise* Longmans (1970).

8 In this case Brooke and Remmers found that defensive motives were the more important.

9 See R. Vernon 'International investment and international trade in the product cycle' *Quarterly Journal of Economics* 80 (1966) p. 190 and R. Vernon 'Future of the multi-national enterprise' in C. P. Kindleberger ed. *The International Corporation op. cit.*

10 See J. Baranson 'Technology transfer through the international firm' *American Economic Review Papers and Proceedings* 60 (1970) p. 435.

11 See K. Pavitt 'The multi-national enterprise and the transfer of technology' in J. H. Dunning ed. *The Multinational Enterprise* Allen and Unwin (1971).

12 An example of the effects of such a policy in reverse is to be found in the decision of the American motor firms to withdraw from the Swedish market when tariff barriers on imports of cars were lowered, see J. W. Sundelson, 'U.S. automotive investments abroad' in C.P. Kindleberger ed. *The International Corporation op. cit.* That the same thing did not happen in Canada is a warning that many factors go to make up a location decision and that one reason may not apply equally in all situations.

13 Though Shell appears to be increasing its control of the allocation of resources but decentralising other functions; see the comment by Sir David Barran in J. H. Dunning ed. *The Multinational Enterprise* op. cit.

14 Monopolies Commission *Colour Film* HMSO (1966) para. 44.

15 M. Z. Brooke and H. L. Remmers *op. cit.*

16 J. H. Dunning 'Foreign investment in the United Kingdom' in I. Litvak and C. J. Maule eds. *Foreign Investment: The Experience of Host Countries* Praeger (1970).

17 Though Dunning shows that the performance of British MNCs in Canada was poor. See J. H. Dunning *Studies in International Investment* Allen and Unwin (1970).

18 For a description of the important role of an MNC (Standard Oil of New Jersey) in the introduction of productivity bargaining in the United Kingdom see A. Flanders *The Fawley Productivity Agreements* Faber (1964).

19 This aspect has been dealt with particularly by Caves and Hymer and Rowthorn. See R. Caves *op. cit.;* S. Hymer and R. Rowthorn 'Multinational corporations and international oligopoly: the non-American challenge' in C. P. Kindleberger ed. *op. cit.*

20 See J. W. Sundelson *op. cit.* p. 246.

21 As for example with the transformation of Procter and Gamble into a keen competitor to Unilever, see Monopolies Commission *Household Detergents* HMSO (1966).

22 National Board for Prices and Incomes, Report No. 66 *Price of Butyl Rubber* HMSO (1968) Cmnd. 3626.

23 National Board for Prices and Incomes, Report No. 64 *Increase in Prices of Mercury Hearing-aid Batteries Manufactured by Mallory Batteries Ltd.* HMSO (1968) Cmnd. 3625.

24 Monopolies Commission, *Colour Film op. cit.*

25 As the PIB recognised; see National Board for Prices and Incomes, Report No. 77 *Third General Report August 1967–July 1968* HMSO (1968) Cmnd. 3715 para. 312.

26 See particularly M. D. Steuer *op. cit.* on this.

27 A. E. Safarian *Foreign Ownership of Canadian Industry* McGraw Hill (1966).

28 A United Nations study concluded that the balance of payments effects were neither clearly positive nor clearly negative, see United Nations *op. cit.*

29 In Canada in 1966 39 of the 100 largest firms in Canada, measured by size of sales, were controlled by foreign MNCs, 26 were American. See I. Litvak and C. J. Maule *op. cit.* p. 88.

30 Monopolies Commission *Chlordiazepoxide and Diazepam* HMSO (1973).

31 Though not all, see M. Watkins *et al. Foreign Ownership and the Structure of Canadian Industry* Queens Printer Ottawa (1968).

32 J. H. Dunning ed. *The Multinational Enterprise op. cit.* p. 33.

33 G. C. Hufbauer and F. M. Adler 'Overseas manufacturing investment and the U.S. balance of payments' *US Treasury Tax Reserve Policy Document No. 1* US Treasury Department (1968). W. B. Reddaway *et al. Effects of U.K. Direct Investment Overseas* Cambridge University Press (1968).

34 The issues are very complex, they are well discussed in J. H. Dunning *Studies in International Investment* Allen and Unwin (1970) and D. Robertson 'The multinational enterprise: trade flows and trade policy' in J. H. Dunning ed. *The Multinational Enterprise op. cit.*

35 A. E. Safarian *op. cit.* p. 306.

Chapter 10

1 For an interesting though brief and largely annotated discussion of some of the relevant issues see G. B. Giles *Marketing* Macdonald and Evans (1969).

2 With the notable exception of the work of Katona and Lancaster who in their different ways have attempted to impart greater realism to economic analysis in this area. See G. Katona *The Powerful Consumer* McGraw Hill (1960) and *Psychological Analysis of Economic Behaviour* McGraw Hill (1951) and K. Lancaster *Consumer Demand – A New Approach* Columbia University Press (1971). For a discussion of this problem see R. Ferber 'Contributions of economics to the study of consumer market behaviour' *Applied Economics* 1 (1969) p. 125.

3 T. Levitt 'Marketing myopia' *Harvard Business Review* 38 No. 4 (1960) p. 45. It must, however, be pointed out that a firm may sometimes deem it to be in its own interest to control supplies of a substitute product and not to introduce it until it has gained full advantage from its existing product.

4 National Board for Prices and Incomes, Report No. 147, *Margarine and Compound Cooking Fats* HMSO (1970) Cmnd. 4368.

5 See, for example, D. Yankelovich 'New criteria for market segmentation' *Harvard Business Review* 42 (1964) p. 83. Yankelovich emphasises that subjective attitudes have an important influence on consumer choice.

6 L. Abbott *Quality and Competition* Columbia University Press (1955); P. W. S. Andrews *Manufacturing Business* Macmillan (1949); J. M. Clark *Competition as a Dynamic Process* Brookings Institution (1961); J. Downie *The Competitive Process* Duckworth (1958); W. Fellner *Competition Among The Few* Reprints of Economic Classics, New York (1965, first published 1949); J. Schumpeter *Capitalism, Socialism and Democracy* Allen and Unwin (1947).

7 Schumpeter *op. cit.* p. 84.

8 Clark *op. cit.* p. 38.

9 See also P. W. S. Andrews *On Competition in Economic Theory* Macmillan (1964) pp. 74–8.

10 J. K. Galbraith *The New Industrial State* Hamish Hamilton (1967). Other ways were through controls of prices and quantities, vertical integration, long-term contracts with suppliers, attempts to avoid price wars, diversification into a conglomerate operation.

11 For a critique of Galbraith see, for example, G. C. Allen *Economic Fact and Fantasy* Institute of Economic Affairs (1967); M. Zinkin 'Galbraith and consumer sovereignty' *Journal of Industrial Economics* 16 (1967) p. 1; J. E. Meade, 'Is "the new industrial state" inevitable?' *Economic Journal* 78 (1968) p. 372; R. Marris, Review of *The New Industrial State American Economic Review* 58 (1968) p. 240.

12 E. T. Mansfield *Industrial Research and Technical Innovation* Norton (1968).

13 See particularly T. Burns and G. M. Stalker *The Management of Innovation* Tavistock (1961); C. F. Carter and B. R. Williams *Industry and Technical Progress* Oxford University Press (1957); J. Langrish *et al. Wealth from Knowledge* Macmillan (1972); D. G. Marquis and S. Myers *Successful Industrial Innovations* National Science Foundation (1970); Science Policy Research Unit, University of Sussex, *Success and Failure in Industrial Innovation* Centre for the Study of Industrial Innovation (1972).

14 For an interesting account of the development of biological detergents see K. van Musschenbroek 'Enzymes invade the weekly wash' *The Financial Times* (31 May 1969).

15 See Science Policy Research Unit, *op. cit.* p. 5. SAPPHO stands for Scientific Activity Predictor from Patterns with Heuristic Origins.

16 F. M. Fisher *et al.* 'The costs of automobile model changes since 1949' *Journal of Political Economy* 70 (1962) p. 433.

17 See the Monopolies Commission *Breakfast Cereals* HMSO (1973) Appendix 2.

18 *Report of the Committee of Enquiry into the Relationship of the Pharmaceutical Industry with the National Health Service 1965–1967* HMSO (1967) Cmnd. 3410.

Chapter 11

1 Advertising Association, *Advertising Expenditure 1960–1972* (1973). Other writers have indicated rather higher proportions, see for example P. Doyle 'Economic aspects of advertising: a survey' *Economic Journal* 78 (1968) p. 570.

2 National Board for Prices and Incomes Report No. 156 *Costs and Revenues of Independent Television Companies* HMSO (1970) Cmnd. 4524.

3 P. J. Donnelly and R. H. Holton 'A note on product differentiation and entertainment expense allowances in the United States', *Journal of Industrial Economics* 10 (1962) p. 134.

4 J. R. Cable 'Market structure, advertising policy and intermarket differences in advertising intensity' in K. Cowling ed. *Market Structure and Corporate Behaviour* Gray Mills (1972); P. K. Else 'The incidence of advertising in manufacturing industries' *Oxford Economic Papers* 18 (1966) p. 88; L. G. Telser 'Supply and demand for advertising messages' *American Economic Review* 56 (1966) p. 457; P. Doyle 'Advertising expenditure and consumer demand' *Oxford Economic Papers* 20 (1968) p. 394.

5 N. H. Borden *The Economic Effects of Advertising* Irwin (1942).

6 Not only is advertising important in helping a manufacturer to introduce a new brand by informing consumers of its availability, it is also likely that manufacturers with established reputations built partly at least through advertising will find it easier for this reason to introduce a new product.

7 P. Doyle 'Economic aspects of advertising' and 'Advertising expenditure and consumer demand' *op. cit.*

8 *Ibid.*

9 The Monopolies Commission *Breakfast Cereals* HMSO (1973).

10 J. J. Lambin 'Is gasoline advertising justified?' *Journal of Business* 45 (1972) p. 585.

11 P. Doyle 'Economic aspects of advertising' *op. cit.*

12 P. K. Else *op. cit.;* N. Kaldor 'The economic aspects of advertising' *Review of Economic Studies* 18 (1950) p. 1; H. M. Mann *et al.* 'Advertising and concentration: an empirical investigation' *Journal of Industrial Economics* 16 (1967) p. 34. See also L. A. Guth 'Advertising and market structures revisited' *Journal of Industrial Economics* 19 (1971) p. 179. Guth adopted a different approach by showing that advertising increased the size inequality of firms in an industry and argued that this complemented findings that advertising increased average profits.

13 J. Cable *op. cit.*

14 W. D. Reekie 'Some problems associated with the marketing of ethical pharmaceutical products' *Journal of Industrial Economics* 19 (1970) p. 33; L. G. Telser 'Advertising and competition' *Journal of Political Economy* 72 (1964) p. 537; J. M. Vernon 'Concentration, promotion and market share stability in the pharmaceutical industry' *Journal of Industrial Economics* 19 (1971) p. 246.

15 J. S. Bain *Barriers to New Competition* Harvard University Press (1956).

16 The Monopolies Commission *Household Detergents* HMSO (1966) para. 94.

17 The Monopolies Commission *Report on the Supply of Cigarettes and Tobacco and of Cigarette and Tobacco Machinery* HMSO (1961).

18 J. L. Simon *Issues in the Economics of Advertising* University of Illinois Press (1970).

19 M. Alemson 'Advertising and the nature of competition' *Economic Journal* 81 (1970) p. 282; W. S. Comanor 'Research and competitive product differentiation in the pharmaceutical industry in the United States' *Economica* 31 (1964) p. 372; J. J. Lambin 'Advertising and competitive behaviour: a case study' *Applied Economics* 2 (1970) p. 231; W. D. Reekie *op. cit.*

20 See D. E. Needham *Economic Analysis and Industrial Structure* Holt Rinehart and Winston (1969) p. 163. Needham argues there is no reason for preferring price to non-price competition in a world of imperfect knowledge and changing tastes and technology.

21 N. Kaldor *op. cit.* Even Telser, a strong defender of advertising, does not dispute that zero price advertising means that more advertising is supplied though he does suggest that it may be more cost effective than an alternative system, see L. G. Telser, 'Supply and demand for advertising messages' *op. cit.*

22 L. G. Telser 'Supply and demand for advertising messages' *op. cit.*

23 The Monopolies Commission *Household Detergents op. cit.*

24 The Monopolies Commission *Breakfast Cereals op. cit.*

25 J. Backman, *Advertising and Competition* New York University Press (1967); W. S. Comanor and T. Wilson 'Advertising, market structure and performance' *Review of Economics and Statistics* 49 (1967) p. 423; R. A. Miller 'Market structure and industrial performance: relation of profit rates to concentration, advertising intensity and diversity' *Journal of Industrial Economics* 17 (1969) p. 104.

26 W. S. Comanor and T. Wilson *op. cit.*

27 L. Weiss 'Advertising, profits and corporate taxes' *Review of Economics and Statistics* 51 (1969) p. 421.

28 Cf. *Final Report of the Committee on Consumer Protection* HMSO (1962) Cmnd. 1781; the Labour Party *Report of a Commission of Enquiry into Advertising* (undated).

29 'Advertising matter is more concerned with emphasising unprovable qualities and building up a "brand image" than with informing the public about the practical attributes of the product and how the best use can be made of it'. The Monopolies Commission *Household Detergents op. cit.* para. 94.

30 National Board for Prices and Incomes Report No. 141, *Costs and Revenues of National Newspapers* HMSO (1970) Cmnd. 4277.

31 The Monopolies Commission *Household Detergents* paras. 125–6.

32 P. Doyle 'Economic aspects of advertising' *op. cit.*

33 The Monopolies Commission *Chlordiazepoxide and Diazepam* HMSO (1973).

Chapter 12

1 See M. Friedman *Essays in Positive Economics* Chicago University Press (1953); C. K. Rowley ed. *Readings in Industrial Economics* vol. I Macmillan (1972) Introduction; F. Machlup 'Theories of the firm, marginalist, behavioural, managerial' *American Economic Review* 57 (1967) p. 1.

2 See, for example, the interesting ideas on consumer choice processes in K. J. Lancaster *Consumer Demand: A New Approach* Columbia University Press (1971).

3 R. F. Lanzillotti 'Pricing objectives in large companies' *American Economic Review* 48 (1958) p. 921.

4 The role of stocks is discussed in P. W. S. Andrews *On Competition in Economic Theory* Macmillan (1964) pp. 105–6.

5 See D. C. Hague *Pricing in Business* Allen and Unwin (1971) for an extensive discussion of this issue.

6 National Board for Prices and Incomes Report No. 75 *Costs and Prices of the Chocolate and Sugar Confectionery Industry* HMSO (1968) Cmnd. 3699.

7 National Board for Prices and Incomes Report No. 136 *Beer Prices* HMSO (1969) Cmnd. 4227.

8 National Board for Prices and Incomes Report No. 80 *Distributors' Margins on Paint, Childrens' Clothing, Household Textiles and Proprietory Medicines* HMSO (1968) Cmnd. 3737.

9 For example, see the Monopolies Commission *Metal Containers* HMSO (1970) para. 169.

10 A. Gabor and C. W. J. Granger 'Price as an indicator of quality' *Economica* 33 (1966) p. 43.

11   R. H. Barback *The Pricing of Manufactures* Macmillan (1964).
12   The Monopolies Commission *Flat Glass* HMSO (1968) para. 264.
13   A. Silberston 'Price behaviour of firms' *Economic Journal* 80 (1970) p. 511.
14   See D. C. Hague *op. cit.*
15   R. L. Hall and C. J. Hitch 'Price theory and business behaviour' *Oxford Economic Papers* 2 (1939) p. 12.
16   P. W. S. Andrews *Manufacturing Business* Macmillan (1949).
17   See A. Silberston *op. cit.;* D. C. Hague *op. cit.*
18   R. L. Smyth 'A price-minus theory of costs' *Scottish Journal of Political Economy* 14 (1967) p. 110.
19   Silberston *op. cit.* p. 542.
20   See, for example, the Monopolies Commission *Metal Containers op. cit.* para. 139.
21   J. Dean 'Pricing pioneering products' *Journal of Industrial Economics* 17 (1969) p. 165.
22   E.g. Counter-Inflation Statutory Instrument 1973 No. 1785 *The Counter-Inflation (Price and Pay Code)* (No. 2) Order 1973.
23   D. C. Hague *op. cit.* p. 61.
24   See J. F. Pickering 'The Prices and Incomes Board and private sector prices' *Economic Journal* 81 (1971) p. 225.
25   The Monopolies Commission *Man-made Cellulosic Fibres* HMSO (1968).
26   National Board for Prices and Incomes Report No. 153 *Tea Prices* HMSO (1970) Cmnd. 4456.
27   National Board for Prices and Incomes Report No. 47 *Prices of Fletton and Non-Fletton Bricks* HMSO (1967) Cmnd. 3480.
28   The Monopolies Commission *Ross Group Ltd. and Associated Fisheries Ltd. A report on the proposed merger* HMSO (1966).
29   The Monopolies Commission *British Sidac Ltd. and Transparent Paper Ltd. A report on the proposed merger* HMSO (1970).
30   The Monopolies Commission *British Insulated Callenders' Cables Ltd. and Pyrotenax Ltd. A report on the proposed merger* HMSO (1967).
31   National Board for Prices and Incomes Report No. 4 *Prices of Household and Toilet Soaps* HMSO (1965) Cmnd. 2791.
32   J. Dean *op. cit.*
33   D. C. Hague *op. cit.* ch. 7.
34   A. Silberston *op. cit.*
35   Richard Baxter, quoted in R. H. Tawney *Religion and the Rise of Capitalism* Pelican (1938) p. 222.
36   See, for example, the account provided of an eighteenth-century businessman's pricing decision in T. S. Ashton *Iron and Steel in the Industrial Revolution* Manchester University Press (1963) p. 219.
37   R. H. Barback *op. cit;* A. Silberston *op. cit.*
38   For an early, critical position on the social responsibility of companies see G. Goyder *The Responsible Company* Blackwell (1961).
39   G. C. Allen *Monopoly and Restrictive Practices* Allen and Unwin (1968) p. 75.
40   *Report of the Committee of Enquiry into the Relationship of the Pharmaceutical Industry with the National Health Service 1965–1967* HMSO (1967) para. 206.
41   Registrar of Restrictive Trading Agreements *Report for the period 1 July 1961– 30 June 1963* HMSO (1964) Cmnd. 2246 para. 17.
42   R. Turvey 'Rates of return, pricing and the public interest' *Economic Journal* 81 (1971) p. 489.
43   Discussions of this question are to be found in C. K. Rowley *The British Monopolies Commission* Allen and Unwin (1966) ch. 17, 18; A. Hunter *Competition and the Law* Allen and Unwin (1966) p. 280–5.
44   The Monopolies Commission *Metal Containers* HMSO (1970) para. 301.
45   J. F. Pickering *op. cit.* p. 238.
46   See, for example, Price Commission *Report for the Period 1 June–31 August 1973* HMSO (1973) para 8.12. See also J. F. Pickering *op. cit.*

Chapter 13

1 D. E. Needham *Economic Analysis and Industrial Structure* Holt Rinehart and Winston (1969) p. 60.
2 D. Yankelovich 'New criteria for market segmentation' *Harvard Business Review* 42 (1964) p. 83.
3 R. H. Holton 'Price discrimination at retail: the supermarket case' *Journal of Industrial Economics* 6 (1957) p. 13.
4 A. C. Pigou *Economics of Welfare* Macmillan (1924) ch. 16.
5 S. Enke 'Some notes on price discrimination' *Canadian Journal of Economics and Political Science* 30 (1964) p. 95.
6 A somewhat different classification of methods of price discrimination is given in F. M. Scherer, *Industrial Market Structure and Economic Performance* Rand McNally (1970) pp. 255–7.
7 The Monopolies Commission *Clutch Mechanisms for Road Vehicles* HMSO (1968) para. 66.
8 The Monopolies Commission *Report on the Supply of Electrical Equipment for Mechanically Propelled Land Vehicles* HMSO (1963) para. 705.
9 The Monopolies Commission *Report on the Supply of Certain Industrial and Medical Gases* HMSO (1956).
10 National Board for Prices and Incomes Report No. 136 *Beer Prices* HMSO (1969) Cmnd. 4227.
11 National Board for Prices and Incomes Report No. 150 *Pay and other terms and conditions of employment in the Fletton Brick Industry and the prices charged by the London Brick Company* HMSO (1970) Cmnd. 4422.
12 See the article by R. H. Holton *op. cit.* for an extensive discussion of supermarket pricing strategy.
13 National Board for Prices and Incomes Report No. 80 *Distributors' Margins on Paint, Childrens' Clothing, Household Textiles and Proprietary Medicines* HMSO (1968) Cmnd. 3737.
14 The Monopolies Commission *Electric Lamps* HMSO (1968).
15 In some situations it may cost less to sell a third unit of a good at the same time, in which case part, at least, of the lower price offered would not constitute price discrimination.
16 National Board for Prices and Incomes Report No. 34 *Bank Charges* HMSO (1967) Cmnd. 3292.
17 The Monopolies Commission *United Drapery Stores Ltd., and Montague Burton Ltd. A report on the proposed merger* HMSO (1967) para. 58.
18 *Op. cit.*
19 National Board for Prices and Incomes Report No. 64 *Increases in Prices of Mercury Hearing-Aid Batteries Manufactured by Mallory Batteries Ltd.* HMSO (1968) Cmnd. 3625.
20 See J. F. Wright 'Some reflections on the place of discrimination in the theory of monopolistic competition' *Oxford Economic Papers* 17 (1965) p. 175.
21 See E. Clemens 'Price discrimination and the multiple-product firm' *Review of Economic Studies* 19 (1950–1) p. 1. 'The firm that does not discriminate in its pricing policy or differentiate its product line or invade new markets (often using price discrimination to do so) dies in the competitve struggle and business management does not commit suicide!'
22 The Monopolies Commission *Report on the Supply of Electrical Equipment op. cit.*
23 The Monopolies Commission *Clutch Mechanisms op. cit.* paras. 186–7.
24 The Monopolies Commission *Man-Made Fibres* HMSO (1968) para. 192.
25 The Monopolies Commission *Industrial Gases op. cit.*
26 In the short run it may be an aid to new entry since short-term losses can be borne by multi-product organisations.
27 The profit maximising condition under price discrimination is, as we have seen, $MR_1 = MR_2 = MC$. Since it is marginal revenues rather than prices that are

equal to marginal cost this is not a welfare optimising condition. See S. Enke *op. cit.* pp. 107–8.

28 For a discussion of American policy see A. D. Neale *The Anti-Trust Laws of the U.S.A.* Cambridge University Press (2nd edition 1970) ch. 9.

29 A. Phillips 'The objectives of economic policy: the contribution of anti-trust' in J. B. Heath ed. *International Conference on Monopolies, Mergers and Restrictive Practices* HMSO (1971).

30 *Small Firms* HMSO (1971) Cmnd. 4811 pp. 292–3.

Chapter 14

1 See C. Kaysen and D. F. Turner *Anti-Trust Policy* Harvard University Press 1959); M. Utton *Industrial Concentration* Penguin (1970) p. 79.

2 O. Morgenstern in preface to M. Shubik *Strategy and Market Structure* Wiley (1959).

3 See, for example, J. S. Bain *Barriers to New Competition* Harvard University Press (1956); P. Sylos Labini *Oligopoly and Technical Progress* English edition Harvard University Press (1969); F. Modigliani 'New developments on the oligopoly front' *Journal of Political Economy* 66 (1958) p. 215; P. W. S. Andrews, *On Competition in Economic Theory* Macmillan (1964).

4 M. Shubik *op. cit.*

5 L. Abbott *Quality and Competition* Columbia University Press (1955) p. 210.

6 W. J. Baumol *Business Behaviour, Value and Growth* Harcourt Brace (1959).

7 K. Rothschild 'Price theory and oligopoly' *Economic Journal* 57 (1947) p. 299.

8 *Ibid.*

9 R. L. Hall and C. J. Hitch 'Price theory and business behaviour' *Oxford Economic Papers* 2 (1939) p. 12.

10 P. Sweezy 'Demand under conditions of oligopoly' *Journal of Political Economy* 47 (1939) p. 568.

11 M. Shubik *op. cit.* pp. 149–50.

12 G. J. Stigler 'The kinky oligopoly demand curve and rigid prices' *Journal of Political Economy* 55 (1947) p. 432.

13 D. F. Turner 'The definition of agreement under the Sherman Act: conscious parallelism and refusals to deal' *Harvard Law Review* 75 (1962) p. 665.

14 J. Markham 'The nature and significance of price leadership' *American Economic Review* 41 (1951) p. 891; G. J. Stigler *op. cit.*; the Monopolies Commission *Parallel Pricing* HMSO (1973) Cmnd. 5330.

15 W. Fellner *Competition Among the Few* Knopf (1949).

16 T. Schelling *The Strategy of Conflict* Harvard University Press (1960).

17 F. M. Scherer *Industrial Market Structure and Economic Performance* Rand McNally (1970) p. 159.

18 A. D. Neale *The Anti-Trust Laws of the U.S.A.* Cambridge University Press (2nd edition 1970) p. 163.

19 W. Fellner *op. cit.*

20 The Monopolies Commission *Parallel Prices op. cit.*

21 The Monopolies Commission *Electric Lamps* HMSO (1968) para. 61.

22 See the Monopolies Commission reports on: *The Supply of Cigarettes and Tobacco* . . . (1961); *The Supply of Certain Rubber Footwear* (1956); *The Supply and Export of Pneumatic Tyres* (1955).

23 W. P. J. Maunder 'Price leadership: an appraisal of its character in some British industries' *The Business Economist* 4 (1972) p. 132.

24 See K. J. Cohen and R. M. Cyert *The Theory of the Firm* Prentice Hall (1965).

25 K. Van Musschenbroek 'Now it's a three-way fight for the bread market' *Financial Times* (15 October 1971) p. 20.

26 The Monopolies Commission *Household Detergents* HMSO (1966) para. 18.

27 For discussions of this in relation to different industries see F. M. Scherer *op. cit.*

pp. 208–9; C. Wilson *The History of Unilever* vol. III Cassell (1968) p. 102; the Monopolies Commission *Electric Lamps op. cit.* para. 61.

28 T. Havrilesky and R. Barth 'Tests of market share stability in the cigarette industry' *Journal of Industrial Economics* 17 (1969) p. 145.

29 J. M. Clark *Competition as a Dynamic Process* Brookings (1961) p. 249.

30 P. Doyle 'Advertising expenditure and consumer demand' *Oxford Economic Papers* 20 (1968) p. 394.

31 M. A. Alemson 'Demand entry and the game of conflict in oligopoly over time: recent Australian experience' *Oxford Economic Papers* 21 (1969) p. 220 and 'Advertising and the nature of competition' *Economic Journal* 81 (1970) p. 282.

32 See G. Maxcy and A. Silberston *The Motor Industry* Allen and Unwin (1959) and D. G. Rhys *The Motor Industry* Butterworth (1972).

33 See the Monopolies Commission *Petrol* HMSO (1965).

34 National Board for Prices and Incomes Report No. 4 *Prices of Household and Toilet Soap* HMSO (1965) Cmnd. 2791; the Monopolies Commission *Household Detergents op. cit.*

35 See the Monopolies Commission *The Supply of Cigarettes and Tobacco op. cit.*; C. L. Pass 'Coupon trading – an aspect of non-price competition in the U.K. cigarette industry' *Yorkshire Bulletin* 19 (1967) p. 124.

36 The Monopolies Commission *Infant Milk Foods* HMSO (1967).

37 The Monopolies Commission *Petrol op. cit.*

38 D. G. Rhys *op. cit.* pp. 310–11.

39 The Monopolies Commission *Man-Made Cellulosic Fibres op. cit.*

40 The Monopolies Commission *Clutch Mechanisms for Road Vehicles* HMSO (1968).

41 The Monopolies Commission *Metal Containers* HMSO (1970).

42 A. D. Neale *op. cit.* p. 48.

43 D. F. Turner 'The Scope of Anti-trust and other economic policies' *Harvard Law Review* 82 (1969) p. 1207.

44 Fair Trading Act 1973 ch. 41, s6(2).

45 D. F. Turner 'The definition of agreement under the Sherman Act . . .' *op. cit.*

46 This case is discussed in D. P. O'Brien and D. Swann *Information Agreements, Competition and Efficiency* Macmillan (1968).

47 W. P. J. Maunder *op. cit.*

48 Referred to in A. D. Neale *op. cit.* p. 163.

49 The Monopolies Commission *Films* HMSO (1966).

50 G. C. Allen *The Structure of Industry in Britain* Longmans (1961).

Chapter 15

1 Most textbooks carry a useful discussion of this issue. See for example P. Asch *Economic Theory and the Anti-Trust Dilemma* Wiley (1970); D. E. Needham *Economic Analysis and Industrial Structure* Holt Rinehart and Winston (1969); D. M. Winch *Analytical Welfare Economics* Penguin (1971) ch. 6.

2 E.g. C. Brock *The Control of Restrictive Practices from 1956* McGraw Hill (1966); J. M. Clark *Competition as a Dynamic Process* Brookings (1961); A. Hunter *Competition and the Law* Allen and Unwin (1966).

3 G. J. Stigler *The Organisation of Industry* Irwin (1968).

4 R. G. Lipsey and K. Lancaster 'The general theory of second best' *Review of Economic Studies* 24 (1956) p. 11. This is also discussed in C. Brock *op. cit.* appendix to Chapter 2.

5 J. M. Clark *op. cit.* p. ix.

6 E.g. G. C. Allen *Monopoly and Restrictive Practices* Allen and Unwin (1968); P. Asch *op. cit.*; J. S. Bain *Industrial Organisation* Wiley (1967); J. M. Clark *op. cit.* and 'Towards a concept of workable competition' *American Economic*

Review 30 (1940) p. 241; C. D. Edwards *Maintaining Competition* McGraw Hill (1964).

7 These criteria are taken from J. F. Pickering 'Effective competition in the television rentals industry: a note' *Journal of Industrial Economics* 18 (1970) p. 141.

8 Registrar of Restrictive Trading Agreements *Report for the period 7 August 1956–31 December 1959* HMSO (1961) Cmnd. 1273.

9 See J. B. Heath *Still Not Enough Competition?* Institute of Economic Affairs (1963) for a discussion of the reasons for the preponderance of price agreements.

10 The case for the advantages of restrictive agreements is extensively argued in various papers by G. B. Richardson, e.g. 'The theory of restrictive trade practices' *Oxford Economic Papers* 17 (1965) p. 432.

11 The history of policy-making in this area has been discussed in a number of books including G. C. Allen *op. cit.;* C. Brock *op. cit.;* P. H. Guenault and J. M. Jackson, *The Control of Monopoly in the United Kingdom* Longmans (1960); V. L. Korah *Monopolies and Restrictive Practices* Penguin (1968); J. F. Pickering *Resale Price Maintenance in Practice* Allen and Unwin (1966); C. K. Rowley *The British Monopolies Commission* Allen and Unwin (1966).

12 Lord Cave in *Sorrell* v. *Smith* (1925) AC 700.

13 *Employment Policy* HMSO (1944) Cmnd. 6527.

14 For discussions of the work of the Monopolies Commission see G. C. Allen *op. cit.;* C. K. Rowley *op. cit.*

15 See A. Hunter 'The Monopolies Commission and price fixing' *Economic Journal* 66 (1956) p. 587.

16 Monopolies and Restrictive Practices Commission *Collective Discrimination* HMSO (1955) Cmnd. 9504. A further, general, inquiry on common prices was in progress at the time of the passing of the Restrictive Trade Practices Act but was then not proceeded with.

17 It also dealt with resale price maintenance by banning outright the collective enforcement of rpm but strengthening the power of individual manufacturers to enforce their own maintained prices; see J. F. Pickering *Resale Price Maintenance in Practice op. cit.* In addition it made consequential alterations to the terms of reference of the Monopolies Commission.

18 As it is a civil rather than a criminal court the Restrictive Practices Court has to be satisfied that a case is proven on the balance of the probabilities.

19 R. B. Stevens 'Justiciability: the Restrictive Practices Court re-examined' *Public Law* (1964) and R. B. Stevens and B. S. Yamey *The Restrictive Practices Court* Weidenfeld and Nicholson (1965) ch. 3.

20 The Reports of the Registrar of Restrictive Trading Agreements published by HMSO are important sources of information on the working of this Act, see (1961) Cmnd. 1273; (1962) Cmnd. 1603; (1964) Cmnd. 2246; (1967) Cmnd. 3188; (1970) Cmnd. 4303; (1973) Cmnd. 5195.

21 Cairns has argued that the court showed signs of assuming that an agreement was *per se* contrary to the public interest if it resulted in unreasonable prices even if it gave benefits under other gateways. Although Sutherland has shown that Cairns' argument is not justified as a general description of the attitude of the court it is clear that in some cases where it has approved agreements the Court has been anxious to satisfy itself that prices have been and may be expected to be reasonable before upholding an agreement. See J. P. Cairns 'The Restrictive Practices Court and reasonable prices' *Journal of Industrial Economics* 12 (1964) p. 133 and A. Sutherland 'The Restrictive Practices Court and reasonable prices: a comment' *Journal of Industrial Economics* 13 (1965).

22 Pleadings under gateway (g) have not been discussed here as they depend upon the successful establishment of a case under one of the other gateways.

23 R. B. Stevens and B. S. Yamey *op. cit.;* A. Sutherland 'Economics in the Restrictive Practices Court' *Oxford Economic Papers* 17 (1965) p. 385 and the references to other comments contained therein. See also C. Brock *op. cit.* and A. Hunter *Competition and the Law op. cit.*

24 R. L. Sich 'Evidence of detriment caused by restrictive trading agreements'

324 Industrial Structure & Market Conduct

Oxford Economic Papers 17 (1965) p. 347.

25 A. Sutherland *op. cit.*
26 See the various reports of the Registrar of Restrictive Trading Agreements.
27 See J. B. Heath *op. cit.*; 'The Restrictive Practices Court on competition and price restriction' *Manchester School* 28 (1960) p. 1; 'Free prices – what progress?' *The Banker* 110 (1960) p. 107; 'Restrictive practices legislation: some economic consequences' *Economic Journal* 70 (1960) p. 474.
28 D. Swann 'The impact of restrictive business practices legislation' *Social Science Research Council Newsletter* No. 19 (June 1973) p. 2; W. P. J. Maunder, 'The glass container industry: a study of the effect of the 1956 Restrictive Trade Practices Act' *Economics* 9 (1972) p. 207 and W. P. J. Maunder 'Price leadership: an appraisal of its character in some British industries' *The Business Economist* 4 (1972) p. 132.
29 For discussions of this see the Reports of the Registrar of Restrictive Trading Agreements; G. B. Richardson *Information and Investment* Oxford University Press (1960); and 'Price notification schemes' *Oxford Economic Papers* 19 (1967) p. 359; D. Swann and D. P. O'Brien 'Information agreements: a problem in search of a policy' *Manchester School* 34 (1966) p. 285 and *Information Agreements, Competition and Efficiency* Macmillan (1968).
30 D. Swann 'The impact of restrictive business practices legislation' *op. cit.*
31 National Board for Prices and Incomes Reports No. 3 *Prices of Bread and Flour* HMSO (1965) Cmnd. 2760; 39 *Costs and Prices of Aluminium Semi-Manufacturers* HMSO (1967) Cmnd. 3378; 80 *Distributors' Margins on Paint, Childrens' Clothing, Household Textiles and Proprietary Medicines* HMSO (1968) Cmnd. 3737.
32 A. D. Neale *The Anti-Trust Laws of the U.S.A.* Cambridge University Press (1970) p. 48.
33 D. F. Turner 'The definition of agreement under the Sherman Act: Conscious parallelism and refusals to deal' *Harvard Law Review* 75 (1962) p. 665.
34 *Ibid.*

INDEX OF NAMES

Note: the first number in bold type refers to the text page to which the reference relates, and the second number in roman type gives the page where the reference is cited; the numbers in brackets give the chapter and note number in which the citation will be found.

Abbott L. **201**, 316 (10.6); **255**, 321 (14.5)

Adelman M. A. **7**, 299 (1.6); **54**, 303 (3.1)

Adler F. M. **193**, 315 (9.33)

Advertising Association **212**, 317 (11.1)

Alberts W. W. **129**, 310 (7.47)

Alchian A. **105**, 308 (6.25)

Alemson M. **218**, 317 (11.19); **265**, 322 (14.31)

Aliber R. Z. **178**, 314 (9.7)

Allen B. T. **28**, 301 (1.53)

Allen G. C. **111**, 308 (6.44); **203**, 316 (10.11); **233**, 319 (12.39); **271**, 322 (14.50); **275**, 322 (14.6); **279**, 323 (15.11); **281**, 323 (15.14)

Andrews, P. W. S. **70**, 304 (4.3 & 4.4); **74**, 305 (4.15); **100**, 307 (6.9); **201**, 316 (10.6); **202**, 316 (10.9); **225**, 318 (12.4); **299**, 319 (12.16); **255**, 321 (14.3)

Annual Report on the Working of the Monopolies Commission **146**, 312 (8.30); **147**, 312 (8.31).

Ansoff H. I. **71**, 304 (4.6); **100**, 307 (6.8); **121**, 309 (7.23 & 7.24); **128**, 310 (7.40); **129**, 310 (7.47); **130**, 311 (7.48)

Armstrong A. **12**, 300 (1.19); **14**, 300 (1.24 & 1.26)

Arnfield R. V. **121**, 309 (7.25); **145**, 312 (8.27)

Arrow K. J. **89**, 306 (5.19)

Asch P. **24**, 300 (1.41); **274**, 322 (15.1); **275**, 322 (15.6)

Ashton T. S. **233**, 319 (12.36)

Backman J. **220**, 318 (11.25)

Bain J. S. **13**, 300 (1.22); **21**, 300 (1.33); **31**, 301 (2.1); **36**, 302 (2.11); **45**, 302 (2.27 & 2.28); **48**, 303 (2.33); **61**, 304 (3.20); **68**, 304 (4.1); **74**, 305 (4.17); **217**, 317 (11.15); **255**, 321 (14.3)

Baldwin W. L. **102**, 307 (6.15)

Baloff N. **39**, 302 (2.12)

Banks Report **82**, 305 (5.2 & 5.4); **89**, 306 (5.16); **91**, 306 (5.25); **94**, 306 (5.35 & 5.36)

Baranson J. **179**, 314 (9.10)

Barback R. H. **228**, 319 (12.11); **233**, 319 (12.37)

Barna T. **65**, 304 (3.30); **109**, 308 (6.37); **115**, 309 (7.3); **118**, 309 (7.16 & 7.18)

Barran D. **183**, 315 (9.13)

Barth R. **264**, 322 (14.28)

Baumol W. J. **104**, 307 (6.19); **111**, 308 (6.43); **112**, 308 (6.45); **255**, 321 (14.6)

Berle A. A. **1**, 299 (1.1)

Bhagwati J. N. **68**, 304, (4.2); **73**, 305 (4.12)

Bhaskar K. **133**, 311 (7.56)

Blair J. M. **88**, 306 (5.13)

Blease J. G. **103**, 307 (6.17)

Board of Trade **136**, 311 (8.4); **137**, 312 (8.10); **140**, 312 (8.18); **145**, 312 (8.27); **149**, 312 (8.35)

Boehm K. **82**, 305 (5.3); **90**, 306 (5.22); **91**, 306 (5.24 & 5.26); **92**, 306 (5.33)

Bolton Committee **250**, 321 (13.30)

Bonini C. P. **12**, 299 (1.18); **117**, 309 (7.7 & 7.8)

Borden N. H. **214**, 314 (11.5)

Briston R. J. **124**, 310 (7.34)

Brock C. **274**, 322 (15.2); **275**, 322 (15.6); **279**, 323 (15.11); **292**, 323 (15.23)

Brooke M. Z. **178**, 314 (9.7 & 9.8); **185**, 315 (9.15)

Brunner E. **70**, 304 (4.3 & 4.4)

Burn D. **55**, 303 (3.8)

Burns T. **205**, 316 (10.13)

Business Monitor **135**, 311 (8.3)

Butters J. K. **124**, 310 (7.33)

Cable J. R. **213**, 317 (11.4); **217**, 317 (11.13)

Cairncross A. **146**, 312 (8.29); **172**, 313 (8.52)

INDEX OF SUBJECTS

Note: numbers in brackets give the chapter and note number in which a reference will be found.